THE MAKERS OF
THE SACRED HARP

MUSIC IN AMERICAN LIFE

*A list of books in the series appears
at the end of this book.*

THE MAKERS OF
THE SACRED HARP

DAVID WARREN STEEL
WITH RICHARD H. HULAN

UNIVERSITY OF ILLINOIS PRESS

Urbana, Chicago, and Springfield

Publication of this book was supported by a grant
from the L. J. and Mary C. Skaggs Folklore Fund.

Library of Congress Cataloging-in-Publication Data
Steel, David Warren.
The makers of the sacred harp / David Warren Steel
with Richard H. Hulan.
p.   cm. — (Music in American life)
Includes bibliographical references and index.
ISBN 978-0-252-03567-8 (cloth : alk. paper)
ISBN 978-0-252-07760-9 (pbk. : alk. paper)
1. Sacred harp. 2. Hymns, English—Southern States—
History and criticism. 3. Church music—Southern States.
4. Shape-note singing. I. Hulan, Richard H. II. Title.
ML3111.S75   2010
782.270975—dc22   2010025591

Come, let us raise our voices high,
And form a sacred song.
—B. Lloyd, *The Primitive Hymns*

CONTENTS

ILLUSTRATIONS

Plates appear after page 176.

INTRODUCTION

David Warren Steel

Sacred Harp singing is a community musical and social event, emphasizing participation, not performance, where people sing songs from a tunebook called *The Sacred Harp*, printed in music notation using four shaped notes. It is the preeminent living reflection of the music of early American psalmody. While not identical to the congregational singing of eighteenth-century New England, it preserves several fundamental characteristics of that era, including a complex of musical skills learned in singing schools and an eclectic repertory of religious part-songs by European and American composers, printed in an oblong book. Since the nineteenth century, Sacred Harp singings have employed a distinctive "hollow square" seating arrangement and rotation of leaders; they begin each song with solmization followed by one or more verses of sung text. Despite its reliance on printed materials, Sacred Harp singing is a form of traditional music that stands on the persistent collaboration of generations of composers, songbook compilers, editors, and revisers, singing teachers, song leaders, and singers of all ages who identify with its sincerity, enthusiasm, devotional strength, and deep historical roots.

The present book is an account of the Sacred Harp songbook and the men and women who made it. Benjamin Franklin White and Elisha James King, who compiled the book in 1844, were members of a tradition that was already several generations old. They were among more than thirty-five southern musicians who issued sacred tunebooks printed in shaped notes between 1816 and 1861.[1] They drew on a repertory of English and American tunes popular in the New England states in the years 1770–1810, and they continued to circulate music from this repertory long after it had lost favor in New England. They reprinted or reset tunes published in previous tunebooks, notably William Walker's *Southern Harmony* (1835).

They collected, notated, and harmonized tunes from a flourishing oral tradition, adapting them for use in churches and singing schools. Finally, White and King added their own compositions and arrangements and those of other composers and teachers in their immediate region.

After King's death in 1844, White supervised successive revisions until 1870. In the twentieth century, revisions by W. M. Cooper, J. L. White, and J. S. James competed for the loyalty of Sacred Harp singers. The 1936 "Denson revision," produced at the depths of the Great Depression by S. M., T. J., and Paine Denson, ultimately won the affection and loyalty of the majority of Sacred Harp singers. The 1991 revision of that book, the *Sacred Harp* best known today, is the subject of this work.

Part One is a collection of essays exploring the Sacred Harp and its creators in a regional context that included Native removal, westward migration, civil war, family life, and trades and professions. The final chapter in this part explores some of the reasons why Sacred Harp music sounds so distinctive today; here the reader may find it helpful to have a copy of the 1991 revision at hand. Part Two consists of an essay by Richard H. Hulan about camp-meetings and their hymnody, along with biographical sketches of five American hymn writers whose work appears in *The Sacred Harp*. Part Three contains a biographical dictionary of composers represented in the tunebook, many of whom were previously unidentified. Part Four lists the songs of *The Sacred Harp* by page number, together with attributions and sources for words and music.

This book draws on the work of many writers and researchers. For information about early figures associated with *The Sacred Harp*, J. S. James's *A Brief History of the Sacred Harp* (1904) long stood as the sole substantial source of first- or even second-hand information. James had the advantage of proximity to his source: he knew the Whites, Absalom Ogletree, J. R. Turner, and the Reeses. Yet he worked at a time when few local histories were available, and he had little direct knowledge of Talbot County and the many figures associated with that region including E. J. King, Zechariah Chambless, Leonard Breedlove, S. R. Penick, J. L. Pickard, and the Lancaster sisters. His extensive industrial, financial, and political interests must have limited his time for direct research, though he had an impressive library of earlier tunebooks, as well as reference works such as Brown and Butterworth, *The Story of the Hymns and Tunes* (1906). James worked much of his information into footnotes printed below each song in the *Union Harp and History of Songs* (1909) and in *Original Sacred Harp* (the James edition of 1911). These quaint notes were retained and supplemented in the Denson revisions of 1936–71. For those seeking reliable information, they represent a scholarly nightmare in which American singing master Amzi Chapin is confused with F. F. Chopin[2] and

Bishop Thomas Ken, misidentified as the author of "O come, loud anthems let us sing," was said to have been "educated at New Oxford" fifty-one years after his own death in 1711 and imprisoned "for refusing to sign the Declaration of Independence."[3] Still, the notes provided continuity of historical and biographical lore from the nineteenth century and preserved anecdotes such as that of John Leland's "Mammoth Cheese"[4] and the death of the composer of ANTIOCH from "a falling tree or limb,"[5] thus keeping generations of Sacred Harp singers aware of the rich and varied history of the repertory that they sing.

Another work produced by a Sacred Harp singer was Earl V. Thurman's manuscript history of the Chattahoochee Musical Convention. Thurman was hardly methodical in the inclusion or treatment of biographical detail; still, he offered useful information about a large number of singers active in the nineteenth and early twentieth centuries, including many composers represented in the Sacred Harp. Circulated in typescript since the 1950s, this study is now available as part of *The Chattahoochee Musical Convention, 1852–2002: A Sacred Harp Historical Sourcebook,* edited by Kiri Miller.

The twentieth century saw the beginnings of academic interest in the Sacred Harp and its history. George Pullen Jackson characterized the Sacred Harp as a folk tradition and examined its contents against the background of American folk song. He also provided historical information about its compilers, composers, and singing conventions, primarily in his *White Spirituals of the Southern Uplands* (1933) and in *The Story of the Sacred Harp* (1944). Buell E. Cobb, in his masterful 1978 study *The Sacred Harp: A Tradition and Its Music,* updated historical aspects of Jackson's work, while clarifying the story of the editions and revisions of the songbook and unveiling substantial and authoritative information about E. J. King and his family. More recently, John Bealle in *Public Worship, Private Faith: Sacred Harp and American Folksong* (1997) has defined the historical and ideological discourse surrounding Sacred Harp singing, while Kiri Miller, in *Traveling Home: Sacred Harp Singing and American Pluralism* (2008), confronts the persistent ability of the Sacred Harp in our own time to attract and engage a diverse community of singers, many of whom did not experience the tradition as children.

The coverage of twentieth-century composers in the present work would have been nearly impossible without the foresight of Hugh McGraw, longtime executive secretary of the Sacred Harp Publishing Company. While preparing the 1966 and 1971 revisions, Mr. McGraw distributed a questionnaire to living composers and to family members of recently deceased ones. The mimeographed forms asked for basic vital information (birth and death dates and places, parents' and children's names) and also for education (including musical training), occupations, and "other information," with a place for survivors to write "something you remember about them singing Sacred Harp." These files, held at the Sacred Harp Headquarters and Museum in Carrollton, Georgia, and updated by the addition of similar information about composers represented in the 1991 edition, proved invaluable in the early stages of this project.

In addition to Hugh McGraw, a large number of individual singers, family members, and other researchers have contributed information and anecdotes about the composers: Blake Adcock, Aldo Ceresa, Velton Chafin, Buell Cobb, Richard DeLong, Robert E. Denson, Jimmie Lou Gilmore, Julietta Haynes, Mike Hinton, Brent Holcomb, Don Howard, David Ivey, Kathryn James, Margaret Keeton, Richard Mauldin, Hugh Bill McGuire, Dollie Miller, Brad Preston, Nathan Rees, Jeff Sheppard, Jonathon Smith, Barbara Swetman, Charlene Wallace, Chloe Webb, Charles Wells, Mike White, Ruth Wyers, and especially the late Amanda Denson Brady, whose keen memory and historical sense brought forth many recollections of her family.

This work incorporates the painstaking labor of the late William J. Reynolds, the dean of Baptist hymnology, in identifying textual sources; he was responsible for the text attributions in the printed songbook. Other scholarly specialists in early American hymnody have also contributed from their research, notably Richard Crawford, Harry Eskew, Thomas B. Malone, Carol Medlicott, David W. Music, and Nikos Pappas.

Two contributors, both skilled researchers, have gone beyond giving of their considerable knowledge of the history of the Sacred Harp: John Plunkett and Robert L. Vaughn have actively pursued original research in libraries, archives, and online, and they have freely contributed their findings to this book. They have worked tirelessly to locate and identify composers in Georgia and Texas, respectively. Among the greatest pleasures in working on this project was the collaboration with these gentlemen in frequent exchanges of electronic mail where each successive reply brought out additional details and questions for discussion, followed by disappointment on encountering blind leads or elation on establishing a secure identification.

As originally conceived, this book was to have contained biographical sketches of all the poets and textual sources of the songs in *The Sacred Harp*. Much of this material would have duplicated that in standard reference works such as John Julian's *Dictionary of Hymnology*, and this approach would have failed to do justice to the large number of anonymous texts, especially spiritual songs from camp-meeting sources, that characterize the tunebook. The contributions of Richard Hulan have addressed this issue. With his unparalleled knowledge of American camp-meeting hymnody, he clarified the role of the preachers and compiler-publishers and has identified a small number of American poets who have left their indelible mark on the Sacred Harp and its singers. He has also reviewed and corrected all the text attributions and sources in Part Four of this work.

This book received continual encouragement from the Sacred Harp Publishing Company and from the Joe Beasley Memorial Foundation, both of which have given it generous financial support. I would also like to thank the L. J. Skaggs and Mary C. Skaggs Foundation for their support. I am grateful to Mike Hinton and Richard Schmeidler, respectively, for their role in negotiating the arrangements with the press. Mr. Schmeidler has also provided invaluable help in copyediting. The University of Illinois Press, with its wide-ranging series Music in American Life, seemed a natural fit as publisher of this study. From the beginning, editor Laurie Matheson has been encouraging, helpful, and knowledgeable in guiding a novice author through the review and editing process and in seeing this book through publication, a task shared by Daniel Nasset, Angela Burton, Copenhaver Cumpston, copyeditor Jane Zanichkowsky, and indexer John Bealle.

All through the making of this book, my wife Anne has been at my side; she has sacrificed much to see this work come to light, and it has been substantially bettered through her keen and sensitive eye. It is to her, my sweet singer of Zion, and to Sacred Harp singers everywhere, that this book is dedicated.

PART ONE
THE BOOK

THE ORIGINS
OF THE SACRED HARP

For more than one hundred fifty years, the Sacred Harp has represented a tradition of community-based music making. It relies on musical participation, rotation of song leaders, and contributions of food for a communal meal. It eschews contentious discussion of politics and denominational religion. The Sacred Harp tradition is often cited as an embodiment of American democracy,[1] but its history reflects the conflicts that formed the nation, as well. Originating in religious pluralism and cultural self-improvement, it has survived wars, political and religious struggles, commercial competition, litigation, and personal slights.

In the years 1801–61, at least thirty-five residents of the southern United States compiled and published sacred tunebooks in shaped notation. *The Sacred Harp* (1844) modeled after existing tunebooks, was intended to compete in a similar cultural, educational, and religious space. Like most other southern tunebooks, *The Sacred Harp* is an eclectic collection containing examples of several different forms, genres, and styles. Like many other compilers, the forty-three-year-old Benjamin Franklin White and his twenty-three-year-old collaborator Elisha J. King played a role more akin to that of anthologists than that of original artists. Although both men composed and arranged music, their primary job was to select tunes from earlier publications, from manuscripts, from their own stock of compositions, and from oral tradition.

Their book, like other published sacred music in the United States, took a form that was typical in the nineteenth century but is highly distinctive today. A standard tunebook was printed in an oblong quarto format, in which four pages of music are printed on each side of a single sheet that is then folded twice and bound on one of the short edges of the folded sheet. The front matter typically included a section of "rudiments" or a pedagogical introduction intended to serve as a reference for those attending singing school or as a guide for those attempting to learn without a teacher. The music itself was printed in two systems reading lengthwise across the page, with one voice part to a staff. In parts of the country, notably the Ohio Valley, the South, and much of Pennsylvania, tunebooks employed a system of four "patent notes," or shape notes, introduced in William Little and William Smith's *Easy Instructor* (Philadelphia, 1801).[2] This system uses four differently shaped note heads to indicate the four singing syllables *fa, sol, la,* and *mi,* which were used in English-speaking lands well into the nineteenth century. Popular tunebooks usually contained a mixture of tunes of various genres, styles and origins, collected by compilers who responded to the tastes of singers and to musical fashions in their respective regions and localities.

It is not difficult to determine the sources of much of the music in *The Sacred Harp:* most of the pieces were copied from other tunebooks. The similarity between the first edition and William Walker's *Southern Harmony* (1835) extends further than the influence and borrowing prevalent in sacred tunebooks. Published in Spartanburg, South Carolina, *The Southern Harmony* was immensely popular among the settlers who were pouring into Georgia and Alabama following the Indian removals. Many of the settlers came from or migrated through South Carolina on their way westward. In 1866 Walker claimed to have sold six hundred thousand copies of his book since 1835. It was natural that White and King should use Walker's book as a model in the way other compilers drew on the work of their predecessors. The ways in which they did so, however, reveal a serious conflict between the two musicians.

White was himself a native of South Carolina; from 1825 to 1842 he lived in Spartanburg, where Walker lived from 1832 until the end of his life. Both men were Baptists, and they were brothers-in-law: White married Thurza Golightly in 1825, and Walker married her sister Amy Golightly in 1832. According to James, who probably heard the story from the White family,[3]

> Major White and his brother-in-law, William Walker, wrote a music book known ... as the Southern Harmony, in four shape notes the same as those used in the Sacred Harp.
>
> Walker and White married sisters and lived not far apart in South Carolina. An arrangement was made between them for Walker to go north and have the book published, there being no publishing houses in the south with plant [sic] suitable to print the book. Walker took the manuscript, and he and the publishers changed the same without the knowledge or consent of Major White and brought it out under the name of Walker, giving Major White no credit whatever for its composition. Walker also entered into a combination with the publishers

and in this way managed to deprive Major White of any interest in the Southern Harmony, although all of the work, or most of it, was done by Major White.

On account of this transaction and treatment, the two men never spoke to each other again. It was such an outrage that Major White would never have any thing to do with Walker and he soon after moved to Harris County, Georgia and engaged in composing and writing the songs in the Sacred Harp.

There are reasons to doubt the foregoing account. Harry Eskew points out that such a conflict among church members likely would have resulted in an investigation and disciplinary procedures that would be reflected in church records, yet he has found no record of such an incident.[4] Walker and White remained members of the same church for some seven years afterward. Yet it is clear that there was trouble between the two men. A White descendant has found court records from June 1841 showing that the Spartanburg sheriff seized and sold a cotton gin owned by White to pay $390 in court costs and damages; Walker, formerly a co-owner of the property, subsequently swore that he had sold his interest two years earlier.[5] We do not have the whole story today, but the timing suggests that disagreement about this incident, rather than the Southern Harmony, may have prompted White's move to Georgia.

The pages of the 1844 Sacred Harp, on the other hand, tend to confirm James's story. White reprinted ten tunes composed or arranged by seven Spartanburg-area musicians who would have been known to both Walker and White.[6] These tunes are copied exactly and attributed to their respective authors. White also reprinted some fifteen tunes that were unattributed in the Southern Harmony. Though some of these were arranged on the basis of versions in earlier sources, White nevertheless quoted them exactly and gave them the same titles as in Walker's collection. They included such favorites as WEBSTER, NEW BRITAIN, ALABAMA, and COLUMBUS. This much might be expected in a book by a compiler who had grown up in the same district. White, however, went further than this: he printed twelve tunes that had been claimed by Walker in Southern Harmony, in identical versions, yet he removed Walker's name and left them unattributed in The Sacred Harp. They include some of Walker's best-known and most distinctive compositions and arrangements: JERUSALEM, PARTING HAND, HALLELUJAH, SWEET PROSPECT, HEAVENLY ARMOR, COMPLAINER, and THE GOOD OLD WAY. Finally, White printed three songs from earlier sources for which Walker had composed the treble part: SWEET HOME, THE TRUMPET, and WARRENTON. Again, the arrangements are identical, except that the name of William Walker is absent. This was so with the 1844 Sacred Harp and any subsequent edition of the Sacred Harp published during White's lifetime.[7] To anyone who can examine both books, the message is clear: White preferred not to get angry, but to get even. James says as much: "[White] was gentle in his nature, lovable in disposition and treated everyone with universal kindness. . . . He had sufficient resentment, however, for his own protection, but he would not allow his wrath or unkind feelings to go any further than to protect his own reputation and his dignity as a gentleman."[8]

In view of White's negative reaction to John McCurry's reprinting of tunes from *The Sacred Harp*, his own appropriation of material from *The Southern Harmony* suggests that he felt much as the Connecticut composer Daniel Read did when he wrote to his brother in 1804, "I feel a reluctance to publish music without the consent of the Authors, . . . [but] those Editors who have made free with mine, have I think, in a degree authorized me to take the same liberty with theirs."[9]

On the title page of the 1844 *Sacred Harp* the compilers promise "nearly one hundred pieces never before published." Although this claim is repeated almost verbatim from the title page of the 1835 *Southern Harmony*, it still bears examination, with the understanding that many "original" tunes may be variant settings of melodies published earlier by others. Of the new tunes in the first edition, twenty-two are claimed by E. J. King and fifteen by B. F. White. Most of the others are credited to Thomas W. Carter and to Jesse Thomas White, B. F. White's nephew, with a couple of tunes each by John Massengale, Zachariah Chambless, and Leonard P. Breedlove and a single tune by J. W. Davis. These total seventy-one, falling well short of the "nearly one hundred pieces never before published." To these might be added one or two unattributed pieces that are nonetheless original, such as CHRISTMAS ANTHEM (later attributed to James M. Denson); on the other hand, a good many of the attributed tunes—especially those claimed by King—are demonstrably derived from tunes printed in earlier books.

Having compiled a tunebook, White and King sought to publish it. Only by means of a capital investment in a work could a tunebook compiler hope to reap the financial rewards of its success. Few publishing houses would extend credit to an unknown author unless he could show an ample subscription list indicating a demand for the work. In 1844 White was recently arrived with his growing family from another state and was still establishing himself as a farmer and landowner. King, however, belonged to a wealthy family on a large plantation. Although it is probable that King provided much of the funding for publication, it is also likely that both compilers were able to solicit subscriptions from a large number of singers and teachers in the area, including composers represented in the book.

Whatever their method of financing the publication, White and King succeeded in bringing out a book of the highest quality. There were printing shops in Virginia and Tennessee capable of printing music in shaped notes, but the work of these provincial centers exhibits rudimentary technology and craftsmanship compared with the work of Cincinnati and Philadelphia printers. *The Sacred Harp*, printed in Philadelphia, embodied the state of the art as reflected in Thomas F. Adams's *Typographia*, an 1837 printing manual illustrating modern mosaic music fonts as well as imposition patterns for oblong music books. In the 1840s, Philadelphia printers were still familiar with shape notes: patent-note tunebooks in English and in German were still popular in parts of Pennsylvania. In 1844, White and King sought out Tillinghast King Collins (1808–70) and his brother Philip Gould Collins (1804–54); the firm of T. K. & P. G. Collins was known for the high quality of its typography and for the lavishly illustrated works of geology and natural history that issued from its presses. The firm had already printed editions of William Walker's *Southern Harmony* from 1838 to 1843.[10] The size of the initial press run is unknown. When King died on 31 August 1844, his estate included one-half of the copyright and seven hundred copies of the book. If, as seems likely, the press run was divided in proportion to the compilers' interest in the book, then it probably consisted of fourteen hundred to fifteen hundred copies.[11]

A major advance in music printing was the use of stereotyped plates, common in music books from about 1820 onward. Adams describes the casting of metal plates "not thicker than the sixth of an inch" from plaster molds of standing type; he explains that the type could be broken up and used for other work as soon as the plates had been cast. According to Adams, "The manufacture of stereotype plates is, therefore, simply a means of keeping up fictitious types to answer future demands, at an expense infinitely inferior to that of keeping the actual pages standing."[12] As a result of this technology, tunebook compilers lost the incentive for the kind of detailed revision found in popular tunebooks before 1820, which were completely reset with each edition, often with changes in content. Although the first edition of *Southern Harmony* was printed directly from type, the book was reset and stereotyped for an 1838 Philadelphia reissue; subsequent editions issued in the years 1840–47 added new material but did not require replacement of old plates until the 1854 edition. It is likely that *The Sacred Harp* was stereotyped from the beginning: new material was added in 1850 and 1859, but no music was deleted until the 1870 edition. Although the stereotyper's name is not indicated in *The Sacred Harp,* it must have been either Lawrence Johnson (1801–60) or John Francis Fagan (1799–1872)—these were the only men practicing this craft in Philadelphia at the time.[13] Both were involved in tunebook production in the 1840s.

The music of the 1844 *Sacred Harp* falls into the following categories:

1. Strophic psalm and hymn tunes. These tunes are designed for multi-stanza poetry: the tune is repeated for subsequent stanzas. Many of these tunes are simple; they are composed of block chords so that everyone sings the same words at the same time (for example, NEW BRITAIN). Tunes "with extension" have some repetition of text in one or more parts (for example, ORTONVILLE), often with one or more parts dropping out (as in CORONATION); "fuging tunes" have at least one section where the parts enter one or two at a time, usually in melodic imitation (BALLSTOWN); in

fuging tunes the words overlap, so that they are not uttered by all the parts at the same time. Some psalm and hymn tunes (called "doubles") contain enough music for two successive stanzas of text (PLEASANT HILL, NEW TOPIA).

2. Revival songs with refrains, often called "choruses." In these songs, each stanza is followed by a constant refrain (for example, ECSTASY). Sometimes there are brief refrains after every couplet (DESIRE FOR PIETY) or every line (SERVICE OF THE LORD).

3. Nonstrophic set pieces, called "odes" on the title page. These are settings of three or more stanzas of poetry, with different music for each stanza, often with musical contrasts. The poem may be on a sacred theme (CHRISTIAN SONG) or on another elevated subject (ODE ON SCIENCE).

4. Anthems, or settings of prose, usually from the Bible. Longer examples (HEAVENLY VISION, ROSE OF SHARON) may have changes of texture, meter, or key. Some anthems are as brief as a psalm tune (DAVID'S LAMENTATION).[14]

The first group, strophic psalm and hymn tunes, comprises examples of several musical styles. *The Sacred Harp* contains (a) eighteenth-century British psalm and hymn tunes, both simple and florid; (b) New England compositions of the period 1770–1810 (including a generous selection of fuging tunes), along with a few newly composed southern tunes in a similar style; (c) "folk hymns" presumably based on oral tradition, including *contrafacta* of various secular melodies; and (d) "reform" tunes in the urban nineteenth-century style of Lowell Mason and his contemporaries. "Revival choruses" and "reform" tunes were relatively new elements in the southern tunebook repertory; although examples of both had appeared since 1820, their number increased greatly during the 1840s. *The Sacred Harp* is distinctive in this treatment of these new genres. It is one of the first musical collections, north or south, to include a large number of revival choruses, as many as thirty in the first edition. This figure compares favorably with the twelve revival choruses in *Revival Melodies* (Boston, 1842), a popular northern tunebook designed for camp meetings. Subsequent editions of *The Sacred Harp* increased the number and proportion of choruses, adding twenty-six in 1850 and another twenty-three in 1859. The large number and variety of revival choruses, one of the most distinctive features of all editions of the work, may account for its enduring popularity in the nineteenth century and beyond.

The abundance of revival choruses in *The Sacred Harp* contrasts with the starkly minimal number of tunes by Lowell Mason and his contemporaries, who rejected vernacular styles and strove to create a chaste, devout style of church music. Since the 1820s such tunes had become ever more prominent in northern collections, as well as in southern tunebooks such as *Genuine Church Music* (Winchester, Virginia,

1832). In the 1844 *Sacred Harp* one can find about half a dozen tunes from British sources that had been favored by earlier reformers but only three songs representing the contemporary reform style: DUANE STREET, by English-born Methodist George Coles, SWEET AFFLICTION (an adaptation of an air by Jean-Jacques Rousseau), and MISSIONARY HYMN ("From Greenland's icy mountains") by Lowell Mason. Some of *The Sacred Harp*'s competitors in the Deep South, including William Hauser's *Hesperian Harp* (1848) and L. J. Jones's *Southern Minstrel* (1849) included a much larger number of reform compositions. Hauser, in particular, may have had *The Sacred Harp* in mind when he wrote in the preface to *The Hesperian Harp*,[15]

> The plan of embracing Sunday-school, Infant, Revival, Missionary, and Temperance pieces in the same volume with Church Music, I deem a new, as well as a good one. And I rejoice now in hope that singers at missionary meetings, especially in the South, will henceforth be able to save persons of taste from the torment of hearing "From Greenland's icy mountains," and "nothing else." Surely the missionary hymn will be allowed to rest awhile, till time shall have renovated it and made it once more agreeable to hearts long since sated with its frequent repetition.

Hauser may have been hinting that collections such as *The Sacred Harp,* with only a single reformed tune by Lowell Mason, might be inadequate for "persons of taste." In addition to the large and varied repertory in his own tunebook, Hauser recommends the works of musical reformers Lowell Mason, Thomas Hastings, and George Hood and, for revival music, William Walker's *Southern and Western Pocket Harmonist* (1846); he makes no mention of *The Sacred Harp.*

After publication, White, the surviving compiler (King died in 1844), organized the Southern Musical Convention and other bodies that expanded the network of composers and teachers who promoted *The Sacred Harp.*[16] Members of these conventions, many of them trained by White, composed or arranged new tunes and served on the revision committees for editions published in 1850, 1859, and 1870. In 1850 Richard F. M. Mann made his appearance, along with David Patillo White, Henry Smith Reese, and a couple of female composers. During the 1850s, B. F. White co-edited a weekly newspaper in Hamilton, Georgia, titled *The Organ,* that took an unusual interest in musical matters, reporting on singing conventions and musical lectures and also printing original music by local composers. Many tunes first printed in *The Organ* became part of *The Sacred Harp* in subsequent editions. Absalom Ogletree made his first contribution in the 1859 edition, as did John Palmer Reese, Edwin Theophilus Pound, Edmund Dumas, and the three Lancaster sisters. With the help of these leaders, White was able to continue promoting *The Sacred Harp* after the Civil War, during a period when new books and new notation systems were increasingly competitive in the region.

In the early twentieth century Wilson Marion Cooper, James Landrum White, and Joseph Stephen James issued separate revisions of *The Sacred Harp* between 1902 and 1911. Each claimed the sanction of one or more singing conventions; each presented the bulk of B. F. White's 1870 edition along with a substantial body of new music. In the case of Cooper and White, the new material included a large proportion of reformed church tunes and contemporary gospel music; most of the new music in the James edition, on the other hand, came from antebellum sources or from contemporary composers who wrote in a similar style. In 1933 T. J. Denson founded the Sacred Harp Publishing Company; its directors appointed a music committee to revise *Original Sacred Harp* (the James edition). Appearing in 1936 as the *Original Sacred Harp* (Denson revision), this book largely supplanted the James edition and itself underwent substantial revision and enlargement in 1960 and 1966, and minor revision in 1971 and 1987, by music committees appointed by the company. *The Sacred Harp* (1991 edition) is the successor to the Denson revision. It is likewise produced under the auspices of the Sacred Harp Publishing Company, but it is no longer officially known as the Denson revision.

The Cooper revision has continued to develop along lines parallel to those of the James-Denson lineage. Following major expansion of the book by Cooper's son-in-law Randall David Blackshear, the Sacred Harp Book Company was established; this body has sponsored the continued publication and enlargement of the Cooper book from 1949 through the 2006 edition. The Cooper revision has had a greater influence on the 1991 edition than previously thought. The *Original Sacred Harp* of 1911 (the James edition) claimed 327 new alto parts composed by musical editor S. M. Denson. In 1914 Cooper sued James, alleging that many of these alto parts were taken from the Cooper revision.[17] Despite the failure of Cooper's lawsuit, close examination of both books reveals that many of the Denson alto parts are, indeed, identical to those in the Cooper revision or differ in only one or two notes. Borrowings of alto lines from the Cooper revision and from earlier books such as William Walker's *Christian Harmony* (1867) are credited in this book as accurately as possible to their original authors and sources.

The 1991 edition of *The Sacred Harp* contains the work of 44 New England composers active before 1810; 112 American composers active in the years 1810 to 1900, almost all in the South; and 72 American composers active since 1900, as well as 17 Europeans, many of whom never visited the United States—a total of 245. Of these, 140 contributed their work directly to *The Sacred Harp* or to *The Organ*, the newspaper edited by B. F. White; 31 others had their work published in other southern tunebooks such as *Southern Harmony*.

Today the Sacred Harp and its singers may be seen as a "lost tonal tribe"[18] whose activities, largely isolated from the commoditization of the musical arts, seem quaintly at odds with those of the commercial mainstream of American culture and music. It is astonishing how little money changes hands in the process of putting on an all-day singing. Many venues where the singing is part of a long-standing church or community observance are free of charge. There is no admission fee, and all are invited to partake of the dinner that the hosts have prepared. Sometimes a hat is passed for "minute money" (a payment to publish the secretary's account of the singing) or for an offering to the host church's maintenance or "graveyard fund." No money is paid to "performers," even those who travel a considerable distance. Visiting singers are instead repaid through reciprocal visits, so that the hosts' expenses will be balanced out by the hospitality at locations they visit. While the Sacred Harp songbook is an essential purchase, its publishers sell the book near cost, and any profits are devoted to keeping the book in print. Pupils at singing schools pay at least a token fee, but such fees are no longer sufficient to support teachers without other occupations.

It is well to recall that *The Sacred Harp* was created as a commercial property from the start. This capitalistic enterprise was an integral part of the history and culture of the young American nation. The composers who contributed to the Sacred Harp represent a cross-section of white males and a few females representing a diverse range of wealth, education, and influence, during the age of Jacksonian democracy, when universal white male suffrage supplanted an earlier franchise limited to holders of substantial land or property. Most of them learned music in singing schools or informally in the family or social circle. They wrote for an audience of singers much like themselves, while working in a variety of trades and professions. They did not mean to found a "lost tribe."

In an era of westward movement and expansion, most Sacred Harp composers died west of their own birthplace, whether they moved from Carolina to Georgia, eastern Georgia to western Georgia, Georgia to Alabama, or Georgia and Alabama to Texas; some composers made two or more of these migrations in their lifetime. As they moved west, these singers and composers followed the "ever-retreating frontier," the land between urbanized civilization and the sparsely populated wilderness. Their singing schools and conventions contributed to "breaking the bonds of custom, offering new experiences, calling out new institutions and activities."[19]

The songs of the Sacred Harp allude to the westward progress of civilization (ODE ON SCIENCE, MURILLO'S LESSON), to the young nation's wars (THE AMERICAN STAR, WAR DEPARTMENT), and to reform movements such as foreign missions (CAN I LEAVE YOU?) and temperance (O COME AWAY). Most of all, they express the religious experience of communities and individuals in the vivid language of camp-meeting revivalism: exhortation to conversion (TURN, SINNER, TURN), prayer for conversions (RETURN AGAIN), despair (COLUMBUS), judgment (MESSIAH), and spiritual pilgrimage (PILGRIM) and warfare (CLAMANDA).

THE
CHATTAHOOCHEE
VALLEY

When B. F. White was born in 1800 in South Carolina, the Georgia land that he and other creators of *The Sacred Harp* would inhabit was the home of the Muscogee, or Creek, confederation. In 1823 George Troup was elected governor of Georgia and immediately began efforts to acquire the remaining Creek lands for white settlement. In February 1825 William McIntosh, leader of the Lower Creek Council and Troup's first cousin, signed the Treaty of Indian Springs, later ratified by the U.S. Senate, ceding all remaining Creek lands in Georgia. After protests from other Creek leaders and the assassination of McIntosh in April 1825, the federal government voided the earlier treaty and negotiated the Treaty of Washington with a larger and more representative Creek National Council; the new agreement called for the cession of most but not all of the area covered by the earlier treaty. Not to be deterred, Governor Troup forcibly removed the Creek from all their remaining Georgia lands, even those excluded by the second treaty, and had the entire area surveyed for a lottery. This large tract includes all the lands between the Flint and Chattahoochee Rivers, along with the lands west of the Chatta-hoochee.[1] The 1826 Creek cession was only one in a westward march of treaties and appropriations of native lands in Georgia and other southeastern states. Plate 1 shows five successive bands of settlement in central Georgia.

The last native group deprived of their Georgia lands were the Cherokee of northwest Georgia. In 1836, by a single vote, the U.S. Senate ratified the Treaty of New Echota, according to which chiefs representing a minority of the Chero-kee nation ceded the Georgia lands of the entire tribe and agreed to move west of the Mississippi. Although the majority of Cherokee, led by chief John Ross, resisted, they were forcibly rounded up by federal troops under Winfield Scott in the summer of 1838 and placed in "removal forts" such as Ross's Landing (later Chattanooga) from which they would embark on the "Trail of Tears." One nineteen-year-old Georgian who volunteered for this removal effort was Levi P. Denson, ancestor of eleven composers represented in *The Sacred Harp*, including S. M. Denson and T. J. Denson.

As the state took control of the Creek cession, the land was divided into five districts organized as Carroll, Coweta, Lee, Muscogee, and Troup Counties. The allotment of lands to individuals, like that in all the new Georgia lands between 1805 and 1832 (encompassing some two-thirds of the land area of the state), was according to a lottery system.[2] With few exceptions, all white male U.S. citizens over eighteen years of age who had lived in Georgia for at least three years, as well as widows and orphans, were eligible to draw for a 202.5-acre lot. "Fortunate drawers" could claim their land on payment of an $18 fee to cover the expenses of the lottery. According to family tradition, John and Elizabeth King of Wilkinson County, parents of *Sacred Harp* co-compiler E. J. King, were among the fortunate drawers in the 1827 lottery; they subsequently claimed land near Upatoi Creek in what would become Talbot County.

The 1827 lottery resulted in rapid development of the region by white settlers and black slaves and the further subdivision into smaller counties as shown in plate 2. The decennial census shows that, as early as 1840, four of the seven most populous counties in Georgia were in this new section, including Troup (15,733), Talbot (15,627), Meriwether (14,132), and Harris (13,933).[3] Talbot County, home to E. J. King and many other composers represented in *The Sacred Harp*, was the fourth-largest county by population only thirteen years after its settlement; slightly more than 43 percent of its residents were enslaved blacks. Harris County, home to B. F. White, was the sixth-largest, with an even greater proportion of slaves.

Thomas Wiggins, born blind and in slavery on a Harris County plantation in 1849 and sold as an infant to Columbus lawyer James N. Bethune, became a national musical prodigy after his pianistic debut in 1857 as "Blind Tom." In the twentieth century, the Chattahoochee Valley, home of *The Sacred Harp*, has been recognized by the folklorists George Mitchell and Fred Fussell as an important source of African American traditional music, including spiritual songs, fife-and-drum music, blues, and gospel music.[4] The decade of the 1840s is marked by the appearance in print of large numbers of "revival spiritual songs" with refrains, a feature that distinguishes the 1844 *Sacred Harp* from earlier southern tunebooks. It is tempting to speculate that some of these may draw on the widespread popularity of such songs in the musical lives of black as well as white pioneers in West Georgia more than twenty years before the national emergence of the Negro spiritual.

THE
WESTWARD
MIGRATION

The west Georgia makers of the Sacred Harp were part of a general and widely recognized pattern of westward migration within the United States. Some, like South Carolina native B. F. White, were immigrants to western Georgia from states further east. Other early Sacred Harp composers born in South Carolina were Reuben E. Brown Sr. (born 1794), Oliver Bradfield (1820), Thomas W. Carter (1822), William Williamson Parks (1823), and John Stringer Terry (1826). From North Carolina came Edmund Dumas (1810), Robert Henry Davis (1824), and Ann Lancaster (1832). Spencer Reed Penick was born in Virginia in 1803. Even among composers born in Georgia, it is possible to trace a movement from the earlier-settled eastern edge of the state to the west-central area where White and King were active. Among them were James R. Turner (born 1807), Richard F. M. Mann (1816), Absalom Ogletree (1817), James Lafayette Pickard (1826), Edwin Theophilus Pound (1833), and Matthew Mark Wynn (1835).

A similar pattern continued across Alabama and Mississippi and beyond: a series of Indian cessions and removals, followed (or preceded) by settlement by white landowners and entrepreneurs with black slaves concentrated in fertile bottomlands suitable for cotton cultivation. Many who were in western Georgia at the publication of the 1844, 1850, 1859, and 1870 editions of *The Sacred Harp* continued to move westward to Alabama, Mississippi, and Texas; only a few moved eastward. One of the first areas colonized by Sacred Harp singers and composers was Alabama's Creek cession of 1832, embracing the east-central part of the state, where the discovery of gold led to a rush of settlement during the 1830s and 1840s. Georgia-born musicians active in Alabama included Reuben E. Brown Sr. (by 1850), Oliver Bradfield, Calvin Ford Letson, James Lloyd Meggs, Richard R. Osborne, Frances Eva Parkerson, William Lafayette Williams, A. J. McLendon, and Millard

Fillmore McWhorter. Later generations included Sidney Burdette Denson, Alfred Marcus Cagle, Willis Alvin Yates, Lee A. McGraw, Thomas Pickens Woodard, O. H. Handley, and Jeff Sheppard.

Some who had grown up or tarried in Georgia or Alabama remained restless and yearned to continue west, mainly to Texas. Among the composers who moved on to Texas were members of the White and King families, as well as many others: David Patillo White, Jesse Thomas White, Elias Lafayette King, Sarah (Lancaster) Hagler, Oliver Bradfield, Reuben E. Brown Sr., W. F. Moore, John Stringer Terry, M. H. Turner, Matthew Mark Wynn, and William Lafayette Williams.

Williams, still living in Tallapoosa, Alabama, in 1869, must have expressed a feeling shared by many who fondly remembered the musical friends of their youth: not only had many perished in the Civil War, but many more were migrating further westward. In a song published in the *Barnesville Gazette*,[1] Williams reminds his friend J. M. Goodwin of their mutual love of music.

> When traveling over the West, Sir,
> Remember the writer of this;
> Who feels the most sensible pleasure,
> When thinking on times we have met[.]
> When sounding harmonious voices
> In concert so pleasant and sweet,
> With treble, and tenor and counter,
> Harmoniously cording with Bass.
>
> Though mountains and rivers may part us
> With many a long tedious mile,
> And winter with all its cold changes,
> And Spring's fragrant flowers may smile[.]
> Yet surely I'll never forget you,
> While reason and sense I retain;
> Nor sever those bright chains of friendship,
> Cemented by music's sweet strains.
>
> I wish you a pleasant location,
> Wherever your choice may befall,
> And hope you will trust a bless'd Saviour,
> And come at his last trumpet's call.
> And hope you will ever remember
> Those friends you have left far behind;
> Though few yet, perhaps they are closer
> Than many perchance you may find.

Ironically, Williams himself would soon move to Texas to join his children.

THE SACRED HARP
AND THE CIVIL WAR

The Sacred Harp arose as part of the culture of a nation and a region in crisis, whose fortunes were frequently disturbed by war. In the Jacksonian era, the United States made impressive strides toward democracy and universal white male suffrage. The enforced removal of the southeastern Indians in the "Trail of Tears" removed the threat of violence to the settlers. The new territories won from the Creek and the Cherokee filled rapidly with settlers from Virginia and the Carolinas. The cotton economy flourished in the Chattahoochee and Flint Valleys, where large plantations produced tons of cotton to feed the mills of the northern states and Great Britain, while rendering the gradual elimination of slavery a political impossibility. The antebellum boom encouraged the growth of industry, the construction of canals and railroads, the founding of schools and colleges, and an increase in printing and publishing. Yet the economic prosperity that made the Sacred Harp possible was based on the rich lands of the Native Americans and the arduous labor of enslaved blacks, despite the fact that fewer than 5 percent of free southerners owned any slaves at all; in Georgia, this figure approached 7 percent.[1] The paradox perceived by James Madison of Virginia remained unsolved: "Next to the case of the black race within our bosom, that of the red on our borders is the problem most baffling to the policy of our country."[2]

The western Georgia home of *The Sacred Harp* was settled in the aftermath of the Indian wars and the Creek cession. In the year the tunebook was published, the election of James K. Polk as president inaugurated a new aggressive stance against Mexico and Great Britain, making the Mexican War of 1846–48 almost inevitable. The decade of the 1850s saw a steadily worsening sectional conflict as the nation teetered toward a devastating civil war. Georgians continued to prosper in this decade, which was also a period of growth for Sacred Harp singing.

The songbook was issued in new editions in 1850 and 1859, expanding the size of the collection from 263 to 432 pages. Yet on the pages of *The Organ,* the Hamilton newspaper founded by B. F. White in 1852, the struggle between the sweet songs of Zion and the clarion call of war is evident. Minutes of singing conventions and lectures on sacred music appear on the same pages as political tracts concerning the Kansas question and advertisements for slaves. In an 1855 lecture reprinted in *The Organ,* Upson County schoolteacher G. H. Perdue praises the healing power of music by invoking the Indians expelled only a quarter-century earlier: "Music has a powerful effect on our feelings, and in this world of care and trouble it would be extremely difficult to get along without this soul-enlivening gift of God. It will be recollected that Aborigines of the country have so great confidence in the charms of music that it was resorted to in cases of extreme sickness, and indeed it often had the desired effect."[3]

In another issue, *The Organ* reprinted (from the Democratic *New York Herald*) an article titled "Union or Disunion" whose intemperate tone and inflammatory language make disunion seem inevitable. In this way *The Organ* took a clear side in the polarization that led to secession, despite the proclamation on its masthead: "neutral in politics and religion, devoted to art, science, education, morality and the advancement of sacred music."[4]

The question of union or disunion was answered for Georgians in January 1861. Despite the pleas of Georgia statesman Alexander Stephens, the state seceded; Stephens soon became vice-president of the Confederacy, and the war was on. Militia major B. F. White, though sixty years of age at the outbreak of the war, is reported to have led in training the local militia during the conflict, and he served as mayor of Hamilton during the war. Of the composers of music in the Sacred Harp, some were preachers or other professionals and were exempt from military service.[5] William Hauser, both a preacher and a physician, served with the 48th Georgia Infantry as a chaplain. The Reverend H. S. Reese remained a civilian, serving as a medical assistant. Yet white men of all classes volunteered for service. At least three composers died in the war: Thomas Waller died of dysentery in Okolona, Mississippi in 1862; James Lafayette Pickard died of measles in a military hospital in Savannah in 1863; R. F. Ball died in unknown circumstances. Carroll County's J. A. Z. Shell was severely wounded in the Battle of Chancellorsville. Willis Dallas Jones, also from Carroll County, was injured while unloading baggage with the 27th Infantry in Quitman, Georgia, in April 1864; he was barely nineteen, and he had to use crutches for the rest of his life. Henry G. Mann, with the 28th Infantry, was wounded in the head at Cold Harbor, Virginia, in 1862; he was not yet nineteen, but he survived until 1920.

While these composers and song leaders were suffering injury and death in the Civil War, at least one child was born who would become a major figure in the Sacred Harp: on 20 January 1863, only days after President Lincoln's Emancipation Proclamation was issued, a boy was born to Levi P. Denson and his wife Julia Ann. He was named Thomas Jackson Denson after General Thomas J. "Stonewall" Jackson, one of the South's most successful commanders, who had captured some twelve thousand Union soldiers at Harpers Ferry in September of the previous year.

The Sacred Harp traveled with at least some of the southern soldiers in their wartime journeys. William Jefferson Moseley (1842–97) of Bibb County, serving in Virginia with the 10th Georgia Infantry, reported to his mother that "we have some of the best singings around the camp fire I have ever heard, since Troupe Edmonds and E. T. Pound used to teach singing school."[6] James Madison "Matt" Jordan (1837–65) wrote to his sister-in-law, the composer Sarah Lancaster, on 7 May 1863 from Guinea Station, near Chancellorsville, to thank her for sending a piece of original music.[7]

At least fourteen of the composers represented in the 1991 edition, and probably many more, served in the Confederate forces. But there were others who fought on the Union side. James William Dadmun, the Massachusetts clergyman who composed REST FOR THE WEARY, joined the war effort as a chaplain while continuing his musical work by providing songs for the troops; he published *Army Melodies* in 1861. Canadian-born William Edward Chute was strongly committed to the Union cause; he enlisted in Minnesota and joined the 14th army corps under the command of General W. T. Sherman in his assault on Atlanta and his March to the Sea. Despite this he developed a warm relationship with Savannah-area composer William Hauser, to whom he loaned old songbooks and with whom he shared information; Hauser called Chute "the greatest hymn and tune antiquary I have ever known"[8] and printed Chute's setting of BABYLON IS FALLEN in his *Olive Leaf* (1878).

When Henry Goodwin Mann, still only twenty-one years of age, stacked his arms with those of his comrades and surrendered to Union troops under Sherman at Greensboro, North Carolina, on 26 April 1865, the war was over. As the survivors hobbled home to their families, they found consolation in the songbook that had sustained them around many a bivouac fire. At one of the first Sacred Harp singings documented in Mississippi, leading singers "met at Poplar Springs church with a few war worn rebs, their noble wives and the children of this neighborhood and engaged in a song service, using the old sacred harp as a text." The reporter adds that "in mingling their voices together in song, the old veterans seemed to forget for the time being, their dilapidated farms, as well as the hardships and dangers through which they had just passed, and the kind old matrons, thankful that their husbands and sons were once again permitted to be with them on the old hill, seemed to pour forth their joy and gratitude in songs of praise."[9]

Like other former Confederate states, Georgia continued to resist, despite the collapse of the cotton economy and the imposition of federal military reconstruction. The General Assembly defiantly refused to ratify the Fourteenth Amendment to the U.S. Constitution, which guaranteed full citizenship to former slaves. On 15 July 1870 Georgia became the last Confederate state to be readmitted to the Union. Meanwhile, in late November 1869, a committee of the Southern Musical Convention met with B. F. White to prepare the fourth edition of *The Sacred Harp,* which emerged from the Philadelphia presses in 1870. Georgia had survived, and so had the Sacred Harp.

MUSICAL
FAMILIES

In Europe, where professions were often hereditary, musical activity and eminence often ran in families over the course of several generations, as with the
Bachs of Germany and the Couperins of France. In the English colonies, with a
relative paucity of musical professions and positions, family ties were nevertheless significant. Nym Cooke has identified familial relationships among American
psalmodists during the period 1770–1820. Teachers often instructed their children
in music; brothers and sisters, together with cousins who lived nearby, often attended singing schools together.[1] A few of these relationships are reflected in the
pages of the 1991 *Sacred Harp*. Amos Munson of Cheshire, Connecticut, composer
of NEWBURGH, was brother to two other composers, Joel Munson and Reuben
Munson, not represented in the Sacred Harp. His first cousin Amos Doolittle was
an active engraver and printer of tunebooks, including several by Daniel Read and
Stephen Jenks. Amos Doolittle's younger brother Eliakim Doolittle is the composer
of EXHORTATION and other tunes. The brothers Lucius and Amzi Chapin, natives
of Massachusetts, were both active in the Valley of Virginia during the 1790s before
settling in Kentucky and Pennsylvania, respectively.[2] Attributions to the Chapins in
published sources are sometimes contradictory because the brothers seem to have
taught a common store of tunes and arrangements, and the published attributions
may reflect the specific manuscript sources available to a given compiler.[3]

As the American tradition of composition advanced to the south and the west,
family connection remained an important vehicle for passing on musical skills to
the next generation. A surprising number of important compilers and composers
had little or no formal training in singing schools but learned music within the
family circle. Spartanburg, South Carolina, was an important early center. William

Walker, author of *Southern Harmony,* and Benjamin Franklin White were brothers-in-law, since both married Golightly sisters (see figure 1). Long before *The Sacred Harp* was conceived, White contributed one tune to Walker's 1835 tunebook; J. S. James, drawing on White family lore, suggests that White's contribution was much greater and that his role was that of an uncredited co-compiler, a circumstance that led to an estrangement between the two men. Two nephews of B. F. White contributed to *The Sacred Harp,* one indirectly. Jesse Thomas White was the son of B. F. White's older brother Robert White Jr. He moved to Georgia about 1840 and contributed ten songs to the first edition of the *Sacred Harp* before moving on to Mississippi and Texas. William W. Bobo was the son of B. F. White's older sister Elizabeth. He remained in the Spartanburg area all his life and contributed a tune to an 1847 edition of *Southern Harmony* that was later added to *The Sacred Harp.*

The contributions of White's nephews suggest that music may have been a significant part of the life he shared with his siblings. More significant is the musical legacy he passed on to his own children. Three of his sons played an important role in the history and revision of *The Sacred Harp.* David Patillo White, born in South Carolina in 1828, moved to Georgia with his parents; he listed "music teacher" as his profession as early as the 1850 census. In that same year, he contributed six tunes to the *Sacred Harp* appendix. Soon after this, he accompanied his father and the Baptist missionary Reuben E. Brown Sr., also a composer, on an extended tour of southeast Alabama. The younger White subsequently married Brown's daughter Celeste in 1852. Brown and the Whites afterwards moved to Texas, leaving behind Celeste's brother Reuben E. Brown Jr., also a music teacher, who contributed a tune to the 1859 *Sacred Harp* appendix.

Two of B. F. White's younger sons were also active as composers and publishers of later revisions of the *Sacred Harp.* Georgia-born B. F. "Frank" White Jr., composed a tune for the 1870 *Sacred Harp.* After the senior White's death, he and his younger brother James Landrum "Jim" White prepared *The New Sacred Harp* (1884), a seven-shape tunebook designed to capitalize on the earlier book's popularity while greatly modernizing its repertory and style. Jim White, who had contributed only a single tune to *The Sacred Harp* during his father's lifetime, became a respected music teacher and composer who continually tried, with varying success, to modernize the old songbook, producing at least two "fifth editions" (1909 and 1910) and a "fourth edition with supplement" in 1911.

Still other White children are not themselves known as composers but helped link White with Richard F. M. Mann, a prolific composer and an important figure in the conventions and the revision committees. White's son Robert H. White married Mann's sister Mary, and White's daughter Malvina Thurza "Mallie" White married Mann's brother Wesley: thus Mann was brother-in-law to two of White's

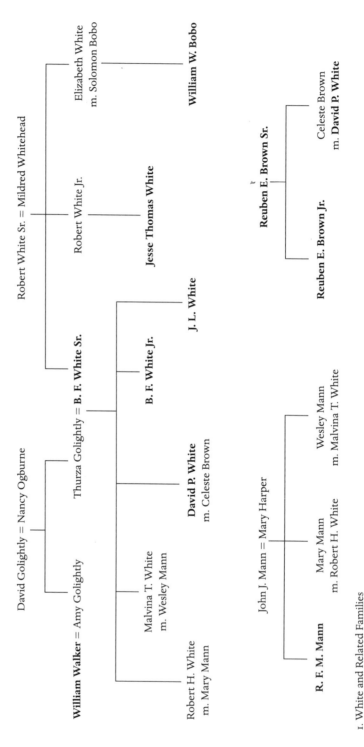

1. White and Related Families

children. One of Mann's compositions, TOLLING BELL, is dedicated to White's youngest daughter, Martha America "Mattie" White, and to his own sister Elizabeth Adeline Mann.

Elisha James King, the junior compiler of *The Sacred Harp*, was a member of a musical family in Talbot County. Though he died in 1844 as the book was being published, at least one member of his family continued to contribute to the tunebook after his death. Elias Lafayette King, only sixteen years of age when *The Sacred Harp* first appeared, contributed six tunes to the 1850 appendix. Other members of King's family played a nonmusical role. Elisha's oldest brother Joel King is listed on the title page as co-proprietor of the first edition of *The Sacred Harp*, perhaps indicating that Elisha was too inexperienced in business affairs, or too sick, to undertake this role. On Elisha's death, his own interest, together with seven hundred copies of the book, was purchased by his brother-in-law Henry Snellings, husband of Elisha's sister Mary.

Another Talbot County family produced at least two Sacred Harp composers. James Lafayette Pickard (1826–63) contributed a tune to the 1850 appendix. His sister Nancy and her husband James William Pound were Talbot County farmers until their deaths in the 1880s. Their son Edwin Theophilus Pound (1833–1919) became an important figure in *The Sacred Harp* as a composer, a teacher, and a pupil, assistant, and ultimately rival of B. F. White.

A father-and-son pair in the early history of *The Sacred Harp* is that of James R. Turner and William Stevens Turner. James, a native of Hancock County, lived most of his life in Villa Rica, in the northerly regions of the 1826 cession. An officer of the Southern Musical Convention and a member of the Sacred Harp revision committee of 1850, he contributed two tunes to that edition, including one cited as a collaboration between "T. & J. R. Turner," presumably indicating a relative. His son W. S. Turner, who became a Methodist preacher, attended his father's singing schools and contributed tunes to the 1859 and 1870 editions.

Among the most active and prominent Sacred Harp teachers and composers were the twin brothers Henry Smith Reese and John Palmer Reese. Born in Jasper County, Georgia, in 1828, they moved to Muscogee County, where they appear with their father's family in the 1850 census; in that year, Henry's first compositions were published in the new Sacred Harp appendix. John, at least, had musical instruction from Talbot County teacher Spencer Reed Penick, and both brothers are listed as Columbus agents for John G. McCurry's *Social Harp* (1855). Here their paths diverged. Henry followed his father's profession: he was ordained to the Baptist ministry in 1853 and served as an itinerant preacher until the beginning of the Civil War, when he settled in Turin, Coweta County. John traveled widely as a singing teacher but also settled down as a farmer in nearby Newnan. Both were active in the early musical conventions, and both were correspondents with the editors of the Newnan *Advertiser* and other newspapers. Both were prolific composers, contributing a total of twenty-seven songs to the 1859 *Sacred Harp;* they played a major role in formulating the style of melody and harmony that would define the Sacred Harp in the twentieth century.

One of the most remarkable musical families in the early history of the Sacred Harp comprises the daughters of James Lupo Lancaster (1810–95). Female composers are not unknown in southern religious music, but it is surprising to find three sisters, all of whom composed songs for publication. Even more surprising is that the Lancaster sisters are descendants of a family of professional musicians active in England in the sixteenth and seventeenth centuries.

Ambrose de Almaliach, known as Lupo, a Jewish string player from Milan (perhaps a Sephardic refugee from Spain or Portugal), was one of six musicians recruited in Venice in 1540 by agents of Henry VIII. He served the English court until his death in 1591 and played at the funeral of Henry VIII and at the coronations of Edward VI and Elizabeth I. His sons Joseph and Peter, born in Venice, did not accompany their father to England but were trained in the Netherlands before entering the service of Queen Elizabeth in the 1560s. Joseph and Peter had sons (both named Thomas) who became court musicians and composers; they joined the elder Lupos as violinists at Elizabeth's funeral in 1603. Compositions of several of the Lupos survive.[4]

Peter Lupo married Katherine Wicke in 1575. Their children included two sons who did not become professional musicians: Albiano (1579–1626) and Philip (1583–1652), both of whom journeyed to Virginia, settling in Elizabeth City County (now part of Hampton). Although Philip, a goldsmith, returned to England, his son, also named Philip Lupo, arrived in Virginia in 1640, taking up land in Isle of Wight County, where he became the progenitor of the Lupo family that produced the Lancaster sisters of Marion County, Georgia.

Anna Lupo, born in Isle of Wight County in 1781, was a descendant of Philip Lupo Jr. She married James Lancaster in 1809 in Edgecombe County, North Carolina. James Lupo Lancaster, their oldest child, was born in 1810. In 1824 James Lancaster died of pneumonia, leaving Anna with seven children and pregnant with an eighth. After remaining in Edgecombe for several years, she moved the entire family to Talbot County, Georgia, around 1833. By this time James Lupo Lancaster had married his cousin Charity Lancaster in 1827, and they had three small children with them when they moved. Six additional children were born in Talbot County, where they grew up amid a large extended family whose neighbors included the Kings, the Reeses, the Pickards, and the Breedloves, and where their lives surely included music making.

Gradually the extended Lupo-Lancaster family dispersed as James's brothers moved on to Alabama, Mississippi, and Louisiana. James and Charity moved to nearby Marion County, where he worked as a farmer and carpenter. Among their children were the three musical sisters, Anna Lucinda Maria Atkinson Lancaster ("M. L. A. Lancaster" in *The Sacred Harp,* "Ann" to her family), born in North Carolina, Sarah ("Sally") Lancaster, and Priscilla R. "Sid" Lancaster, the last two born in Georgia. By the mid-1850s all three were composing music, and Sarah was developing a lifelong interest in the art. An 1854 letter from Sarah to Ann shows that she was attending the Hamilton Female Seminary (a kind of finishing school) and apparently was boarding with B. F. White and his family. While she may have attended one of White's singing schools, she certainly received musical instruction at school, including private piano lessons. The letter reveals a somewhat shallow and petulant young woman with an intense interest in, almost an obsession with, music. A few months later Ann received a letter from Columbus, apparently from J. P. Reese, commenting on compositions that she and Priscilla had sent him for advice and approval. The surviving letter is incomplete, but it appears that the compositions in question are those published in the 1859 *Sacred Harp* appendix: NEW HARMONY and OH, SING WITH ME! Sarah's work is not mentioned, but it is clear that by 1859 she had formed the habit of including one or more original compositions in her letters to close friends and family members.[5]

A close friend of the Lancaster sisters was Nancy Bradfield, a South Carolina native who had come to Coweta County with her family, including her brother, the composer Oliver Bradfield, who had founded the Chattahoochee Musical Convention in 1852. In an 1860 letter to Ann Lancaster, Nancy writes that she is composing a piece of music to send along. In a postscript she encourages Sarah to continue sending pieces of music: "I don't care how many tunes you send me if it is one hundred." A letter to Sarah from a brother-in-law in the Confederate Army shows that she had sent him a piece as well: "I am a thousand times obliged to you for the song you sent me. . . . I think I can learn it tolerable easy. O, I haven't language to express how proud I am of it."[6]

In 1866 Sarah Lancaster married George Washington "Wash" Hagler; ten years later the couple, with their five children, moved to Freestone County, Texas, where Sarah continued to send music with her letters and to inquire about "the singings" back home. On 28 October 1877 she wrote to Ann, "I have tunes running in my mind all the time, day and night, tell me what you think of that."

Members of the Lupo family served six English monarchs from 1540 to 1650, separated by two centuries from the musical activities of their Georgia descendants. Present-day descendants of James Lupo Lancaster include piano teachers and amateur musicians, and they still regard themselves as a musical family.

Another family in which the musical gene has run unusually true, and which played a crucial role in the development and survival of the Sacred Harp tradition, includes descendants of William Howard Denson (see figure 2). Joseph Denson, like Anna Lupo, was a native of Isle of Wight County, Virginia, and had moved to North Carolina and then South Carolina, where William Howard Denson was born around 1785. The son went on to Georgia, where he married Catherine Melinda Phillips in 1809. Their third child, James M. Denson (1816–55), was raised in Walton County, a little to the east of the western Georgia heartland of Sacred Harp activity, yet he contributed an anthem to the first edition of the book and served as president of the Southern Musical Convention in 1847 before emigrating to Louisiana.

James Denson's younger brother Levi Phillips Denson (1819–89) likewise grew up in Walton County; after his marriage in 1838 to Julia Ann Jones, the couple moved to the gold fields of eastern Alabama, where they settled in Arbacoochee, Randolph County (now Cleburne County) around 1845. Levi became a miner, farmer, mechanic, and Methodist lay preacher; though he was not, like his brother James, involved in the original foundations of the Sacred Harp, two of his sons, their wives, and their numerous descendants occupy a unique place in its continued development. Seaborn McDaniel Denson, the third son, was born at Arbacoochee in 1854 and educated in common schools only a few months per year. His brother Thomas Jackson Denson, nearly twelve years younger, was born in 1863.

Among the other residents of Randolph County was the family of William Howard Burdette of Wilkes County, Georgia, and his wife Julia Ann Prather. Married in 1843, the Burdettes came to the gold-bearing regions of Alabama after the rush had subsided, around 1853; they had one son who lived to adulthood and seven daughters. The Burdette girls were afforded a more thorough education than the Denson boys: daughter Sidney attended a boarding school in Troup County, Georgia, while her younger sister Amanda was a student at the nearby Chulafinnee Academy. Both were trained in music; their brother James Alexander Burdette was a singing teacher and a leader of the Chattahoochee Musical Convention. Music, and perhaps singing schools, must have been an important element in the courtship of Densons and Burdettes: in 1874 Seaborn Denson married Sidney Burdette and also taught his first singing school. In 1878, the fifteen-year-old Tom Denson led a thirty-minute lesson at the Chattahoochee Convention in Georgia; at the end of that year, before reaching his sixteenth birthday, the boy married Amanda (plate 3). At the Chattahoochee convention two years later, Sidney caused a sensation as the only female song leader. During the 1890s both families moved to Winston County, Alabama, where Seaborn and Tom were farmers for part of the year and taught singing schools in the remaining months. They continued to travel to Georgia and eastern Alabama to visit friends and attend singings with their growing families. Seaborn was especially active as musical editor of the *Union Harp and History of Songs* (1909) and *Original Sacred Harp* (1911), both sponsored by the United Sacred Harp Musical Association of Atlanta. In the latter collec-

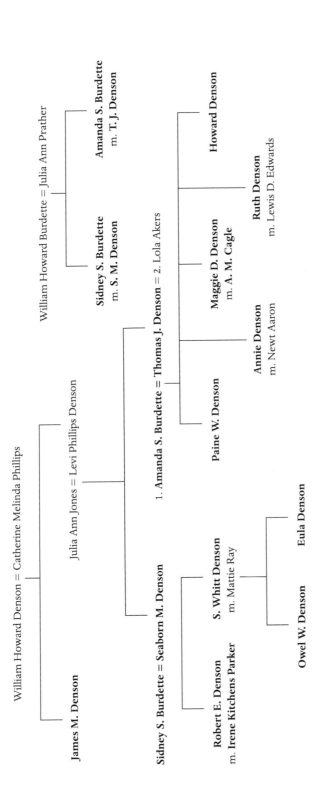

William Howard Denson = Catherine Melinda Phillips

Julia Ann Jones = Levi Phillips Denson

James M. Denson

William Howard Burdette = Julia Ann Prather

Sidney S. Burdette
m. **S. M. Denson**

Amanda S. Burdette
m. **T. J. Denson**

1. **Amanda S. Burdette = Thomas J. Denson** = 2. Lola Akers

Paine W. Denson

Annie Denson
m. Newt Aaron

Maggie D. Denson
m. A. M. Cagle

Ruth Denson
m. Lewis D. Edwards

Howard Denson

Sidney S. Burdette = Seaborn M. Denson

Robert E. Denson
m. **Irene Kitchens Parker**

S. Whitt Denson
m. Mattie Ray

Owel W. Denson

Eula Denson

2. Denson and Related Families

tion Seaborn added alto parts to most of the songs that had lacked them, while Sidney added scriptural quotations below the title of each song. Tom Denson was a founder of the Sacred Harp Publishing Company in 1933, which purchased the rights to *Original Sacred Harp* and began to revise that book in a much smaller format given the conditions of the Depression. Tom died in 1935 and Seaborn in 1936, about seven months later, just before the publication of the *Original Sacred Harp* (Denson revision).

After their deaths, their children came to the fore. Tom's son Paine Denson (1882–1955) completed the "Denson revision" as musical editor and wrote a new set of rudiments for it. His younger brother Howard Denson (1897–1950) also served on the revision committee. In addition, three of their sisters are credited with music in the Denson revision of the *Sacred Harp*: Annie Denson (1885–1962), wife of Winston County sheriff N. B. Aaron, Maggie Denson (1887–1969), wife of Sacred Harp composer A. M. Cagle, and Jarusha "Ruth" Denson (1893–1978), Cullman schoolteacher and wife of Lewis D. Edwards. All these were children of Tom and Amanda Denson. Tom Denson's children by his third wife, Lola Akers, included the active singers Tommye Mauldin, Vera Nunn, and Violet Hinton, but no composers represented in the *Sacred Harp*.

The children of Seaborn and Sidney Denson were likewise active singers and composers. Their son S. Whitt Denson (1890–1964) was a Church of God preacher and composer who sang in quartets, contributed to gospel music publications, and trained his children to sing. He was also a key figure in a series of small-group Sacred Harp recordings spanning the period 1928 to about 1960 in which he adapted a gospel quartet style, with piano accompaniment, to traditional Sacred Harp songs. The Denson Quartet of 1928 consisted of Whitt, his brothers Robert and Evan Denson, and J. C. "Cadd" Brown. Later incarnations of the quartet included his daughters Eula and Delilah, his cousin Howard Denson, and gospel publisher Orin Adolphus Parris. Whitt's daughter Eula Denson Johnson is credited with a song in the *Sacred Harp,* as is his son, gospel composer and publisher Owel W. Denson; Whitt's brother Robert E. Denson of Addison was a familiar sight at Sacred Harp singings until his death in 1983 at the age of ninety-one. A grandson of S. M. Denson was Otis Leon McCoy (1897–1995), son of Denson's daughter Ida. He became well known in the gospel music industry as a member of the Vaughan Quartet, as an instructor of sight-singing at the Vaughan School of Music, and as founder of Tennessee Music and Printing Company in 1931. Otis's brother Charles W. McCoy (1906–98) was a noted Sacred Harp singer and contributed a tune to the 1960 Denson revision, but it was removed from later editions.

In Europe, musical leadership and employment frequently passed from father to son-in-law, to the extent that applicants for the position were expected to marry the incumbent's daughter. Although leadership in the publication and promotion of Sacred Harp singing did not come with a title or a stipend, it is tempting to see Tom Denson's son-in-law Alfred Marcus Cagle (1884–1968) in this light. Born in Georgia and abandoned by his father at an early age, young Marcus accompanied his mother to Alabama, where he met Seaborn and Tom Denson. As a young employee on the latter's farm, he received instruction and advice on his early compositions. He also made the acquaintance of Tom Denson's daughter Maggie, whom he married. Although this marriage ended in divorce, Cagle remained close to the family and continued to collaborate with the Denson children in songbook revision and publication. After his death in 1968, Maggie's sister Ruth Denson Edwards wrote an obituary in the 1971 Denson revision stressing Cagle's musical accomplishments.

Another protégé of Tom Denson was James Elmer Kitchens (1912–79) of Parrish, Alabama. Kitchens accompanied Denson on a teaching tour of Texas in 1930. Among his many pupils were his own brothers and sisters, including Irene Kitchens. Late in life Irene married Seaborn Denson's son Robert E. Denson after both had lost their first spouses.

Another important musical family comprises the descendants of Roland Jackson McGraw (1859–1910) and Augusta Ann Savannah Entrekin (1865–1940). After marrying in 1879, this couple lived in Carroll and in Haralson Counties, Georgia, where their children were born. Three were composers: Lee A. McGraw, a member of the Denson revision committee of 1935, H. N. "Bud" McGraw (who served on the 1935 and 1960 committees), and their younger brother Tom McGraw, who lived long enough to serve on the revision committees of 1935, 1960, and 1966 (see figure 3). Their cousin Thomas Jesse Entrekin (1879–1974) of Tifton, Georgia, contributed a tune to the 1960 Denson revision, but it was removed from later editions. The grandsons of Roland Jackson McGraw are represented by Lee's son Edgar Leon McGraw of Auburn, Alabama, and Bud's son Buford McGraw of Mt. Zion, Georgia. Buford's wife Gladys was the sister of the composer Charlene Wallace.

One of the best-known McGraws is a second cousin to Leon and Buford. A grandson of Roland Jackson's brother William Alexander McGraw (1862–1930), Hugh McGraw (plate 4) played a crucial role in the revitalization and spread of Sacred Harp singing in the late twentieth century. He began singing as an adult; under the guidance of A. M. Cagle and Raymond Hamrick he quickly became an accomplished composer of several memorable songs. He will be chiefly remembered, however, for his long service with the Sacred Harp Publishing Company as executive secretary from 1958 to 2002, for his role in the revisions of 1960, 1966, 1971, and 1991, and for his leadership in bringing hundreds of new singers, many from outside the South, into the tradition while helping to establish singings and conventions in many states.

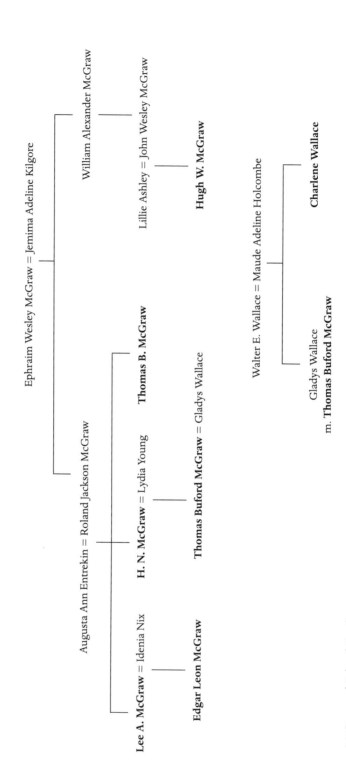

3. McGraw and Related Families

In the early years of the twentieth century, Marion County in western Alabama supported many singings and conventions; both Tom and Seaborn Denson taught schools in the county. Among the singing families of the area, the Frederick family of Hackleburg produced three composers, all pupils of Tom Denson, whose works are represented in *The Sacred Harp*. Oscar H. Frederick, born in 1885, was the grandson of Marion County pioneers; he farmed, worked in insurance, and taught singing schools. His son Elbert Foy Frederick went to college, then returned to the county as a schoolteacher and agricultural agent. Oscar's nephew Floyd Monroe Frederick was an active teacher until his death in 1960.

Another Alabama family that contributed to the Sacred Harp was the Parris family. Hosea Anderson Parris, born in Georgia, moved at an early age to Winston County, where he lived near the Densons. He contributed an arrangement to the *Union Harp* (1909). His nephew Orin Adolphus Parris, who also resided in Winston County, became a major figure in southern music as a publisher, teacher, and composer in varied styles for the *Sacred Harp, Christian Harmony,* and shape-note convention music. He was a quartet singer and a member of the Denson-Parris Quartet, which recorded for Columbia in 1934. He served on the 1935 *Sacred Harp* revision committee, revised the *Christian Harmony* in 1954, and founded the Parris Music Company and the Convention Music Company.

The DeLongs were early settlers of Hall County, Georgia, but spread through much of the northern part of that state during the nineteenth century. Doris W. DeLong (1906–86), a native of Roswell, wrote more than forty songs, two of which were published in the 1960 Denson revision. He also recorded with the Roswell Sacred Harp Singers on a private label during the 1950s. His grand-nephew Richard L. DeLong learned music from family members, began teaching singing schools in his teens, and chaired the United Sacred Harp Convention at the age of twenty. He accompanied Hugh McGraw in his journeys to organize and support singings in distant parts and contributed an original composition and an arrangement of an English song-tune to the 1991 edition.

PROFESSIONS
AND OCCUPATIONS

In the history of European music since the Renaissance, the art of musical composition has been practiced by persons in a variety of livelihoods. Aristocratic courts, churches, and many municipalities provided livings for the vast majority of European musicians known as composers before 1800. Many of these served as singers, instrumentalists, music directors, and teachers for whom composing was a qualification for employment or at least a desired activity. Spanish and Portuguese colonies in the New World made early attempts to re-create this system of patronage, at least in the church, but the English colonies to the north offered few vocational opportunities to talented musicians, especially outside the major towns on the Eastern seaboard, where, by 1800, musical societies, theatre, and some semblance of concert life flourished, largely staffed by immigrants from England and other European lands. A persistent theme in the history of music in the United States, then, has been the effort of American musicians, lacking traditional sources of patronage, to search out or if necessary create a market for their skills and to cobble together a career or profession for themselves while gradually laying the foundations of musical institutions. Those who succeeded as musicians are distinguished as unusually enterprising, versatile, and flexible. Among the musical professions most often pursued in early America, that of singing-master stands out.[1]

During the period 1770–1810, most compilers of sacred tunebooks pursued at least a part-time career as a teacher of psalmody or sacred music. In many cases, however, this was not full-time work: among early composers represented in *The Sacred Harp*, William Billings was a tanner, and Daniel Read a general merchant and comb-maker. Timothy Swan and Amariah Hall were hatters; Justin Morgan, Supply Belcher, and Jeremiah Ingalls innkeepers; Elihu Carpenter, Oliver Holden, and

Lucius Chapin carpenters; and Samuel Holyoke, Elihu Carpenter, Eliakim Doolittle, and Jacob Kimball schoolmasters. A minority of singing-masters pursued an itinerant life, moving frequently to conduct singing schools in fresh territory, but as Nym Cooke has shown, most New England singing teachers (including 70 percent of the 149 composers and tuneboook compilers for whom biographical information is available) appear to have taught school primarily near their settled home.[2]

As these musical activities became prevalent in the Middle States and the South in the nineteenth century, they came to be seen as especially suited to young men, who taught singing schools, composed music, and perhaps published tunebooks in their youth and then went on to other pursuits in later life. Among compilers credited with tunes in *The Sacred Harp,* Ananias Davisson, James P. Carrell, Alexander Johnson, William Caldwell, and John G. McCurry are not known to have continued their musical activities into their old age, whereas William Walker, William Hauser, and B. F. White were among the exceptions who made music a lifelong, if not exclusive, occupation.

Nearly all the composers associated with the Sacred Harp in the nineteenth century were farmers at least part of the time; this is hardly surprising, given the prominence of agriculture in the southern economy. Of these, most were small farmers employing mainly family members or just a few slaves or hired hands. A few, such as Leonard P. Breedlove and James Lafayette Pickard, were relatively large planters and slaveholders.

Next to farming, the employment most frequently mentioned among composers represented in *The Sacred Harp* is the teaching of music in singing schools. For many, this was a seasonal employment, since singing schools clustered around convenient times in the agricultural calendar, usually winter in New England and midsummer ("laying-by") in the South. Leaving spouse and children at home, some men were able to teach several singing schools per year while maintaining a farm. Among these were Seaborn and Tom Denson. Tom's wife Amanda recalled that she taught her children to sing at home while her husband was off teaching everybody else in the country how to sing. On other occasions, family members might accompany the teacher, serving as "section leaders" for scholars attempting to learn various voice parts. In 1892 Seaborn apparently brought his wife and children to Prentiss County, Mississippi, to teach singing schools in a community where his uncle William Cicero Denson had settled; Seaborn's son Robert E. Denson was born there in August of that year. Bob Denson later recalled accompanying his father in a mule wagon to a singing school in Hamilton, Alabama, where the mule died, stranding father and son until the local mayor graciously provided a replacement mule.

A substantial number of composers were well-educated persons pursuing prominent and respected professions. Ministers and preachers include Samuel Wakefield

of Mount Pleasant, Pennsylvania; Stephen Bovell of Abingdon, Virginia; James
P. Carrell of Lebanon, Virginia; Andrew Grambling of Pacolet, South Carolina;
and William Hauser of Georgia. Those directly associated with the Sacred Harp
in the nineteenth century include Henry Smith Reese, Edmund Dumas, Reuben
E. Brown Sr., Lewis Ledbetter, William S. Turner, Willis Dallas Jones, and John
Smith Searcy, who officiated at the third marriage of the composer Leonard P.
Breedlove. In the twentieth century, ministers and preachers credited with tunes
in the Sacred Harp include Elmer Kitchens, Roy Avery, B. E. Cunningham, Whitt
Denson, Priestly Miller, and J. M. Denton. A great many more were deacons or
other local church leaders. Physicians included Truman S. Wetmore, William
Hauser, Thomas W. Carter, William L. Williams, and Robert Henry Davis; Lewis
Ledbetter and Richard R. Osborne were dentists.

Magistrates (ordinaries and justices of the peace) include E. T. Pound, S. R.
Penick, Leonard P. Breedlove, Edmund Dumas (who also served in the General Assembly), D. P. White, B. F. White Jr., and Paine Denson. Benjamin Franklin White
Sr. was mayor of Hamilton, Georgia, while Robert Denson and Palmer Godsey
both served as mayor of Addison, Alabama. Millard Fillmore McWhorter served
as sheriff of Cleburne County, Alabama, where he was remembered as the last
non-gun-toting sheriff in the state. Many more served as county commissioners
or tax collectors.

Early American musicians Oliver Brownson and Ananias Davisson worked as
printers, while Joseph Stone worked as a bookbinder. Newspaper publishers and
editors included B. F. White, E. T. Pound, and J. S. James. The brothers Henry
and John Palmer Reese were frequent contributors to newspapers in their com-
munities, and Matilda (Durham) Hoy was the author of Baptist religious tracts.
Musicians who compiled or published music books other than *The Sacred Harp* include E. T. Pound, J. L. White, J. S. James, O. A. Parris (reviser of William Walker's
Christian Harmony in 1954 and 1958) and Owel Denson, and, more recently, Neely
Bruce, Bruce Randall, Glen Wright, and others.

For many farmers and part-time musicians, the business of buying and selling
proved attractive and profitable. Just as Daniel Read and Oliver Holden were successful merchants in New England, many southern musicians acted as merchants
at times. William Walker operated a bookstore in Spartanburg, South Carolina.
Other merchants included R. F. M. Mann and E. T. Pound in the nineteenth century and James A. Ayers, B. E. Cunningham, Floyd Frederick, Cecil Gilliland, O.
H. Handley, and Terry Wootten in the twentieth. Other singers and teachers kept
inns and hotels, including Justin Morgan, Jeremiah Ingalls, Solomon Chandler,
Amariah Hall, Abner Ellis, James M. Denson, J. T. White and Eula Denson Johnson. The Sacred Harp even has two barbers among its composers: Doris DeLong
and Toney Smith.

Teaching common or literary school was a widespread profession among early American psalmodists. Schoolteacher-composers represented in *The Sacred Harp* include Supply Belcher and Abraham Maxim of Maine, Eliakim Doolittle and Justin Morgan of Vermont, Nehemiah Shumway of New York, and Joseph Stone, Samuel Holyoke, and Jacob Kimball of Massachusetts. Among *Sacred Harp* composers, schoolteachers included Leonard P. Breedlove, M. Mark Wynn, and C. F. Letson, and, later, the sisters Sidney Burdette and Amanda Burdette Denson, as well as Amanda's daughter Ruth Denson Edwards, John Marion Dye, Foy Frederick, Palmer Godsey, and Richard DeLong.

TEACHERS
AND TRADITION

Since around 1700, singing schools have provided a model and a mechanism to transmit not only a book and a repertory of music but also an array of distinctive practices that are considered correct by singers, though they may seem archaic or uncouth to outsiders. Some of these practices are prescribed or introduced in outline form in the theoretical introductions ("rudiments") in *The Sacred Harp* and other tunebooks. Still others reside in the oral teaching of successive generations of singing-masters as well as those teaching informally.

For example, when keying music by ear, a song leader may disregard the notated pitch as determined by a keyboard or tuning fork. It is necessary for the keyer to scan the voice parts and offer a pitch that will enable all voice parts to lie in a comfortable or at least possible range for the voices at hand. This practice is recommended in the first book containing music printed in the English colonies, the "Bay Psalm Book" of 1698: "First observe of how many Notes compass the Tune is. Next, the place of your first Note; and how many Notes above & below that: so as you may begin the Tune of your first Note as the rest may be sung in the compass of your and the peoples voices, without Squeaking above, or Grumbling below."[1]

Like many other teachers, Hugh McGraw warns against keying music too high or low, leading to "screeching and growling," a phrase that echoes the "squeaking and grumbling" of early teachers and singing manuals. As another example of a shared teaching technique, many present-day teachers offer a homely image to teach the correct manner of beating time, in which the hand falls during the first half of the measure and rises in the second half. The bar line is likened to a low fence encountered by a dog that finds he can neither go through nor under, but must leap over the fence to continue on the other side.

Many excellent Sacred Harp singers, including B. F. White, never attended a singing school or learned most of the essentials of the art before attending a formal school. Some learned to sing in the family circle. Irene Denson learned from her brother J. E. Kitchens, and Toney Smith was taught music by his father. Others, such as John T. Hocutt, attended at least one singing school to learn the rudiments of singing but were self-taught in harmony and composition.

Singing schools offer a clear vehicle for continuity of musical tradition between the generations. The Canadian singing-master W. E. Chute, who knew many of the major figures in nineteenth-century American sacred music (he attended the institutes of Lowell Mason, George F. Root, and P. P. Bliss and corresponded with William Hauser, Samuel Wakefield, and H. P. Main), wrote proudly that he received his first musical instruction from his father, who was instructed by one Captain Dean, who was himself a pupil of William Billings![2] In the same way, many living singers and composers can trace their musical roots to Seaborn and Tom Denson.

Although White is known to have taught E. J. King, E. T. Pound, and perhaps Sarah Lancaster, it is difficult to establish such direct teacher-pupil relationships between White and his contemporaries (J. R. Turner, S. R. Penick), on one hand, and the great teachers and composers of the twentieth century, on the other. James Denson left Georgia in 1848, far too early to instruct his nephews Seaborn and Tom Denson, whose musical instructors remain unidentified. Alabama singer O. H. Handley studied in his youth with I. M. Shell, born in 1828, a neighbor of and collaborator with J. P. Reese, himself a pupil of S. R. Penick. Joe S. James, editor of *Original Sacred Harp* together with S. M. Denson, attended one of Turner's schools in Douglas County, Georgia. A large number of twentieth-century composers proudly identified themselves as pupils of Seaborn or Tom Denson or both: in addition to their children, these include A. M. Cagle, B. E. Cunningham, H. N. McGraw, O. A. Parris, G. S. Doss, and Oscar, Floyd, and Foy Frederick.

To Earl V. Thurman, organizations such as the Chattahoochee Musical Convention, rather than individual schools, represented the most potent means of transmitting the distinctive styles and practices of Sacred Harp singing from patriarchs such as White, Turner, J. P. Reese, Bradfield, and Ogletree to later generations. When Seaborn and Tom Denson began singing and teaching in the 1870s, B. F. White was still alive, and Absalom Ogletree and the Reeses were still active in the Chattahoochee and other conventions.

If the past is any guide, it may be that the future vitality of the Sacred Harp tradition ultimately depends on all three multigenerational activities: family musical life, singing schools (including Camp Fasola, founded in 2003), and singing conventions. It may be that another generation of singers can say with Chattahoochee Convention patriarch James Martin Hamrick (1838–1907) of Villa Rica:

For the past 40 years I have been a lover of sacred music and have traveled hundreds of miles to attend our conventions, and at my present age, it fills my soul with love to sing God's praises; and if a man were to pass my house with a sacred harp under his arm, he can return, eat my ham and sweetened coffee, and slumber on my best bed. . . . And after my time, I hope my musical friends will hold a memorial singing in memory of me.[3]

THE STYLES OF
SACRED HARP MUSIC

Newcomers to the Sacred Harp frequently comment that the music sounds archaic, like an echo from the past. Newspaper and magazine accounts, as well as many scholarly articles, confirm these impressions, suggesting that the music shows a striking resemblance to music of the Middle Ages,[1] that it is "brought down from Elizabethan England,"[2] or that it represents "an indigenous American music that has lived since the eighteenth century."[3] Sacred Harp singing is hailed as an expression of the common folk, a musical vernacular that has been attacked and suppressed by the "better music boys,"[4] the reformers who would replace it with a smoother, more cultivated style of religious music. *The Sacred Harp* is an eclectic tunebook containing examples of many styles and genres of music, yet when Sacred Harp singers sing it, it constitutes a distinctive sound that strikes many hearers as exotic, archaic, or elemental. It is well to remember that the Sacred Harp, its singing schools and conventions, its compilers and composers, are themselves descended from an earlier form of "better music," an attempt to bring congregational song into line with notated music books and the musical standards of educated clergy and musicians. The sound of today's Sacred Harp singing reflects the musical cultures, both European and American, urban and rural, that have contributed to it. The following essay attempts to trace the historical background of the Sacred Harp, its musical style and performance practice.

In England, the Reformation left in place trained choirs of men and boys, at least some organs, and a liturgy that allowed complex polyphonic settings in English of texts from the Bible and the Book of Common Prayer. Such music, however, was limited almost exclusively to cathedrals, universities, and churches and chapels under royal patronage and control. In the vast majority of parish churches, music was neglected. More radical reformers, many of them trained in John Calvin's

Geneva, stepped into the gap, promoting the unaccompanied unison singing by the entire congregation, of metrical psalms, that is, psalm texts set in strophic poetry such as that found in *The Whole Book of Psalms, Collected into English Metre* (1562). The tunes, including many imported from the Continent, supplied music for four, six, or eight lines of poetry, after which they could be repeated as needed. On Sundays and holy days, the parson and the clerk (a literate layman) read the services of morning and evening prayer, including psalms in prose, without any singing. Before and after the service, or before and after the sermon, the congregation, led by the parish clerk or other lay leader, sang a metrical psalm.[5]

During the English Civil War the Puritan Party gained ascendancy and remodeled the Church of England on Presbyterian lines, abolishing choirs and Prayer Book worship and removing many church organs. The musical element of worship in parish churches, however, changed little; one of the few innovations was the 1644 introduction of "lining out," a practice in which the clerk or other leader spoke or chanted the psalm in call-and-response fashion, one line at a time, answered by the congregation.[6] In this way Reformed psalmody in England, Scotland, and North America took a distinctive form: the singing was led by parish clerks or other leaders chosen "more for their poverty than skill and ability";[7] the repertory was increasingly limited to a small number of tunes that the congregation knew by heart; interrupted by the leader's promptings, the melody lost its rhythmic momentum and tended to slow down; the tune came to be freely embellished by members of the congregation and developed into an oral tradition bearing little resemblance to the printed tunes.[8] This practice, known in both England and America as "the old way of singing," may be heard today in the churches of the Isle of Lewis in Scotland, among some groups of Primitive and Old Regular Baptists in the United States, and in a large number of African American churches, where singers regard the richly ornamented tunes as a precious legacy handed down by their ancestors. It was precisely this oral tradition, disdained by educated musicians but loved by its adherents, that singing schools and tunebooks were designed to counteract, replacing these unregulated oral melodies with written music, in parts, with fixed note values.

Many of the practices associated with the Sacred Harp may have their origin at London's Temple Church, originally built by the medieval Knights Templar. Here, in the Norman porch of the round nave, John Playford rented in 1642 a booth or stall where for more than forty years he sold music books to customers such as Samuel Pepys, John Blow, Henry Purcell, and Nahum Tate and became the most prominent music publisher of his time.[9] Here, in 1653, Playford was admitted as clerk of the Temple Church, and so took charge of leading the music, which under the Commonwealth consisted solely of psalm tunes sung in unison by the congregation. In 1654 he published *A Brief Introduction to the Skill of Mu-*

sick, a hodgepodge of instructional resources, including rudiments of music, the principles of composition, and a selection of vocal and instrumental pieces. In the 1658 edition he added a collection of psalm tunes for two voices. The 1672 edition included the letters *F, S, L,* and *M* written below the notes of the melody to indicate the musical syllables *fa, sol, la,* and *mi.* These letters, reminding singers of the scale degrees and the intervals between them, had long formed the basis of musical instruction in England.

In 1671 Playford brought out the ambitious *Psalms & Hymns in Solemn Musick,* presenting psalm tunes set for four male voices, with the suggestion that trebles might double the tenor melody an octave higher. Although these settings were beyond the skill of most congregational singers, Playford presented several copies of his book to the Company of Parish Clerks for their weekly "singing practice."[10] Finally, in 1677, Playford issued his *Whole Book of Psalms* in three-voice settings: *cantus* (air), *bassus,* and *medius,* a counter-melody occupying a similar range to that of the melody. All three voices could be doubled at the octave by male and female voices; to facilitate this, Playford printed both upper parts with the G clef rather than the traditional C (tenor) clef. The availability of these harmonized psalm-books coincided with the growth of religious societies and singing schools and led to a demand for more ambitious music among singers in city and country.

John Playford introduced several concepts on which the singing school movement was founded and which survive in the Sacred Harp today: he promoted the singing of psalm tunes in parts, using musical notation; he experimented with printing tunes so that the fasola syllables could be identified on sight; he pioneered the use of the G clef for male voices and suggested that parts be doubled at the octave by men and women (or boys); finally, he participated in "singings" where he and other men learned to sing psalms in parts in order to introduce them to their congregations. After Playford's death in 1686, his son Henry Playford continued to bring out new editions of the *Introduction* and of the *Whole Book of Psalms;* in 1701, he added *The Divine Companion,* a collection of psalm and hymn tunes along with original anthems by several composers. Although George I would not accede to the throne until 1714, *The Divine Companion* marks the first fruits of the singing school in England and the beginning of a school of composition known today as "Georgian psalmody" or West Gallery music.

In England's American colonies, the "old way of singing" prevailed well into the eighteenth century. Led by a single "chorister," the entire congregation attempted to sing together a melody that most of them had learned by ear. English-born magistrate and diarist Samuel Sewall (1652–1730), though hardly chosen for his poverty, acknowledged his inadequacy and frustration while attempting to "set the psalm" in his local meeting house during the years 1693–1718: "[The preacher] spake to me to set the Tune; I intended Windsor, and fell into High-Dutch, and then essaying to set another Tune, went into a Key much too high. So I pray'd Mr. White to set it; which he did well, Litchf[ield] Tune. The Lord humble me and Instruct me, that I should be occasion of any Interruption in the Worship of God."[11]

The earliest music publications in the American colonies drew on John Play-ford's *Brief Introduction to the Skill of Musick* for their methods and their reper-tory. The ninth edition of the Bay Psalm Book (1698) included a supplement of thirteen tunes in two parts, with the fasola letters *F, S, L,* and *M* written below the notes of both voices. A brief introduction to this supplement addressed a problem that had so vexed Sewall, explaining how to "begin the tune of your first note as the rest may be sung in the compass of your and the peoples voices, without Squeaking above or Grumbling below."[12] According to Irving Lowens, the contents of this supplement, including the directions for keying, the fasola letters, and the tunes themselves, were taken from various editions of Playford's *Introduction* from 1667 to 1674.[13] By 1720 the "regular singing" movement began in earnest, spreading from Boston. Singing masters held schools in many com-munities, where young people learned the rudiments of music and sight-reading and went on to lead music in their churches, sometimes forming choirs. A flurry of printed pamphlets and sermons appeared, as well as two tunebooks: Thomas Walter's *Grounds and Rules of Musick* and John Tufts's *Introduction to the Art of Singing Psalm-Tunes.* Both books ran through several revisions after their initial appearance in 1721. Both drew largely on the collections of John Playford, as well as on more recent British sources. The Tufts collection introduced a new way to keep the fasola syllables in the singers' view: the letters *F, S, L,* and *M* replaced the note-heads on the staff itself.

Today's *Sacred Harp* contains only four tunes printed in America before 1770: OLD HUNDRED (page 49), MEAR (page 49), AYLESBURY (page 28), and WELLS (page 28). All are plain settings, in which all parts move together. The parts fol-low, for the most part, the "rules of descant" outlined in Playford's *Introduction* and other treatises. They produce consonant intervals on strong beats, while al-lowing dissonances on weaker beats for the sake of graceful voice leading (for example, WELLS, the last beat of measures 3 and 11; MEAR, tenor in measure 14). Parallel fifths, octaves, and unisons are largely avoided, though OLD HUNDRED has a striking example in the tenor and bass of measure 3.

The appearance of William Billings's *New-England Psalm-Singer* in 1770, with its 126 original compositions, including fuging tunes and anthems, represents a milestone in American music and the beginning of the "first New England school" of composers. Although in his introduction Billings declared, "I don't think myself confin'd to any Rules for Composition laid down by any that went before me," it is clear that he had studied the works of English psalmodists such as William Tansur and Aaron Williams, whose tunebooks had been reprinted in Massachusetts during the 1760s. Between 1770 and 1810 the music of nearly three hundred American composers, nearly all from New England, appeared in print, including many represented in *The Sacred Harp*. The style of these compositions varies, but a few points are clear: the parts are generally conceived one at a time, beginning with the tenor, as Billings explained in *Continental Harmony*:

> Musical composition is a sort of something, which is much better felt than described. . . . Although I am not confined to rules prescribed by others, yet I come near as I possibly can to a set of rules which I have carved out for myself; but when fancy gets upon the wing, she seems to despise all form, and scorns to be confined or limited by any formal prescriptions whatsoever; for the first part [tenor] is nothing more than a flight of fancy, the other parts are forced to comply and conform to that, by partaking of the same air, or, at least, as much of it as they can get: But by reason of this restraint, the last parts are seldom so good as the first; for the second part [bass] is subservient to the first, the third part [treble] must conform to first and second, and the fourth part [counter] must conform to the other three; therefore the grand difficulty in composition, is to preserve the air through each part separately, and yet cause them to harmonize with each other at the same time.[14]

Billings describes a tension between melodic independence and harmonic intelligibility. Although some, like Billings, Oliver Holden, and Jacob Kimball, were able to balance these conflicting tendencies relatively smoothly, other composers—Daniel Read, Eliakim Doolittle, Stephen Jenks, and Truman Wetmore—frequently favored melody over smooth harmonic progression. CHESTER (page 479), though published in Billings's first collection, succeeds in avoiding serious errors in voice leading and dissonance treatment (that is, the rules of descant), while exhibiting strong melodies in three of the four voices; only the counter is relatively weak, obliged, as the composer admits, to "conform to the other three." Wetmore's FLORIDA (page 203), on the other hand, is replete with parallel fifths, octaves, and unisons, as well as a few clashing dissonances on strong beats. The fifths between bass and counter (measure 2) and between bass and treble (measures 3–4) are conspicuous enough, but the octaves between tenor and treble in measures 3–4 and 13 represent more than part-writing errors, hinting at unison writing or even heterophony, in which the tenor and treble (measure 13) represent two simultaneous versions of the same melody. The unprepared dissonance on the third quarter note of measure 15, where F-sharp, G, and A sound at once, seems inexcusable by the rules of descant, but it may merely represent an incidental clash among four strongly melodic voices. Even the counter seems more melodic and more fun to sing than many of the counters of Billings or Holden (for example, that of CONCORD, page 313).

In adopting fuging tunes, set pieces, and anthems, American composers gained rhythmic flexibility and more varied textures. They also developed a close attention to the text that was quite alien to the utilitarian demands of strophic psalmody, in which texts and tunes of the same meter could be freely interchanged, and music suitable to one text had to accommodate the text of other verses as well. Although elaborate fuging tunes could be, and were, sung in multiple verses by choirs and congregations in the meeting house, some composers seem to have rediscovered some of the intimate connection of music and words that had marked much of the greatest European music for voices. Composers began to select texts from outside the bounds of parish psalmody, such as those of MOUNT VERNON (page 110) or PILGRIM'S FAREWELL (page 185), or to select individual stanzas because of their evocative words. In short, music became once again an art and gradually surpassed the bounds of psalmody in the pathos of DAVID'S LAMENTATION (page 268), the solemnity of MORNING and CHINA (both on page 163), the grandeur of HEAVENLY VISION (page 250), and the sweetness of ROSE OF SHARON (page 254), as well as in pictorial gestures such as the twinkling stars of NEWBURGH (page 182), the towering waves of OCEAN (page 222), the thirsty pilgrims of MONTGOMERY (page 189), or the leaping lover of SWANTON (page 352). Such images clearly fascinated the young people who sang them in singing schools or heard them in the meeting house, "where 'Mortality,' 'Greenwich,' and the 'Judgement Anthem' were the glory of the front gallery; where 'Oh for a cooling' chased itself round the circle like a dog after its tail, to the amusement of all the mischievous boys present, especially on a July Sabbath."[15]

Perhaps it was this sense of enthusiasm and amusement that provoked a wave of musical reform in the 1790s among clergy and educated composers. As early as 1791, Samuel Holyoke, himself a prolific composer of fuging tunes, wrote of the "trifling effect produced by that sort of music; for the parts, falling in, one after another, conveying a different idea, confound the sense, and render the performance a mere jargon of words."[16] Connecticut compiler Andrew Law, who had brought a large number of American tunes into print, began to criticize the music of his countrymen in the preface to his *Musical Primer* (1793), not for its dissonance but for its lack of dissonance, which, he suggested, represented an attempt to compensate for their rough, untrained voices: "European compositions aim at variety and energy by guarding against the reiterated use of the perfect cords. Great numbers of the American composers, on the contrary, and as it were, on purpose to accommodate their music for harsh singing, have introduced the smooth and perfect cords, till their tunes are all sweet, languid and lifeless."[17]

Today's singers are unlikely to hear the music of Read and Jenks as "languid and lifeless," but Law's point seems to be that the Yankee composers used too many perfect consonances, including open fifths and octaves, while neglecting the dissonances associated with European art music, for example, the dominant seventh chord, the suspension, and the appoggiatura. By 1810, the American religious establishment and most tunebook compilers had adopted an ideology that favored solemn, dignified, even bland music from European sources, while avoiding fuging tunes.[18] An example is PLEYEL'S HYMN (page 143), adapted from a symphonic work by a Viennese composer and first published in America in *The Columbian Sacred Harmonist* (Dedham, Massachusetts, 1808). In the Sacred Harp setting, only the melody, clearly intended for soprano, is tuneful; the other parts serve mainly to emphasize the simple harmonic progression. The appoggiaturas in measures 8 and 22 (printed as grace notes in *The Sacred Harp*) add graceful dissonance, while both halves progress through a second inversion and a dominant seventh chord to reach the final tonic chord. Though these effects seem entirely conventional today, they are rare in the music of Yankee composers.

Just as musical reform and European music began to tighten their hold on the urban centers of the eastern United States, another trend arose, primarily in the hinterlands of northern New England, the Ohio Valley, and the South. Here the New England repertory of 1770–1810, including fuging tunes, was still popular, but composers and teachers also showed interest in a new kind of sacred setting: melodies from oral tradition including ballads and dance tunes or original melodies resembling them, harmonized in much the same manner as the earlier repertory. These tunes are often termed "folk hymns," although many of the texts are identical to those in printed hymnbooks. In this repertory, the "composer" often acted as an arranger of a pre-existing melody. Some of the melodies in Amos Pilsbury's *United States' Sacred Harmony* (1799) show the characteristics of folk music, but a larger body of folk material appeared in *The Christian Harmony, or Songster's Companion* (1805), by the Vermont compiler Jeremiah Ingalls. Many of the unattributed tunes bear distinctive folk traits that are otherwise rare in the New England repertory: patterns of repeated phrases such as AABA, "gapped" melodies lacking one or more scale degrees, and melodies ending on notes other than the tonic or key note. MOURNING SOULS, from Ingalls's collection but not printed in *The Sacred Harp*, illustrates all these characteristics. The melody is a variant of that seen in THE CHURCH'S DESOLATION (page 89). The second phrase is the same as the first; the third is distinct, and ranges higher than the first two, and the fourth phrase begins like the third but ends like the first and second phrases, in a kind of musical rhyme, on the fifth note above the tonic. The melody lacks the seventh degree entirely; the fourth degree occurs only once, and not at all in the Sacred Harp setting. The minor differences between the two settings represent another feature of this repertory: tunes may migrate from one collection to another or one region to another as complete settings with identical title, attribution, text, and voice parts, or they may be recomposed or reset from the oral tradition by different individuals, resulting in a confusing array of variants of the same tune. KINGWOOD (page 266), for example, was set by R. D. Humphreys and first printed in *Supplement to the Kentucky Harmony* (1820) by Ananias Davisson of Virginia. A year later, another version of the same tune appeared: NASHVILLE (page 64), set by Alexander Johnson in the second edition of his *Tennessee Harmony* (1821). The rhythms differ slightly, as do the titles, the texts, and the accompanying parts. Another "doublet" in the 1844 *Sacred Harp* consists of YE WEARY SOULS by J. T. White (page 72) and FLORENCE by Thomas W. Carter (page 121), clearly variant settings of the same melody. Another piece in *The Sacred Harp* shows the uneasy conflation of two distinct settings of the same melody. PISGAH, by J. C. Lowry (page 58), was printed in the second edition of Davisson's *Kentucky Harmony* (1817) in four voice parts, including a counter (alto) in the normal range. A three-voice setting of the same tune, under the name CHRISTIAN TRIUMPH, was claimed by Johnson in *Tennessee Harmony* (1818). *The Sacred Harp* (1844), like Walker's *Southern Harmony* (1835), contains PISGAH, still attributed to Lowry, but with the treble part of CHRISTIAN TRIUMPH substituted for Lowry's counter—as it stands, the tune has two treble parts and no alto, and it produces a rather unruly effect.

The widespread popularity of folk hymns coincided with two other developments in American culture: the rise of the religious camp meeting, with its distinctive body of spiritual song, and the invention of shaped notation. The camp meeting and its influence are discussed by Richard H. Hulan in Part Two. The invention of shaped note-heads in Philadelphia before 1790[19] was the culmination of earlier attempts by John Playford and John Tufts to keep the sol-fa syllables in the singer's mind at all times, while retaining the visual cues for pitch (placement on the staff) and duration (color, stems, and flags). First published in 1801, *The Easy Instructor* inspired imitation by publishers on the migration routes westward and southward who adopted its notation for their own collections in Harrisburg, Pennsylvania, by 1810, in the Ohio Valley by 1813, and in Virginia by 1816. By the 1820s "patent notes" came to dominate sacred tunebook publication in the West and South, regardless of whether the compiler favored folk hymns and New England standards or tunes by Europeans and reformers.

The addition of settings of folk and folk-like melodies to the early nineteenth-century tunebook did not result in a wholesale replacement of one repertory or style with another, nor did it mean the total replacement of original composition with arrangements of pre-existing tunes. Yet there are noticeable differences between compositions and arrangements of many southern and western singing-masters and those of New Englanders such as Billings or even Ingalls. Published tune settings were more likely than before to have three voice parts or fewer, though this was not a universal trend. Teachers or audiences may have grown tired of the male counter voice, and there was some doubt among both urban and rural singing-masters as to who should sing the part when printed. Ezekiel Maynard of Norfolk, Virginia, wrote in his *New Selection of Sacred Music* (Baltimore, 1822): "The Counter, I consider no advantage to a School, and is very seldom used by those who publish. In consequence of which I have left it out. It injures more voices that attempt to perform it, than it improves."[20] Some compilers, such as John Wyeth and Ananias Davisson, maintained four parts in books dominated by the older repertory, while experimenting with fewer parts in less formal settings of camp-meeting hymns.

Another simplification that appeared in several nineteenth-century shape-note books was the elimination of some notational signs, including the accidental sharp, flat, and natural, on the grounds that they "have no other tendency, than to swell the rudiments and perplex the learner with a crowd of mysteries which are in my opinion useless." In justifying these omissions, Ananias Davisson implies that they were routinely ignored by singers and teachers: "The gentleman from whom I received my instruction, had been in the constant habit of teaching for fifteen years; and was pronounced a teacher of first eminence; and by that gentleman to the best of my recollection, I never was stopt by the interposition of an accidental flat, sharp, or natural, either to sink half a tone, raise half a tone, or make any primitive restoration."[21]

New England composers certainly had used accidentals in their music, and Ingalls had used them in his arrangements of folk melodies that otherwise could be called modal. Davisson not only avoided them in his own compositions and those of his associates but also purged them from the works of earlier American and European composers. His omission of these symbols implies a musical system that was purely diatonic and modal, without raised leading tones in the minor modes or accidentals to mark modulations to dominant or subdominant harmonies. Davisson's practice, though not universal, was followed by authors such as William Moore (*Columbian Harmony*, 1825) and William R. Rhinehart (*American or Union Harmony*, 1831).

The compilers of *The Sacred Harp* did not follow Davisson's example in purging accidental sharps and flats from existing compositions. Although White and King did not include accidentals in their own compositions, they seemed content to follow their immediate sources for older songs in the book, including them in some songs (Vermont, page 180) and not in others (Russia, page 107). In his musical writings, however, B. F. White took a strong position against "artificial" constructs such as the harmonic minor scale: the seventh degree of the minor key should remain a whole tone below the tonic and should retain the name *sol;* he appears to endorse the statement of the anonymous "Georgia Boy" that "sharping the seventh sound of the minor scale is an artificial composition," even in such tunes as Greenwich (page 183) and Phoebus (page 173).[22]

Whether tunes were printed in three or four voices, other stylistic changes emerged in the music of the southern and western tunebooks. These include a greater sense of tunefulness in the accompanying parts, along with a relaxed attitude toward parallel fifths and octaves and a greater tolerance of the perfect fourth as a consonance. PRIMROSE (page 47), first published in 1812, is usually attributed to Amzi Chapin, a Massachusetts-born singing-master who spent the years 1800–31 in Westmoreland County, Pennsylvania. Although the setting is in four parts, the lack of triads is conspicuous, especially in the final notes of phrases. The second phrase (measures 5–7) begins and ends on a fourth against the bass, an effect that would be highly unusual in New England music. There are instances of parallel octaves in measure 6 (tenor and alto, with a strong clash on the second beat) and 8 (alto and bass). There is, however, a strong melodism in all parts, even the alto (only the first phrase is static); this and an abundant use of contrary motion (including voice-crossing in tenor and treble) combine to leave an elegant impression. GARDEN HYMN (page 284), printed as BALTIMORE without attribution in the third edition of Davisson's *Supplement to the Kentucky Harmony* (1826), is a variant of a melody in Ingalls's *Christian Harmony* (1805); the three-part setting may be by Davisson. Again, contrary motion is strongly present. Parallel octaves are more conspicuous (four notes in a row between tenor and bass in measures 3–4), as are fifths (measure 2, bass and treble). The consonant fourth appears in the very first measure and introduces phrases at measures 6 and 15. The folk-based tenor ranges widely but is crossed by both bass and treble, each of which spans a full octave.

Many elements of this folk-informed style can be found in tunes printed in southern books before the Civil War, including *The Sacred Harp*. In a 1940 article, the musicologist Charles Seeger noted, with some relish, that

> the style of the three-voice shape-note settings of which I speak are outrageously heterodox, violating such basic and centuries-old prohibitions as those against:
>
> 1. parallel fifths, octaves, and unisons
> 2. parallel fourths between outer voices or between upper voices without a third in the bass
> 3. unprepared and unresolved dissonances
> 4. cadences on 8/4
> 5. crossing of voices.
>
> Were these violations only occasional, one might easily pass them by. But they are so frequent that they clearly constitute essential elements in the style.[23]

These observations were based on the study of three three-voice settings, including two tunes in *The Sacred Harp*: WONDROUS LOVE (page 159) and PARTING FRIENDS (page 267). Acknowledging these violations, Seeger concludes of the best of these settings, "[H]ere is true style! There is a rigorous, spare, disciplined beauty in the choral writing that is all the more to be prized for having been conceived in the 'backwoods' for which many professional musicians have such scorn, and in the face of the determined opposition of sophisticated zealots in no small number, from Lowell Mason down to those of this very day."[24]

Dorothy Horn and William Tallmadge have expanded on Seeger's remarks to suggest that the printed three-voice folk hymns in southern tunebooks represent an alternative harmonic system of "quartal harmony" based on pentatonic melodic modes and employing "dyads," two-note chords, in the same way that ordinary diatonic music employs triads. Tallmadge heard echoes of this style in the improvised or orally transmitted harmonies in Appalachian churches and in the harmonies of modern bluegrass vocals.[25]

The composer of PARTING FRIENDS was John G. McCurry, compiler of *The Social Harp* (1855), one of the few southern tunebooks to offer advice to those composing in this folk-influenced style. McCurry mentions neither dyads nor triads; he makes it clear that the rules of "descant" had changed little since the eighteenth century. The emphasis is on writing melodies and then checking for dissonances. The parts are still composed consecutively.

> After you have written your tenor, then commence your bass by placing your notes a proper distance from the tenor, and be careful always not to place any note within one degree of the corresponding note in the other part, or within seven degrees, it being within one degree of the octave. Also avoid ninths, as they have the same effect as seconds and sevenths. Any two notes of the same name will make an agreeable sound[;] you may place notes in unison if you see proper. The intervals that produce harmony (when sounded together) are thirds, fourths, fifths, sixths and eighths, or unison. Those that produce a disagreeable sound are seconds, sevenths and ninths. . . . After having written the bass and tenor, commence the treble by observing both parts already written; be careful not to place any note on the next sound to the notes in either part that are already located.[26]

McCurry then advises the composer to write independent lines with frequent voice-crossing and to avoid restricting the final part (the treble, in three-part music) by "taking all the good ground" in the other parts.

> Be careful not to let the treble have the same turn with the bass, for it is very injurious, if not ruinous, to any piece of music. Variety and turn is the chief thing in making good music. If the tenor runs high, let the treble take a medium position. If the tenor runs on a medium line, let the treble run above or below. It is not best to place the treble too high throughout, but let it run high, and low, and on a medium line. . . . When the tenor runs low, the bass should always run

above the tenor. . . . Be careful when writing bass, not to take all the good ground from the treble. Always when writing have an eye to the treble, so you may not be excluded when you come to writing treble.[27]

The three-voice settings of folk melodies by Walker, White, and King are a far cry from the products of musical reform whose number increased in later editions. It is wise to be cautious in examining the tunes composed by reformers such as Lowell Mason, Thomas Hastings, or H. K. Oliver, since some have been re-edited or even "southernized" in their Sacred Harp settings. The treble part of Hastings's ORTONVILLE (page 68), composed by B. F. White, exhibits a more lively melodic sense than Hastings's original, which was intended as a tenor part for male voices. The treble of Mason's HEBRON (page 566) may also be by White: it is wider-ranging and more interesting than the original. Mason's SHAWMUT (page 535), however, preserves the composer's own harmonies. The limited range of the melody and the repeated notes in each phrase may have been inspired by Anglican chant.[28] The part-writing is exceptionally chaste, with none of the voice-crossing recommended by McCurry. When the reformers published their hymn tunes, they placed the melody in the soprano voice but continued to print this melody directly above the bass, for convenience in playing a keyboard accompaniment. If the melody of SHAWMUT is played on a keyboard with the right hand in the soprano range, the alto and tenor ("treble") can also be played at the same time with the right hand, in parallel motion throughout. The two inner parts (treble and alto in the *Sacred Harp*) are devoid of melodic interest: the downward treble resolutions in measures 2–3 and 9–10 seem especially awkward. Only the bass has any independence, though even that serves mainly to state the harmonic root of each chord. The fourth against the bass appears in measure 5, but this is a textbook example of a dissonant suspension followed by a resolution to the dominant of the relative minor, complete with inflected leading tone. Finally, the dominant seventh appears in the final beat of measure 11. SHAWMUT was not part of the White and King *Sacred Harp;* it was added only in 1960 at the request of Ruth Denson Edwards, whose name appears as the composer in the 1960 appendix. This error was corrected in subsequent editions.

That a tune by Lowell Mason was submitted to the revision committee by Ruth Denson Edwards is an important reminder that Sacred Harp music is not a single distinctive style. For many traditional singers in the southern United States, any song in the book is a Sacred Harp song, even if it was made by a composer who was opposed to shape-notes and disdained most of the music in the book. For many singers, the stylistic variety of the repertory is a strength—a folk hymn such as DETROIT (page 39) may be followed by a rollicking fuging tune such as THE LAST WORDS OF COPERNICUS (page 112), a revival shout such as ANTIOCH (page

277), a reform tune such as FEDERAL STREET (page 515), or a gospel song such as THE MARRIAGE IN THE SKIES (page 438).

Most of the original music in the southern tunebooks published in the 1840s and 1850s consists of three-part settings—B. F. White, E. J. King, and their contributors published only three-part music in the first two editions of *The Sacred Harp* and largely avoided fuging tunes. Instead, they concentrated on plain tunes, often with folk elements, along with a large number of "revival choruses," tunes with refrains such as SWEET CANAAN (page 87) and DONE WITH THE WORLD (page 88). In the 1850 version the editors, perhaps smarting from the implied criticism of William Hauser, added several tunes by British composers and by reformers such as Lowell Mason, among them HEBRON, ORTONVILLE, CAMBRIDGE (page 287), and CARMARTHEN (page 473). They also added several complex and difficult tunes, for example, MORGAN (page 304), NEW JORDAN (page 442), and ALL SAINTS NEW (page 444); though many of these were in four parts, they were all taken from much earlier sources. As Buell Cobb recognized, starting with the 1859 edition, Sacred Harp composers such as Absalom Ogletree and H. S. Reese began to publish new four-part compositions and to experiment with original fuging tunes.[29] This trend was yet more evident in the 1870 edition. A revived interest in the alto part and in relatively complex music may reflect an abundance of young, capable singers who attended the schools and conventions set up by White and his associates. Sarah Lancaster, M. M. Wynn, Henry G. Mann, and B. F. White Jr., all born in the years 1834–45, wrote four-voice compositions.

Among the fuging tunes introduced in the 1870 edition are several examples of a type that would exert a strong influence on Sacred Harp composers well into the twentieth century. Among these pieces are FILLMORE by J. P. Reese (page 434), SARDIS by Sarah Lancaster (page 460), and SAVE, LORD, OR WE PERISH by M. M. Wynn (page 224), all for four voices. Among their distinctive qualities is a strong emphasis on the tonic chord. FILLMORE, if published in *The Organ,* was composed by the 1850s and may represent a prototype of the genre. In a piece 28 measures long, measure 23 is the first that begins on anything other than the tonic sonority. There are a few chords on the relative minor, but these are emphasized only in measures 23 and 26. All parts are strongly pentatonic: the fourth degree appears in the treble at measures 16 and 24, and the seventh appears briefly in the final flourish in measures 25 and 26. Dominant harmony is almost absent, even at the cadences, belying the conventional bass leaps that would typically accompany the dominant. In SARDIS, only a single measure (3) begins with a chord containing notes outside the tonic triad. There are strong dominant chords on the first and third beat of measure three, as well as much more transient dominants at measures 5, 6, and 17; a chord on the sixth degree is relatively strong in measures 5, 14, and 17 and weaker elsewhere. The strong, almost obsessive predominance of a single chord makes it easier to follow McCurry's rules while providing a hypnotic chiming or droning effect that tends to create a sense of security and inevitability. The range of the alto part is as great as that of the tenor. Note that in both the cadence before the fuging section (measure 7) and at the final chord, there was no third degree—the alto part was altered in 1911, presumably by S. M. Denson, to add thirds at both locations. SAVE, LORD, OR WE PERISH, with its minor mode and unusual poetic meter, varies somewhat from the previous examples, but the emphasis on the tonic and the sense of inevitability are maintained. The bass leads the harmony to sonorities on the third, fourth, fifth, and seventh degrees, often enforcing its will through parallel fifths and octaves in the upper parts, as in bass and tenor at measures 3, 6, and 7 (fifths) and 9 and 10 (octaves), while avoiding the second and sixth degrees. Dominant harmony is avoided; there are strong passing dissonances at measures 4, 22, and 26, all resolving to the tonic. The third degree is rarely heard in the tonic chord, as in the alto at measure 5; usually the tonic is an open fifth. These fuging tunes, published in 1870, and others like them, have little of the diatonic scope of Billings or Read, but their distinctive sound influenced much of the music of the later composers Seaborn and Tom Denson, A. M. Cagle, and Paine Denson.

The next great wave of musical influence to affect the Sacred Harp was that of gospel music. Drawing on the Sunday school songs of William B. Bradbury, the Victorian parlor song, and the music of northern gospel composers such as Ira Sankey and Philip P. Bliss, southern gospel composers such as Aldine S. Kieffer of Virginia published songs in character notes (a system using seven shapes) that featured recurring refrains in a much smoother style than the revival choruses favored in *The Sacred Harp.* Almost all songs were in major keys and featured smooth, predictable harmonies; the texts emphasized the assurance of God's love and avoided thorny issues such as divine judgment and punishment. Through tunebooks like *The Temple Star* (1877), music normal schools, conventions, and a periodical called *The Musical Million,* Kieffer and his associates became evangelists for character notation in seven shapes and for a repertory of southern gospel song that competed directly with *The Sacred Harp.* Later publishers such as A. J. Showalter, James D. Vaughan, and Virgil O. Stamps printed small paperback books of gospel songs that became staples of the convention circuit and succeeded in making gospel music a big business. In the late nineteenth century such books competed for the loyalty of Sacred Harp singers and enjoyed some use in Sacred Harp conventions.[30]

In the early twentieth century, and especially during the Great Depression, gospel music, including the sale of songbooks and live quartet performances, represented a supplementary income for talented southern musicians. Several Sacred Harp composers took up the call, namely, Whitt, Owel, and Howard Denson; O. A. Parris; A. A. Blocker; and J. M. Dye. The influence of gospel music is especially strong in the revisions of *The Sacred Harp* by W. M. Cooper (1902) and J. L. White (1909); these revisions replaced many traditional songs with favorite gospel numbers, and so they greatly changed the musical character of Sacred Harp singing in the areas where these books were adopted. *Original Sacred Harp* (the James edition, 1911) consciously limited the influence of this new music, insisting that any new songs be written in what the editors considered true "dispersed harmony," a phrase that may be interpreted as melodic part-writing not suited to keyboard accompaniment. Some of the new songs, however, showed gospel influence. The rollicking rhythm and repeated bass notes of THE MARRIAGE IN THE SKIES are characteristic of the genre, as are the emphasis on tonic, dominant, and subdominant, the dominant seventh chords, the *dal segno* repeats, and the cheerful original text by the composer, Sidney Denson. THE BETTER LAND (page 454), by O. A. Parris, is ostensibly a traditional fuging tune, but the clear harmonic progressions and the use of accidental sharps and flats show gospel influence. In addition to his Sacred Harp activities, Parris was a composer and publisher who expanded the gospel repertory with such songs as THE GRAND HIGHWAY (*Christian Harmony*, 1954). But he, Blocker, the Densons, and others understood the distinction between gospel and Sacred Harp music.

The influence of gospel music can be seen in recent compositions such as MY HOME by Roy Avery (page 560) and WOOTTEN by Hugh McGraw (page 548), but such influence may be waning as new composers emerge. Recent compositions that have become popular at singings include LLOYD by Raymond Hamrick (page 503), A THANKFUL HEART by John T. Hocutt (page 475), and NATICK by Glen Wright (page 497). None of these evokes the droning sound of Reese or Lancaster, nor the gospel cadences of Sidney Denson or O. A. Parris. An inspired melody, LLOYD is harmonized meticulously on both strong and weak beats, although the treble is consistently higher and crosses the tenor less often than in many earlier compositions in this style. A THANKFUL HEART has its parallel fifths and consonant fourths but seems almost effortless in its flow. Finally, NATICK, by Massachusetts-born Wright, evokes the spirit of folk hymnody in a setting that, though not pentatonic, shows both rich melody in all parts and dyadic harmony between many, beginning on a consonant fourth and ending on an open fifth. All three can engage a class of good singers and inspire the promise of another generation of composers who can make their contribution to future revisions while remaining true to the essential though varied character of Sacred Harp singing.

PART TWO
THE WORDS

FRONTIERS OF THE
AMERICAN HYMN

Richard H. Hulan

For the past seventy-five years, serious scholarly attention to early American religious folksong has overwhelmingly approached the material as music. Of the few scholars who have expressed any deep interest in the hymns—that is, the words—perhaps a majority have done so in periodicals catering to a particular denominational audience or to working professionals in the area of church music. These specialized references are, of course, available to those who search them out, but they are easily overlooked by someone inquiring more generally into American folk hymnody and shape note traditions.

Yet some of the same criteria that give the music a widespread appeal today might also be applied, in a comparably forgiving way, to the poetry. One need not share the theology, worldview, or social system of a semiliterate frontier preacher in order to recognize in his writing—and recognize it often—simple truths, simply and memorably expressed. It may not be couched in the loftiest English we have seen, but it is worth saying—and worthy of being sung. In many instances we are singing it, still, precisely because it is in *The Sacred Harp*.

It is true that a good portion of the hymnic content of *The Sacred Harp* is the work of well-known British evangelical poets. Because most of them lived and wrote somewhat more than two hundred years ago, even their efforts may seem a little quaint and, by now, perhaps unfamiliar outside these pages. But the authors are not obscure and did not in their own day seek anonymity. Notices of them are to be found in many standard biographical and hymnological sources, and they need not consume much of the research time of the Americanist.

Very much harder to identify as authors—and also harder to flesh out as real people, once identified—are the American frontier preachers. And with few exceptions those who penned the vibrant and ecstatic camp-meeting spirituals that became so quickly and widely popular during the early nineteenth century were preachers. Their works are to a large extent the texts that distinguish *The Sacred Harp* among the oft-winnowed genre of nineteenth-century singing school books that are still in use. So this is the body of hymnody on which the present essay aspires to shed some new light.

CHASING RAINBOW MAKERS

We may well know the physical, and especially optical, laws governing the creation and perception of a rainbow, but its chief qualities, going hand in hand, are beauty and impermanence. Now we see it, now we don't. Camp-meeting spirituals, the best of them, were like that. The people who made them and first sang them were well aware of the fact, and in some cases went to considerable lengths to catch them for posterity. Perhaps they copied what they had heard at a camp meeting into a diary or sent it in a note to some acquaintance with access to a press. Almost nothing of this *experiential stage* has survived in this literary genre. A few sample lines may occur in the writings of a diarist or religious journalist: Francis Asbury, Lorenzo Dow, Jesse Lee, and Thomas S. Hinde (all Methodists, though very un-equally disciplined) come to mind. As far as we know, Dow wrote one pretty good hymn, Hinde wrote several pretty bad ones, and the others wrote prose.[1]

But the folk geniuses—the virtuoso performers in this genre—tended to keep the light of their individual identities under their respective bushels. As a result, the number of these virtuosi whose names are known, and whose personal con-tributions can be considered numerically great as well as popularly successful, may be counted on one hand—with, perhaps, an asterisk on the thumb. They are John Leland, John Adam Granade, Caleb Jarvis Taylor, George Askins, and John Poage Campbell. Other known authors may be identified for an individual hymn or two, but only these five have been credited with several examples that entered widespread traditional usage.

That has much to do with the second and third stages in the process by which these new hymns entered the mainstream. Very soon after a spiritual song came to exist in *manuscript* form—the author's or some early hearer's—it commonly found its way to a printer and was able to reach a wider audience in the form of a *broadside*. This was a text, usually that of a single hymn (or two hymns set in columns), printed on only one side of a sheet of paper. If the printer was one of those who issued his own broadside series, it might be offered alongside many secular ballads and sold on the streets by a hawker, who knew a tune for it and would sing a sample verse for prospective customers.

For a number of the camp-meeting hymns that exist in broadside form, this standard and venerable, essentially British model seems unlikely to have been followed. It is more credible that they were printed at the expense of an author or other interested person who then sold them at the camp meeting (or other large gathering of the pious). In this way they were available to the target audience when brand new, and they were dispersed fairly widely, almost at once, as the event's participants returned to distant homes. There is anecdotal and circumstantial evidence that this practice was common, but it is not well documented. For that matter, neither are the much more commonplace phenomena surrounding the diffusion of secular song broadsides in America.

The broadsides, sacred and secular, were in any case routinely and quickly incorporated into small topical collections, usually called *songsters* at the time but often referred to as *chapbooks* in the book trade. Camp-meeting songsters were being published soon after the very first camp meetings were held. Thirty years ago, while researching and writing my dissertation, I found it necessary to define this genre in order to study its earliest core repertoire. Reasoning that there could not be a camp-meeting songster before there had been a camp meeting, I opened my list of eligible collections with the year 1801; being under some pressure to keep my data manageable, I closed it in 1805. I found eighteen qualifying songsters and analyzed their contents.

My search, though more diligent than any that had preceded it, was not perfect. I now know of a few relevant collections that I simply missed, and two or three known examples—known to have been published but not to have survived—still have not surfaced. The present study is subject to no such chronological boundaries, and I am allowed to admit, as I always knew, that a good bit of the new and American content of the earliest camp-meeting songsters was not, in fact, brand new. Some of it was about ten years old. But it was popularized, diffused, and made nondenominational under the influence, and in the milieu, of the early camp meetings. That was where the latest revivalistic hymns and their infectious tunes were shared, and learned, by a wide cross-section of the populace—white and black, northern and southern, Methodist and Baptist, and everybody else.

EARLIER REVIVAL SONGSTERS THAT MATTER TO US

The first of the American revivalist collections whose direct impact on the tradition may still be felt were compiled by Baptists in Virginia and in New England, almost at the same time and with considerable sharing of the same new material. Much of it was, of course, British, and was a little older; but when in 1790 the cousins Richard and Andrew Broaddus of Caroline County, Virginia, published their *Collection of Sacred Ballads,* among its 107 hymns were five new ones by Elder John Leland. This Massachusetts native was at the time entering the last year of his extended residence and ministry among the Virginia Baptists during the years

1776–91. A few other new hymns that would be important as the tradition grew were also found for the first time in this Broaddus collection.[2] We have no proof that it was at first widely circulated or adopted, but much of its content was to be found in Andrew Broaddus's *Dover Selection* (1828) and *Virginia Selection* (1836). Both of these were demonstrably popular and influential.

In the same year in which Leland returned to his native New England (1791), Joshua Smith, an itinerant Baptist evangelist working in southeastern New Hampshire, published his *Divine Hymns or Spiritual Songs, for the Use of Religious Assemblies, and Private Christians.* This was arguably the most popular American-based selection of spiritual songs during the 1790s and well into the first decade of the following century. It began modestly enough, with 145 texts. By 1816 a number of successors to Smith (chief among them Samuel Streeter and William Northup) had independently issued nearly thirty revisions and editions; the number of hymns issued over the name of "Joshua Smith, and others" had grown to about 600. By 1805 Smith's lengthy title also had been appropriated for at least two completely unrelated collections. They make no claim to be his own selection, but one can only assume that the adoption of his very popular title was no coincidence.[3]

Smith's collection was notable for a number of Bible stories set to verse. It was lyric verse, intended to be sung, although perhaps more appropriately by an individual than by a congregation. His book shared more than two dozen songs with the earlier (and far rarer) work of his fellow New England preacher, Samson Occum. Much of the latter's *Choice Collection of Hymns and Spiritual Songs* (1774) is of British origin, and the fresher material written or collected by Occum is likely to have entered the broader tradition primarily because Joshua Smith included it in *Divine Hymns.* The same might be said about the incorporation into Smith's collection of new material from a much smaller one compiled by his friend and colleague John Peak, *A New Collection of Hymns and Spiritual Songs, from Various Authors—Some Entirely New* (1793). Although Peak seems to be the source, Smith's book—mainly the many editions published after his death in 1795—is the medium through which it became widely traditional.

Smith's several "experience" songs (along with "free grace" texts in editions not under the control of William Northup) indicate that he was most comfortable among the "general" rather than the "particular" Baptists. That distinction would very soon prove to be a key to the diffusion of this part of the tradition. Simply stated, Calvinist Baptists did not condone camp meetings, nor were they in fellowship with those who did. It would not be long before new denominations, notably the Freewill Baptists and the Christian Connexion, would step in to fill this niche. The principal exponent in print of the latter group (and, in nominal partnership with Abner Jones, compiler of its popular hymn book) was Elias Smith. He had spent a year as Joshua Smith's companion in the traveling ministry. After

1804 the Elias Smith and Abner Jones collection *Hymns, Original and Selected, for the Use of Christians* (with many places of publication and editions) would stand firmly with those of the late Joshua Smith, as with the newer songsters that were directly beholden to the nascent camp-meeting movement and to the Methodists who, numerically were its principal champions.

Apart from their informality and their theological leaning toward the individual experience of personal salvation, independently printed revivalist collections such as Joshua Smith's have a somewhat different family tree than the contemporary hymnals of the established denominations. It is typical (not universal) for each hymn or a majority of them to be headed with some sort of title: The Good Shepherd, Blind Bartimaeus, The Bold Pilgrim, Affliction, Free Grace, for example. In later years, this title may also have become the tune name. It is not surprising that in the cases in which a broadside version of the hymn in question is known, that broadside is headed by the same title. One might argue (but I shall not) that the broadside could derive from the hymn book and not the other way around. In any case, the broadside seldom carries either a date or a publisher's name, whereas the songster typically has both. The question of precedence can rarely be proved beyond any doubt. Nor, in most cases, can that of authorship.

This brings us to the other characteristic wherein most revivalist songsters differ from the more formal hymnals: rarely is much attention given to the worldly task of associating a particular text with the name of its author. The exceptions, important as such (if not also for their contribution to the growing corpus), are few enough in number to be described within this essay. One of these exceptions, Benjamin Cleavland's *Hymns on Different Spiritual Subjects,* might antedate Smith's *Divine Hymns;* in neither case is the first imprint dated with great confidence. Cleavland's Baptist selection was advertised for sale, not necessarily for the first time ever, in the *Windham* [Connecticut] *Herald* of 14 May 1791. The only surviving copy seems to be from the fourth edition (1792). Individual authors, or at least compilers, were responsible for its two main sections, and a few additional hymns are attributed. On the basis of this little book we can identify Cleavland himself, Anna Beeman of Warren, Connecticut, and Elder Daniel Hibbard as credible candidates for authorship of several strong hymn texts that entered the broader tradition.

It appears that the first compiler of a collection of this sort who made a diligent effort to identify his sources was Josiah Goddard. His efforts anticipated those of this volume: he named the author, or if he did not know who the author was, he cited an earlier publication in which he had found a given text. Goddard issued the first of at least three editions of *A New and Beautiful Collection of Select Hymns and Spiritual Songs* at Conway, Massachusetts, in 1798. (The title was modified slightly in the editions of 1801 and 1809.) A longtime resident of Conway, he was remembered there: "Elder Goddard was a man of excellent sense, of a strong mind. He was a worker withal with his hands; and he has left the reputation of being the swiftest reaper the town ever produced."[4] More pertinent to our concerns is the fact that he had grown up in John Leland's home church in Cheshire.

Among many similar services to posterity, Goddard attributed eleven hymns to Leland in the 1809 edition. Nearly a century later, in compiling his own list of twenty-one Leland hymns, the respected Baptist hymnologist Henry S. Burrage began with ten texts identified by Goddard. Most of the ten are familiar still to shape note singers, whereas almost all of the rest (identified primarily on the basis of notes in an 1845 collection of Leland's prose writings) are virtually unknown in the broader tradition. For some reason, Burrage missed one of Goddard's attributions to Leland, "See th'eternal Judge descending," which is among those that became popular. For this essay, it is enough to suggest that Goddard's immediate contact with the earlier American authors (especially his fellow Baptists, such as Leland) and their new hymns makes him the most credible witness for such attributions. William Parkinson added to the data in *A Selection of Hymns and Spiritual Songs, in Two Parts* (New York, 1809), a collection of parallel importance for Baptist hymnology.

So matters stood as the nineteenth century dawned, bringing in its opening years two phenomena that were to walk hand in hand through the following two centuries. First, the camp meeting movement began on the southwestern frontier of Kentucky and Tennessee and moved rapidly throughout the new nation, most of which lay to the north and the east. Its trove of new and exciting hymns, often set to exuberant folk tunes, multiplied and spread along with the expanding waves of evangelical fervor. Second (or perhaps simultaneously, but elsewhere), the new American technique of teaching vocal music with shaped notation was very quickly adapted to the task of capturing these hymns. From publishing centers in Philadelphia and Albany, the production of shape-note tunebooks spread rapidly to the south and the west. It was fitting and proper, one might almost say foreordained, that the first solid marriage of the camp-meeting hymn repertoire and music in shape notes was to occur in Harrisburg, Pennsylvania, with John Wyeth's 1813 *Repository of Sacred Music, Part Second.*[5]

CAMP-MEETING HYMNS, AS SUCH

There is credible and well-documented evidence that the nondenominational camp-meeting movement began in Logan County, Kentucky, and neighboring Sumner County, Tennessee, in the summer of 1800.[6] Almost immediately this movement began to produce a new body of hymns suitable for the new context of worship. The fact that many of the new ones were recorded later as short passages of text interspersed with refrains and choruses, has sometimes obscured the much broader repertoire of such meetings, as reported by eyewitnesses, and as apparent from the content of songsters designed specifically for camp meeting use. The older hymns by British evangelical authors (Isaac Watts, Joseph Hart, John Newton, William Cowper, John Cennick, Charles Wesley, and many more) remained popular. Newer American ones, lately made available by Joshua Smith and others, found a fertile soil in which to grow. And those on the ground at the earliest camp meetings expressed themselves in verse. To the extent that this verse survives, it has much more in common with its evangelical models than with the "call-and-response" form into which many such hymns would be broken for outdoor worship settings in which little besides a chorus could actually be heard by the thousands of participants.

Most of the first camp meetings were convened under the auspices of "New Light" Presbyterian and Methodist clergy; both groups had (unlike the Baptists) been heretofore prohibited by the authorities of their respective denominations from publishing any such unofficial hymn collections. The single exception may be a collection of original hymns by the Methodist laywoman Sarah Jones, issued perhaps in the vicinity of Norfolk, Virginia, probably before her death in 1792.[7] The existence of such a compilation is strongly suggested in later works, but no copy has been discovered. In any case, the camp-meeting movement was, in this and other ways, beyond the control of Methodist bishops and Presbyterian synods. Its adherents needed a new hymnody; it was not found in their standard hymnals, and it was swiftly supplied. Although its publishers were often simply the nearest available job printers, the collections were compiled, in most cases, by members in good standing of the participating clergy—most promptly and aggressively, it would seem, by the Methodists.

The first identifiable collections of camp-meeting songs came out in 1801 in Philadelphia and Baltimore. The first tells us much more on its title page: *A Collection of Spiritual Songs and Hymns selected from Various Authors*, by Richard Allen, African Minister (Philadelphia, 1801). The second edition was printed in the same year and city, and the third in 1802. With each revision Allen's little book grew by several hymns—from fifty-four to sixty-four to eighty-six. Richard Allen was not a native of Africa; he was born in 1760 as a slave of Benjamin Chew (later chief justice of Pennsylvania) in Germantown. As a small child he was sold, along with both parents and two brothers, and he grew up on a Delaware farm. There he became a Methodist and a lay preacher in his late teens; by 1783 he had earned enough to purchase his own freedom and that of his brothers. Returning to Philadelphia, he became the organizer of what is now called Mother Bethel A.M.E. Church. In 1799 he became the first black minister ordained by Francis Asbury and founder of the African Methodist Episcopal Church in 1816.

For most of the past century a presumption has been maintained in the scholarship concerning folk hymnody that American camp-meeting spirituals are defined by the "revival choruses" that are found attached to many of them. It is in some instances further asserted that these choruses reflect African American antecedents. These assertions are not supported by the surviving print record, which for the new hymn texts typically antedates that of their music by about two decades. Camp-meeting spiritual songs, like other hymns, differ widely in form, as they do in subject matter. Many have been thought through and organized with great care, notably for the purposes of evangelism and argument. Choruses may routinely have been added on the camp-meeting grounds, as the hymns were sung in large groups, but this was not widely reflected in print until about 1809. Richard Allen's 1801 collection contains a few revival choruses, but they are no more prominent than in other works of its genre already discussed that have no camp-meeting antecedents (and, in several New England Baptist examples, no known exposure to the worship or other practices of the black population).

On the other hand, the presence of black worshipers was very strong in the early decades of the camp-meeting movement. The influence of this presence on the performance practices of the movement in general is especially well documented in Methodist sources; a notable case in point is the smooth blending of Allen's very early effort into the long-lived and influential Baltimore Collection. Some forty years later *The Sacred Harp* and a handful of comparable collections, particularly but not exclusively those from the South, would reflect this multicultural background of camp-meeting hymns in a great variety of melodic and rhythmic patterns barely hinted at by the words-only broadsides and songsters.[8]

The other important Methodist contribution to the nascent camp-meeting hymn genre was compiled anonymously. *Hymns and Spiritual Songs for the Use of Christians, Including a Number Never Before Published* (Baltimore, 1801) was published as a commercial venture, apparently with great success. Several of its numerous editions were printed in several other cities, but it was generally cited by those who borrowed its popular new hymns as the "Baltimore Collection." Not until 1812 (the eleventh edition, printed in New Haven) would any of its publishers deign to mention the fact that these hymns were used "Particularly by the Methodist Societies." Ironically, by 1812 that may no longer have been the case; in the first edition, however, most of the new content was, indeed, of Methodist origin. Its second edition (Baltimore, 1802) included a wholesale importation of well over half the content of the second edition of Allen's collection; most of these hymns are unmodified, and they occur in the same order.[9]

One of the early secondary imprints of the Baltimore Collection is an 1803 edition from the Lexington, Kentucky, press of Joseph Charless. This printer was rather busy issuing little books and pamphlets of hymns during the early years of the new century. In some respects the most important of his offerings was a booklet of only thirty pages, titled simply *Spiritual Songs* (January 1804); its twenty hymns are all originals by Caleb Jarvis Taylor. A much larger publication, also with groundbreaking content, is *The Lexington Collection, being a Selection of Hymns and Spiritual Songs, from the Best Authors. Together, with a Number Never Before Published*, second edition (Lexington, 1805). At least two of the hymns that first appear in this book are the work of Barton W. Stone, whose church had hosted the great Cane Ridge revival of 1801 not far from Lexington. An 1805 title that is not known to have survived but was advertised by Charless at the end of a theological tract by Stone is *The Christian's Hymn Book*: almost certainly this was the prototype for the popular *Christian Hymn-Book*, the denominational hymnal of the western branch of the Christian Church. No copy of that work earlier than an 1813 second edition from Nashville has been found. The first hymn book printed in Tennessee, it is the repository of a few camp-meeting hymns that appear nowhere else. Stone's tract about the Atonement was attacked in print, with a good bit of vitriol, by John Poage Campbell; this exchange, essentially one of conflicting opinions about Calvinist orthodoxy, continued into two more little books. Campbell, another fine frontier hymn writer, had until 1804 been Stone's brother in the Presbyterian ministry.[10]

What would prove to be the most influential of all the new collections from Lexington was published not by Charless, but by a competitor: *The Pilgrim's Song-ster* by John Adam Granade (Daniel Bradford, 1804). It was advertised for sale in Bradford's *Kentucky Gazette* on 3 April 1804. No copy of the tract has survived, but at least thirty of Granade's own hymns were copied from it, along with the title, and published, with credit to the author, by his fellow Methodist minister Thomas S. Hinde. The first edition of this 1810 publication is lost, but the second edition of Hinde's *Pilgrim's Songster* (Chillicothe, Ohio, 1815) is extant, as is a Cincinnati third edition of 1828. In these enlarged, eclectic compilations, Hinde attempted to do for the Methodists of the South and West what Josiah Goddard had done in 1809 for the Baptists of the North and East. In Hinde's case, the volume rescued from anonymity many original and important camp-meeting hymns: not only Granade's but also some by Caleb J. Taylor, Sarah Jones, and George Askins.

It is regrettable that no such champion of authors' rights appeared among the Kentucky Baptists. The first of their collections may have been the one tersely advertised in Bradford's *Kentucky Gazette* in 1804: "A Collection of Spiritual Songs, by Joshua Morris, For sale at this Office." Because no copy has been located, we cannot be certain, but this publisher appears to have been the pastor of the Mill Creek Baptist Church in Nelson County, a little east of Bardstown. Early collections by Starke Dupuy (1811), Silas M. Noel (1814), and Absalom Graves (1825) identify much of the work they had received from European authors—but not their own, nor that of their fellow Baptists in Kentucky.

The same cloak of anonymity conceals the identity of most hymn writers among the newly formed frontier congregations of the Cumberland Presbyterians and the "Stoneite" Christians. Oddly enough, the Shakers preserved a couple of the latter because the gifted hymnist Richard McNemar apparently wrote them early, while he was still associated with Barton W. Stone. Most of McNemar's adult life was spent as a Shaker; it was their historians, not those of the Christian Church, who credited this author of hymns preserved in both groups (and in *The Sacred Harp*).[11] Finally, the western Presbyterian mainstream is represented—quite late in the development of this repertoire—by Thomas Cleland (1826); he attributes hymns to a number of his fellow American ministers, not all of them members of his denomination.

On Sunday, 9 October 1804, Daniel Bradford mentioned in his *Kentucky Gazette* that Lorenzo Dow, "the celebrated pedestrian and itinerant preacher," had arrived in town the preceding Thursday. This dates his visit a bit more closely than Dow himself does (though his own account provides several interesting details). It is almost a certainty that Dow picked up a copy of Granade's six-month-old songster, and possibly Taylor's; fellow ministers whom he subsequently visited in Virginia and North Carolina were to be among the first to reprint the new hymns from Kentucky. Dow carried the work to England and Ireland on his second trip there in the winter of 1805. Within a year of his arrival he had published more than half of Granade's known hymns (with others by unknown authors) in Dublin and Liverpool, before they were very widely known in America; indeed, they became the bedrock of the hymnody of the new Primitive Methodist Church. For the present study the point is that some *Sacred Harp* material for which we cite works compiled by David B. Mintz (1805 and 1806) and by Stith Mead (1807) may well have reached them via their known associate, likewise known to have been an energetic spreader of the camp meeting and of its hymnody: Lorenzo Dow. That is most apparent with respect to brand-new hymns they reprinted by Granade and Taylor; for those texts, however, we have been able to cite the actual authors.

Among other recently emancipated publishers of officially unsanctioned but clearly popular revivalist material for the Methodists, John C. Totten looms larger than most. The work that is cited as a source for the *Sacred Harp* first appeared as *A Collection of the Most Admired Hymns and Spiritual Songs, With the Choruses Affixed as Usually Sung at Camp-Meeting, &c., With Others Suited to Various Occasions* (1809). Before launching this popular songster (which enjoyed at least twenty-two editions by 1830), Totten had in 1807 reprinted *A Choice Selection of Hymns and Spiritual Songs, Designed for the Use of the Pious* (1805). Although these collections are not cited as sources of any Sacred Harp hymns, they were among the first to supply Granade's and Taylor's western hymns (anonymously) to revivalists in the northeastern states in a form other than the broadside.

One more initiator of a series of camp-meeting songsters for a predominantly Methodist clientele deserves notice: John J. Harrod. To him belongs the distinction of having first printed, in *Social and Camp-Meeting Hymns, for the Pious* (1817), the best-known hymn by the recently deceased circuit preacher George Askins. This may have been an accident of geography and timing. Thomas S. Hinde had attributed one hymn to him in 1815 (perhaps already in 1810, but we do not have that edition to check); this is the only one that has come to light that was published during Askins's lifetime. Publishing in the year after his death, Harrod attributed only two to Askins, one of which is in *The Sacred Harp*. These and four more were identified by Askins's close neighbor at the time of his death, George Kolb, in *The Spiritual Songster: Containing a Variety of Camp-Meeting, and Other Hymns* (Frederick-Town, Maryland, 1819). Sad to say, this total of seven attributed texts makes Askins one of the best-documented hymn writers of his generation and genre.

Harrod's collections had a success and a longevity similar to those of Totten before him and many others after him such as Orange Scott, Peter D. Myers, and Thomas Mason. Though not unimportant, these later series have decreasing value for the present study as first sources. It is an oversimplification, but true, to state that far more Americans learned their folk hymnody from such pocket-sized songsters as Harrod's *Social and Camp-Meeting Hymns, for the Pious* than from such singing-school books as *The Sacred Harp*. The former was an artifact of folk religion (in which this hymnody was a vibrant central element); the latter, of music education (in which it was becoming an increasingly isolated subset). These two arenas of cultural activity are deeply indebted to each other for, on one hand, the creation, and on the other, the preservation of some of the fleeting rainbows of early American religious and musical interaction. This did not happen by accident; people who heard these hymns in crowds of ten or twenty thousand outdoor worshippers felt a need that we might perceive as almost folkloristic to record them for posterity. There is much more in print about the "songcatchers" who were musicians than about those who only took down the words; it seems appropriate to let a few of them who actually expressed themselves concerning the matter have their say.

The best place to look for commentary is a compiler's preface, but a majority of these songsters lack one. Often something like the outline of a missing preface may be detected in the wordy subtitle incorporated into the title page of many examples of this genre. Totten, for instance, mentions the fact that he has left "the Choruses Affixed as Usually Sung at Camp-Meeting"; although he does not really include very many such examples, he is one of the pioneers of this practice. A more cultured approach is taken by the Congregationalist Joshua Spalding of Salem, Massachusetts, who gave us *The Lord's Songs: A Collection of Composures in Metre, Such as Have Been Most Used in the Late Glorious Revivals; Dr. Watts's Psalms and Hymns Excepted (1805).* One might think, That says it all; but in fact he has a preface, and it says a good bit more. "The editor, having spent several years in travelling among the churches in the late remarkable season of Divine Influences, has witnessed the great benefit of the use of Hymns and Spiritual Songs, which has been prevalent with this glorious work." But seeing room for improvement on many of them, he proceeds to do exactly that, and then claims a number of good songs—already in widespread use—as being "originally composed, or materially altered, by the editor." This sort of thing was common; he is just more articulate and candid about his own role than most.

Another very popular northern collection (though not a direct source for *The Sacred Harp*) is *Hymns and Spiritual Songs, on Different Subjects, Collected from a Variety of Authors. By Miss Harvey, now Mrs. Stevens. To which is added, a Collection, Suitably Adapted to the Edification of Christians, and the Public Worship of God. By Herman Harvey, and others.* (Hudson [New York], 1804). The compilers were the children of Deacon Obed Harvey (usually spelled "Hervey" where they lived) of Durham, New York. Herman (also spelled Hermon) was pastor of the Baptist church there for more than thirty years. Of the many excellent and interesting hymns in their frequently reprinted collection, one that especially catches the eye (in Herman's part of the book) is "The Virginian song, about the glorious day." This piece is by John Leland, who had already been back in Massachusetts for thirteen years; he had, indeed, published many of his hymns in Virginia, but we have no surviving evidence that this is one of them. None, that is, but the fact that Harvey seems to imply that it was. The hymn begins, "The glorious day is drawing nigh, / When Zion's light shall come."

Perhaps the best title page of the entire genre is found in a book known from a single surviving copy: *A Choice Collection of Hymns and Spiritual Songs. Designed for the Use of the Pious of All Denominations. Being a Selection from the Following Pamphlets, to-wit: Mintz's first and second—John A. Granade's, ditto—Meads', ditto—Jones', ditto. And some Original Hymns.* (Newbern [North Carolina], 1807). The compiler is not named, but given that one of the printers is Salmon Hall (whose own 1804 collection is a first source for *The Sacred Harp*), he is perhaps our unself-conscious hymn collector. Nominally for "all denominations," the book is compiled entirely from Methodist sources; the only one we cannot be positive about is "Jones." Examination of the content excludes Abner Jones, partner of Elias Smith in New England, and the book includes everything we know by Sarah Jones of Virginia. (Unfortunately, we only know of her authorship through Stith Mead, and he is represented in this *Choice Collection* as well.) In the absence of strong evidence to the contrary, I am inclined to assert that Sarah Jones probably published a pamphlet-hymn collection, that this compiler probably had a copy, and that the 1807 *Choice Collection* is the quintessential southern folk hymn collection of its era.

Thomas S. Hinde seems as worthy as any of our compilers to have the last word. We know—because he tells us so in the preface to his *Pilgrim's Songster* (1815)—that he had in hand the published hymns of both Taylor (whom he knew intimately) and Granade (who was well known at least to Hinde's father). Far from "correcting" their original language, as would a Spalding, he tried his best to restore it. Here are a few of his comments: "It has been said of Luther, that among the greatest rewards he shall receive for his labors of love at the Last Day, will be that for having made and published Hymns and Spiritual Songs suitable to the meanest capacity of his countrymen, and in a language most familiar to them. . . . In this selection are condensed the choicest Spiritual Songs, agreeably to my judgement, that we have, or that I have ever seen. Nor have my means been scanty in forming the collection."

After naming many collections that he owned, and specifically excluding the Methodist Hymn Book (very well known by the target audience for his songster), he focuses on Granade and Taylor. "These two poets composed their songs during the great revivals of religion in the states of Kentucky and Tennessee about the years 1802, 3 and 4. They appear to have been written in the midst of the Holy Flame. . . . The peculiar turn of these two interesting poets . . . is very particularly adapted to the minds and dispositions of the western people. Their language is that of the church in the wilderness."

Hinde closes this unusually perceptive contextual analysis of the Western Bards (and of many other successful vernacular lyricists with whom we may yet become acquainted in *The Sacred Harp*) with an extended quotation and paraphrase of several verses from Isaiah 35 and 55—most of them song-related. It begins, "The wilderness and the solitary place shall be glad for them; and the desert shall rejoice, and blossom as the rose." To restate an axiom from the beginning of this essay: one does not need the mind and belief system of a frontier evangelist to see, through the lens of another two hundred years, that he got that right.

SKETCHES OF SELECTED POETS AND HYMN WRITERS
Richard H. Hulan

JOHN LELAND

John Leland was born 14 May 1754 in Grafton, Massachusetts. Four generations of his family had lived in that colony since 1652; they were Congregationalists, and as a child of three he was baptized in that church. (In later years he was pleased to report that they first had to send the maid to catch him.)[1] He was a bright child and a good student but did not receive an advanced education. The preaching of the Baptist evangelist Elhanan Winchester (later a pillar of the Universalist denomination) had a strong influence on him when he was eighteen. Leland was again baptized, in what he deemed the correct way, in June 1774; before that month was over he had preached his first sermon. In the spring of 1775 he was licensed to preach by the Bellingham Baptist Church. After a preaching tour to Virginia during the following fall and winter, he returned briefly to Massachusetts, where he married Sally Devine of Hopkinton at the end of September. They set out immediately for Virginia and did not resume residence in the state of their birth for nearly fifteen years.

A brief stopover in Fairfax and a few months' ministry in Culpeper were followed by a lengthy residence on an Orange County farm he had purchased, initially in partnership with Elhanan Winchester. Leland spent much of his time on evangelistic trips to South Carolina, Philadelphia, and elsewhere. Management of the farm (and of their nine children) was left largely to Sally. Both of the Leland hymns that are found in *The Sacred Harp* appear to have been first published in Virginia. "The day is past and gone" is set to two tunes, on pages 209 and 302; it was printed in Broaddus and Broaddus, *Collection of Sacred Ballads* (1790). "O when shall I see Jesus, and reign with him above," or some part of it, is found in no fewer than six tunes, on pages 82, 85, 106, 129, 319, and 410. It is first noted in Eleazar Clay's *Hymns and Spiritual Songs* (1793).

During the last five years of his stay in the Old Dominion, Elder Leland became much more prominent in Baptist circles, and to some extent was involved also in state and national politics. He endorsed James Madison's candidacy as a representative to the Virginia Convention to ratify the new United States Constitution in 1788, on the assurance that additional guarantees of religious liberty would be added to that document. Madison won the election, with strong Baptist backing—and in opposition to James Monroe and Patrick Henry. It has been suggested on the basis of credible evidence that Leland influenced Madison's thinking about his subsequent Bill of Rights, the third article of which (prohibiting, among other limitations of freedom, the establishment of a state religion) became our First Amendment.

An early historian of the Baptist Church, David Benedict, is among those who preserved the following unusual highlight of Leland's career as a public figure.

> Cheshire is famous for its excellent cheese, and in 1801, a number of farmers united their efforts, and made one of the astonishing weight of thirteen hundred pounds! . . . This was called the Mammoth Cheese; it was designed as a present to Mr. Jefferson, then President of the United States, and Mr. Leland was commissioned to conduct it to Washington. In the journey he was gone four months, in which time he preached seventy-four times, and multitudes everywhere flocked to hear the Mammoth priest. Mr. Leland is remarkable for his singularities, and also for his success in the ministry. In 1810, he had baptized eleven hundred and sixty-three persons, about seven hundred of them in Virginia. From this Cheshire church have proceeded . . . Josiah Goddard, now of Conway, the compiler of a Hymn Book, which is well esteemed . . . and a number of other ministers.

The anecdote is told at greater length elsewhere, but this 1813 source is the one that most clearly links Goddard (discussed in chapter 9 with regard to his contributions to hymnology) and the longtime minister of his home church. John Leland (see plate 6) preached his last sermon in Cheshire on 8 January 1841; he became ill and died six days later, in his eighty-seventh year.[2]

JOHN ADAM GRANADE

John Adam Granade was born 9 May 1763, in Jones County, North Carolina. We have no actual record of his first thirty years, although he later confessed to his fellow Methodists that this period had been intemperate. In any case, his father died in 1791; not long after his mother passed away in 1796, he moved with the family of a married sister to a part of Sumner County, Tennessee, that is now Trousdale County. Granade was subject to extreme emotional highs and lows, not unusual among Methodists of his day. He was perhaps bipolar. He spent the winter of

1797–98 wandering in the woods, howling for mercy; thus he earned the nickname "the Wild Man of Goose Creek," which was to follow him throughout his career. Eventually settling across the Cumberland River in Wilson County, he taught school for the children of the Wynne, Babb, and Still families. In August 1800, at one of the very first camp meetings (at Blythe's Big Spring, about eight miles northeast of Gallatin, Tennessee), he had a powerful conversion experience during a sermon on John 3:8 by John Rankin, who in about five years would become a founder of the Cumberland Presbyterian Church. Granade's conversion was later described in his own words, both verse and prose, and by others present at the scene.

Although he had not left much of a mark in his first thirty-seven years, Granade made up for this during the next four—a meteoric career that was to ruin his physical health. He became an exhorter at once and was officially under supervision on the Cumberland circuit (including his home neighborhood) in 1801. Admitted as a circuit minister on a trial basis by Bishop Francis Asbury in October 1801, he spent the following year on the Green circuit and the next on the Holston circuit; both were in East Tennessee, along with adjacent parts of Kentucky and southwestern Virginia. He was "pretty well broken down" by March 1803; having begun his brief circuit ministry a "corpulent thunder of a man," he finished it weak, slender, and unable to speak much above a whisper.[3] In full standing for 1804, he was appointed to the Hinkstone circuit in Kentucky; this included the Cane Ridge vicinity. However, he was not physically able to continue the traveling life; instead he studied medicine during 1804 under the tutelage of Doctor Thomas Hinde (father of the hymn publisher) in Lexington, Kentucky.

It was during this period that he published his *Pilgrim's Songster.* We do not know whether the thirty-odd hymns (some are in two parts, and the parts have not uniformly been treated as separate hymns) that Thomas S. Hinde attributes to Granade include his whole collection, but that seems unlikely. (Taylor's contemporary work, for example, contained twenty texts, only eleven of which are repeated by Hinde.) To the extent that we can identify Granade's hymns, *The Sacred Harp* contains four of them, one of which appears twice. They are "Sweet rivers of redeeming love" (page 61); "Ye weary, heavy-laden souls" (page 72 and the last two verses on page 121); "See how the scriptures are fulfilling" (page 102); and "Come, all ye mourning pilgrims dear" (page 201). The last was one of several that circulated independently in broadside form, and it may be the only one found in a songster (an 1803 imprint of the Baltimore Collection) before Granade published his own in 1804. Many of his other hymns were widespread in the tradition, found both in songsters and in singing-school books but almost never credited to him.

Returning to his old Tennessee home, Granade began to practice medicine. He married Polly Wynne (perhaps one of his former pupils) in 1805; they had two sons, one of whom was born after he had died (December 6, 1807). Lorenzo Dow visited

Granade's widow in the fall of 1813. His journal notes that because his route included Lebanon, Tennessee, "I saw the wife of the 'wild man of the woods.' I strove to obtain his journal, but in that I was disappointed, though they had agreed on certain conditions to let me have it; he died in peace." Dow would almost certainly have published this journal, which might be of great interest. It remained in the Granade family for about a hundred years but then disappeared; only a few brief passages from it were preserved in an article by his grandson, Hervey M. Granade.[4]

CALEB JARVIS TAYLOR

Caleb Jarvis Taylor was born on 20 June 1763 in St. Mary's County, Maryland. His parents, who were Irish, raised him in the Roman Catholic Church. Leaving home at the age of eighteen to pursue a career as a schoolteacher, he first settled in Washington Bottom, now Perryopolis, Pennsylvania. There he became a Methodist and was soon licensed as a local preacher in the vicinity of Uniontown. He moved to Mason County, Kentucky, by 1795, and then to a farm in nearby Campbell County. Throughout his life he continued to teach school for the support of his considerable family (his will, proved in August 1817, names his wife Sarah, five daughters, and three sons). He was from time to time a circuit preacher for brief periods during the illness of a colleague or some temporary vacancy, but the pay for such service was in his opinion inadequate to the needs of his family. His earliest preserved poetry is not a hymn but a comic reflection on his economic circumstances. Another work of his that saw print was an ironic, humorous pamphlet titled *News from Infernal Regions* (Lexington: Joseph Charless, 1803), in which it is learned (by eavesdropping on a business conference of demons) that the institution of slavery was a plot to make Americans indolent and weaken their morals generally: essentially, a recruitment plan from hell. There is strong circumstantial evidence that Lorenzo Dow used this tract at a camp meeting the following year in the Mississippi Territory.

Taylor spent most of his ministerial and teaching career at Maysville, Kentucky. A number of his spiritual songs became widely popular after their publication in January 1804. A single surviving copy of this booklet in the Cincinnati Public Library preserves the hymns he is known to have authored to that time. Thomas S. Hinde (who had reprinted many of the 1804 texts and at least one of his later hymns) was entrusted not only with Taylor's personal papers but also with the care and raising of one of his sons, Thomas Hinde Taylor. Hinde's own papers (including a few of Taylor's) were acquired by Lyman Draper and are preserved in the Wisconsin Historical Society. Another interesting imprint is the undated broadside issued by Richard Allen of Philadelphia's African Methodist Episcopal Church, of Taylor's dialogue between a person going to a camp meeting and one returning from it.

Two of Taylor's hymns appear in *The Sacred Harp.* "Oh, Jesus, my Savior, I know Thou art mine" (page 125), is his variation on a theme originated by Mrs. Sarah Jones in a hymn beginning, "Oh Jesus, my Savior, to thee I submit." (Much better known as it was anonymously revised in the 1860s to begin "My Jesus, I love thee, I know thou art mine," this text is very rarely credited to Taylor.) His other contribution is "Come, and taste, along with me, / the weary Pilgrim's consolation" (page 326); this one has in many sources been erroneously credited to John Leland. Taylor was indeed indebted to Leland for the first line, but the latter's slightly older hymn (in a different poetic meter) begins "Come and taste, along with me, / Consolation running free." Besides several hymns that were widely reprinted and are still sung today, Taylor left a stirring poetic description of the 1801 Cane Ridge camp meeting, in which he was a participant; this meeting, near Millersburg, was about halfway between his home and Lexington.[5]

GEORGE ASKINS

George Askins was born in Ireland, but the date and place of his birth are unknown; the most likely family of origin seems to be in the vicinity of Larne, County Antrim. The name was formerly spelled Erskine, and both forms are found in Antrim. It is believed that he came to the United States as an adult, and already a Methodist, in 1801. At any rate, he was a recent immigrant in that year, when he was admitted on trial to the ranks of itinerant preachers and assigned to the Montgomery circuit of the Baltimore Conference. His subsequent appointments (with his name inconsistently spelled) are as follows:

1802	Remained on trial; Ohio circuit (Pittsburgh Conference)
1803	Full connection; Shenango circuit (Pittsburgh Conference)
1804	Deacon; Muskingum & Little Kanawha circuit (Ohio Conference)
1805	Deacon and Elder-elect; Limestone circuit (Kentucky Conference)
1806	Elder; Hinkstone circuit (Kentucky Conference)
1807	Lexington circuit (Kentucky Conference)
1808	Danville circuit (Kentucky Conference)
1809	Shelby circuit (Kentucky Conference)
1810	Scioto circuit (Miami Conference)
1811	Staunton circuit (Virginia Conference)
1812	Berkeley circuit (Baltimore Conference)
1813 and 1814	Chambersburg circuit (Baltimore Conference)
1815	Frederick circuit (Baltimore Conference)

Elder George Askins died in Frederick, Maryland, on 28 February 1816, leaving a widow. She is credited in George Kolb's *Spiritual Songster* with having provided that compiler with some of her late husband's verse. As late as 1843 she received a small pension from the Baltimore Conference. Askins was physically handicapped, and it was with considerable difficulty that he traveled some of the most mountainous circuits east of the Mississippi. He is considered the founding pastor of the First United Methodist Church in Lexington, Kentucky. Albert H. Redford's *History of Methodism in Kentucky* (1870) has a lengthy section about George Askins, but most of it is devoted to his death and is not in the broader sense biographical. It does preserve this anecdote, quoted from an elderly former acquaintance, Jonathan Stamper:

> He was a man of small stature, and a cripple, one of his legs being withered up to the hip; yet he was more active on foot than any cripple I ever saw. Notwithstanding this bodily infirmity, he was full of spirit, and a stranger to fear. No threats could deter him from speaking his sentiments, no matter who might hear them, and he would reprove sin wherever or by whomsoever committed. In doing this, he often gave great offense, and on one or two occasions suffered personal injury.

Apart from the seven hymns credited to Askins, several of which are outstanding, little else is known of him. "Brethren, we have met to worship," set to HOLY MANNA, has long been featured as the opening hymn at the annual "Big Singing" from the *Southern Harmony* at Benton, Kentucky.[6]

JOHN POAGE CAMPBELL

John Poage Campbell was born in 1767 in Augusta County, Virginia. His father, Robert Campbell, moved the family to Kentucky (still a frontier in this period) when John was fourteen. Raised in a prominent family of Scotch-Irish Presbyterians, John was sent back to Virginia for his higher education. His childless uncle, Major John W. Campbell, having adopted him, he attended Hampden-Sidney College, graduating in 1790. This places him on that campus during a historically important revival of religion that was centered there beginning in 1787. Campbell continued his studies in divinity and in medicine a few counties to the southwest at a sister academy, Liberty Hall, to which the Hampden-Sidney revival had quickly spread. (Liberty Hall was the germ of what is now Washington and Lee University.) Among the many links between these two Virginia schools (and David Caldwell's academy in Guilford County, North Carolina), none was more crucial than the preaching of James McGready. Hymn singing was also a strong element of this revival, both in the schools themselves and while traveling by foot to the larger union meetings. In this cause, the important singing-master Lucius Chapin (several of whose arrangements are in *The Sacred Harp*) was brought to southwest Virginia by the founding rector of Liberty Hall, William Graham.

Campbell assumed the duties of co-pastor with his former professor Moses Hoge in the Presbyterian congregations of Lexington, Oxford, New Monmouth, and Timber Ridge. Elected a trustee of Liberty Hall in 1793, he was before the age of thirty closely acquainted with many of the New Light Presbyterian preachers— and Methodist and Baptist clergy with similar approaches—whose evangelism would lead to the birth of camp meetings a few years later and a few hundred miles farther west. Campbell himself moved back to Kentucky in 1795, his first pastorate being at Smyrna and Flemingsburg, in present-day Fleming County. He later served at Danville, Nicholasville, Cherry Springs, Versailles, and Lexington before removing to Chillicothe, Ohio, shortly before his death in 1814. He was a medical doctor as well as a pastor and was usually given the title "Doctor" instead of an ecclesiastical title. A prolific writer, sometimes a polemicist, Campbell early published *Sermon on Sacred Music: Preached before a Public Concert, in Washington* (Washington, Kentucky: Hunter and Beaumont, 1797). This earned him a niche in the annals of shape-note hymnody when it was used, without attribution to its author, as the introductory essay ("On the origin, nature, and moral tendency of music") in Samuel L. Metcalf's *Kentucky Harmonist* (1818), the first shape-note tunebook that originated in the old Southwest Territory.

A number of strong revivalist hymns have been ascribed imprecisely to "Campbell," but only recently has it been possible to say which Campbell wrote these texts. This is largely thanks to his fellow Kentucky Presbyterian, Thomas Cleland (1778–1858), who knew Campbell for about the last fifteen years of his life and succeeded him at one pastorate (Danville). Three hymns in Cleland's collection of 1826 are attributed to "Campbell," one of them specifically to "J. P. Campbell." This example is the only hymn I have ever seen that was clearly written for the Scotch-Irish Presbyterians' semiannual sacramental services: great gatherings (especially in the summer), sometimes open to other denominations, that in the 1790s had served as the immediate forerunners of the still larger and longer camp meetings. Though the text is not found in the *Sacred Harp*, its suggested tune is PILGRIM'S FAREWELL. It is worthwhile to quote a bit of this unusual hymn; these verses are the first and fifth of eleven:

> Happy place, happy place, happy place,
>   where our dear Lord is seen,
> In sacred emblems newly slain,
> Through all the soul sweet transport pours,

Or peace distils in gentle showers.
    Chorus.
Or peace, or peace, or peace,
Distils in gentle showers.

Ling'ring round, ling'ring round, ling'ring round,
    still our fond hearts would stay,
And sing our peaceful days away:
But sterner duties call anew;
Here hours of rapture must be few.
    Chorus.
Here hours, here hours, here hours,
Of rapture must be few.

Campbell might not have been thrilled by the association of revivalist texts with his name, though he had in his younger days penned some very good ones. By 1805 he was entering a phase of his career in which he defended Presbyterian positions (concerning, for example, predestination and the "ransom" interpretation of the Atonement) that were not widely shared by the more revivalistic general population. He was particularly hard on his former colleagues Barton W. Stone (who had helped found the new Christian Church) and James McGready (who had a similar role among the Cumberland Presbyterians). But Campbell died in 1814 at the age of forty-seven. Cleland was heir apparent to his task of defending the Westminster Confession, and he did so ably for a number of years. But even he yielded to the temptation of getting out a hymn book when a secondary wave of revivals broke out among Kentucky's Presbyterians in 1826–29. And it is thanks to that late revival—among people who really knew better—that we can with some confidence name John Poage Campbell as one of our rare examples of a known, important, and gifted camp-meeting hymnist.[7]

PART THREE

THE COMPOSERS

BIOGRAPHICAL
SKETCHES OF
THE COMPOSERS

In the following section I have attempted to describe what is known about the composers associated with *The Sacred Harp,* 1991 edition. Where a wealth of information is available in accessible and authoritative sources, this information is merely summarized. In many more cases where information is scarce, it is presented in fuller detail. Although the names of the composer's parents and spouse may not be of interest to all, they may aid in establishing a firm identity for future researchers. Places of burial are of particular interest to the singers and family members who cherish their memory.

Many of the details about the composers are drawn from local and family histories, including a large number of online sources. It is prudent to exercise caution with such sources and to acknowledge their shortcomings and their reluctance to judge their subjects. It is natural that, in particular, descendants of the composers should stand in awe of the hardships and primitive conditions that were overcome by ancestors who, often lacking formal education and inherited wealth, achieved local eminence through persistence and toil.

Many of these individuals would have remained unidentified without the online archiving of local and family records by amateur genealogists and historians. Inaccuracies may be found in the sketches presented here, and I take full responsibility for these. The present work cannot claim to present the last word on the subject. It is hoped instead that it represents only the first word, a guide for future researchers who will flesh out the histories of the early Sacred Harp composers and the world they inhabited.

Many songs in the Sacred Harp are variants of songs known from printed collections or manuscripts or collected from oral tradition. Hence, the concept of authorship may be somewhat vague and may refer to an original melody, an original setting, a setting of a melody from oral tradition, or an arrangement of an earlier setting, whether a hymn tune, secular song, or instrumental piece. As a result, some pieces have not been traced to an individual composer or arranger; in other cases more than one composer may be connected with a song. Some tunebook compilers acknowledged as much. In his *Union Harmony* (1837, 3–4), William Caldwell advanced claims of authorship that might seem extravagant, had he not stated in the preface:

> Many of the tunes over which the name of the Subscriber is set are not entirely original, but he has harmonised, and therefore claims them. Many of the airs which the author has reduced to system and harmonized, have been selected from the unwritten music in general use in the Methodist Church, others from the Baptist and many more from the Presbyterian taste.

In his *Southern Harmony* (1835, iii), William Walker likewise explained:

> I have composed the parts to a great many good airs, (which I could not find in any publication, nor in manuscript,) and assigned my name as author. I have also composed several tunes wholly, and inserted them in this work, which also bear my name.

There is one additional form of authorship that I have rarely encountered outside the Sacred Harp tradition. A few songs are credited to an individual as a form of tribute or dedication, but are actually composed by another person, perhaps a well-known Sacred Harp composer who already has many tunes to his credit. This has the effect of recognizing a person for his or her service to the cause of Sacred Harp singing by transferring credit for a given song, while modestly reducing the share of songs credited to any one author. It is not known for certain whether such tributes existed in the nineteenth century—though standard dedications exist, for example, "in honor of J. P. Rees"—but a few examples of these "dedicatory attributions" are noted below.

Following each composer sketch is a list of compositions in the 1991 edition. Quotation marks indicate attributions from early editions, with editorial information in brackets.

AARON, ANNA EUGENIA "ANNIE" DENSON (17 March 1885–23 June 1962), was the daughter of T. J. and Amanda Denson. Born at Arbacoochee, Cleburne County, Alabama, she spent part of her childhood in Georgia before her family moved to Winston County, Alabama. She married Newton Byrd Aaron and lived in Double Springs, and her husband was sheriff of Winston County for sixteen years; the couple had five children. Annie Denson Aaron usually sang treble. Her tune

CONSOLATION was first printed in the Denson revision of 1936. She was buried in Fairview Cemetery, Double Springs.

367 Consolation

AIKIN, BURWELL STEPHEN (30 May 1849–6 April 1918), son of Elisha Clay Akins and Martha Welden, was born in Orchard Hill, Pike County, Georgia, later Spalding County. In 1870 he married (1) Emma Ella Georgia Williamson in Pike County. After Emma died in 1916 he married (2) a Miss Bennett of Barnesville, only six weeks before his death. Aikin served as a county commissioner and tax equalizer. He was a Primitive Baptist, and, according to J. S. James, "a fine singer and a great lover of music." A member of the United Sacred Harp Musical Association and of the revision committees for *Union Harp* (1909) and *Original Sacred Harp* (1911), he "rearranged" L. P. Breedlove's SHEPHERDS REJOICE in 1908, changing a few notes and adding an alto part. He died in Zebulon after suffering a heart attack, leaving a widow and seven sons; he was buried in the Williamson family cemetery.

152 SHEPHERDS REJOICE [rearranged, alto added]

ARNE, THOMAS AUGUSTINE (12 March 1710–5 March 1778), was born in London, the son of an upholsterer. Educated at Eton College, he studied the violin but learned composition on his own and became the major English theatrical composer of the eighteenth century. Like his mother, he was a Roman Catholic. His sister Susannah Cibber was the greatest tragic actress of her day, and his wife Cecilia Young was a prominent soprano singer. Arne is best known today for the patriotic song "Rule, Britannia!" composed in 1740. His opera *Artaxerxes* (1762) was the first full-length serious opera in English; an air in the overture was arranged after Arne's death as a hymn tune, later known as ARLINGTON, by Ralph Harrison (1784). He was buried in the churchyard of St. Paul's, Covent Garden.

73 ARLINGTON

ARNOLD, JAMES D. (9 November 1838–16 June 1910), was born at Barnesville, Georgia, the son of Owen and Louvicie Arnold. He moved to Coweta County, where he married Nancy Seay Owens in Forsyth on 15 January 1857. A member of Ebenezer Baptist Church, Forsyth, he was ordained a deacon in 1867. He served in the First Georgia Cavalry from 1862 to 1865. Arnold composed or arranged three tunes for the 1870 edition of *The Sacred Harp:* BALDWIN and SHADY GROVE (both deleted) and HIGHLANDS OF HEAVEN, an arrangement of a Scots song.

175 HIGHLANDS OF HEAVEN [arranged]

AVERY, HARVEY ROY (14 February 1906–5 June 1999), of LaFayette, Alabama, the son of Robert H. Avery and Mattie Price, was a Primitive Baptist elder and singing teacher. Ordained to preach in 1929, he served churches in several states. He was an active teacher whose pupils included his three brothers. In the 1960s he led a group of east Alabama singers in a studio recording of Sacred Harp songs, later reissued on compact disc as *Eternal Day*. He said that his greatest delight in life was to preach the Gospel and to sing Sacred Harp. He was buried at Rocky Mount Primitive Baptist Church, Daviston, Alabama. A SONG OF PRAISE (later deleted) and MY HOME were first published in the 1960 Denson Revision.

560 MY HOME

AYERS, JAMES ADRIAN (28 February 1905–3 December 1987), was born at Indian Creek, near Bowdon, Georgia, one of five children of James William Ayers and Mary Ella Skinner. He married Liley Bell Lee on 27 February 1926 and had a daughter and a son. Jim Ayers was a farmer, brickmason and contractor, a Methodist, and an avid fisherman. After his retirement, he and his wife operated Lake Side Curb Market. He sang bass, and his wife sang treble. He taught singing schools and traveled widely to singings; he chaired the United Convention in 1960, 1961, and 1975. He contributed SEWELL (later deleted) to the 1960 Denson Revision and THE ARK to the 1966 revision. He was buried in Bowdon City Cemetery.

506 THE ARK

BALL, R. F. (died about 1862), was a member of the 1859 revision committee; according to Ogletree, he was a staunch Methodist and died in the Civil War. Together with a man named Drinkard he wrote a setting of "The Dying Californian," a popular ballad about a Forty-Niner who died on the way to the goldfields. He also contributed VALLEY GROVE and I AM PASSING AWAY to the 1859 appendix, but these were removed in the 1870 edition.

410 THE DYING CALIFORNIAN "Ball & Drinkard"

BARNETT, SHADRACK P. "SHADE" (13 April 1826–4 April 1896), singing teacher, moved to Carroll County, Georgia, in 1843, perhaps from Coweta County; he married Martha Ann Fielder and appears on the 1870 census. He was buried at Pleasant View Cemetery, Carrollton. He was president of the Chattahoochee Convention from its first session in 1852 until 1854, and served as vice president in 1866–67. ARKANSAS was composed for *The Organ* and published in the 1870 *Sacred Harp*. Another song, MECHANIC'S CALL, co-written with James P. Story, appeared in *The Organ* on 28 February 1855. According to the *Atlanta Constitution* of 11 October 1891,

> he has taught a school in the old Sacred Harp in nearly every community in the county. Nearly all the old people of Carroll have been students of Uncle Shade's

schools. Indeed he was the pioneer patent note–singer in this part of Georgia. There is but one older four-note teacher, and no other system teacher in Georgia than S. P. Barnett, and that man is Professor Absolom Ogletree, near Griffin.

The old Sacred Harp is full of old-fashioned church or sacred music, just such as Uncle Shade loves to sing and hear, hence he says that is a reason he always sang in the book; he taught the book, and will advocate it as long as he lives. He says he believes the angels sing such songs as are contained in the old Sacred Harp. Uncle Shade has been a resident of the community near Mt. Carmel church on Snake's for many years, and has conducted five different music schools at that place. The people of that community concluded to have an old-fashioned fa-sa-la [*sic*] singing at that place the other day. A large crowd greeted Uncle Shade, and he led a lesson of old-time music, such as our people sang 100 years ago, for an hour or more. Although Uncle Shade is sixty-five years old and seems to have lost the old-time vigor, yet he sings like a boy of twenty. He sang three pieces in the Harp, the last one being "Parting Hand." During the singing of the last song Uncle Shade passed around and shook hands with the vast audience. Very few dry eyes were seen.

271 ARKANSAS

BASS, CYNTHIA, may be Cynthia A. Bass (born about 1831), of Warren County, Georgia, the daughter of Buckner Bass and Anne E. Dozier. I. M. Shell of Coweta County recalled that "she was a fine leader" and a member of the Southern Musical Convention who "often led music before the Singing Conventions."

275 ROLL ON

BAYLY, THOMAS HAYNES (13 October 1797-April 1839), was born in Bath, Somerset, and educated at Winchester College and St. Mary's Hall, Oxford. In 1826 he married Helena Becher, an Irish heiress, and pursued a literary career as a playwright, poet, novelist, and a very popular songwriter. He died at Cheltenham, Gloucestershire, and was buried there. Among his best-known songs are "I'd Be a Butterfly," "Oh, No, We Never Mention Her," "She Wore a Wreath of Roses," "The Mistletoe Bough," and "Long, Long Ago." The last of these was arranged by M. H. Turner as WHEN I AM GONE.

339 WHEN I AM GONE

BELCHER, SUPPLY (29 March 1751–9 June 1836), farmer, tavernkeeper, and schoolteacher, was born in Stoughton, Norfolk County, Massachusetts, the son of Clifford Belcher and Mehitable Bird. As a young man he may have received instruction from William Billings, who taught in Stoughton before the Revolution. In 1775 he married Margaret Johnson More and served as a private in the war. From 1778 to 1785 he farmed and operated a tavern in South Canton, Massachusetts, but in

1785 he moved to the district of Maine, settling first in Hallowell and later (1791) in Sandy River, now Farmington, where he served his community as selectman, town clerk, magistrate, and state representative. He also played the violin and organized the town's first choir. He was the author of *The Harmony of Maine* (1794), consisting entirely of his own compositions. His tuneful, intricate sacred compositions earned him the title "The Handel of Maine."

297 CONVERSION

BELKNAP, DANIEL (9 February 1771–3 October 1815), the son of Jeremiah Belknap Jr. and Hepzibah Stone, was born in Framingham, Massachusetts. Belknap was a farmer, mechanic, militia captain, poet, and singing teacher in his native town. He taught his first singing school at the age of eighteen. A Mason, he composed an ambitious piece for the installation of the Middlesex Lodge of Framingham; this MASONIC ODE was in the *Sacred Harp* until the current edition. In 1812 he and his family moved to Pawtucket, Rhode Island, where he died. He compiled four sacred tunebooks in the years 1797–1806 and also issued a book of secular songs with music. His first published tune, LENA, was printed in *The Worcester Collection*, 5th edition (1794).

210 LENA

BILLINGS, WILLIAM (7 October 1746–26 September 1800), was born in Boston, Massachusetts, the son of William Billings and Elizabeth Clark. He lived his life in Boston as a tanner, singing teacher, and civil servant. In 1774 he married Lucy Swan of Stoughton, where he conducted singing schools. He was the first American-born composer to bring out a collection of his own music, *The New-England Psalm-Singer* (1770); he continued to publish sacred tunebooks from 1778 to 1794. He taught singing schools at several Boston churches and from Rhode Island to Maine. He had an original mind and a rare talent but died in poverty, unappreciated in his native city; he was buried in an unmarked grave in the Central Burying Ground on the Boston Common. Diarist William Bentley noted his death, calling him "the father of our New England music," who "spake and sung and thought as a man above the common abilities."

66 JORDAN

91 ASSURANCE

173 PHOEBUS

174 PETERSBURG

178 AFRICA

180 VERMONT

236 Easter Anthem

254 Rose of Sharon

268 David's Lamentation

269 Bear Creek "Arranged by B. F. White"
   [originally called Washington]

291 Majesty

320 Funeral Anthem

479 Chester

486 Beneficence

BISHOP, HENRY ROWLEY (18 November 1786–30 April 1855), was born in London, the son of a watchmaker and merchant. After early efforts as a composer of songs and stage music, he served as musical director of the Covent Garden theatre from 1810 to 1824; he was also a founder of the Philharmonic Society in 1813. In later life he was appointed to chairs of music at Edinburgh and Oxford and was knighted in 1842. He married twice, both times to a singer: (1) Elizabeth Sarah Lyon in 1809 and (2) Anna Riviere in 1831, who abandoned him and their children to elope with her accompanist. He is best known today for his ballad "Home, Sweet Home" from the opera *Clari, or The Maid of Milan* (1823), which became one of the most popular songs of the nineteenth century. He died in London and was buried in East Finchley Cemetery.

161 Sweet Home

BLACKMON, HENRY MARTIN (23 December 1888–24 February 1966), was the youngest of eight children of Simeon Daniel Blackmon and Mary Elizabeth Bradley. Trained in music by John Eady, George D. Phillips, A. M. Cagle, and Hugh McGraw, he lived in Villa Rica, Georgia where he farmed and worked as a railroad employee; he was a Baptist and a Mason. He married Dura Campbell, whom he met at a Sacred Harp singing in Douglas County in May 1952; they married on 28 December of that year. She wrote the prayer that he set to music as Dura, first published in the 1960 Denson revision, though he was assisted by A. M. Cagle in this composition. He was buried at Holly Springs Church.

531 Dura

BLOCKER, ABRAHAM ALLEN (9 January 1886–15 January 1963), the son of George Asberry Blocker and Easter Ann Peacock, was a native of Alabama, probably Coffee County, but grew up in Holmes County, Florida. In later life he lived in Crystal Lake, Florida; he was buried in Whitewater Cemetery, Holmes County.

Although he sang from the Cooper revision of the *Sacred Harp*, he contributed tunes to O. A. Parris's *Christian Harmony* (1954) and to the 1960 Denson revision of *Original Sacred Harp*. He also contributed songs to seven-shape gospel songbooks. The melody of SHOWERS OF BLESSINGS was taken from a tune called IF CHRIST BE IN MY ARMS in the Cooper revision, itself an adaptation of GRAFTON by Joseph Stone.

528 SHOWERS OF BLESSINGS

BOBO, WILLIAM W. (17 November 1814–15 November 1887), was the son of Solomon Bobo (1794–1851) and Elizabeth White (1793–1845), the older sister of B. F. White. He was born in New Prospect, Union County, South Carolina, and lived in Cross Keys. He married Mariah Ray; the couple had two sons and four daughters. He joined Padgett's Creek Baptist Church in 1832 and served as a deacon and "music clerk" (chorister) for more than forty years, earning him the nickname "Singing William Bobo." He also became a deacon of the church and a Sunday school superintendent. He was buried at Padgett's Creek. He contributed the tune LONG SOUGHT HOME to the 1847 edition of Walker's *Southern Harmony*.

235 LONG SOUGHT HOME

BOLEN, J. H. co-wrote the tune CUBA with H. S. Reese. James wrote that Bolen was a member of the Southern Musical Convention from 1850 to 1860. Presumably Bolen sang the melody and Reese wrote down the melody and composed the remaining parts. The setting was published in the 1859 appendix to *The Sacred Harp*. The attribution to "J. A. Bolen" was corrected to "J. H. Bolen" in the 1870 edition.

401 CUBA "J. H. Bolen and H. S. Rees"

BOVELL, STEPHEN (1770-December 1840), was born in Cumberland County, Pennsylvania, the son of John Bovell and Margaret Day-Watson. He was active as a Presbyterian minister in Bourbon County, Kentucky, from 1795 to 1798, and served on the board of trustees of Kentucky Academy. In 1798 he moved to Washington County, Virginia, where he married Esther Vance on 8 March 1798, and served for many years as a Presbyterian minister in Abingdon. In 1821 he published *A sermon delivered at Salem Church, October 28th, 1820, on the death of the Rev. John W. Doak, D.D. pastor of Salem and Leesburg churches*. He retired in 1826 but continued to perform marriages and serve other functions until 1835. In 1836 he moved to Edgar County, Illinois, "when very old and feeble, to find a home with his children." He died in Paris, Illinois. He contributed several tunes to Ananias Davisson's *Kentucky Harmony*.

68 SALEM

BOYD, ROBERT (25 December 1771–1822), the son of William Boyd and Elizabeth McTeer, was born in Pennsylvania. He moved to Knox County, Tennessee, where he married Margaret Meek in 1793, and where in the years 1792–95 he rose from ensign to captain in the Knox Regiment. Later in 1795 Captain Boyd moved with his family to Blount County, where he was a farmer, militia captain, and singing teacher. He contributed eight tunes to the publications of Ananias Davisson and is credited with assisting Davisson in the compilation of the second edition of *Kentucky Harmony* (1817). ALBION was first published in the first edition of *Kentucky Harmony* (1816).

    52 ALBION

BRADFIELD, OLIVER S. (8 March 1820–28 April 1895), was born in Edgefield District, South Carolina, son of James and Nancy Bradfield. He married (1) Jane Carter in Edgefield District in 1840. Around 1845 he emigrated to Coweta County, Georgia, where he was a founder of the Chattahoochee Convention in 1851. He later moved to Alabama, where he taught singing schools, and then to northern Upshur County, Texas (Camp County since 1874), where he remained active in singings and conventions. A few months after Jane's death in 1887 he married (2) Elvira Levant in Camp County. He died in Pittsburg, Texas, and is buried in Matinburg Cemetery.

    Oliver Bradfield's sister Nancy Bradfield (1824-ca. 1910) was called by J. S. James "one of the best treble singers" of the Southern and Chattahoochee conventions. A girlhood friend of the Lancaster sisters, she encouraged their interest in composition. Single for much of her life, around 1884 Nancy married James H. Moore, the widowed husband of her sister Emily Bradfield. Oliver Bradfield's tunes CHEVES (dated 1857) and WE'LL SOON BE THERE were first printed in the 1870 *Sacred Harp.* HOPE and WILLIAMS were deleted in the Denson revision.

    97 WE'LL SOON BE THERE "Alto by J. P. Rees"

    432 CHEVES

BRADSHAW, WILLIAM (1 September 1797–26 July 1861), was probably born in Virginia, but settled in east Tennessee as a young man, where on 8 August 1818 he married Melinda Wear (born 1800), daughter of Sevier County pioneer Colonel Samuel Wear (1753–1817). The couple moved to Lauderdale County, Alabama, where they appear on the 1830 and 1840 censuses and where most of their nine children were born. Some time after 1840, the family moved to Texas, finally settling in 1849 in Ioni, Anderson County, where Bradshaw's brother James had settled as early as 1835. Here William pursued farming and appears on the 1850 and 1860 censuses as a substantial landowner. Melinda died 14 December 1852; she and her husband are buried in Denson Springs cemetery. The composer, whose first name is given by William Walker in *The Christian Harmony* (1867), contributed nine tunes to the first and third editions of Ananias Davisson's *Supplement to the Kentucky Harmony* (1820, 1826). If Walker is correct, this William Bradshaw represents a plausible, though highly uncertain, identification.

> 39 DETROIT

BREEDLOVE, LEONARD P. (ca. 1803–9 August 1864), was a leader in the early years of the Sacred Harp, along with White and Turner. He may have been born in Jones County, Georgia, where his father, Nathan Breedlove, died in 1829. Leonard married (1) Sarah S. Johnston, née Boynton, on 9 September 1828, (2) Ann Bradbury on 15 July 1852, and (3) Henrietta Mason on 17 September 1860, all in Talbot County. In 1830 he was named as a trustee of the Centreville Academy in Talbot County. During the 1830s he was a prosperous planter and slaveholder, who built an impressive house in 1836 but sold it the following year, along with six hundred acres of land, for $7,300. From 1838 to 1840 he was the owner of the Franklin House, a hotel in downtown Talbotton, which he sold for $1,500. He also served as justice of the peace. The 1860 census lists him as a teacher living in Daviston, Taylor County, near the Talbot line (Taylor County was formed in 1852). He was a Baptist: he and Sarah were admitted as members of Bethel Church in 1829. He died in Taylor County. A bass singer, he was secretary of the Southern Musical Convention, 1845–50, and a member of the 1850 revision committee. He contributed two tunes to the 1844 *Sacred Harp* and ten tunes to the 1850 appendix. He also contributed at least two tunes to *The Organ* in 1854. Of these, CHARLTON was added to *The Sacred Harp* in 1859 and I WOULD SEE JESUS in 1870.

> 75 I WOULD SEE JESUS
>
> 123 CROSS OF CHRIST
>
> 152 SHEPHERDS REJOICE
>
> 282 I'M GOING HOME
>
> 285 ARNOLD
>
> 290 VICTORIA
>
> 326 WEARY PILGRIM
>
> 337 MERCY'S FREE
>
> 342 THE OLD-FASHIONED BIBLE
>
> 407 CHARLTON

BRITTAIN, PHILIP DANIEL (born 16 April 1946), was born in Phoenix, Arizona. A musician in the U.S. Army who earned the rank of major, he retired from the service to become a band and church choir director. Dan Brittain has lived in Abilene, Texas; Hampton, Georgia; Heidelberg, Germany; Hampton, Virginia; Conway, Arkansas; and Cazenovia, New York; he currently resides in Harrison, Arkansas. An Episcopalian, he was introduced to Sacred Harp music in 1970 and learned Sacred Harp composition from Loyd Redding, Jim Ayers, Hugh McGraw, and Raymond Hamrick.

313 COBB

353 McGRAW

472 AKIN

481 NOVAKOSKI

BROWN, BARTHOLOMEW (8 September 1772–14 April 1854), son of John Brown and Ginger Hutchinson, was born in Danvers, Massachusetts, He graduated from Harvard College in 1799 and married Betsy Lazell in 1801. A Unitarian, he was a lawyer, editor, and a teacher of vocal and instrumental music, and was a founding member of the Handel and Haydn Society of Boston. He was the chief compiler of the *Bridgewater Collection,* which went through twenty-seven editions from 1802 to 1834. He was also the author, for many years, of the calendar pages in *The Farmer's Almanac* (now known as *The Old Farmer's Almanac*). He died in Boston. MOUNT ZION was published in the fourth edition of *The Worcester Collection* (1792) when the composer was only twenty years of age.

220 MOUNT ZION

BROWN, JACKSON C. (March 1849–after 1913), was a son of S. M. Brown and Elizabeth Chandler, born in Haralson County, Georgia. On 11 December 1873 he married (1) Elizabeth A. Monroe in Haralson County. As early as May 1881 (shortly after his father's death), he was reported as near death from "heart dropsy," but he recovered and lived at least another thirty years. He married (2) Sarah F. Ayers on 28 November 1893, with whom he had a son around 1900; all are listed in the 1910 census. He was a Baptist deacon. A member of the United Sacred Harp Musical Association, he was on a committee appointed by that body to compile the *Union Harp and History of Songs* (1909), to which he contributed THE BLIND GIRL in collaboration with his brother John M. Brown. This tune was reprinted in *Original Sacred Harp* (1911), with the note that the Brown brothers resided in Buchanan, Georgia. Jackson C. Brown also served on the revision committee for that book. In 1913 Brown is credited with the tune ROCKY ROAD, arranged by S. M. Denson, in J. S. James, *Sacred Tunes and Hymns,* even though this tune had appeared (as

RUGGED ROAD) in J. L. White and B. F. White Jr.'s seven-shape *New Sacred Harp* in 1884. Finally, ROCKY ROAD, still credited to Brown, made its appearance in the Denson revision of 1936 in a new arrangement by Paine Denson.

The composer J. C. Brown of Georgia should not be confused with another J. C. Brown, also associated with the Denson family, and a pioneer in the recording of Sacred Harp music. James Cadmus Brown (2 January 1886–29 May 1931) was born in Bibb County, Alabama. The son of James Marion Brown and Margaret Ellajane Deason, he was raised by his grandparents Robert Martin Brown and Martha Adeline Shuttlesworth. "Cadd" Brown married Nancy Jane Tommie in Bibb County on 15 May 1905; the couple moved to Birmingham and then to Gadsden, where he was a clerk in a furniture store. He was president of the B. F. White Sacred Harp Convention of Alabama. George Pullen Jackson, who encountered him at conventions in Georgia, Alabama, and Texas, reported that "he could not sing or lead more than a few minutes before his tears were streaming. The greater emotion seemed to call forth the greater vocal exertion. He was known as the most zealous of all the Sacred Harpers." With Whitt Denson he led a group of Sacred Harp singers who recorded several songs in Atlanta in October 1928 for the Columbia label; he also sang tenor in the Denson Quartet, along with Whitt, Bob, and Evan Denson. He was an active singing teacher with many young pupils. He planned to take them to Mineral Wells, Texas, in August 1931, but he died of tuberculosis in Gadsden, Alabama, and was buried in Haysop Baptist Cemetery in Bibb County.

294 ROCKY ROAD

BROWN, REUBEN ELLIS (ca. 1794–1864), was born in South Carolina but moved to Georgia. A Methodist, later a Baptist minister, Brown traveled to southern Alabama with B. F. and D. P. White in 1850, and settled in Barbour County. He was pastor of Bethlehem Baptist Church in Louisville, Alabama, and preached at revivals in the area, where he was described as "a noted vocalist." His daughter, Celeste V. Brown, married D. P. White in 1852. He emigrated to Texas with his wife Elizabeth around 1855–56, settling in Polk County among others from southeastern Alabama, first in the Providence community, then in Livingston, the county seat. He died in Galveston during the Civil War. His FAMILY CIRCLE (written with B. F. White) was published in the 1850 *Sacred Harp*.

> In person he was very tall, and, like Saul, "from his shoulders and upwards he was higher than any of the people." His voice was clear as a trumpet, and of great strength and endurance. In sacred song he had but few if any equals, and frequently melted large congregations to tears under the strains of music from

his single voice. . . . He died at his post as a preacher in the city of Galveston, during the late war, in hope of blessed immortality.

According to J. S. James, Reuben Ellis Brown was a ventriloquist.

333 FAMILY CIRCLE

BROWN, REUBEN ELLIS, JR. (ca. 1827-after 1880), was the son of the Reverend Reuben Ellis Brown. He moved with his family to Barbour County, Alabama, around 1850, but did not follow them to Texas. He was listed as a music teacher in the 1850 census; in 1880, he and his family lived at the county "poor house," where he served as "keeper" or overseer. He contributed CONVERTING GRACE to the 1859 *Sacred Harp*.

230 CONVERTING GRACE

BROWN, S. M. (1811–29 March 1881), was born in South Carolina and moved to Georgia in 1834, settling in what would become Haralson County. His given name is something of a mystery as it is given as Silas in the 1870 federal census, but Samuel in the 1880 census. He married Elizabeth Chandler (called Eliza or Lucy) in 1836. A farmer, he served as justice of the peace in 1868–69. Brown was the first secretary of the Tallapoosa Musical Convention in 1867 and also participated in the Chattahoochee Convention. He contributed several truly memorable tunes to the 1870 *Sacred Harp*, all marked "original," indicating that they had not been published previously. His obituary in the 15 April 1881 *Carroll County Times* reads:

> We regret to chronicle the death of Hon. S. M. Brown of Haralson county. He died of chronic liver disease. He was well known to all the old citizens of Carroll and adjoining counties and was thought well of far and near. He was a good singer and a composer of music. He had several pieces of music in the Sacred Harp and we hope Bro. Ripples [J. P. Reese] will sing two of his compositions found on page 138 and 384 of the Sacred Harp, in remembrance of Bro. Brown, as it was his request to have them sang before his death by his friends.

Later that year, on 14 August, the Tallapoosa Musical Convention passed a memorial resolution stating:

> Since our last meeting, Death has visited our musical family. Bro. S. M. Brown was born in South Carolina in 1811 and moved to Georgia in 1834 and in 1836 was married to Miss Lucy Chandler. He never made any public profession of religion, but his walk and conversation imitated that of a christian. He was a dear lover of music. Just before his death he raised his hands toward heaven and said "I want to go up yonder." He breathed his last on March 29th, 1881. He was a kind father

and an affectionate husband. He has left a kind wife, eight children and many friends to mourn his loss.

1. Resolved, that in the death of Brother Brown, the convention has lost one [of] its best standards.
2. Resolved, that we would say to the children to try and imitate the steps of their father.
3. Resolved, that our prayer is that when we leave this land of toil we may strike hands with him beyond the river of Jordan.
4. Resolved, that we sing the tune "Span of Life" led by Bro. C. J. Cook and engage in prayer, led by Bro. T. L. Lassiter.
5. Resolved, that the proceedings be recorded on the convention book and a copy sent to the Carroll County Times for publication and request that the Cedartown paper to copy, and a copy be sent to the family of the deceased Brother.

J. M. Hamrick / B. O. Monroe / S. Edwards, Committee

138 OGLETREE

322 MAN'S REDEMPTION

379 SPAN OF LIFE

384 PANTING FOR HEAVEN

BROWNSON, OLIVER (13 May 1746–20 October 1815), singing master and printer, was born in Bolton, Connecticut. From 1775 to 1793 he was active as a singing teacher and composer in Litchfield, Simsbury, and New Hartford. Around 1802 he moved to Smithfield, New York, settling in the village of Peterboro, where he died. He published *Select Harmony* in 1783 and *A New Collection of Sacred Harmony* in 1797; he was a Baptist. VIRGINIA was printed in Simeon Jocelin, *The Chorister's Companion* (1782).

191 VIRGINIA

BRUCE, FRANK NEELY (born 21 January 1944), is an American composer, pianist, conductor, and music historian. Born in Memphis, Tennessee, he attended the University of Alabama (B.M. 1965) and the University of Illinois (M.M. 1966, D.M.A. 1971). Since 1974 he has taught at Wesleyan University in Connecticut. A composer of major works in a variety of styles, Neely Bruce first heard Sacred Harp singing in 1967; in the early 1970s he recorded a Sacred Harp album with the American Music Group at the University of Illinois. He was a founder of the New England Sacred Harp Singing Convention in 1976. Since 1989 he has contributed tunes to several books in four-shape notation; in 1992 he issued a four-shape collection, *Hamm Harmony*, containing solely his own compositions. HEAVENLY UNION was composed for the 1991 edition of *The Sacred Harp*.

484 HEAVENLY UNION

CAGLE, ALFRED MARCUS (5 October 1884–19 December 1968), was the son of Jesse Martin Cagle and Samaria Duke. Born at Cedartown, Georgia, he grew up in Cullman County, Alabama, where he learned music from S. M. Denson. He also learned much from T. J. Denson, on whose farm he was employed, and to whom he showed his first compositions, NEW HOPE and PRESENT JOYS; these were published in the *Union Harp* (1909) and *Original Sacred Harp* (1911). As an adult he lived in Cullman, Birmingham, and (from 1937) Atlanta, where he worked as a bookkeeper, bank employee, and traveling salesman before retiring to Villa Rica, Georgia. He married (1) Maggie Frances Denson, daughter of T. J. and Amanda Denson; this marriage produced three children but ended in divorce. He subsequently married (2) Lena Rose Drake (died about 1959), daughter of L. B. Drake of Coweta County, Georgia, and (3) Inez Lee. A bass singer and a skilled and prolific composer, he contributed SACRED MOUNT and SOAR AWAY to the 1936 Denson revision. He can be heard keying much of the music on the recordings of the 1959 United Convention at Fyffe, Alabama. He was chairman of the music committee for the 1960 revision and a member of the music committee for the 1966 revision. His obituary, written by Ruth Denson Edwards, appeared in the introduction to the 1971 Denson revision:

> On December 19, 1968, death claimed Alfred Marcus Cagle, the senior member of the *Original Sacred Harp* Music Committee, and he was laid to rest in the New Georgia Church Cemetery, near Villa Rica, Georgia, where his wife, Inez Lee Cagle, presently resides.
>
> Mr. Cagle was born in Polk County, Georgia, on October 5, 1884. He was the older son of Jesse and Samaria Duke Cagle. When he was quite young, his parents moved to Cullman County, Alabama, and he grew to manhood on a farm near Cullman, Alabama. He was deeply interested in Sacred Harp Music and attended singing schools taught by Seaborn M. Denson.
>
> He became a leading singer and, except for the Cooper book, his compositions appeared in all editions and revisions of the Sacred Harp since the 1911 James revision. His authority on Dispersed Harmony was undisputed and unsurpassed. He prepared a manuscript on the subject which was never published.
>
> Mr. Cagle was an outstanding singer, leader, teacher, and writer of Sacred Harp music.

316 NEW HOPE

318 PRESENT JOYS

CAGLE, MARGARET FRANCES "MAGGIE" DENSON (4 July 1887–13 April 1969), daughter of T. J. and Amanda Denson, was born at Cedartown, Polk County, Georgia, and raised in Winston County, Alabama. She married A. M. Cagle, and they had three children, born between 1906 and 1912. After their marriage ended in divorce, she remained single until her death, settling in Selma, Alabama. She was a tenor singer with a wide vocal range, also known for her cooking, gardening, and handcrafted lace and embroidery. Her tune SAMARIA was named for her mother-in-law, Samaria Duke. When it was completed, the 1936 Denson revision was already in press; Howard Denson drove the manuscript to the printers in Tennessee, and space was found for it at the end of the rudiments, before BETHEL, which had been the first tune in all previous editions of *The Sacred Harp*. Maggie Denson Cagle was buried in Live Oak Cemetery in Selma.

CALDWELL, WILLIAM (24 October 1801–10 July 1857), was the son of Anthony Caldwell (1764–1832) and Elizabeth Aiken; he was born near New Market, Jefferson County, Tennessee, where his parents had settled after the Revolutionary War and where he spent most of his life; he was a farmer and a Presbyterian. He noted in 1835 that he had been "employed in the business of teaching Vocal music for the last 12 or 14 years," that is, from about the age of twenty. On 30 December 1829 he married (1) Cindrilla Blackburn in Jefferson County; the 1840 census shows him as a widower with three children under the age of ten. On 9 November 1841 he married (2) Harriet Rebecca Meek (born 1816), who bore him six additional children. Around 1856 he and his family moved to Fannin County, Texas, where he died the following year, leaving behind several young children.

Caldwell's *Union Harmony* was a long time coming: in 1833 he began soliciting subscriptions for a songbook; by 1834, when he registered the copyright, the book was apparently complete. In March 1835 he wrote of problems in finding an East

Tennessee printer willing to invest in music types; the book was finally printed in Maryville in 1837. He acknowledged that not all the tunes he claimed were of his own composition, but that some were "selected from the unwritten music in general use among the Methodist Church, others from the Baptist, and many more from the Presbyterian taste."

CANANT, REMUS ADOLPHUS (16 August 1883–17 April 1984), was the son of William H. Canant Jr. and Mary Matilda Lowery. Raised on a farm in Cullman County, he attended his first Sacred Harp singing at age seven at Prospect Church. In 1940 he moved to Birmingham, where he was a steelworker and singing teacher; he taught singing schools in Alabama and Mississippi. An officer of the Ryan's Creek convention of Cullman County, R. A. Canant was chairman of the Doss Creek singing in 1951. He enjoyed a long and active life after his retirement at the age of seventy-three and continued to hunt rabbits until the age of ninety. On his one hundredth birthday he stood on his lawn and released one hundred balloons and proceeded to sing three of his favorite songs, including NEVER TURN BACK (page 378). He died eight months later and was buried in Elmwood Cemetery in Birmingham. He contributed a tune to O. A. Parris's *Christian Harmony* in 1954, and PARTING FRIENDS to the 1960 *Sacred Harp* appendix.

CARNES, JAMES P. (born 3 August 1955), is a native of Columbus, Mississippi, who began singing Sacred Harp in that state in 1974. A 1977 graduate of the University of North Carolina, he has lived in Chicago, Nashville, and Birmingham. He currently lives in Montgomery, Alabama, where he is a writer and editor. In 1992 he married Erin Kellen; they have one daughter.

CARPENTER, ELIHU (18 December 1752–5 July 1827), the son of Eleazar Carpenter and Elizabeth Warfield, lived in Rehoboth, Massachusetts. After serving in the Revolutionary War during the years 1775–77, he married Martha Hutchins in 1783; they had eleven children. A farmer and schoolmaster, he served as a deacon in the Congregational church. He was buried in Newman Cemetery in East Providence, Rhode Island. His SOUTHWELL was published in *The American Musical Magazine* in 1786 by Daniel Read and Amos Doolittle. A family historian recounts:

He did not attend school until he was 16 years of age. He was then a tall boy, and had to go into a class of small children, which was very humiliating to him. He made good progress, and soon mastered the common branches and became a teacher; his success as a teacher was remarkable—one of the best. Many of the liberally educated men of the town owe their success to him. It was a credit to a student to state that he had obtained his early education under the tutorship of Elihu Carpenter. He also taught singing school, and as the old lady, Mrs. Perry, said in the 92d year of her age, . . . "he taught singing school for nothing and found candles." He used to sing when about the house and his work. Someone asked his mother one day what made him sing so much, when she replied: "To plague the devil." He sang pious hymns. He was also a deacon of the church.

365 SOUTHWELL

CARRELL, JAMES P. (13 February 1787–1854), was born in Washington County, Virginia, the son of Charles Carrell and Agnes Peery. In 1809 he married his first cousin Martha George Peery. Carrell was a substantial farmer, Methodist minister, and county clerk in Lebanon, Russell County, Virginia. He was author of the unlocated *Songs of Zion* (1821) and co-author of *Virginia Harmony* (1831).

131 MESSIAH

332 SONS OF SORROW

CARTER, THOMAS W. (22 December 1822–13 July 1869), was born in South Carolina. Around 1842 he married Sarah Ann Wall (1828–88), daughter of a wealthy planter in Tazewell, Marion County, Georgia, only a short distance from the home of E. J. King. He sought medical training, and appears as a physician in the 1850 census for Atlanta, DeKalb County, Georgia (now Fulton County). The family moved before 1866 to Terrell County, where he died. He was associated with White and King in the first edition of *The Sacred Harp*, to which he contributed thirteen tunes. James titles him both Doctor and Professor, and says he was a member of the Southern Musical Convention from its founding in 1845 until 1860, and also a member of the Chattahoochee Convention.

79 THE OLD SHIP OF ZION

106 ECSTASY

121 FLORENCE [arranged]

170 EXHILARATION

229 IRWINTON

CARWELL, JOHN, according to J. S. James, was a member of the Southern and Chattahoochee conventions in the 1850s and 1860s and a "splendid singer and leader of music." One John Carwell who married Louisa P. Miles in Baldwin County, Georgia, on 26 July 1832 may possibly be identified with the composer, whose arrangement of NEVER PART appeared in the 1850 appendix to *The Sacred Harp.*

94 NEVER PART

CASTLE (flourished 1804–10) may have lived in upstate New York. He contributed music to Thomas Atwill's *New York and Vermont Collection* (Albany, 1804), where SARDINIA was first published, and to the sixth edition of the *Easy Instructor* (Albany, [1808–10]).

296 SARDINIA

CHAMBLESS, ZACHARIAH (7 July 1814–ca. 1850), was the son of John D. Chambless (1785–1857) and Obedience Ledbetter. He should not be confused with Zachariah Chambless (1775–1874) of Forsyth, Georgia, nor with another Zachariah Chambless in Marion County. A Georgia native and a resident of Talbot County, the composer married Sarah Jane Howell on 4 December 1835. He contributed three tunes to the 1844 *Sacred Harp,* including BELLEVUE, named for the community in Talbot County spelled Belleview today. He was buried in Chambless Cemetery in Talbot County.

72 BELLEVUE

CHANDLER, SOLOMON (17 January 1756–ca. 1827), was born in Enfield, Connecticut, the son of Henry Chandler and Mercy Colton. He was a tailor in his native town, but later moved to the Hudson valley, first to Amenia, where he married about 1791, then to Catskill, where he was an innkeeper and merchant known for his love of psalmody. He was a member of the vestry of St. Luke's (Episcopal) Church in Catskill. He suffered from a club foot and walked with a cane. His EN-FIELD was published in the 1785 edition of Brownson's *Select Harmony.* Timothy Swan, as reported by his daughter, recounted that Chandler "made several tunes, tho' he was no singer," and suggested that Chandler was assisted by two others in composing ENFIELD.

184 ENFIELD

CHAPIN, AMZI (2 March 1768–19 February 1835), son of Edward Chapin and Eunice Colton, was born in Springfield, Massachusetts; a cabinetmaker, he taught music in Virginia, North Carolina, and Kentucky from 1791 to 1800. In 1800 he married Hannah Power in Westmoreland County, Pennsylvania, and settled there, remaining until 1831; he died in Northfield, Ohio. PRIMROSE, also known as TWENTY-FOURTH and ORANGE, appeared in an untitled supplement of tunes printed for Virginia singing-master John Logan in 1812.

47 PRIMROSE

95 VERNON

CHAPIN, LUCIUS (25 April 1760–24 December 1842), son of Edward Chapin and Eunice Colton and older brother of Amzi Chapin, was born in Springfield, Massachusetts. He served in the Continental Army in the Revolution. In 1791 he married Susannah Rousseau, then taught music in Virginia during the 1790s. In 1797 he settled near Mason, Kentucky, at a home named Vernon. He died in Glendale, Hamilton County, Ohio, and is buried in Spring Grove Cemetery, Cincinnati. NINETY-THIRD PSALM, printed in 1813, is a variant of a tune called DELAY, printed in Jeremiah Ingalls, *Christian Harmony* (1805).

31 NINETY-THIRD PSALM

CHRISTOPHER, JAMES (21 May 1815–9 October 1844), lived in Spartanburg, South Carolina, and appears on the 1840 census. In 1843 he purchased land on the Enoree River, but he died the following year and was buried at Sharon Cemetery, Reidville. Christopher contributed several tunes to the 1840 appendix to William Walker's *Southern Harmony*.

159 WONDROUS LOVE

CHUTE, WILLIAM EDWARD (24 April 1832–7 September 1900), was born at Clements, Nova Scotia, but moved with his parents to Upper Canada (Ontario). His father, Andrew Chute, was a Baptist deacon and a singing-master who had learned music from one Captain Dean, a pupil of William Billings. While visiting Nova Scotia in 1855 William taught his first singing school, using *The American Vocalist*. During a long career he taught nearly two hundred singing schools using thirty different books in Nova Scotia, Ontario, New York, Michigan, Minnesota, and Missouri. Chute attended three musical institutes under Mason, Root, Bliss, and others, and collected four hundred hymnbooks and six hundred tunebooks. After his marriage in 1861 he settled in Minnesota (1862–69), Missouri (1869–75), St. Thomas, Ontario (1875–79), and Michigan (1879–90), then retired to Massachusetts to work on family history. He died in Chicago, Illinois, and was buried in Oak Woods Cemetery on Chicago's South Side.

While living in the United States he volunteered in the Union forces in the Civil War and fought in the 14th Army Corps, participating in W. T. Sherman's march through Georgia and the Carolinas. He corresponded with William Hauser, William

Walker, Aldine S. Kieffer, Samuel Wakefield, and H. P. Main. Some of the tune-books he owned, kept at the Newberry Library, Chicago, and elsewhere, contain handwritten annotations with historical information. His tune BABYLON IS FALLEN was printed in *The Musical Million* 6 (December 1875) and in Hauser's *Olive Leaf* (1878), where Hauser states that Prof. William E. Chute, then living in St. Thomas, Ontario, "composed the tune out of an old theme, and is too modest to claim any originality, but I do it for him." In the acknowledgments, Hauser calls Chute the "greatest hymn and tune antiquary I have ever known, and the correctness and excellence of the book in this department is owing almost entirely to him."

   117 BABYLON IS FALLEN

CLARK, ALEXANDER C., of South Carolina, according to J. S. James, may have been related by marriage to B. F. White and William Walker. He contributed several tunes to the revisions of Walker's *Southern Harmony* and *Christian Harmony* and to Andrew Johnson's *American Harmony*.

   157 ESSAY

   162 PLENARY

COAN, SIMEON (April 1767–5 November 1815), the son of John Coan and Mabel Chittendon, was born in North Guilford, Connecticut, and christened on 19 April 1767, although his tombstone reads "aged 43 years," suggesting a birth around 1772. On 4 February 1794 he married Parnel Fowler; they had several children, and she died giving birth to twins in 1813. In 1804 Coan joined the Episcopal church in Guilford, where he served as chorister for the rest of his life and as organist from 1807 to 1811. He died in Branford, New Haven County; he was buried in Westside Cemetery, Guilford. His tunes were published by Daniel Read and others. DE-LIGHT was published in Asahel Benham's *Social Harmony* (1798).

   216 DELIGHT

COLES, GEORGE (2 January 1792–1 May 1858), was born in Stewkley, Buckingham-shire. He became a Methodist preacher before he emigrated to America in 1818. He settled in New York, where he edited the *Christian Advocate and Journal* and worked for the Methodist Publishing House. In 1820 he married Belinda Wilson of South Salem, New York. He is buried in Ivandell Cemetery, Somers, Westchester County, New York. Coles revised the *Methodist Harmonist* in 1833. He should not be confused with gospel songwriter George Coles Stebbins (1846–1945), who often used the pen name "George Coles."

   164 DUANE STREET

   231 THOU ART PASSING AWAY [arranged]

COMMUCK, THOMAS (18 January 1804–25 November 1855), a Narragansett Indian, was born at Charlestown, Washington County, Rhode Island. As a young man he joined the remnant of Mohegans and Pequots at Brothertown, Oneida County, New York. In 1831 he married Hannah Abner, a Pequot, and migrated with the rest of the Brothertown band to Calumet County, Wisconsin. In 1845 he brought out *Indian Melodies,* containing original compositions harmonized by Thomas Hastings. This book contains the first printing of the tune known as LONE PILGRIM, which was arranged by B. F. White for the 1850 appendix to *The Sacred Harp.* Commuck also wrote a brief "Sketch of the Brothertown Indians" in 1855. He drowned in the winter of 1855 after falling through a hole in the ice near his home.

341 LONE PILGRIM

CRANE. This composer is completely unknown. His setting of FEW HAPPY MATCHES was printed in the second edition of Simeon Jocelin's *Chorister's Companion* (1788). The version in *The Sacred Harp* is by B. F. White and E. J. King.

96 FEW HAPPY MATCHES

CUNNINGHAM, BENJAMIN EDWARD (23 October 1863–29 October 1948), of Vernon, Alabama, was a farmer, merchant, and for forty years, a Baptist preacher. He attended singing schools of T. J. Denson, who stayed on his farm when he was teaching in Fayette County. He was active in the Fayette and Lamar County convention in the 1920s and served as chaplain in 1930. He married (1) Martha Melinda Hankins and (2) Sophronie Swindol. He was buried at Fellowship Cemetery, Lamar County. The song HAPPY CHRISTIAN, published in the 1936 Denson revision, is his arrangement of an older tune called SOLICITATION.

399 HAPPY CHRISTIAN [arranged]

CURTIS. Nothing is known about this composer, whose tune PROVIDENCE was printed in the 1820 edition of *Wyeth's Repository of Music, Part Second.*

298 PROVIDENCE

DADMUN, JOHN WILLIAM (20 December 1819–6 August 1890), was born in Hubbardston, Worcester County, Massachusetts. He joined the Methodist Church at the age of sixteen and attended the Wilbraham Wesleyan Academy; he was licensed as a preacher in 1846 and stationed in the Springfield area, where he became a noted evangelist. Dadmun published several music books, including *Revival Melodies* (1858); *The Melodeon* (1860) sold more than four hundred thousand copies. During the Civil War he served as a military chaplain and published *Army Melodies* (1861). After the war he became chaplain at a prison on Deer Island in Boston

Harbor, where he died while conducting a chorus of inmates during a visit by dignitaries. He was a Mason, serving as Grand Master of the Natick Lodge from 1863 to 1865. One of his best-known songs was REST FOR THE WEARY, published in *The Melodeon;* it was arranged by B. F. White for the 1870 *Sacred Harp.*

    154 REST FOR THE WEARY

DANIELL, GEORGE BYRON (21 February 1860–24 September 1933), son of William Robert Daniell and Henrietta Virginia Jennings, was born in Tallapoosa, Georgia, but spent most of his life in Atlanta, where he was a singing teacher and a laborer. On 11 October 1881 Daniell married Olive Adelaide "Addie" Hamby. Daniell served as clerk of a Primitive Baptist church, and J. S. James reports that "seven of his grandfather's brothers were Primitive Baptist ministers." He died in Atlanta and is buried in Hollywood Cemetery. Daniell was a founder of the United Sacred Harp Musical Association and a member of the revision committee for *Original Sacred Harp* (the James edition) of 1911. He contributed SOLDIER OF THE CROSS to the *Union Harp* in 1909 and composed the alto part of BEAR CREEK for the 1911 James edition.

    325 SOLDIER OF THE CROSS

DAVIS, B. F. (died before 1848), was a resident of Alabama. According to E. K. Davis, "he fell a victim to bilious fever in the midst of his youth, and usefulness." He wrote a song beginning, "Young people all, now at the ball," a warning against social dancing, printed in *The Hesperian Harp;* he may also be responsible for the words of DAY OF WORSHIP.

    60 DAY OF WORSHIP "B. F. and E. K. Davis"

DAVIS, C. A., was a member of the Southern Musical Convention from 1850 to 1860. He contributed LIVING LAMB to the 1850 appendix of *The Sacred Harp.*

    309 LIVING LAMB

DAVIS, E. K., lived in Cedar Bluff, Cherokee County, Alabama. He contributed several tunes to the *Hesperian Harp* (1848) and collaborated with B. F. Davis on the song DAY OF WORSHIP.

    60 DAY OF WORSHIP "B. F. and E. K. Davis"

DAVIS, MARTIN C. H. (ca. 1795–after 1880), a South Carolina native, was a clockmaker and silversmith. He grew up in Newberry County, where he married Melinda Goggans (1808–79) before 1834, and where he is listed in the 1850 and 1860 censuses. He and Melinda retired to their daughter's home in Concord, Cabarrus County, North Carolina, where he is listed in 1870 and 1880. M. C. H. Davis contributed both music and a religious poem titled "M.C.H. Davis' Experience" to *Southern Harmony*. His tune LIVERPOOL is based on BENEVOLENCE in J. M. Boyd's *Virginia Sacred Musical Repository* (1818).

37 LIVERPOOL

DAVIS, ROBERT HENRY (1824–7 April 1890), born in North Carolina, was the son of William Davis and Lydia Garner; his father, known as "Euchee Bill" Davis, was a noted Indian fighter. Robert married Mary Ann Law on 20 June 1846 in Pike County, Alabama, where his children were born. Davis was one of the first physicians in Pike County—he was not trained in a medical school but learned by assisting an experienced doctor in another region. He is listed as a physician in the 1880 census for Dixons, Pike County. He died in Pike County and was buried in the cemetery at Springfield Baptist Church, where he served as clerk from 1859. His tune HEAVEN'S MY HOME, co-authored with fellow Alabama resident John S. Terry, was printed in the 1870 *Sacred Harp*. His son Robert M. Davis (born around 1864) is credited with a tune called DAVIS in the Cooper revision of the *Sacred Harp*, actually an arrangement of the well-known hymn tune LONSDALE, itself derived from a sonata movement by Arcangelo Corelli.

119 HEAVEN'S MY HOME "Dr. R. H. Davis
     and J. S. Terry"

DAVISSON, ANANIAS (2 February 1780–21 October 1857), was a printer, farmer, and singing teacher in Rockingham County, Virginia. He was born in Shenandoah County, the son of Ananias and Jemima Davisson. A ruling elder in the Presbyterian Church, he compiled and published four tunebooks, including *Kentucky Harmony* (1816) and, "for his Methodist friends," *Supplement to the Kentucky Harmony* (1820), containing many camp-meeting songs. Davisson cultivated a network of composers and singing teachers in Virginia, Kentucky, and Tennessee who sold his books and whose compositions he introduced into print. These include James P. Carrell, Stephen Bovell, J. C. Lowry, William Bradshaw, Reubin Monday, R. D. Humphreys, and Robert Boyd. He was buried at Massanutten Cross Keys Cemetery, Rockingham County.

47 IDUMEA

DAY, J. M. Nothing is known of J. M. Day, who contributed VILLULIA and two other compositions to the 1850 appendix to *The Sacred Harp*.

56 VILLULIA

DELONG, DORIS WINN (1 February 1906–10 February 1986), of Roswell, Georgia, was one of a pair of twin brothers whose father, James Marion DeLong, had moved to Georgia from Laurens County, South Carolina. Doris DeLong was a barber, house painter, and singing teacher; he married Winnie Barnett. A pupil of Elder E. I. McGuire and Posey Reed, he led music at the Union Musical Convention in 1926 and began teaching singing schools in 1951; he composed more than thirty songs, twenty-six of which he published as *Sacred Songs*. A tenor singer, he was a member of the Roswell Sacred Harp Singers, who recorded in the 1950s. He served as treasurer and clerk of Ebenezer Primitive Baptist Church in Dunwoody and was buried in Ebenezer Cemetery.

465 WHERE THERE'S NO TROUBLE AND SORROW

541 HOME OF THE BLEST

DELONG, RICHARD LEE (born 28 February 1963), a native of Atlanta, is the son of James Harold DeLong and Ellen Janette Thaxton and the grandnephew of Doris DeLong. His grandparents, Dollie Corley and Albert DeLong, met at a Sacred Harp singing. Richard was instructed in Sacred Harp music by his grandmother and by Hugh McGraw, Loyd Redding, Buford McGraw, and Charlene Wallace. A graduate of West Georgia College (now the University of West Georgia), he resides in Carroll County, where he is a schoolteacher. Since 1982 he has taught singing schools all over the United States and in England. A member of the music committee for the 1991 revision, he served as president of the United Sacred Harp Musical Association in 1983, at the age of twenty, and again in 2004. He is a member of the board of directors of the Sacred Harp Publishing Company. Richard Lee DeLong should not be confused with the organist and composer Richard Paul DeLong (1951–94).

494 BIG CREEK

510 CORLEY [arranged]

DENSON, AMANDA SYMINGTON BURDETTE (7 January 1861–19 September 1910), daughter of William Howard Burdette and Julia Ann Prather, was born in Calhoun, Lowndes County, Alabama, but grew up in Cleburne County, where she attended the Chulafinnee School. On 28 December 1878 she married T. J. Denson, brother of her sister's husband S. M. Denson, and moved to Winston County. She was a schoolteacher; she also taught piano and accordion and assisted her brother James Alexander Burdette (1851–1923) and her husband in teaching Sacred Harp music. She told her grandchildren that she taught her children to sing at home while her husband was "off teaching everybody else in the country how to sing." She was an alto singer and assisted her brother-in-law S. M. Denson in collecting and composing alto parts for the 1911 *Original Sacred Harp.* Though she married a Methodist and raised several Methodist children, she remained a lifelong Baptist and was buried at Fairview Cemetery near Double Springs, Alabama.

426 KELLEY

DENSON, HOWARD BURDETTE (4 August 1897–30 January 1950), the youngest son of T. J. and Amanda Denson, was born near Helicon, Winston County, Alabama. He married (1) Myrtle L. Price and had one son; their marriage ended in divorce. He subsequently married (2) Marjorie Goodwin; they had two daughters. Howard Denson lived in Cullman, Jasper, Birmingham, and Tuscaloosa, where he was a correspondent, agent, and district manager of the *Birmingham News and Age-Herald;* he was a Methodist and a Mason. Taught music at an early age by his father and mother, he often sang bass, and he sang in the Denson-Parris Quartet on their 1934 Bluebird recordings. He was a member of the 1935 revision committee. He died of throat cancer at the age of fifty-two and was buried at Fairview Cemetery near Double Springs, Alabama.

373 HOMEWARD BOUND

DENSON, JAMES M. (1816–55), was born in Georgia, the son of William Howard Denson and Catherine Melinda Phillips. He grew up in Walton County, where he married Permelia Catherine Owens on 7 March 1838. He was president of the Southern Musical Convention in 1847. Around 1848 he emigrated to Bienville Parish, Louisiana, where he was listed in the 1850 census as an innkeeper; he also served as postmaster in the parish seat of Sparta. In 1851 he was secretary of a Masonic lodge in Sparta, and in 1853 he was chosen as the town's first marshal; he died there in 1855. Family tradition holds that he composed CHRISTMAS ANTHEM for the 1844 *Sacred Harp.* His younger brother Levi Phillips Denson (1819–89) was the father of S. M. Denson and T. J. Denson.

225 CHRISTMAS ANTHEM

DENSON, OWEL W. (6 December 1912–24 January 1969), the oldest son of Whitt Denson, lived in Addison, Alabama. He studied music as a child with his father and later at the Vaughn School of Music in Lawrenceburg, Tennessee, and at the University of Alabama. A member of the Church of God, he was a tenor singer, composer, teacher, and promoter of modern gospel music. He also was the owner of Denson Music Publishing Company, which published such collections as *Keys to the Kingdom* (1959) and *Songs of Zion* (1961). Owel Denson printed the 1960 edition of *Original Sacred Harp* (Denson revision), to which he contributed LORD, WE ADORE THEE. In 1964 he brought out a reprint of the 1911 *Original Sacred Harp*

(James edition) at the request of singers in southern Georgia. He was buried at Nesmith Cemetery, Winston County.

    477 LORD, WE ADORE THEE

DENSON, PAINE W. (8 October 1882–30 January 1955), was the eldest surviving child of T. J. and Amanda Denson. Born at Arbacoochee, Alabama, he attended public schools in Carroll County, Georgia, and Winston County, Alabama. He then worked as a store clerk in Cullman and Haleyville before entering law school at the University of Alabama, where he received the LL.B. degree in 1910. He married (1) Emma Janie Gibson on 7 September 1903; she died in 1908. He then married (2) Mary Lee Horton on 30 April 1913. Paine Denson worked as an attorney in Eutaw, Cullman, Jasper, and Birmingham, finally retiring to Double Springs, Alabama, around 1950 after suffering serious burns in an accident. He served as justice of the peace and was a member of the Masonic lodge. He was chief editor of the Denson revision of 1936 and wrote the rudiments for that collection. Paine Denson was remembered as an excellent composer and leader who inherited much of his father's musical ability and charisma. He was buried in Fairview Cemetery near Double Springs.

    292 BEHOLD THE SAVIOR

    294 ROCKY ROAD [arranged]

    330 HORTON

    330 FELLOWSHIP

    392 MANCHESTER

    396 NOTES ALMOST DIVINE

    447 WONDROUS CROSS

    502 A CHARGE TO KEEP

    518 THE HEAVENLY ANTHEM

    524 THE TWENTY-THIRD PSALM

    532 PEACE AND JOY

    553 ANTHEM ON THE BEGINNING

DENSON, ROBERT E. (12 August 1892–30 August 1983), born in Booneville Mississippi, was the son of S. M. Denson; he attended boarding school in Haleyville, Alabama, and Snead College in Boaz before settling in Addison. A prosperous farmer, he served as a commissioner of Winston County and as mayor of Addison from 1960 to 1964; a member of the Church of God, he served for many years as chaplain for the Chattahoochee and other conventions. An excellent treble singer, he was a member of the Denson Quartet from its earliest days and is remembered for his wit and charm. He married (1) Belle Cleghorn (1890–1970) in 1913 and (2) Irene Kitchens Parker, but had no children. He was buried at Pisgah Church Cemetery near Nesmith in Winston County.

505 WHERE CEASELESS AGES ROLL

DENSON, SEABORN MCDANIEL (9 April 1854–18 April 1936) was born in the gold-mining settlement of Arbacoochee, Randolph County, Alabama (now in Cleburne County), the son of Levi Phillips Denson and Julia Ann Jones; he was a nephew of James M. Denson. According to Ruth Denson Edwards, "he spent his early years working on his father's plantation, and searching for nuggets in the gold mine there." He gained his education by attending local schools "a few months each year." On 26 June 1874 he married Sidney Seward Burdette and began to establish a reputation as a singing teacher, with schools in Alabama, Georgia, and Mississippi. Among their children were S. Whitt Denson and Robert E. Denson. Before 1900 he moved to Winston County, Alabama, where he farmed and continued to teach. He also played the violin and the fife. His first two published tunes (one written in collaboration with his brother T. J. Denson) appeared in the seven-shape *New Sacred Harp* (1884) by J. L. White and B. F. White Jr. He was co-editor of the *Union Harp* (1909) and musical editor of the *Original Sacred Harp* (James revision) of 1911; he also added many alto parts to that revision. He was a member of the 1935 revision committee but died in the year the book was published; he was buried in Pisgah Church Cemetery near Nesmith in Winston County. Of his compositions in *The Sacred Harp*, CLEBURNE, ARBACOOCHEE, JESTER, McKAY, and RESURRECTED were composed for the *Union Harp and History of Songs* (1909), while PRAISE GOD, MORNING SUN, ETERNAL HOME, and TRAVELING ON were composed for the 1911 James edition. The Denson revision of 1936 called him "a great Sacred Harp singer, leader and teacher, and the most profound writer of dispersed harmony yet known."

153 RESURRECTED

208 TRAVELING ON "S. M. Denson
     and J. S. James"

314 CLEBURNE

328 PRAISE GOD

331 JESTER

336 ETERNAL HOME

430 ARBACOOCHEE

433 McKAY

436 MORNING SUN

DENSON, SIDNEY SEWARD BURDETTE (11 October 1853- 2 May 1928), daughter of William Howard Burdette and Julia Ann Prather, was born in Georgia, probably in Wilkes County. She was educated at a female academy in Troup County, Georgia, became a schoolteacher, and accompanied her family to Cleburne County, Alabama, where she married S. M. Denson on 26 June 1874. At the 1880 session of the Chattahoochee Convention she was the only female song leader, possibly the first ever in that convention's history. J. A. Robertson reported in the *Carroll County Times:*

> One remarkable thing, calculated to excite the curious, was the rendition of a lesson on Sunday at eleven o'clock, conducted by a Mrs. Denson, of Alabama. When it was announced by the chair that a lady would conduct a lesson, the house was filled to overflowing instanter. People mounted the benches with eager eyes and itching ears, so as to be able to see and learn all that passed. . . . Mrs. Denson's lesson was conducted with skill and good taste, and void of that embarrassment peculiar to women. Your reporter ventures the opinion that it was the best lesson of the convention.

According to family members, it was Sidney Denson who selected a scriptural quotation to be printed below the title of each piece in the James edition (1911). Although she usually sang treble, she and her sister Amanda aided S. M. Denson in collecting and composing alto parts for that revision. She joined the Church of God and gave lectures and taught Bible classes for that denomination. She was buried at Pisgah Church Cemetery near Nesmith, Alabama. Her song THE MARRIAGE IN THE SKIES, published in the *Union Harp* (1909), was composed in a contemporary gospel style.

438 THE MARRIAGE IN THE SKIES

DENSON, SIDNEY WHITFIELD "WHITT" (25 February 1890–17 May 1964), born at Arbacoochee, Alabama, was a farmer, preacher, singing teacher, gospel singer, and composer, the son of S. M. and Sidney Burdette Denson. As a young man he traveled with his father, assisting him in his singing schools. He married Mattie Ray in 1908 and lived in Helicon, Arley, and Haleyville, Alabama. Although J. S. James described him in 1911 as "a consistent member of the Missionary Baptist Church," he later joined the Church of God and became a preacher. Like many leading singers of his time, Whitt Denson sang and composed gospel quartet music; he also taught his children to perform as a quartet. As founder and guiding spirit of the Denson Quartet (with his brothers Robert and Evan Denson), he could play the piano and sing any part, but he was known especially for his ability to sing the alto part with a clear voice in its proper range. His overdubbed recording (with piano accompaniment) of his father's composition MORNING SUN was played at his own funeral, and remains a favorite. He was a member of the 1936 Denson revision committee and contributed the well-known WILL YOU MEET ME? to O. A. Parris's *Christian Harmony* (1954). BURDETTE and SIDNEY were printed in *Union Harmony*; AMANDA RAY and two other tunes (later deleted) appear in the 1960 appendix. He was buried in Nesmith Cemetery, Winston County.

> 422 BURDETTE
>
> 437 SIDNEY
>
> 493 AMANDA RAY

DENSON, SUSIE IRENE KITCHENS PARKER (21 September 1908–24 March 1987), of Parrish, Alabama, grew up in a family that produced many fine singers. Irene Kitchens was the second child of Wiley L. Kitchens and Emily B. Posey. A music pupil of her younger brother J. E. Kitchens, she was a fine treble singer. Her younger sister Mary Maxine Kitchens (born 1924), wife of Robert Franklin Gardner, was also a composer, contributing a song, IN THY PRAISE, to the 1960 Denson revision, but this was removed in the 1991 edition. Irene married (1) Asburn Lafayette Parker and (2) Robert E. Denson. She ran a dry cleaning business and was a jewelry store clerk in Jasper. She died in Leesburg, Florida. She contributed LORD, HEAR MY PLEA (later deleted) and THE PILGRIM'S WAY to the 1960 Denson revision.

> 545 THE PILGRIM'S WAY

DENSON, THOMAS JACKSON (20 January 1863–14 September 1935), was born in Randolph County, Alabama, the youngest of four sons of Levi Phillips Denson and Julia Ann Jones—he was named for Confederate general Thomas J. "Stonewall" Jackson. When he was only fifteen years of age, he led a thirty-minute lesson at the 1878 session of the Chattahoochee Convention. On 29 December of that year he married (1) Amanda S. Burdette, sister of his brother Seaborn's wife Sydney Burdette; their children included Paine, Annie, Maggie, Ruth, and Howard Denson. Following Amanda's death in September 1910 he married (2) Lillie Florida Cagle (born 1883), an older sister of A. M. Cagle. This marriage was swiftly dissolved, and Tom Denson married (3) Lola Mahalia Akers of Logan, Cullman County, on 29 December 1912; they had three daughters, Vera, Violet, and Tommye, all fine singers. Raised in the Methodist church, he later joined the Missionary Baptist faith of the Burdette family; he was also a member of the Masons and the Odd Fellows.

As a young man Tom Denson farmed for ten years in Polk and Carroll Counties, Georgia, before moving to Winston County, Alabama in 1895. He resided near

Double Springs and Cullman, Alabama; Leoma and Lawrenceburg, Tennessee; and in southern Georgia: in all these places he farmed in the spring and fall and traveled to teach singing schools in the summer. Tom Denson was renowned as a charismatic song leader and teacher. When he attended singings with his children, he took pride that they distributed themselves among all the voice parts. He told his pupils, "I can teach you to sing, but only God can teach you to sing with the spirit."

In 1930 he undertook an eight-month teaching tour in Texas, where he returned for additional teaching in 1934. A member of the music committee for the James edition of 1911, he founded the Sacred Harp Publishing Company in 1933 and was a member of the 1935 revision committee. In August 1935 he attended the Chattahoochee Convention in Georgia with four of his grown children, all singing different parts. As he led WHEN I AM GONE he walked to each of his children and shook their hands as he sang. The following month he died suddenly at his home in Manchester, Alabama, while preparing to attend a singing; he was buried at Fairview Cemetery near Double Springs. The Denson revision of 1936 called him "the greatest Sacred Harp singer, leader, teacher and writer of all time."

293 AKERS

302 LOGAN

340 ODEM

380 LAWRENCEBURG

382 COSTON

397 THE FOUNTAIN

411 MORNING PRAYER

426 JASPER

DENTON, JESSE MONROE (25 December 1898–4 February 1979), son of Elder John Bartlett Denton and Zilpha Melissa Taylor, was born in San Saba, Texas, and attended a Sacred Harp singing school in Coryell County as a child. During World War I he served in Europe, where he recalled singing THE LONE PILGRIM at the grave of a fallen comrade. He married Mary Elizabeth Barton on 7 November 1920 and raised three children. Ordained to the Primitive Baptist ministry in 1935, Monroe Denton served several churches in Texas and taught many singing schools. In 1943 he was called to the Macon, Georgia area, where he continued to teach Sacred Harp; he is credited with helping preserve the singing in that region. He died in Macon and was buried in Glen Haven Memorial Gardens.

354 LEBANON

DEOLPH OR DEWOLF. Charles (9 April 1747–16 December 1814), Amasa (26 December 1748-ca. 1820), and Mark Anthony DeWolf (born 9 March 1751/52) were sons of Simon DeWolf and Esther Strickland of Middletown, Connecticut. Simon DeWolf was born in Guadaloupe; he and his sons occasionally used variant spellings of their family name that included Deaolph, Deolph, and Dolph. "Charles Deaolph" of Brooklyn, Connecticut, was listed as a singing master as early as 1775. "Mark Anthony Deaolph" of Norwich and "Amasa Deaolph" of Pomfret were listed as handling subscriptions for Andrew Law's *Select Harmony* in 1778. Mark Anthony DeWolf was remembered by Charles's descendants as "quite a composer of music and poetry." Any of these, or a combination of two or more, may have been the men to whom four tunes were attributed in American tunebooks between 1778 and 1803. The remarkable "flying" tune MOUNT PLEASANT is attributed to "Deolph" in Nehemiah Shumway's *American Harmony* (1793).

218 MOUNT PLEASANT

DOOLITTLE, ELIAKIM (29 August 1772–April 1850), the son of Ambrose Doolittle and Martha Munson, was born in Cheshire, Connecticut. His older brother Amos Doolittle (1754–1832) was a celebrated silversmith and engraver who printed and published several tunebooks for Daniel Read, Stephen Jenks, and others; Eliakim's first cousins, Reuben and Amos Munson, were also composers. After attending Yale University without graduating, Eliakim Doolittle became a schoolteacher and singing master. He later moved to Hampton, Washington County, New York, where he married Hasadiah Fuller in 1811; the couple had a son and five daughters. Known for a "roving disposition," he eventually suffered from dementia, "wandering the streets in tattered garments, with untrimmed locks and long beard." He spent his last years in Pawlet, Vermont, and in the Washington County Poorhouse in Argyle, New York, where he died and was buried. He was a devout Congregationalist. In 1806 he published *The Psalm Singer's Companion*, containing forty-one of his own compositions.

272 EXHORTATION

315 IMMENSITY

538 HAMPTON

DOSS, GEORGE SEBRON (4 February 1882–18 February 1970), the son of John A. Doss and Irene Spradling, was born near Morris, Alabama, and grew up in Jefferson County; he studied music with S. M. and T. J. Denson. He married (1) Ellen Jordan in 1905 and lived in Morris, Birmingham, and Gardendale, where he raised ten children; Ellen died in 1945. He subsequently married (2) Florence Nunnelly of Holly Pond, Alabama. Sebron Doss was a carpenter and foreman for DuPont for twenty-one years; he was a Baptist, and a Mason. In addition to the Sacred Harp, he also sang Christian Harmony and gospel music. OUR HUMBLE FAITH was first published in the 1960 appendix to the Denson revision.

463 OUR HUMBLE FAITH

DRINKARD. A composer of this name collaborated with R. F. Ball on a setting of THE DYING CALIFORNIAN. John Smith Drinkard (1808–ca. 1865) was a South Carolina native who appears in the 1830 census for Newton County, Georgia, and in the 1840 census for Heard County. By 1850 he was in Chambers County, Alabama, where he died. Smith Drinkard is a possible identity for the composer.

410 THE DYING CALIFORNIAN "Ball & Drinkard"

DUMAS, EDMUND (15 February 1810–22 October 1882) (plate 7), the son of Benjamin F. Dumas and Martha Ussery, was descended on his father's side from Huguenot refugees who settled in Jamestown, Virginia, in 1700. He was born in Richmond County, North Carolina (in what is now Montgomery County), and moved with his family to Putnam County, Georgia, in 1814 and then, with the Creek cession of 1821, to Monroe County. He was a Primitive Baptist minister for more than forty years and a member of the Masons. He served as a local magistrate and as a member of the Georgia legislature. He married Isabel Martha Gibson in 1830 and fathered thirteen children.

An early composition by Dumas is THE BOTANIC DOCTOR, a humorous song about the dangers of calomel, a mercury compound then used in medicine; the piece appeared in *The Organ* on 14 February 1855. Dumas was a member of the 1869 revision committee of *The Sacred Harp*. Among his compositions are several named after friends and fellow musicians: WHITE (B. F. White), REESE (J. P. or H. S. Reese), EDMONDS (Jeremiah Troup Edmonds), and MULLINS (Rev. John Mullins). Dumas died in Monroe County and was buried in the cemetery of Union Primitive Baptist Church in the Goggins community, a church he had founded in 1837.

34 THE GOSPEL POOL

83 THE DYING MINISTER

111 To Die No More

115 EDMONDS

288 WHITE

310 WEEPING SAVIOR [arranged]

323 MULLINS

329 VAIN WORLD ADIEU

DURHAM, MATILDA T. (17 January 1815–30 July 1901), was born in Spartanburg County, South Carolina, the daughter of George Durham and Susan Hyde. In 1843 she married Andrew C. Hoy in a ceremony conducted by the Reverend John Gill Landrum, who was, like herself, a composer and contributor to Walker's *Southern Harmony*. Durham was a singing teacher and author of Baptist religious tracts and articles, "the serious content of which did not obscure the wit for which she was known." After the Civil War she moved to Cobb County, Georgia, where she died and was buried at Fowler Cemetery. At her death she was survived by two children, nine grandchildren, and five great-grandchildren. As a young woman she contributed several tunes to William Walker's books between 1835 and 1846.

DYE, JOHN MARION (1 January 1875–17 March 1957), schoolteacher, gospel singer, and songwriter, was the son of George Washington Dye and Nancy Lassiter. Born in Shelby County, Alabama, he was educated in the public schools and at Thorsby Institute in Chilton County. He was a Methodist. From the age of fifteen he attended singing schools and normal institutes taught by A. J. Showalter, J. M. Bowman, J. D. Patton, Adger M. Pace, and William Burton Walbert. He married (1) Lottie Pearl Farr on 24 December 1902, and they had five children. Their son Homer Showalter Dye (1902–77) was named for the renowned gospel songwriters Homer Rodeheaver and A. J. Showalter. After Lottie's death in 1929 he married (2) Georgia A. Farr in 1931. He taught in public schools for more than twenty years and divided his spare time between the Sacred Harp and modern gospel music. He wrote more than two hundred songs, many of which were published by Stamps-Baxter, Vaughan, and other publishers. He was a founder of the Alabama State [Gospel] Musical Convention and served as its president for two years. In December 1928 he led a group of Sacred Harp singers who went to Richmond, Indiana, to record for the Gennett label; at least ten sides were issued, several featuring Dye on piano. He was president of the Alabama State Sacred Harp Musical Association for several years from 1930, and he played the piano to accompany evening sessions of that convention. He continued to write music until his final years, and was buried in Mt. Era cemetery in Shelby County. His arrangement of the spiritual song WAYFARING STRANGER was published in the 1936 Denson revision.

EDMONDS, JEREMIAH TROUP (born about 1828), son of Georgia natives Amos Edmonds and Senah Mapp, was likewise born in Georgia, perhaps in Pike County, where his family lived in 1850, and where J. S. James recalled his origin. At this time, however, census records show that the twenty-two-year-old Edmonds was employed in Butts County as a farm hand. Troup Edmonds became a singing teacher; according to James, he "was a bachelor and taught music awhile with Prof. Pounds [E. T. Pound]." A member of the 1859 revision committee, he later moved to Newton County, Mississippi, where his parents had settled before 1860. The 1880 census lists him as a music teacher, then living with his sister's family in Newton County, where he probably died before 1890, if James is to be believed, writing that he "died when he was about 60 years old." Although he is not credited as a composer, the song EDMONDS, by Edmund Dumas, is named in his honor.

EDSON, LEWIS (22 January 1747/48–1820), son of Obed Edson and Keturah Willis, was born in Bridgewater, Massachusetts. In 1770 he married Hepzibah Washburn. From 1776 to 1791 he lived in Lanesboro, Massachusetts, and Mink Hollow, New York, where he worked as a blacksmith. He later moved to Woodstock, New York, where he died; he was an Episcopalian. His LENOX and BRIDGEWATER, both printed in Simeon Jocelin, *The Chorister's Companion* (1782), were among the most popular early American compositions. His son Lewis Edson Jr. published some of his father's music in his *Social Harmonist* (1801).

40 LENOX

276 BRIDGEWATER

EDWARDS, JARUSHA HENRIETTA "RUTH" DENSON (3 July 1893–25 April 1978), was the youngest daughter of T. J. and Amanda Denson. Born in Carrollton, Georgia, raised near Helicon, Alabama, and educated at high school in Cullman, Ruth Denson was an honors graduate of the Peabody College for Teachers in Nashville. She learned Sacred Harp music from her parents. She married the traveling salesman Lewis D. Edwards in 1917; this marriage produced no children and ended in divorce. An elementary school teacher for forty-five years in Cullman, she retired in 1962 and moved to Jasper. She sang in the choir at First Methodist Church in Cullman for many years. A member of the 1960 and 1966 revision committees, she chaired the United Convention in 1967 and was the long-time secretary of the Sacred Harp Publishing Company. She was buried at Fairview Cemetery, and is recognized as a "music achiever" in the Alabama Music Hall of Fame.

446 INFINITE DAY

534 NEW GEORGIA

543 THOU ART GOD

ELLIS, ABNER (4 January 1770–14 December 1844), son of Abner Ellis and Meletiah Ellis, was born in Dedham, Massachusetts. In 1790, when he was a young man, the parish voted to "admit an instrument of music [presumably a bass violin or violoncello] into public worship to strengthen the bass" and appointed Abner Ellis to play it. On 18 December 1793 he married (1) Mary Gay; she died in 1806. On 10 May 1807 he married (2) Polly Newell of Sturbridge, a schoolteacher. Abner Ellis worked as a schoolteacher, tavernkeeper, sawmill operator, and state legislator. He was buried in a mausoleum at Third or Clapboard Trees Parish, Dedham, now First Parish, Westwood. Ellis contributed several tunes to books compiled by Daniel Read, Stephen Jenks, and Daniel Peck printed in Dedham during the years 1805–08; in 1806 he also apparently compiled a supplement to the unauthorized third edition of Read's *Columbian Harmonist*. HARMONY first appeared in Jenks's *Delights of Harmony; or, Norfolk Compiler* (1805).

172 HARMONY

FREDERICK, ELBERT FOY (16 January 1906–6 July 1974), the son of Oscar H. Frederick, was born in the Wigginton community of Marion County, Alabama. He learned music from his father, from T. J. Denson, and from J. D. Wall. As a student at the Alabama Polytechnic Institute (now Auburn University) in the 1920s, he attended Sacred Harp singings in eastern Alabama. After completing his B.S. degree, Foy Frederick taught mathematics and coached basketball at Marion County High School in Guin, then became agricultural agent and inspector for the Alabama Department of Agriculture. He was partial to minor music.

511 THE GREAT REDEEMER

FREDERICK, FLOYD MONROE (12 April 1893–9 October 1960), was the son of John Thomas Frederick and Asenath Elizabeth Wood, and a nephew of Oscar H. Frederick. Floyd Frederick grew up in the Fairview community near Bear Creek, Alabama, and was a Tennessee Coal and Iron employee, a farmer, and a grocer. He married Sara Alice Mullins in 1913. A music pupil of T. J. Denson, he taught singing schools in Alabama and Mississippi, mainly singing treble. He was president of the Barn Creek convention of Marion County in 1928 and vice president in 1929–30. He contributed tunes to O. A. Parris's *Christian Harmony* (1954) and to the 1960 Denson revision of *The Sacred Harp*. In 1960, while leading ANTHEM ON THE SAVIOR (page 355) at a Sacred Harp singing at the Itawamba County courthouse in Fulton, Mississippi, he collapsed suddenly; he never regained consciousness, and died the following day at the hospital in Hamilton, Alabama.

499 AT REST

539 SUPPLICATION

FREDERICK, OSCAR HUSTON (27 April 1885–5 April 1955), youngest son of Heze-kiah Gideon Frederick and Penelope Burleson, was born in Marion County, Ala-bama. He married Acinith Wetherly in 1903 and became a farmer and insurance agent. A music pupil of T. J. Denson, he taught singing schools in Marion, Fay-ette, and Lamar Counties, Alabama, and in Mississippi. In 1925–27 and 1929–30 he was chairman of the Barn Creek singing convention of Marion County, and he was vice chairman of the Hamilton courthouse singing in 1925 and 1930. He was a bass singer.

    389 FREDERICKSBURG

FRENCH, JACOB (15 July 1754–May 1817), son of Jacob French and Miriam Downs, was born at Stoughton, Massachusetts, where in 1774 he attended a singing school of William Billings. After serving in the Revolutionary War, he married Esther Neale and became a farmer and singing-master. He published three tunebooks from 1789 to 1802, including *Harmony of Harmony* (1802). He died in Simsbury, Con-necticut, where he had moved in 1815. Along with William Billings, he is regarded as one of the finest composers of anthems in the New England tradition.

    250 HEAVENLY VISION

    260 FAREWELL ANTHEM

GIARDINI, FELICE (12 April 1716–8 June 1796), was an Italian violinist and com-poser. Born in Turin, he was a chorister at Milan cathedral; he studied singing, composition, and violin in Turin under G. B. Somis. In the 1750s he settled in London, where he was music master to the Duke of Gloucester, the Duke of Cumberland and the Prince of Wales. He died in Moscow. His glee for men's voices, "Viva tutte le vezzose," known in English as "Here's a health to all good lasses," was arranged by White and Searcy for *The Sacred Harp* as "Here's my heart, my loving Jesus."

    361 LOVING JESUS

GILLILAND, CECIL HOUSTON (17 November 1898–28 October 1968), was born in Gallant, Alabama, the son of John Gilliland and Mary Scott. He was trained in music by J. R. Smith, Lee Smith, Elmer Kitchens, and A. M. Cagle. He keyed the music at singings in his area. He joined Clear Creek Church in 1921 and became a deacon in 1934. He was a farmer, school bus driver, and storekeeper at Boaz.

    478 MY RISING SUN

GILMORE, TIMOTHY RANDALL (born 11 August 1959), son of Ronald Gilmore and Lavada McGough, was born and raised in Jasper, Alabama, graduating from Walker High School in 1978. He attended singing schools of John T. Hocutt and

Toney Smith and learned from Robert Aldridge how to key music. For several years he worked in the wholesale food distribution business. He wrote ALEXANDER in 1986, dedicating it to Mr. and Mrs. Roie Alexander of Oneonta.

393 ALEXANDER

GODSEY, PALMER (11 September 1898–17 August 1983), son of Robert W. Godsey and Emily Jackson, was born in Winston County, Alabama, and graduated from Winston County High School in 1921. A graduate of the Alabama Polytechnic Institute at Auburn, he taught vocational agriculture and served as mayor of Addison from 1952 to 1960. In 1922 he married Era T. Tidwell (17 June 1897–14 February 1986), also a schoolteacher; they had no children, but they endowed and built a children's home in Double Springs, Alabama. In the spring of 1939, Palmer Godsey led a group of singers that recorded Sacred Harp songs for a Library of Congress folklore project. He was buried at Fairview Cemetery near Double Springs.

490 MY SHEPHERD GUIDES

GOFF, EZRA WHITING (26 May 1760-August 1828), son of William Goff and Rebecca Whiting, was a native of Rehoboth, Massachusetts. After serving as a fifer in the American Revolution, he moved to Winchendon, Massachusetts, where he married Mehitable Bliss in 1789, and to Windham County, Vermont, where he appears on the 1790 census. He moved after 1810 to New York State, and in 1826 to Blissfield, Lenawee County, Michigan Territory, where he was the first town clerk in 1827, and where he died the following year. He is buried on a farm in what is now Palmyra Township. Twelve of his tunes appeared in others' books from 1786 to 1809, beginning with STRATFIELD in the *Worcester Collection* (1786); his DEDICATION ANTHEM, presented to the Musical Society in Dorchester, Massachusetts, was published separately in 1807.

142 STRATFIELD

GRAHAM. Nothing is known of this composer, who is credited with the tune PROSPECT in *The Southern Harmony* (1835). He was probably a resident of South Carolina, and is not to be confused with J. C. Graham.

30 PROSPECT

GRAHAM, J. C. Little is known of this composer, who is credited as the arranger of PARTING FRIEND in the 1859 appendix to *The Sacred Harp*. James reports that he lived in Alabama and attended the Southern Musical Convention from 1850 until the Civil War. H. S. Reese reported that he was a fine leader of music and a fine-looking man as well.

414 PARTING FRIENDS "Arranged by J. C. Graham"

GRAMBLING, WILLIAM ANDREW (21 November 1783–14 May 1874), was born in Orangeburg, South Carolina, to Bavarian immigrants Adam Gramling and Christina Chloanna Gassaway. A Methodist, he was licensed to preach on a trial basis in 1810. After his marriage to Rebecca Foster in 1811, his full admission to the ministry was delayed until 1812. He then settled in Pacolet, South Carolina. Before 1850 he retired to Cherokee County, Georgia, where he died at the age of ninety; he was buried in Riverview Cemetery, Canton, Georgia. Grambling is credited as the composer of MISSION in *The Southern Harmony* (1835), though this tune is a variant of ROAN by Seaton in *Supplement to the Kentucky Harmony*, third edition (1826).

204 MISSION [arranged]

GRANT, DAVID RUSSELL (born 1 April 1932), is a native of Macon, Georgia, and a 1959 graduate of Mercer College. He served as an instructor and computer systems specialist with the United States Air Force for thirty-three years until his retirement in 1987. He resides in Macon and enjoys Sacred Harp singing, square dancing, bridge, and growing flower bulbs. His tune in the *Sacred Harp* was composed by Raymond C. Hamrick and attributed to Grant by way of dedication.

50 HUMILITY

HALL, AMARIAH (28 April 1758–8 February 1827), farmer, innkeeper, and singing master, was born in Raynham, Bristol County, Massachusetts, the son of Amariah Hall and Hannah White. He married Sybil White in 1788 and moved in 1798 to Wrentham, where he was one of the first to manufacture straw bonnets. He lived three years in Providence before retiring to Bridgewater, Massachusetts, where he died; he was buried in Pleasant Street Cemetery in Raynham. He contributed tunes to several books published in New England between 1790 and 1800. His long and difficult tune ALL SAINTS NEW was much admired.

444 ALL SAINTS NEW

HAMRICK, RAYMOND COOPER (born 14 June 1915), was born in Macon, Georgia, to Horace Clifford Hamrick and Ida Eugenia Berry. A jeweler and watchmaker, he has been owner of Andersen's Jewelers in Macon since 1963. A 1933 graduate of Lanier High School in Macon, he served in the U.S. Army Air Corps from 1942 to 1946, and in 1950 married Joyce Darlene Rape. In 1946 he attended his first singing school, taught by Elder Monroe Denton, in Bibb County. A bass singer, he has been an active singing teacher and has served several times as president of the South Georgia Sacred Harp Convention. He was president of the Sacred Harp Publishing Company from 1986 to 2002 and a member of the music committee for the 1991 revision. A perceptive and articulate observer of Sacred Harp singing, Raymond Hamrick has been a source and a consultant for countless articles, books, and dissertations; he was one of the first to document changes in singing tempos over the course of his lifetime. He owns a large collection of tunebooks and related literature covering American music from about 1770, and has been active in barbershop quartet singing for more than thirty years. He composed two songs for the 1971 revision, five for the 1991 edition, and two for the *Sacred Harper's Companion* (1993). While sleeping one night, he dreamed of a great throng of singers, their faces hidden by cowls, singing a melody that he recalled on waking. He jotted down the tune, and later harmonized it and named it LLOYD after his friend and fellow singer Loyd Redding. His *Georgian Harmony*, issued in 2008, comprises seventy-seven of his own compositions, many bearing dates ranging from 1969 to 2007.

347 CHRISTIAN'S FAREWELL

492 INVOCATION

503 LLOYD

540 NIDRAH

569 EMMAUS

571 PENITENCE

HANDLEY, OTTO ERASTUS "O. H." (5 March 1879–16 February 1967), was born in Carroll County, Georgia, the son of William Handley and Nancy Hunter. He married (1) Malinda Jane Beard in 1898 and moved to Cullman, Alabama, in 1903, where he farmed, operated a general store and restaurant, and served as justice of the peace. Malinda died in 1933, and he married (2) Mrs. Francis in 1940. He began attending singing schools at the age of eleven and was a pupil of Enoch Marlow, W. A. Yates, I. M. Shell, and Bob Hendon in Georgia and of T. J. Denson in Alabama before teaching his own schools in Cullman County and elsewhere. He was vice president of the Rock Creek Convention in 1928 and 1930, was chairman of the Arab and Cullman courthouse singings in 1951, and was president of the Alabama State Convention in 1953. His funeral included an hour of Sacred Harp singing; a memorial singing, held annually until 1995, was established in his honor. Among his children, Millard H. Handley (1901–82) was a Sacred Harp singer and composer. In addition to singing, he loved to fish in the Tennessee River. He was buried at Macedonia Cemetery in Cullman County.

488 AS WE GO ON

HARRISON, JOYCE DARLENE RAPE (born 1 March 1929), daughter of Victor Franklin Rape and Gladis Gertrude Greene, was born in Houston County, Georgia, and raised in the Sacred Harp tradition. A graduate of Mercer University, she was an elementary school teacher for twenty years. She married (1) Raymond C. Hamrick in 1950; they had two daughters before their marriage ended in divorce. She later married (2) James O. Harrison.

466 HAYNES CREEK

HARRISON, RALPH (1748–1810), the son of William Harrison and Anne Cooper, was a Unitarian minister, teacher, composer, and linguist in Manchester, England. As minister of Cross Street Chapel, he built a schoolhouse behind the church, where he conducted an academy. His *Sacred Harmony* (London, 1784) contained several original tunes; his arrangement of an air from Arne's opera *Artaxerxes* has become known as ARLINGTON.

73 ARLINGTON

HASTINGS, THOMAS (15 October 1784–15 May 1872), son of Seth Hastings and Eunice Parmele, was born in Washington, Litchfield County, Connecticut. In 1796 he moved with his family and several neighbors to Clinton, Oneida County, New York. A self-taught musician, he taught his first singing school in 1806, directed a church choir, and began to publish collections of sacred music. He married Mary Seymour in 1822. In the same year he published *A Dissertation on Musical Taste,* the first book-length musical treatise by an American-born musician. In 1823 he settled in Utica, where he edited *The Western Recorder,* a religious newspaper. He moved in 1832 to New York City, where he was director of musical societies and teaching institutes; he was awarded an honorary doctorate in music by New York University in 1858. An albino, he suffered from extreme nearsightedness. He was buried in Greenwood Cemetery, Brooklyn. A Presbyterian, Hastings published more than fifty collections of sacred music and composed more than a thousand sacred pieces; he was also a prolific hymn writer. Among his hymns is "Bleeding hearts, defiled by sin" (page 497). Hastings was associated with Lowell Mason in the reform of American church music, and attempted to wean Americans away from the "unscientific" harmonies of the early New Englanders and of the southern shape-note books. Vehemently opposed to shape notes (he called them "dunce notes"), he nevertheless published one collection in seven shapes.

68 ORTONVILLE "Arranged by B. F. White"

HAUFF, JUDY (born 11 August 1943), the daughter of Edwin Prentiss Hauff and Cecilia Stoltz, is a native of Watertown, South Dakota. She has resided since 1964 in Chicago, where she has worked in several fields, including that of music producer. A Sacred Harp singer since 1983 along with her sister Melanie Hauff, she is self-taught in composition.

348 AINSLIE

368 STONY POINT

504 WOOD STREET

547 GRANVILLE

HAUSER, WILLIAM (23 December 1812–15 September 1880), physician, pharmacist, Methodist minister, and singing teacher, was born in Bethania, North Carolina; his father Martin Hauser, a Moravian who had become a Methodist, died when William was only two years old. Licensed to preach in 1834, he became a circuit rider for several years, and in 1837 married Eliza M. Renshaw. Soon after his marriage, he moved to Georgia, where in 1841 he studied medicine in Richmond County with Samuel B. Clark; he opened his own medical practice in 1843. In 1846 he settled near Wadley, Georgia, on a farm he named "Hesperia." In 1859 he became professor of physiology at Oglethorpe Medical College, Savannah. In the Civil War he served as chaplain with the 48th regular Georgia infantry, and was wounded at Chancellorsville. He and his wife are buried at Hesperia. His *Hesperian Harp* (1848) is one of the largest tunebooks ever printed in four shapes. In 1878 he published *The Olive Leaf* in seven shapes. Early in life he spelled his name "Houser," writing in the preface of *Hesperian Harp*, "This name is of Germanic origin. The original spelling is Hauser, and the pronunciation *How' zer.*" Later in life, however, he returned to the original spelling.

332 SONS OF SORROW "Treble by Wm. Houser"

334 O COME AWAY "Treble and Alto by Wm. Houser"

109 CARNSVILLE "2d Treble by Wm. Houser"

HENDON, M. A., may be Melissa Ann Hendon (23 December 1836–15 September 1881), daughter of William A. Hendon Sr. and Mary "Polly" Lassetter. Melissa was born in Troup County, Georgia, and moved with her family as a child to Carroll County. In 1854 she married James M. Wester in Coweta County. Their children were born in Coweta County through 1869 at least, but the Westers returned by 1875 to Carroll County, where she died.

448 THE GRIEVED SOUL

HERITAGE, ELPHREY (25 January 1812–1875), the son of Daniel Heritage Jr. and Ann Coles, was a native of New Jersey, where his brother Jason Heritage (1820–1902) was a strawberry farmer in Burlington County. Elphrey, raised a Quaker, married (1) Caroline Clement in 1833 and (2) Jane Denny in 1846; he had children of both marriages. He settled in Philadelphia, where he and Jason contributed tunes written in the style of Lowell Mason to several books, all published in Philadelphia by T. K. Collins: *The Christian Minstrel* (1846), *The Hesperian Harp* (1848), *The Timbrel of Zion* (1853), *The Social Harp* (1855), and *The Sacred Harp* (1870). He died in Philadelphia.

    213 WARNING

    489 THE SAVIOR'S CALL

HIBBARD probably lived in Windham County, Connecticut; he may be the composer of a popular tune called NORWICH, first printed by Andrew Law in 1779; other tunes attributed to him were printed by Jacob French and Elijah Griswold in the years 1793 and 1796.

    171 EXHORTATION

HITCHCOCK was the composer of two tunes in Andrew Law's *Rudiments of Music.* FAIRFIELD first appeared in the variant second edition of 1787–90.

    29 FAIRFIELD

HOCUTT, JOHN TILMON (28 February 1916–16 February 2005), the son of Tilmon E. Hocutt and Elizabeth Barton, grew up in Oakman, Walker County, Alabama. He was a farmer, carpenter, and singing teacher. From the age of fourteen he attended schools of Elmer Kitchens, J. D. Wall, Johnny Payne, O. A. Parris, and others, but was self-taught in harmony and composition. He taught singing schools throughout Alabama in *The Sacred Harp* and *Christian Harmony,* which published some of his compositions in 1954. He married Agnes Wall; they had no children. He died in Jasper, Alabama.

    475 A THANKFUL HEART

    480 REDEMPTION

    498 THE RESURRECTION DAY

    564 ZION

HOLDEN, OLIVER (18 September 1765–4 September 1844), the son of Nehemiah Holden and Elizabeth Stevens, was born in Shirley, Massachusetts. He grew up in Groton, Massachusetts, where he attended school and learned cabinetmaking. During the War of Independence he served as a marine on the frigate *Dean* and participated in the capture of five British warships. In 1783 he attended a singing school for two months and tried his hand at composing music. In 1785 he settled in Charlestown, where he was a carpenter, merchant, and land developer. In 1791 he married Nancy Rand. Holden became a prominent and wealthy citizen and a trustee of many civic and philanthropic organizations. He served several terms in the state House of Representatives and was also a justice of the peace. Raised a Congregationalist, he joined the Baptist Church in 1790; also a Mason, he was a member of King Solomon's Lodge in Charlestown.

From 1792 to 1807 Oliver Holden wrote some 230 compositions and published more than fifteen collections of music, including *Sacred Dirges* (1800), a book of pieces in memory of George Washington. He also wrote sacred poetry, including the hymn "Weeping sinners, dry your tears" (page 108). In his later years he regretted that his compositions had been published before he had a proper grasp of "musical science." Despite this, his CORONATION may be the best-known hymn tune from early America. He was buried in the Phipps Street burying ground in Charlestown.

    63 CORONATION

    168 COWPER

    313 CONCORD

HOLDROYD, ISRAEL, was a psalmodist at Halifax, West Yorkshire, England. Little is known about his life. His *Spiritual Man's Companion* (ca. 1722), containing psalm tunes and anthems, was issued in at least five editions, the last in 1753.

    28 WELLS

HOLYOKE, SAMUEL (15 October 1762–7 February 1820), schoolteacher, singing master, and composer, was born in Boxford, Massachusetts, the son of Rev. Elizur Holyoke and Hannah Peabody. As a student at Harvard College he compiled his first tunebook, *Harmonia Americana* (1791); his secular songs appeared in the *Massachusetts Magazine* in 1789 and 1790. After taking his master's degree in 1792, he taught school in Groton, Massachusetts, then moved to Charlestown, where with Hans Gram and Oliver Holden he edited *The Massachusetts Compiler* (1795). Holyoke devoted much of his life to musical activities and never married. He taught singing schools throughout New England but mainly in Essex County, where he was a founder of the Essex Musical Association (1797). He was an unusually prolific composer of sacred and secular music: his *Columbian Repository of Sacred Harmony* (1803) contains 733 pieces, about half of them his own. Although he opposed fuging tunes because of the confusion of sense and "jargon of words," he continued to compose examples of this type. Though he was a Congregationalist and a Mason, his *Christian Harmonist* (1804) was intended specifically for Baptists. Lacking a pleasing singing voice, he sometimes used the clarinet in vocal instruction. He brought out two volumes of *The Instrumental Assistant* (1800, 1807) also published pieces for voices and instruments together. Late in life he became a heavy drinker but retained the love and respect of his friends in East Concord, New Hampshire, whom he asked a few days before his death to sing one of his compositions for the last time. The 29 February *New Hampshire Patriot* refers to him as "celebrated as a teacher and composer of sacred music." Although he is not credited with any music in *The Sacred Harp*, the White family may have had access to a copy of his *Columbian Repository,* since B. F. White and one of his sons arranged songs from that source.

   120 CHAMBERS "arranged by B. F. White"
    [from SAVOY]

   362 NORWICH "D. P. White"
    [arranged from MALABAR]

HOWD. Nothing other than the surname is known of the composer of WHITES-TOWN, first published in Stephen Jenks's *Musical Harmonist* (1800). The song's title denotes a tract in Oneida County, New York, intensively settled by emigrants from Connecticut around 1800. Samuel Howd (1779–1862), a native of Branford, Connecticut, who moved to Camden, New York, and married Eunice Fuller in 1797, is at least a possibility in identifying this composer.

   211 WHITESTOWN

HUMPHREYS, R. D., contributed five tunes to *Kentucky Harmony* and *Supplement to the Kentucky Harmony*. In 1817 Ananias Davisson named him among "gentlemen teachers" in Virginia, Tennessee, and Kentucky. The melody of KINGWOOD, in the *Supplement* (1820), is almost identical to that of NASHVILLE, printed in Johnson's *Tennessee Harmony* two years earlier.

   266 KINGWOOD

INGALLS, JEREMIAH (1 March 1764–6 April 1838), born in Andover, Massachusetts, was the son of Abijah Ingalls and Elisabeth Hutchinson. Orphaned at the age of fifteen, he settled in Newbury, Vermont, around 1789, where he married Mary Bigelow (also an orphan) on 28 September 1791. Ingalls was a farmer, tavern-keeper, and singing teacher; as a deacon and chorister in the Congregational church, he played the "bass viol" (violoncello) at divine service. In 1810 he was dismissed from the Newbury church due to a "lack of repentance" for marital infidelity; he moved with his family to a farm near Hancock, Vermont, where he lived the rest of his life and continued his musical activities. His *Christian Harmony, or Songster's Companion* (1805) contains many folk and popular melodies set to hymns and spiritual songs used in early revivals and camp meetings.

   24 THE YOUNG CONVERT

   155 NORTHFIELD

240 CHRISTIAN SONG

299 NEW JERUSALEM

IVEY, DAVID (born 15 August 1955), son of Coy Ivey and Marie Jones, was born into a family of Sacred Harp singers in Henagar, Alabama; he received instruction from Leonard Lacy, Hugh McGraw, and Joyce Walton. A 1977 graduate of Auburn University, he married Karen Isbell in 1978 and settled in Huntsville, where he is program director for the Alabama Supercomputer Center. The Iveys have raised three children, all singers. In 1985 he founded the annual singing at the Burritt Museum, Huntsville; he chaired the United Convention in 1981, 1989, and 1999. He was on the music committee for the 1991 edition and served on the board of directors of the Sacred Harp Publishing Company. In 2003 he founded Camp Fa-sola, a weeklong residential singing school for all ages. David Ivey directed a group of fifty-five singers that recorded two songs for the soundtrack of the Miramax film *Cold Mountain* (2003).

415 EASTER MORN

JAMES, JOSEPH STEPHEN (20 March 1849–20 January 1931), born in Campbell County, Georgia (now Douglas County), was one of many children born to sing-ing teacher Stephen James (1821–72) and Martha Shipley. His middle name is given as Summerlin in some sources, including a publishers' directory from 1908, but family sources agree on Stephen. In 1869 he married Margaret Anna Elizabeth Maxwell (1845–1927). Largely self-educated, he attended only a log schoolhouse near his home, yet he was admitted to the bar in 1875 and became an attorney, politician, and land speculator in his hometown of Douglasville. He served as a surveyor for the Georgia Pacific Railroad, as a state representative, as the first mayor of Douglasville, as a U.S. district attorney, and as editor of a local newspa-per, *The New South*. He was a Methodist and a Mason.

In his youth James attended a singing school of J. R. Turner; later in life he became a tireless promoter of Sacred Harp singing in the Atlanta area. He was a founder of the United Sacred Harp Musical Association and presided over it for many years. In 1904 James wrote and published *A Brief History of the Sacred Harp;* in 1909 he compiled *Union Harp and History of Songs,* and in 1913 produced *Sacred Tunes and Hymns,* combining shaped notes with keyboard accompaniments. His most enduring contribution was the 1911 collection titled *Original Sacred Harp,* known as the James edition. In all three music books he was aided by musical editor S. M. Denson. In 1920 James issued a pamphlet titled *An Explanation of the Sacred Harp,* a spirited defense of his 1911 *Original Sacred Harp* against the claims of competing revisers W. M. Cooper and J. L. White. At his death a memorial service in Atlanta attracted several hundred singers. He was buried in Douglasville Cemetery. While not known as a composer, he was given credit as a collaborator with S. M. Denson on the songs THE GREAT ROLL CALL in *Union Harp* and TRAVELING ON in *Original Sacred Harp.*

> 208 TRAVELING ON
> "S. M. Denson and J. S. James"

JARMAN, THOMAS (21 December 1776–19 February 1861), was a tailor and singing teacher of Clipston, Northamptonshire, England, where he was the chorister (song leader) of the Baptist chapel for most of his life. He played instruments in several church bands in the area and organized village choral festivals. His first publication, *Sacred Harmony,* vol. 1 (ca. 1803) contains his fuging tune NATIVITY, which appears in the 1991 *Sacred Harp* with the fuging section removed.

> 350 NATIVITY

JENKS, STEPHEN (17 March 1772–3 June 1856), the son of John Jenks and Lydia Lucinda Bucklin, was born in Glocester, Rhode Island, and grew up in Ellington, Connecticut; he taught singing schools in Connecticut, Massachusetts, and New York. He published ten collections of sacred music between 1799 and 1818, which included 125 of his own compositions, along with the work of many other rural New England composers; he also published two books of secular songs. He later retired to Thompson, Geauga County, Ohio, where he farmed and made drums. Jenks left behind a manuscript containing almost a hundred compositions, mainly from his later years. James called him "a ready composer." His MOUNT VERNON was written to commemorate the death of George Washington in December 1799; the music was pasted into copies of Jenks's first publication, *The New-England Harmonist.*

> 110 MOUNT VERNON
>
> 126 BABEL'S STREAMS
>
> 137 LIBERTY
>
> 169 DARTMOUTH
>
> 209 EVENING SHADE
>
> 440 NORTH SALEM

JOHNSON, ALEXANDER (25 February 1791–December 1832), son of John Johnson and Martha Alison, was born in South Carolina and moved with his family to Maury County, Tennessee. He served as a private in the War of 1812 and married Nelly Craig on 25 January 1816. His *Tennessee Harmony* (1818), the first music book in Middle Tennessee, had a profound influence on *The Missouri Harmony* and other collections. DEVOTION was published in the first edition of *Tennessee Harmony*; NASHVILLE was introduced in the second edition of 1821.

48 DEVOTION

64 NASHVILLE

JOHNSON, EULA DENSON (ca. 1910–1998), oldest daughter of Whitt Denson, grew up in Helicon, Winston County, Alabama, where she was taught music by her father. She was a saleslady and operated a motel and restaurant in Nesmith. She composed OH, WHAT LOVE for the 1960 appendix of the Denson revision.

491 OH, WHAT LOVE

JOHNSON, THEODORE WALLACE (born 6 August 1928), was born in Evanston, Illinois, the son of Donald Southwood Johnson and Kathryn Purcell. Educated at Loyola (B.A. in sociology, 1966) and Northwestern University (Ph.D. in English, 1975), he taught at Michigan State and at Indiana University Northwest (Gary) before becoming a writer and editor of textbooks. On 14 June 1966 he married Marcia Klein. He began singing in *The Sacred Harp* in the early 1980s. A treble singer, he travels widely to singings with his wife, who sings alto. NEW AGATITE was first published in the 1991 edition of *The Sacred Harp*.

485 NEW AGATITE

JONES, WILLIS DALLAS (25 March 1845–18 April 1921), the son of Thomas Benjamin Jones and Celia Susanna Velvin, lived his entire life in Carroll County, Georgia. He was a county tax collector, a Baptist preacher, and a member of the Chattahoochee Musical Convention for forty years. In the Civil War Jones served as a private in Company B, 27th Georgia Volunteer Infantry. In April 1864 he received an injury that permanently disabled him, so that he walked with crutches for the rest of his life. Despite this, he married Margaret Jane Hanson in 1875, had several children, and continued to preach and sing. He was buried at Consolation Baptist Church, where he had served as pastor. His tunes GAINSVILLE and SACRED REST were first printed in the 1870 *Sacred Harp*.

70 GAINSVILLE "Original"

435 SACRED REST "Original"

KIMBALL, JACOB (15 February 1761–6 February 1826), was born in Topsfield, Massachusetts, the son of Priscilla Smith and of blacksmith and chorister Jacob Kimball Sr. At the age of fourteen Jacob served as a military fifer and drummer in the Revolutionary War; he graduated from Harvard College in 1780. After a few years as a schoolteacher and a lawyer, he returned to his native town and to the occupation of singing-master; he was also a poet. Kimball published two collections of music: *The Rural Harmony* (1793) and *The Essex Harmony* (1800) and left behind compositions in manuscript. As a member of the Essex Musical Association, he advocated reform in church music; his own music exhibited a more refined style and more "correct" harmony than that of many of his contemporaries. He became an alcoholic in his later years and died in the Topsfield Alms House. INVITATION was his first published tune, appearing in the second edition of Daniel Bayley's *Select Harmony* (1784).

   327 INVITATION

KING, ELIAS LAFAYETTE (11 March 1828–9 February 1876), was born in Wilkinson County, Georgia; he was the son of John King and Elizabeth Dubose and a younger brother of E. J. King. He grew up in Talbot County, where he was a farmer and a Mason. James reports that "he was a young man in 1850; a splendid director of music." A member of the 1850 revision committee, he contributed six tunes to the 1850 appendix of *The Sacred Harp.* He married (1) Arianna Virginia Gray (1837–56) on 24 November 1853; she died of consumption at the age of eighteen. He then married (2) Cynthia "Cissy" Glaze on 24 March 1857. About 1870 he moved to Geneva, Sabine County, Texas, where he died in a firearms accident; he was buried in King Family Cemetery.

   308 PARTING FRIENDS

KING, ELISHA JAMES (1821–31 August 1844), co-compiler of *The Sacred Harp,* was the son of John King and Elizabeth Dubose. He was probably born in Wilkinson County, Georgia, but his parents moved in 1828 to Talbot County, settling in the Box Springs community in the southwest corner of the county. A farmer and singing teacher with "bright prospects as a musician," he died on 31 August 1844, the same year the book was completed; his father died only two weeks later, on 15 September. According to J. S. James, King was trained in music by B. F. White. King was credited with twenty-four tunes in the book, though several of these were arranged from earlier sources. Though James suggests that he may have had some help from Major White in composing some of his tunes, his work shows a distinctive style in such classics as BOUND FOR CANAAN, SWEET CANAAN, and FULFILLMENT.

   33 WEEPING SAVIOR

   33 ABBEVILLE [arranged]

   76 HOLINESS

   77 THE CHILD OF GRACE [arranged]

   80 SERVICE OF THE LORD

   82 BOUND FOR CANAAN

   87 SWEET CANAAN

93 Frozen Heart [arranged]

96 Happy Matches
　[arranged by] "B. F. White & King"

98 Dull Care [arranged]

99 Gospel Trumpet [arranged]

100 The Bower of Prayer [arranged]

101 Canaan's Land

102 Fulfillment

104 The Lovely Story [arranged]

109 Carnsville

113 The Prodigal Son

116 Union

123 The Dying Christian [arranged]

160 Turn, Sinner, Turn [arranged]

227 Ode on Life's Journey

234 Reverential Anthem

KING, J., probably lived in South Carolina and is not to be identified with Joel King (1809–71), E. J. King's older brother, who was listed as co-proprietor of the 1844 *Sacred Harp*. His tune The Saints Bound for Heaven, co-authored with William Walker, appeared in the 1840 appendix to *Southern Harmony*.

35 Saints Bound for Heaven
"by J. King and W. Walker"

KITCHENS, JAMES ELMER (16 June 1912–13 June 1979), was born in Parrish, Walker County, Alabama, one of ten children of Elder Wiley Leander Kitchens and Emily Birdie Posey. He married Elma Morrow in 1932; they had four daughters. Elmer Kitchens was a carpenter, brickmason, and housewright (he built several church houses) and a Primitive Baptist preacher ordained in 1937; he taught singing schools for more than thirty years. In 1930 he accompanied T. J. Denson for eight months on a teaching tour of Texas. He was a member of the music committee for the 1960 and 1966 revisions and was president of the Sacred Harp Publishing Company at the time of the 1966 revision. The Shepherd's Flock, published in the 1936 Denson revision, was his first composition.

279 The Shepherd's Flock

512 The Spirit Shall Return

568 I Want to Go to Heaven

LANCASTER, M. L. A., P. R., AND SARAH (so designated in the pages of *The Sacred Harp*), were daughters of James Lupo Lancaster (1810–95) and Charity Lancaster (1804–85), of Edgecombe County, North Carolina, who removed to Talbot County, Georgia between 1832 and 1834, then settled in Marion County before 1860. James was a descendant of Peter Lupo (1535–1608), one of an originally Jewish family of musicians that served the Tudor and Stuart monarchs of England. Charity was James's first cousin, once removed. The Lancaster sisters grew up in Talbot County and were instructed in music by B. F. White and J. P. Reese. They were assisted by J. P. Reese in their compositions, which were first published in the 1859 *Sacred Harp*. Sarah continued to compose, and contributed two well-known fuging tunes, THE LAST WORDS OF COPERNICUS and SARDIS, to the 1870 edition.

ANNA LUCINDA MARIA ATKINSON "ANN" LANCASTER (18 February 1832–9 November 1922) was born in Edgecombe County, North Carolina. Never married, she died in Marion County, Georgia, and was buried in Providence Cemetery. Her diary and other letters and family papers are in the Georgia State Archives. I. M. Shell reported that Ann and her sister Sarah attended singing conventions and that he had "never heard finer voices than those two women have."

    406 NEW HARMONY "Arranged by
        Miss M. L. A. Lancaster"

PRISCILLA R. "SID" LANCASTER (14 July 1838–28 September 1916) was born in Talbot County, Georgia. She married (1) Jack Hagler, who died in 1864; she then married (2) John L. Benson. She died in Marion County and was buried at Ramah Cemetery.

    374 OH, SING WITH ME!

SARAH "SALLY" LANCASTER (28 April 1834–13 April 1918) was born in Talbot County, Georgia, and educated in Hamilton, apparently at the Hamilton Female Institute, where she studied piano and was intensely interested in music. From a letter dated 1854 it appears that she boarded with the family of B. F. White while studying in Hamilton. As a young woman, she formed the habit of sending pieces of original music along with letters to friends and family. She married George Washington "Wash" Hagler on 28 November 1866; the couple had five children. On 27 December 1876 the family left Georgia, arriving 5 January 1877 in Butler, Freestone County, Texas, where they appear in the 1880 census. After her move to Texas, Sally continued to send music to her family and to inquire about "the singings" back home; to her sister Ann she wrote, on 29 October 1877, "I have tunes running in my mind all the time, day and night, tell me what you think of that." By 1886 the Haglers had moved to Oakwood, Leon County, where she died; she was buried in

Oakwood Cemetery. James reported that she was a "sweet singer" and "a Christian woman, of a lovable disposition."

112 THE LAST WORDS OF COPERNICUS "Original"

345 I'M ON MY JOURNEY HOME "Original"

460 SARDIS "Original"

LEDBETTER, LEWIS L. (12 September 1817–9 June 1867), the son of Washington Ledbetter and Lucy Bostick, was born in Greene County, Georgia. He trained as a dentist and settled in McDonough, Henry County, by 1840. On 20 December 1842 he married Cornelia Jones Byrd (born 27 April 1828 in DeKalb County); their first five children, born between 1843 and 1850, were born at McDonough. In 1851 he established his practice in Atlanta, where he remained until 1857, and where daughters were born in 1852 and 1856. In the years 1857–1862 he lived in Troup and Meriwether Counties, then a hotbed of Sacred Harp activity. His song, co-authored with B. F. White, was published in the 1859 appendix to *The Sacred Harp*. In addition to dentistry, Ledbetter was a Methodist preacher, licensed by the North Georgia Conference. He was also a master Mason. After 1862 he moved to eastern Georgia, settling near Alexander, Burke County. He died in Washington, Wilkes County, under mysterious circumstances. Among his sons, one became a Methodist minister, one a mayor of Cedartown; his daughter Alice became the editor of the Meriwether *Vindicator*. Lewis Ledbetter was buried at Habersham Methodist Cemetery, Perkins, although a 1989 census of that cemetery revealed no trace of his monument.

369 SEND A BLESSING "B. F. White &
    L. L. Leadbeater"

LETSON, CALVIN FORD (15 April 1833–1902), was born in Jackson, Butts County, Georgia, one of twin sons of South Carolina natives Robert M. Letson and Susanna McClain. According to J. S. James he was raised in Carroll County, where he taught singing schools. He married D. Anna Bridges (1839–1930) of Pike County; they had eight children. At some time between 1864 and 1870 they moved to Alabama, where he appears as a farmer and schoolteacher in Tuscaloosa County. He died in McCalla, Jefferson County, where he was buried in Pleasant Hill Cemetery. His tunes first appeared in the 1870 edition of *The Sacred Harp*.

51 MY HOME

402 PROTECTION "Original"

LOWRY, JAMES C., contributed nine tunes to *Kentucky Harmony* and *Supplement to the Kentucky Harmony*. In 1817 Ananias Davisson named him among "gentlemen teachers" of music in Virginia, Tennessee, and Kentucky. He probably lived in

Kentucky, since two additional tunes are credited to him in *Columbian Harmony* (1829) by Kentucky residents Benjamin Shaw and Charles H. Spilman.

58 PISGAH

165 FAMILY BIBLE

MANN, HENRY GOODWIN (21 August 1843–1 January 1920), no relation to R. F. M. Mann, was the son of Joel Mann and Amanda Goodwin and lived in Meriwether County, Georgia. On 10 September 1861 he enlisted in the 28th Georgia Infantry, Company E. He was wounded in the head at Cold Harbor, Virginia, on 27 June 1862, and surrendered at Greensboro, North Carolina, on 26 April 1865. He married Sarah M. Brown in 1868 and had numerous offspring. He was buried in Salem Cemetery, Raleigh, Georgia. He contributed tunes to the 1870 *Sacred Harp.*

176 BLOOMING YOUTH

348 FLEETING DAYS

MANN, RICHARD F. M. (26 October 1816–11 July 1891), was born in Elbert County, Georgia, the eldest son of John J. Mann and Mary R. (Polly) Harper; he lived near Griffin, Pike County, Georgia in 1850 but moved to Spalding County before 1860. When his father died in 1841 he and his mother took responsibility for his younger brothers and sisters. In the Civil War he served first in Georgia's Tenth Regiment, of which he was elected captain on 14 January 1862 and was mustered out in May 1862. He later enlisted as a private in Company B of the Fifth Georgia Infantry. A farmer, merchant, singing teacher, and a Methodist, he was a member of the Southern and Chattahoochee Conventions and a member of the 1850 and 1869 revision committees. James reports that he "had a very strong voice." Married at least twice, but with no children, he enjoyed close family ties with B. F. White. His sister Mary married Robert H. White and his brother Wesley married Melvina Thurza White. Richard F. M. Mann contributed a single tune to the 1850 appendix of the *Sacred Harp*, but none to the 1859 appendix. The 1870 *Sacred Harp* contains fourteen dated compositions, some written much earlier, as shown in figure 4.

Mann's TOLLING BELL was dedicated to Miss M. A. White (Martha America White, B. F.'s daughter) and E. A. Mann (Elizabeth Adeline Mann, his unmarried sister). As of August 1888 he was still living in Spalding County, where his name appears on a list of voters. About this time he began to suffer from dementia—James wrote that "he became diseased in body and mind"; on 7 September 1889 he was admitted to the Georgia State Asylum in Milledgeville, where he died less than two years later.

105 JEWETT

111 JOURNEY HOME

394 THE MESSIAH'S PRAISE "By R. F. M. Mann
   and Jas. A. Spark"

459 TOLLING BELL

4. Dated Compositions of R. F. M. Mann, 1853–1869.

SACRED MUSIC	March 4, 1853
HEAVENLY LAND	July 19, 1857
CHARMING SOUND	January 28, 1858
JEWETT	August 3, 1858
HILL OF ZION	April 12, 1868
HAPPY DAY	September 5, 1868
TOLLING BELL	November 1, 1868
JOURNEY HOME	November 15, 1868
ST. PAUL	December 13, 1868
THE SKY	June 13, 1869
THE KINGDOM	June 17, 1869
FUNERAL HYMN	July 16, 1869
BIRTH OF CHRIST	October 22, 1869
FESTIVAL DAY	October 22, 1869
HOLY LAND	November 20, 1869

MARSH, SIMEON BUTLER (1 June 1798–14 July 1875), was born in Sherburne, New York, the son of Eli Marsh and Asubah Butler. He married Eliza Carrier in 1820. He was a pupil of Thomas Hastings, as well as a newspaper editor and singing teacher in various towns in upstate New York. He died in Albany and was buried in Vale Cemetery, Schenectady. He wrote MARTIN in 1834; the tune was published by Thomas Hastings in 1836.

452 MARTIN

MASON, LOWELL (8 January 1792–11 August 1872), was born in Medfield, Massachusetts. His parents, Johnson Mason and Catherine Hartshorn, both sang in the church choir; Lowell attended his first singing school at the age of thirteen and directed the Medfield choir by the age of sixteen. In 1812 he moved to Savannah, Georgia, where he studied composition with Frederick L. Abel and directed music at a Presbyterian church while employed as a dry-goods merchant and a bank clerk. Following the success of his first tunebook, the *Boston Handel and Haydn Society Collection* (1822), he returned to Boston in 1827, where he married Abby Gregory, directed music at Bowdoin Street Church and Central Congregational Church, and founded the Boston Academy of Music. After visiting Europe in 1851–53, he settled in Orange, New Jersey, where he died. He was buried in Rosedale Cemetery, Orange; his music books and manuscripts are in the Yale University library. One of the great musical reformers, he introduced music instruction to the Boston public schools in the years 1838–45 and conducted institutes and normal schools for the training of music teachers. He published more than fifty music books and composed more than one thousand hymn tunes.

145 SWEET AFFLICTION [arranged]

147 BOYLSTON

147 LABAN

535 SHAWMUT

566 HEBRON

MASSENGALE, JOHN, was listed with B. F. White as co-proprietor of *The Sacred Harp* in the 1850 and 1859 editions. Little is known of his life, but he probably lived in or near Talbot County, Georgia. He advertised in the Columbus *Enquirer* in 1841 seeking lost saddlebags; among his tunes with distinctive geographical names, CUSSETA is near Columbus, Georgia, and AUTAUGA is a county in south central Alabama. He contributed three tunes to the 1844 *Sacred Harp* and six to the 1850 appendix.

32 CORINTH

73 CUSSETA

88 MOUNT ZION

306 OXFORD [arranged]

312 SING TO ME OF HEAVEN

338 SAWYER'S EXIT [arranged]

MAXIM, ABRAHAM (3 January 1773–28 March 1829) was born in Plympton (now Carver), Massachusetts. He may have attended a singing school of William Billings. In the 1790s he settled in Turner, Maine (then part of Massachusetts), where he was a schoolteacher and singing master and played the bass viol. He was a Universalist. In 1827 he moved to Palmyra, Maine, where, according to *The Old Stoughton Musical Society* (1928), he "dropped dead in the street with [manuscripts of] music and a Spelling Book in his pocket." His best-known tune, TURNER, was later arranged for the 1859 appendix to the *Sacred Harp* by Absalom Ogletree.

371 HEAVENLY DOVE [arranged by Ogletree]

556 PORTLAND

MAYFIELD, ISRAEL (ca. 1812–ca.1868), was born in North Carolina. A farmer, he lived in Hueytown, Jefferson County, Alabama, and married (1) Clarky Meggs, sister of J. L. Meggs, and (2) Ann Price. He collaborated with J. L. Meggs on the tune STILL BETTER in the 1870 *Sacred Harp*, but his name was there erroneously printed as "Israel Bradfield." He died before that book was published, and was buried in Valley Creek Cemetery, Hueytown.

166 STILL BETTER

MCCURRY, ALEXANDER WASHINGTON (22 November 1826–22 July 1885), the youngest son of J. G. McCurry Sr. and Sarah McCurry, was the brother of J. G. McCurry Jr. and like him a farmer in Hart County, Georgia, and a member of the Masonic fraternity. He married Nancy E. Roberts in 1850. He is credited with two compositions in *The Social Harp*, including ROLL, JORDAN, ROLL.

274 ROLL, JORDAN "W. and
John G. McCurry, 1853"

MCCURRY, JOHN GORDON, JR. (26 April 1821–4 December 1886), son of John Gordon McCurry Sr. and Sarah McCurry, was born in Elbert (now Hart) County, Georgia, where he was a farmer and singing teacher in the Bio community. Though raised in the Presbyterian Church, he became a staunch Baptist who taught Sunday schools and donated land for the building of Bio Baptist Church. He was a Mason. He married Rachel S. Brown in 1842. Although they were childless, they raised several orphans. He was remembered for maintaining a centralized post box for the residents of the Bio community and for his ability to estimate accurately the size of a plot of land after walking around it once. He was also a tailor and quilt designer. He was buried in Bio Baptist Cemetery.

In 1855 McCurry compiled *The Social Harp*, containing 222 pieces, many of them camp-meeting songs and revival choruses. As with most southern tunebooks, many of the tunes he claims as composer are arrangements of earlier songs. Others are directly taken from *The Sacred Harp*, a fact that did not escape the notice of B. F. White, who wrote in *The Organ*, 2 February 1855, "We now remark in self defence, that this work contains some thirty-five or forty pieces of music which belongs [sic] to the proprietors of the Sacred Harp, under copyright protection, which has been inserted in the Social Harp without consent or consultation." Edmund Dumas, however, wrote in the same paper, 5 April 1856: "Musical brothers in Georgia and elsewhere, you ought to have it in connection with the Sacred Harp, Hesperian Harp, and all good Harps, — There is one or two new pieces in the Social Harp that is richly worth one dollar. Come boys, test what I say." "H.S. & J.P. Rees" of Columbus, Georgia, are named on the covers of *The Social Harp* as wholesale and retail agents for the book. Tunes credited to McCurry were not added to *The Sacred Harp* until the twentieth century. The melody of PARTING FRIENDS, dated 1846, is almost identical to that of FULFILLMENT by E.

J. King (1844), while RAYMOND (1855) is a major-mode version of NORTH SALEM by Stephen Jenks.

267 PARTING FRIENDS [arranged]

274 ROLL, JORDAN "W. and
John G. McCurry, 1853"

441 RAYMOND

McGRAW, EDGAR LEON (21 July 1917–10 December 1987), was the youngest son of Lee A. McGraw. Born in Anderson, Alabama, he married Johnnie Faye Richardson in 1938 and raised three daughters. A graduate of Alabama Polytechnic Institute (later Auburn University), he was information director of Auburn's agricultural research station from 1968 to 1982. He was buried in Auburn Memorial Park.

295 ODEM

McGRAW, HENRY NEWTON "BUD" (18 November 1883–27 January 1969), was a younger brother of Lee A. McGraw. Born in Bowden Junction, Georgia, he had only four years of formal schooling. He married Alabama native Lydia E. Young in 1905 and lived in Mt. Zion, Carroll County, where he was a railroad worker and singing teacher. He was a Mason. Bud McGraw studied music with T. J. Denson. He was a member of the 1935 and 1960 music committees and chairman of the United Convention in 1957. He died at his home only five days after his wife's death and was buried at Mt. Zion Cemetery.

283 SABBATH MORNING

453 HOLLY SPRINGS

483 ETERNAL LIGHT

544 PRAISE HIM

McGRAW, HUGH WINFRED (born 20 February 1931), born near Centralhatchee, Georgia, and raised in Villa Rica, is a retired clothing manufacturer living in Bremen, Georgia. The son of John Wesley McGraw and Lillie Mae Ashley, he married Donnie Mert Todd; they had two daughters. Coming to Sacred Harp singing as an adult, he learned music from H. N. McGraw and A. M. Cagle. He made rapid progress as a singer and composer and was recognized for his strong skills as a businessman and as an interpreter of the Sacred Harp to the world at large. In 1958 he became executive secretary of the Sacred Harp Publishing Company, a position he held until 2002. As an ambassador of Sacred Harp singing, he presented lectures and workshops to academic, religious, and other organizations and taught singing schools and sold songbooks throughout the United States.

He appeared as a singer in the 1980 film *The Long Riders*. Hugh McGraw founded the National Sacred Harp Convention in 1980 and chaired numerous singings and conventions. He received a National Heritage Fellowship Award in 1982. He was the guiding spirit behind three editions of the *Sacred Harp*: a member of the music committee for the 1960 revision, chair of the 1966 and 1971 music committees, and "general chairman" of the 1991 edition.

225 REYNOLDS

500 LIVING HOPE

516 DELONG

517 MARS HILL

527 MY LIFE AND BREATH

548 WOOTTEN

549 PHILLIPS FAREWELL

570 FAREWELL TO ALL

MCGRAW, LEE ANDREW (4 March 1882–15 June 1957), was the oldest son of Roland Jackson McGraw (1859–1910) and Augusta Ann Savannah Entrekin (1865–1940). Born in Bremen, Georgia, he settled in Anderson, Alabama, near the Tennessee line. He is buried in Mitchell Cemetery, Lauderdale County, Alabama. A farmer, carpenter, brickmason, rural mail carrier, and clerk of a cotton gin company, he was a member of the Masonic Lodge and a deacon and treasurer in the Baptist Church. He married (1) Louisa Idenia "Lou" Nix in Cullman, Alabama in 1902; they had six children, and Lou died in 1955. Lee then married (2) Lou's widowed niece Ida Bertha Nix in 1956. He was buried in Mitchell Cemetery, Lauderdale County, Alabama. Lee McGraw was a member of the music committee for the 1935 Denson revision.

395 NEW BETHEL

MCGRAW, THOMAS BEATRICE (15 July 1890–13 November 1970), was the younger brother of L. A. and H. N. McGraw. Born at Mt. Zion, Georgia, he married Octavia Bishop in 1914 and later moved to Atlanta. He was a carpenter. Tom McGraw was a member of the 1935, 1960, and 1966 music committees. He was buried in Westview Cemetery, Atlanta.

197 GEORGIA

381 SING ON

386 CHRIST OUR SONG

420 BISHOP

471 THE SAVIOR'S NAME

530 A GLAD NEW SONG

558 LIVING STREAMS

562 INFINITE DELIGHT

McGRAW, THOMAS BUFORD (25 March 1911–6 January 1982), was the second son of H. N. and Lydia McGraw. Born in Anderson, Alabama, Buford McGraw grew up in Bowden Junction, Georgia. He went to school at Mt. Zion, Georgia, where he settled and worked in construction. Like his father, he was a member of the Masons. He married Florence Gladys Wallace in 1929. He was an excellent treble singer.

476 THE THRONE OF GRACE

McLENDON, AUGUSTUS JACKSON (25 March 1853–24 December 1929), was born in Meriwether County, Georgia, the son of Isaac Newton McLendon (1832–1915) and Mary Anne Eliza Rowe (1832–1915). Raised in the Veal community of Carroll County, Jackson McLendon married three times: (1) Eugenia Pentecost of Carroll County, on 25 March 1884; (2) Minnie Lee Beavers of Coweta County on 7 January 1888; and finally (3) Ida Viola Laminack (1872–1942) of Cleburne County, Alabama, on 31 March 1895. He was a Primitive Baptist and an influential Sacred Harp singer, serving as secretary of the Chattahoochee Convention in 1894–96 and president in 1900, 1906, 1908, and 1913. His brothers William Beauregard McLendon, Clifton Warner McLendon, and Thomas Simpson McLendon were also active in this convention and served as officers. His third wife Ida was among three women who led a lesson at the Chattahoochee Convention in 1902. She was remembered as a remarkable treble singer. Jackson McLendon was active in the United Sacred Harp Musical Association, and was a member of the editorial committee for the 1909 *Union Harp* (where A SISTER'S FAREWELL was first published) and the 1911 *Original Sacred Harp* (James revision). He died in Cleburne County, Alabama, where he was buried in Old Harmony Cemetery near Hopewell.

55 SISTER'S FAREWELL

McWHORTER, MILLARD FILLMORE, SR. (21 November 1858–16 March 1940), the son of Moses McWhorter (1824–58) and Mary A. McElroy (1833–1906), was a native of Georgia but came as a child to Cleburne County, Alabama; there he studied music with S. M. and T. J. Denson. He became a farmer, businessman, county commissioner, and sheriff, and was a singing teacher for fifty years. He was a member of Mars Hill Primitive Baptist Church. He married (1) Martha Jane Hayes (1861–1931) in 1877 and (2) Bertha B. Mills in 1932. He contributed four songs to the *Union Harp* (1909) and at least two to J. L. White's "fifth edition" of *The Sacred Harp* (1909); he had additional unpublished music, but this was lost after his death. He was buried at Mt. Paran cemetery, Cleburne County.

317 JACKSON

MEGGS, JAMES LLOYD (18 January 1833–14 October 1895), was born in Georgia, the son of Isaac Meggs and Anna Blankin. He moved to Jefferson County, Alabama, by 1858, when he married Vesta Waldrop; he appears as a farm laborer on the 1860 census for Hueytown, where he died. He was buried at Pleasant Ridge Cemetery. He collaborated with his next-door neighbor and brother-in-law Israel Mayfield in composing STILL BETTER for the 1870 appendix to *The Sacred Harp*.

166 STILL BETTER

MERCER, JOHN (October 1776–25 March 1852), was the son of James Mercer (1713–90) and Sarah Simmons. Born in at Kiokee, Columbia County, Georgia, he served as a colonel in the Creek wars in Alabama. He married Sarah Chivers in 1802 in Wilkes County. While living in Greene County he served as a trustee of a preparatory school in Penfield, which was later named Mercer University after his nephew, the Reverend Jesse Mercer. The latter was author of a hymnbook titled *The Cluster,* named on the title page of William Walker's *Southern Harmony* as a source of hymns for which the book provided music. In 1838 John Mercer married the widow Sarah Towns (née Greene) in Lee County and settled in Palmyra, where he was a deacon in the Baptist church. He died in Lee County and was buried in the cemetery of Palmyra Baptist Church. Colonel Mercer contributed a single tune to the 1850 appendix, making him one of the oldest composers of music first printed in *The Sacred Harp*. The name GREENSBOROUGH refers to the county seat of Greene County (now Greensboro).

289 GREENSBOROUGH

MERCER, THEODORE CHELTON, JR. (born 27 December 1946), was born in Chattanooga, Tennessee, the son of Theodore Chelton Mercer and Ora Alice Moore; he received his baccalaureate degree from Bryan College, Dayton, Tennessee, where he encountered a copy of *The Sacred Harp* in the library. After receiving the M.B.A. degree from the University of Chicago, Ted Mercer became a real estate broker in Chicago, Illinois. Introduced to Sacred Harp singing in 1983 by Philip Trier of Evanston, Illinois, he was instrumental in organizing and supporting singings throughout the Midwest: he chaired the first Midwest Convention in 1986 and the United Convention in 1990. In recent years, Mercer has collected more than two hundred tunebooks from the eighteenth and nineteenth centuries.

464 SHEPPARD

501 O'LEARY

MERRILL, DAVID (12 November 1768–31 January 1859), the son of Jacob Merrill and Elizabeth Wyatt, was born in Plymouth, New Hampshire. He married Sarah Lee in 1806 and settled in Holderness, New Hampshire, where he was a farmer. He is the likely author of *The Psalmodist's Best Companion* (Exeter, N.H., 1799), which included six of his compositions. An additional tune appeared in the second edition of Abraham Maxim's *Northern Harmony* (1808). Although there were other men of this name in New Hampshire, the names of tunes attributed to him (including GILMANTON, CLAREMONT, and VERMONT) suggest a resident of northern New Hampshire, and his proximity to Dartmouth College would provide an opportunity to meet Samuel Temple, with whom he collaborated on two tunes, including CLAREMONT.

245 CLAREMONT

MILLER, PRIESTLEY (5 September 1905–23 January 1969), was born in Huntingdon, Tennessee. In 1922, at the age of sixteen, he attended the Vaughan Music Normal School in Lawrenceburg and became a skilled song leader. He subsequently studied music at Belmont Conservatory and divinity at Vanderbilt School of Religion. Originally a Methodist, he later became a Presbyterian minister, serving as pastor of Harpeth Presbyterian Church from 1948 until his death. He was introduced to Sacred Harp singing by George Pullen Jackson and later founded the *Harpeth Valley Sacred Harp Newsletter*. In 1966 he chaired the United Convention. THE LAMB OF GOD, the brief anthem credited to him in the 1966 Denson revision, was actually composed by T. B. McGraw and dedicated to Miller in recognition of his service to Sacred Harp singing.

572 THE LAMB OF GOD

MONDAY, REUBIN, was a militia captain and singing teacher in Knox County, Tennessee. His tunes were published in Ananias Davisson's *Kentucky Harmony* (1816) and its *Supplement* (1820), and in William Moore's *Columbian Harmony* (1825). Davisson acknowledged his assistance in the compilation of the second edition of *Kentucky Harmony* (1817).

215 NEW TOPIA

MOORE, W. F. (ca. 1830–August 1898), lived in Cleburne County, Alabama, where he was the first president of the Tallapoosa Singing Convention in 1867 and was president again in 1873. He later moved to Texas; the *Cleburne New Era* of 10 August

1893 reported that he was then living in Alvarado, Texas and had recently visited Alabama. In Alvarado he served as an alderman and was a deacon in the Baptist Church. If he is the W. F. Moore who died of consumption at the age of sixty-eight and is listed in a 31 August 1898 obituary in the *Dallas Daily Times Herald*, he was born around 1830.

46 LET US SING [arranged]

176 RAGAN [arranged]

177 THE CHRISTIAN'S FLIGHT

301 GREENLAND

MOORE, WILLIAM, was a resident of Wilson County, Tennessee, in 1825, when he compiled *Columbian Harmony*. In this book Moore introduced his own compositions and arrangements, including THE CONVERTED THIEF, HOLY MANNA and SWEET RIVERS.

44 THE CONVERTED THIEF

59 HOLY MANNA

61 SWEET RIVERS

MOORS, HEZEKIAH (3 December 1775–1814), son of John Moors and Hannah Sawtel, was born in Shirley, Massachusetts. Around 1798 he moved to Mount Holly, Vermont, where he was a farmer and surveyor. He died in Union, New York. His *Province Harmony* (1809) contains only his own compositions and is the source of both the tunes by him in *The Sacred Harp*, which were added in the 1991 edition.

351 PITTSFORD

352 SWANTON

MORELLI is the presumed composer of a march tune well known to nineteenth-century fifers and published in several instrumental collections as "Morelli's Lesson" or "Lesson by Morelli." As a military fifer, B. F. White surely knew the tune at an early age; he arranged it for the 1850 appendix to *The Sacred Harp* as MURILLO'S LESSON.

358 MURILLO'S LESSON

MORGAN, JUSTIN (28 February 1747–22 March 1798), son of Isaac Morgan and Thankful Day, was born in West Springfield, Massachusetts. In 1774 he married his cousin Martha Day in Springfield, where he farmed, kept a tavern for boatmen on the Connecticut River, and served as tax collector. In 1788 he moved with his family to Randolph, Vermont, where he became a schoolteacher, singing teacher (in locations as far away as New York and Pennsylvania), farmer, tavern-keeper, town clerk, and owner of Figure, a stallion that became the progenitor of the Morgan horse breed. The composer was also known for his fine penmanship. He died of consumption and was buried in Randolph. Only nine of his pieces survive, but these include several acknowledged favorites.

151 Symphony

189 Montgomery

193 Huntington

391 Sounding Joy

MUNSON, AMOS (ca. 1774–5 January 1810), was born in Cheshire, Connecticut, the son of Peter Munson and Elizabeth Hall. Amos grew up in a musical family: his father was a drum major in the Revolutionary War, and two of his brothers played stringed instruments. His first cousin was the composer Eliakim Doolittle. Amos Munson died in New York City. Little is known about his life, but he and his brothers Reuben and Joel Munson contributed tunes to the books of Daniel Read and of Lewis and Thaddeus Seymour from 1793 to 1801.

182 Newburgh

NICHOLSON, WILLIAM, contributed four tunes or arrangements to *Supplement to the Kentucky Harmony* (1820). William Hauser, in *The Olive Leaf* (1878), possibly drawing on information from W. E. Chute, describes him thus: "Wm. Nicholson, of Va. and Ohio. Captured by the British at Fort Malden, in the War of 1812." A music manuscript from Adams County, Ohio, contains nine tunes attributed to Nicholson, some unpublished, suggesting activity in that region.

205 Pleasant Hill

OGLETREE, ABSALOM (25 October 1817–2 August 1910), was born in Wilkes County, Georgia, the son of Absalom Ogletree and Eleanor Grey. He should not be confused with his first cousin, the Reverend Absalom Ogletree (1811–61), also born in Wilkes County, who moved to Monroe County and was a founder of the Congregational Methodist Church. The singer married (1) Amanda G. Terry, and by 1842 had moved to Fayette County, where he came into contact with B. F. White and *The Sacred Harp*. His wife Amanda died in 1849 after bearing him two children. In 1851 he married (2) Martha A. E. Harper; in the same year, Spalding County was formed, where he appears on the 1860 census. Ogletree was a farmer in the Birdie community, a singing teacher, a Methodist, and a Mason. A close friend and pupil of B. F. White and J. R. Turner, Ogletree was Major White's right-hand man in all the revisions of the *Sacred Harp*, serving on revision committees in 1850, 1859, and 1869, as well as the committees for *Union Harp and History of Songs* (1909) and *Original Sacred Harp* (1911). He was an officer of the Southern and Chattahoochee conventions. Ogletree was buried at County Line Cemetery, Spalding County. A "very stout" man, he was remembered for leading CLAREMONT at the 1866 Chattahoochee Convention. According to J. S. James,

> He did so without looking in the book, either to sing the words or the notes, and he repeated the entire five pages of this long tune with perfect ease and with great satisfaction to the large concourse of people present and credit to himself, and while he was singing the words of the same his eyes flashed and his countenance changed several times and accented the words as he spoke them. Any one at a reasonable distance could hear him speak the words distinctly, and we have heard many people speak of the elegant and impressive manner with which he rendered this piece of music.

    108 THE TRAVELER [arranged]

    371 HEAVENLY DOVE [arranged]

OLIVER, HENRY KEMBLE (24 November 1800–10 August 1885), was born in Beverly, Massachusetts, the son of the Reverend Daniel Oliver and Elizabeth Kemble. A graduate of Dartmouth College, he became a schoolteacher, militia officer and mayor of Salem, and state treasurer. He died in Boston. An organist and choir director, he organized glee clubs and musical societies. His FEDERAL STREET, composed in 1832, was published in Lowell Mason's *Boston Academy Collection* (1836).

    515 FEDERAL STREET

OSBORNE, RICHARD RUSSELL (born 1824), the son of Yerby Osborne and Jane Ottwell, was raised in Troup County, Georgia. On 24 August 1845 he married (1) Julia Ann Heard (1830–51), sister of his brother's wife, in Troup County. James wrote that he belonged to the Southern Musical Convention and was "a very fine singer, so reported." He later moved to Alabama, where he became a dentist, and where he married (2) Pickens County native Rachel Ann Gore (born 1837). In 1860 he lived in Carrollton, Pickens County, when the house he rented was sold at public auction. He appears as a private on the muster roll of the 41st Alabama Volunteer Infantry, Company C (the Pickensville Grays) from 1862.

    324 NORTH PORT

PARKERSON, FRANCES EVA (ca. 1833–1904), was born in Georgia, probably in Wilkes County, the daughter of John Cook Parkerson and Amanda Shields. She appears with her family in the 1840 census for Monroe County and the 1850 census for Harris County. She married Jack Williams. According to J. S. James, Miss

Parkerson was a pupil of J. P. Reese, and a participant in the Southern Musical Convention. She later moved to Cleburne County, Alabama. She collaborated with Reese in arranging the tune NEVER TURN BACK, published in *The Organ* in the 1850s, and in the 1870 *Sacred Harp*.

> 378 NEVER TURN BACK "Arranged . . .
> by J. P. Rees & Miss F. E. Parkerson"

PARKS, WILLIAM WILLIAMSON (23 April 1823–1 December 1897), was born in Abbeville District, South Carolina, and married Martha Camp in Walton County, Georgia, in 1851. According to J. S. James, he was a member of the Chattahoochee and Southern conventions. With his fellow Walton County resident M. H. Thomas, he arranged A HOME IN HEAVEN for the 1859 appendix. Parks also composed ADORATION for *The Organ* in the 1850s; the tune was added to *The Sacred Harp* in 1870. He died in Hall County.

> 41 A HOME IN HEAVEN [arranged by]
> "W. W. Parks & M. H. Thomas"
>
> 138 ADORATION

PARRIS, HOSEA ANDERSON (14 June 1867–2 May 1954), was born in Paulding County, Georgia, the son of Nathan Parris and Sarah Elizabeth Wisner. He moved to Alabama at an early age, married Emily Isabelle Rhodes in 1888, and settled in Helicon, Winston County, where their numerous children were born, and where he died. He was a Baptist. His arrangement of CHRISTIAN'S HOPE was published in *Union Harp and History of Songs* (1909). James wrote that "none can be found who loves music better than Mr. Parris." He was buried at Liberty Baptist Church in Cullman County.

> 206 CHRISTIAN'S HOPE [arranged]

PARRIS, ORIN ADOLPHUS (26 December 1897–13 April 1966), singing teacher and music publisher, was the son of Oscar H. and Ada Ovelia Parris and a nephew of H. A. Parris. Born near Warrior, Jefferson County, Alabama, he moved as a young man to Winston County, where he married Mae Lewis on 28 September 1919 and appears in the 1920 and 1930 census. The couple had two sons and two daughters. He attended the Vaughn School of Music in Lawrenceburg, Tennessee. His teachers included major figures in Sacred Harp and gospel music: James D. Vaughan, S. M. Denson, C. A. Brock, J. D. Wall, Virgil O. Stamps, W. W. Combs, William Burton Walbert, and Adger M. Pace. He made Sacred Harp recordings in the 1930s and served as a member of the 1936 Denson revision committee. He edited a partial revision of William Walker's *Christian Harmony* in upright format in 1954, then collaborated with John Deason to complete the revision in oblong format in 1958. In 1997 he was posthumously inducted into the Southern Gospel Music Hall of Fame, which published the following sketch:

> A native of Jefferson County, Alabama, Oren A. Parris devoted his entire life to gospel music. A key figure in the publishing business, he studied music under the direction of James D. Vaughan and Adger M. Pace. In 1932, Parris founded the Parris Music Company in Jasper, Alabama, and, over the next 13 years, tackled such tasks as revising the original Sacred Harp and Christian Harmony songbooks. He also composed hundreds of gospel songs, including "When The Home Gates Swing Open," "A Happy Meeting," and "Hallelujah, I'm Going Home." In 1947, Parris joined the Stamps Quartet Music Company as the organization's southeastern office manager and served in that capacity for 15 years. Late in life, he also organized the Convention Music Company and served as that organization's president for three years.

> 349 A Cross for Me

> 377 Eternal Praise

> 454 The Better Land

> 546 My Brightest Days

PENICK, SPENCER REED (17 April 1803–1875), was born in Cumberland County, Virginia, the son of Nathan Hill Penick and Zilla Allen. He married Martha Augusta Booker in Prince Edward County, Virginia. He lived for a while in Talbot County, Georgia, but he appears on the 1850 census for Crawford County, and soon afterward settled in Houston County, where he was an officer of Perry Presbyterian Church in 1854, served as a magistrate, and appears on the 1860 census. He is referred to as "Judge S. R. Penick" in the minutes of an 1854 singing in Crawford County. He was a Mason. Penick taught music to J. P. Reese, and served as secretary of the Southern Musical Convention from 1851 to 1854. Penick's name appears on the roll of Georgia's 6th infantry regiment during the Civil War. He died in Houston County, where he was buried in Evergreen Cemetery, Perry.

> 275 Loving Kindness "By J. L. P. & S. R. Penick"

PICKARD, JAMES LAFAYETTE (1826–2 June 1863), was born in Hancock County, Georgia, the son of Robert Micajah Pickard and Sarah Barksdale. He lived in Talbot County, where he married Nancy Ann Haseltine Ross on 27 February 1849 and where he appears as a planter in the 1850 census. Pickard's sister, also named Nancy, was the mother of E. T. Pound. He later moved to Upson County, where he and his wife joined Good Hope Primitive Baptist Church on 19 August 1854. Described in *Baptist Biography* as "a prosperous planter and a noble specimen of the Christian gentleman," he appears as a farmer on the 1860 census for Upson County. His son William Lowndes Pickard (1861–1935), born in Upson County, became a Baptist minister and president of Mercer College. A member of the 32nd Georgia Infantry, J. L. Pickard died at the Confederate Hospital in Savannah during a measles epidemic, leaving behind five children; he was buried in Griggers Cemetery in Upson County. He collaborated with fellow Talbot County resident S. R. Penick on the song LOVING KINDNESS in the 1850 *Sacred Harp*: the book gives only the initials J.L.P. He contributed two songs to the 1859 edition.

275 LOVING KINDNESS "By J. L. P. & S. R. Penick"

425 GOLDEN STREETS

PILSBURY, AMOS (15 October 1772–19 October 1812), was the son of Samuel Pilsbury and Mary Hackett. A native of Newbury, Massachusetts, he lived in Charleston, South Carolina, where he was a silversmith, a schoolteacher, and a clerk in the Presbyterian church. He was the compiler of *United States Sacred Harmony* (1799), where his tune MORNING first appeared.

163 MORNING

PLEYEL, IGNAZ JOSEPH (18 June 1757–14 November 1831), was an Austrian composer, music publisher, and piano manufacturer. The son of a village schoolmaster, he studied composition with Franz Joseph Haydn and established himself in Strasbourg, where he became a renowned and prolific composer, producing forty-one symphonies and seventy string quartets. In 1795 he moved to Paris, where he was a music publisher and piano maker. He was buried in Père Lachaise Cemetery in Paris. The hymn tunes connected with his name were arranged from his instrumental works: PLEYEL'S HYMN (page 143) is based on the *Andante grazioso* of the Symphonie Concertante in E-Flat (Benton 111, 1786); PLEYEL'S HYMN (page 523) is based on the *Andante* from his String Quartet in G Major (Benton 349, 1788).

143 PLEYEL'S HYMN

523 PLEYEL'S HYMN

POUND, EDWIN THEOPHILUS (2 February 1833–24 June 1919), was born in Hancock County, Georgia. He grew up in Talbot County, where his parents, James William Pound and Nancy Pickard, were "substantial and influential citizens." He married Elizabeth Bloodworth in 1855 and settled in Pike (now Lamar) County, where he became a merchant, magistrate, singing teacher, and founder and editor of the Barnesville *Gazette*, later the *Pike County News*. In 1884 he began a musical journal titled *Musical Tidings*. He was a Methodist and a trustee of Gordon Institute (now Gordon College); he and his family also boarded young men and women from other communities who were attending Gordon. He died at his daughter's home in Shellman, Georgia, and was buried in Greenwood Cemetery, Barnesville. A pupil of B. F. White, he contributed THE CHRISTIAN'S NIGHTLY SONG to *The Organ* on 17 May 1854 and served on the 1859 *Sacred Harp* revision committee. As a leader of the Southern Musical Convention, Pound favored opening the convention to systems of musical notation other than the four patent notes; when this position was adopted around 1867, B. F. White and his followers withdrew; many joined the Chattahoochee Convention. Pound then assumed leadership of the Southern Musical Convention, and began to promote the use of seven-shape notation; he published several music books and developed a new system of musical notation. According to the author of a local history,

> Judge Pound was an ardent lover of music and a thorough musician and to the day of his death rejoiced in singing the good gospel songs. Many there are throughout the state who recall his devotion to the cause of music and his efforts in extending musical knowledge. While editor of The Gazette he wrote many editorials on music and questions of the day and in its early days published music in its columns which gave it a circulation in widely separated sections. . . . He was the author of several song books which had a wide popularity and large sale throughout the South, among them "Songs for All," "Gospel Voices" and "The Vocal Triad" 1 and 2.

413 THE LOVED ONES [arranged]

416 THE CHRISTIAN'S NIGHTLY SONG

POWER, WILLIAM THOMAS (26 November 1817–ca. 1864), son of Jesse Power and Esther Tuggle, was a singing teacher and, according to James, a member of the Southern and Chattahoochee musical conventions. He lived in Madison County, Georgia, where he is listed in the 1850 census as a "teacher of vocal music." He then moved to Elbert County, where he married Susan Mildred Oglesby on 25 November 1852. He contributed THE ROYAL BAND to the 1859 appendix of *The Sacred Harp* and may be the "Power" who in 1852 co-authored a tune with John G. McCurry printed in McCurry's *Social Harp* (1855). He died in Elbert County, Georgia, leaving his widow with small children.

360 THE ROYAL BAND

PRICE, F., may be identified with Frederick Freeman Price (10 October 1797–3 November 1851). Born in Rutherford County, North Carolina, the youngest child of John Ernest Price, a native of Wales, and Leanna Lively, he moved to South Carolina, where he appears on the 1820 and 1830 censuses for Spartanburg County; he married Elizabeth Potter Kennedy on 11 December 1824 in Union County,

South Carolina. Freeman Price contributed music to William Walker's *Southern Harmony* in 1835. He died in Greene County, Alabama.

    57 CHRISTIAN SOLDIER [arranged]

    74 KING OF PEACE [arranged]

    114 SAINT'S DELIGHT

RAIFORD, L. M., of Harris County, Georgia, has not been identified, though this surname was prominent in the area. He composed PROMISED DAY for the 1859 *Sacred Harp*. He was a member of the Southern Musical Convention.

    409 PROMISED DAY

RANDALL, BRUCE (born 2 November 1958), the son of Melvin Randall and Marilyn Johnson, was born in Haverhill, Massachusetts, where he has spent much of his adult life. He graduated from the University of Lowell (B.M. in music education, 1981), and established himself as a freelance professional musician, directing many ensembles, both vocal and instrumental. He plays the trombone, baritone, recorder, and serpent. Bruce first heard Sacred Harp singing in 1982; he is a member of Norumbega Harmony and a pioneer in the performance of English West Gallery music (Georgian psalmody) in the United States. He has composed more than four thousand pieces of vocal music, and is the author of *Valley Harmony* (1993), containing a sampling of his compositions.

    474 MOUNT DESERT

RANDALL, JOHN (26 February 1717–18 March 1790), was an organist, choral director, and composer. Trained as a chorister in the Chapel Royal, he studied at Cambridge, where he held several positions as organist and took the degrees of bachelor and doctor of music; he held the music professorship from 1755. He married Grace Pattison on 5 October 1756. John Randall published his collection of psalm and hymn tunes in 1794.

    287 CAMBRIDGE

READ, DANIEL (16 November 1757–4 December 1836), son of Daniel Read and Mary White, was born in Rehoboth, Massachusetts (now Attleboro), where he grew up on a farm with little formal schooling, but was composing music as early as 1774. In 1782 he settled in New Haven, Connecticut, where he married Jerusha Sherman in 1785; he died in New Haven and was buried in Grove Street Cemetery. Read was a comb-maker, general merchant, and singing teacher, naming his oldest son George Frederick Handel Read. He published several tunebooks, including *The American Singing-Book* (1785), and is regarded as one of the greatest early American composers. He composed little after 1800, and seems to have taken to heart the criticism of the early American idiom, which, he wrote, "has had its day and is gone."

38 WINTER

38 WINDHAM

50 MORTALITY

78 STAFFORD

107 RUSSIA

150 AMITY

183 GREENWICH

186 SHERBURNE

280 WESTFORD

300 CALVARY

467 LISBON

REDDING, LOYD RICHARD (13 October 1915–13 November 1985), of Bremen, Georgia, was a tailor and merchant, as well as a singing school teacher who frequently keyed the music at singings in West Georgia. He chaired the Chattahoochee Convention in 1960–61 and 1978 and the United Convention in 1968. He was buried at Holly Springs Cemetery.

470 THE MERCY SEAT

REESE, HENRY SMITH (23 November 1828–11 November 1922) (plate 8), was born in Jasper County, Georgia, one of twin sons of the Reverend James Reese and Rebecca Smith. Like many of his contemporaries, he lacked formal education, never having more than "six months' training in an old-field school." Ordained to the Baptist ministry in 1853 by the Columbus Association, he preached for sixty-seven years, serving churches in Talbot, Harris, Meriwether, Heard, and Fayette Counties before settling in Turin, Coweta County. During the Civil War he served the civilian population as a medical assistant. After the war he helped African Americans to organize Baptist churches and associations. He was a Mason. He married (1) Almeda Brawner in 1857, with whom he had one daughter, and (2) Martha Jane Leavell, widow of Dr. Lewis Brooks, in 1865, with whom he had seven children. He contributed to the *Newnan Herald and Advertiser* under the name "R.A.T." (Round About Turin) and contributed tunes to *The Organ*, including HUMBLE PENITENT, on 28 June 1856. He was buried in Tranquil Cemetery, Turin. According to *Baptist Biography* (1920), "He was a teacher of singing, and a composer of a number of songs, both of the words and the music, in the 'Sacred Harp' and other song books."

156 JESUS ROSE

278 TRAVELING PILGRIM

285 LAND OF REST

359 THE BRIDE'S FAREWELL

398 THE DYING BOY

400 STRUGGLE ON

401 CUBA "J. H. Bolen and H. S. Rees"

412 NEW HOSANNA [arranged]

419 MELANCHOLY DAY

421 SWEET MORNING

428 WORLD UNKNOWN

REESE, JOHN PALMER (23 November 1828–13 May 1900), the twin brother of H. S. Reese, was born in Jasper County, lived in Columbus, Georgia, during the 1850s, and finally settled in Coweta County in 1855, in a location two miles north of Newnan. "Squire Reese" was a farmer, a tax collector, and a member of the Masonic fraternity. He married Elizabeth Mosley and was the father of ten children. A pupil of S. R. Penick, he taught singing schools for more than thirty years in Georgia and Alabama. As early as 1855 he was contributing tunes to *The Organ,* including YOUTH WILL SOON BE GONE on 6 June 1855 and CELESTIAL LIGHT on 31 October 1855. He was a member of the 1859 revision committee and longtime president of the Chattahoochee Convention. He lost his library and music manuscripts in a fire at his home. He contributed to E. T. Pound's *Barnesville Gazette* under the name "Rubin" and to the *Newnan Herald and Advertiser* under the name "Ripples." He died of pneumonia and was buried with Masonic honors in Oak Hill Cemetery, Newnan. During the Civil War Reese served in Company I of the 37th Georgia Infantry. Like B. F. White, he was a student of the "freaks of nature": while composing WEEPING PILGRIM outdoors, he troubled over the last tenor note in the 3/4 section until he heard the lowing of a cow in a nearby field; he then incorporated this note into his composition. His obituary in the *Herald and Advertiser,* 18 May 1900, states

> He was devoted to the art of song, and enjoyed a wide reputation as a vocalist, having served for several years as president of the Chattahoochee Musical Association. He had probably presided over more singing conventions than any

man in Georgia. He took part in these meetings, not for amusement, but in a sprit of earnest worship, and was never happier than when leading an exercise of this character.

He contributed four tunes to *The New Sacred Harp* (1884).

    39 SHARPSBURG "By J. P. Rees and J. A. T. Shell"

    69 FAREWELL TO ALL

    97 WE'LL SOON BE THERE "Alto by J. P. Rees"

    108 WEEPING SINNERS

    132 SINNER'S FRIEND

    274 THE GOLDEN HARP

    321 NEWNAN

    343 HAPPY HOME

    345 JESUS IS MY FRIEND

    375 LOVE THE LORD

    378 NEVER TURN BACK "Arranged . . . by
       J. P. Rees & Miss F. E. Parkerson"

    383 ETERNAL DAY "Music original, by J. P. Rees"

    385 FIGHT ON (Original)

    385 CAN I LEAVE YOU? [original]

    404 YOUTH WILL SOON BE GONE [original]

    408 WEEPING MARY

    417 WEEPING PILGRIM

    423 GRANTVILLE

    424 SWEET UNION

    434 FILLMORE "For the Organ, by John P. Rees."

    482 MULBERRY GROVE

    567 THE GREAT DAY "As sung by
       Judge Falkerner, of Ala."

REEVES, ROBERT H. (born ca. 1847), was born in Fayette County, Georgia, the son of William Reeves and Martha Ann Black. In May 1864, still a teenager, he enlisted in the First Georgia Reserves at Andersonville when they were mustered into active duty for the defense of Atlanta. According to James, R. H. Reeves belonged to the Chattahoochee Convention from 1867 to 1869; he arranged LOVER OF THE LORD for the 1870 appendix to *The Sacred Harp*.

    124 LOVER OF THE LORD

RICH, A. The tune A HOME IN HEAVEN, printed in William Hunter's *Select Melodies* (1843), is attributed to A. Rich, where it is "used by permission," suggesting that it had previously been published. The composer is otherwise unknown. In the 1859 appendix to *The Sacred Harp,* the tune is arranged by W. W. Parks and M. H. Thomas.

41 A HOME IN HEAVEN

ROLLO, JOHN HALL (25 May 1774–29 September 1847), was born in Hebron, Connecticut, the son of William Rollo and Lucy Hall. In 1795 he married Philomela Trumbull in Hebron. Around 1798, after the birth of their first child, they moved to central New York, where their remaining children were born. He died in Summer Hill, Cayuga County, New York. John Hall Rollo is the likely composer of the tunes attributed to "Rollo": REPENTANCE in Griswold and Skinner's *Connecticut Harmony* [1796], two tunes in Ephraim Reed's *Musical Monitor* (Ithaca, N.Y., 1820), and an arrangement in J. Leavitt, *The Christian Lyre* (New York, 1830).

214 REPENTANCE

ROUSSEAU, JEAN-JACQUES (28 June 1712–2 July 1778), Enlightenment philosopher, composer, and music critic, was born in Geneva to Isaac Rousseau and Suzanne Bernard. He was associated with Diderot's *Encyclopédie,* for which he wrote articles on musical subjects. His musical ideas, like his philosophy, showed Enlightenment ideals and were highly controversial. He died on a morning walk near Paris; sixteen years later, his remains were moved to the Panthéon in Paris. One of Rousseau's most successful musical works was the pastoral comic opera *Le Devin du Village* (1752). Among the instrumental dances in this work is a rustic gavotte. J. B. Cramer (1771–1858) arranged this air as *"Rousseau's Dream: An Air, with Variations for the Piano-forte."* Lowell Mason adapted the piano piece as a hymn tune. William Hauser recounts a fanciful anecdote to explain the name:

> This poor French infidel fell asleep one day, and dreamed that he was taken to heaven, where he saw the angels of God standing about the throne, and heard them singing this tune. As soon as he awoke, being a musician, he wrote down the tune. Hence it ought always to be called 'Rousseau's Dream.'

145 SWEET AFFLICTION

RUSSELL, HENRY (24 December 1812–8 December 1900), English composer, pianist, and singer, was born in Sheerness, Kent, on the Isle of Sheppey, to a distinguished Jewish family. He studied in Italy with Gioachino Rossini and Vincenzo Bellini, then traveled in 1834 to Canada and the United States, where he settled in Rochester, New York, as organist of the First Presbyterian Church. At the same time he established a career as a concert artist, singing his own sentimental and dramatic songs while accompanying himself on the piano. He returned to England about 1845. He died in London. Among his best-known songs are "Woodman, spare that tree," "The Maniac," "The Gambler's Wife," and "Wind of the Winter Night." The last of these, composed and dedicated to the Rochester Academy of Sacred Music in 1836, was arranged by George Coles as THOU ART PASSING AWAY.

231 THOU ART PASSING AWAY

SEARCY, JOHN SMITH (20 March 1820–13 April 1896), son of William and Sarah Searcy, was born in Milledgeville, Georgia, at that time the state capital. He was educated at Oglethorpe College in Milledgeville, and moved with his parents to Talbot County, where he continued his education for three years at the Collinsworth Institute. He also attended Mercer College, but did not graduate. He was a farmer (holding fifty-two slaves in 1860) and a Missionary Baptist preacher, and is listed in the 1850 and 1860 Talbot censuses. He officiated at the third marriage of Leonard P. Breedlove. He married Martha Jane Thweatt (1824–1900). He died in Prattsburg; his obituary was published in the 21 April 1896 *Butler Herald* (Taylor County). He may be plausibly identified with the Searcy who collaborated with B. F. White in arranging the music for LOVING JESUS in the 1850 *Sacred Harp*, a *contrafactum* of a glee by Felice Giardini.

361 LOVING JESUS

SHELL, JOHN ABNER ZACCHEUS (16 January 1829–7 May 1918), was the son of I. M. Shell Sr. and Mary Wright. He spent his life in Coweta County, Georgia, making his home at Standing Rock, near Senoia. He married (1) Emily Carr Cole in 1855 and (2) Sarah Ann Drewry in 1867. He fought in the Civil War and was severely wounded at Chancellorsville. He was a Royal Arch Mason. He was buried in Tranquil Cemetery near Turin, Georgia. John Shell collaborated with J. P. Reese on the tune SHARPSBURG in the 1870 *Sacred Harp*, where his name is given as "J. A. T. Shell."

His brother, Ivey Isham Malone Shell (1826–1906), born in Newberry County, South Carolina, moved with his parents a year after his birth to the newly settled Coweta County. He was a notable singing instructor, teaching regularly from 1847 to 1879 in Georgia and Alabama, and an active member and officer of the Chattahoochee Convention for more than ten years. Ivey M. Shell died at Turin and is buried in Tranquil Cemetery. His tune WARNERVILLE, also in the 1870 *Sacred Harp*, was deleted from the Denson revision. He also contributed a tune to the seven-shape *New Sacred Harp* (1884).

39 SHARPSBURG "By J. P. Rees and J. A. T. Shell"

SHEPPARD, WILLIAM JEFFERSON (born 11 September 1930), was born in Tifton, Georgia, the youngest of nine children of Frank Sheppard and Ellen Henley. He grew up in Opelika, Alabama, and served in the Korean War. After retirement in 1976 from a long career with Sears, Roebuck and Company, he opened a shipping business in Anniston. He attended a singing school of T. J. Denson in Ashland, Alabama, as a small child, but was trained in music by his father and has taught numerous singing schools. In 1955 he married Shelbie Cates, also a singing teacher. Jeff Sheppard was a member of the music committee for the 1991 revision and a founder of the Sacred Harp Musical Heritage Association.

    303 HEAVENLY LAND

SHERMAN, P., is known only as the composer of seventeen tunes in Daniel Peck's *Musical Medley* (1808). Philo Sherman (16 June 1787–20 April 1875) is a possible candidate. The son of Lewis Sherman and Sarah Glover, he was born in Newtown, Connecticut, also the home of Daniel Peck, who was slightly older. He married Phoebe Masters in 1808 and moved in 1822 to Wakeman Township, Huron County, Ohio. In 1854 he sold his farm and moved to nearby Berlin Heights, Erie County, where he died.

    181 EXIT

    187 PROTECTION

    202 NEW LEBANON

SHUMWAY, NEHEMIAH (26 August 1761–July 1843), was a farmer and schoolteacher. Born in Oxford, Massachusetts, to Amos Shumway and Ruth Parker, he graduated from the College of Rhode Island (now Brown University) in 1790. He became principal of an academy in Freehold, New Jersey, where he married Sarah Tice in 1795. He moved to Albany, Schenectady, and Jefferson Counties, New York, where he farmed for a while. Losing his farm through a legal technicality, he returned to Freehold, where he died. He published *American Harmony* (Philadelphia, 1793) and later contributed tunes to *The Easy Instructor*, the book that introduced the four patent notes. In addition to the tunes listed below, Ananias Davisson attributes to him NEW JORDAN (page 442), one of the most remarkable tunes in *The Sacred Harp*. While Davisson's attributions are not always accurate, this is at least plausible, as the tune was first published in an 1815 edition of *The Easy Instructor*.

    192 SCHENECTADY

    217 BALLSTOWN

SIKES, MATTHEW (2 February 1825–September 1900), the son of Matthew Guilford Sikes and Sarah Wood, was born in Houston County, Georgia. He married Jeanette Bone on 1 January 1846 in Bibb County, but later lived in Montgomery County, where he lived when he contributed the song PENICK to the 1859 *Sacred Harp.* According to H. S. Reese, he taught music and was a member of the Southern Musical Convention. He may be the Mr. Sikes who raised questions of musical theory that B. F. White answered in *The Organ* of 25 April 1855.

387 PENICK

SMITH, ISAAC (ca. 1734–14 December 1805), a London linen-draper, was clerk (song leader) at Alie Street Baptist Meeting House in the East End of London. He published *A Collection of Psalm Tunes in Three Parts* around 1780. He died in Walworth, Surrey (now London).

311 SILVER STREET

SMITH, TONEY E., (born 21 September 1927), was born in Fayette County, Alabama, the youngest of six children of Earl T. Smith and Myrtie Mosley. After serving in the United States Army, he married Lavoy Stokes in 1948 and settled in Tuscaloosa, where he worked as a barber until his retirement in 1989. He began singing at age four, and was taught music by his father and by his brother V. P. Smith; both were pupils of T. J. Denson. He later attended schools of Hugh McGraw, Bennie Keeton, and Rupert Yarbrough. He was a member of the music committee for the 1991 edition.

278 LOVE SHALL NEVER DIE

SPARK, JAMES A., is listed as collaborator with R. F. M. Mann on the song MESSIAH'S PRAISE, claimed as "original" in the 1870 *Sacred Harp.*

394 THE MESSIAH'S PRAISE "By R. F. M. Mann
and Jas. A. Spark"

STEPHENSON, JOSEPH (1723–19 July 1810), was a singing-master of Poole, Dorset, England. In 1766 he succeeded his father as clerk of the Unitarian meeting, where he served for forty-five years and, according to his monument, "manifested a steady attachment to the cause of Religious Liberty, the right of Private Judgment, and the practice of Rational Religion." The third edition of his *Church Harmony* was published in 1760. His fuging tunes served as a model for the music of Edson, Read, Jenks, and other American composers.

273 MILFORD

STONE, JOSEPH (20 March 1758–2 February 1837), was born in Worcester, Massachusetts, the son of Jonathan Stone and Ruth Livermore. During the Revolutionary War he served in the defense of Dorchester Heights in 1776. Some time after his marriage in 1779 to Hannah Nichols he settled in Ward (now Auburn), near Worcester, where he was a schoolteacher, surveyor, and bookbinder. He also served as town clerk, constable, and assessor and as a delegate to the General Court (legislature). Although Stone composed hundreds of psalm tunes and anthems, and left behind many compositions in manuscript, only fifty-five of his tunes were published between 1786 and 1800. In 1793, he and Abraham Wood published *The Columbian Harmony.* His fuging tune GRAFTON, under another title, was credited to another composer in the Cooper revision of the *Sacred Harp;* this tune was subsequently rearranged by A. A. Blocker for the 1960 appendix to the Denson revision.

528 SHOWERS OF BLESSINGS

SUMNER, JAZANIAH (1753–20 August 1835), son of John Sumner and Temperance Crane, was born and died in Taunton, Massachusetts. He married (1) Abigail Carver and (2) Joanna Fuller. Sumner was remembered as "a noble hearted, unpretending, patriotic man; a deacon of the [Congregational] church, who loved his country more than his political party." He wrote both the words and the music of "Ode on Science" for the opening of Bristol Academy, Taunton, in 1798, dedicating the piece to Simeon Daggett, then principal of the academy. In his letter to Daggett, Sumner refers to composing "this small piece of music, together with the lines."

242 ODE ON SCIENCE

SWAN, TIMOTHY (23 July 1758–23 July 1842), born in Worcester, Massachusetts, was a hatter, merchant, poet, and composer. A fifer in the Revolutionary War, he settled in Suffield, Connecticut, where he married Mary Gay in 1784 and remained until 1807; he later moved to Northfield, Massachusetts, where he died. After contributing several popular tunes to others' collections, he published his own *New England Harmony* in 1801. He also published a collection of secular duets around 1786. He had an unusual melodic gift; his CHINA was a favorite at New England funerals for several generations. RAINBOW, BRISTOL and POLAND were printed in Oliver Brownson's *Select Harmony* (1785). CHINA, though composed as early as 1790, was not printed until 1801.

86 POLAND

163 CHINA

344 RAINBOW

468 BRISTOL

TABER, PHILIP A. (14 June 1932–21 March 2005), was an engineer and taxi driver who lived in Alabama, Michigan, Tennessee, and New York. He died in Lookout Mountain, Tennessee. He was an avid collector of music books. Around 1960 he prepared a facsimile reprint of *The New Harp of Columbia* for East Tennessee singers. He submitted versions of two tunes to the 1991 edition of *The Sacred Harp* that vary considerably from the originals: Jarman's NATIVITY has the original fuging section removed, and the treble and alto of Swan's RAINBOW have been altered or exchanged in several places.

344 RAINBOW [arranged]

350 NATIVITY [arranged]

TEMPLE, SAMUEL (23 May 1770–19 September 1816), was the oldest child of Hananiah Temple and Elizabeth Learned. His birthplace is unknown, but he grew up in Orange, Franklin County, Massachusetts. A graduate of Dartmouth College, he settled in Lower Mills, Dorchester, Massachusetts, where he kept a store and taught school. He married Phebe Mann. He was the author of a popular schoolbook titled *A Concise Introduction to Practical Arithmetic* (1803). He died in Randolph, Massachusetts, and was buried in Oakland Cemetery. Temple collaborated with David Merrill in composing two pieces in Merrill's *Psalmodist's Best Companion* (1799), including the long and difficult ode CLAREMONT.

245 CLAREMONT

TERRY, JOHN STRINGER (11 January 1826–23 October 1886), singing teacher, was born in Edgefield District, South Carolina, the son of Stephen Clement Terry and Elizabeth Strom. He married Mary "Polly" Cockcroft in Pike County, Alabama, in 1845; he later lived in Covington County, Alabama, where he was listed in the 1860 census as a "teacher of vocal music." He served in the 18th Alabama Infantry, Company B. The family moved to Texas in 1875 and settled in Hill County in 1880. He died at Covington, Hill County. His son William Harrison Terry (born 1848) was also a musician.

37 ESTER

119 HEAVEN'S MY HOME "Dr. R. H. Davis
   and J. S. Terry"

403 HEAVENLY REST

THOMAS, M. H., and W. W. Parks arranged A HOME IN HEAVEN for the 1859 appendix to *The Sacred Harp*. An M. H. Thomas married Elizabeth J. Mitchell in

Walton County in 1856; he is likely the composer, since his collaborator Parks also lived in Walton County.

41 HOME IN HEAVEN [arranged by]
"W. W. Parks & M. H. Thomas"

TURNER, JAMES R. (8 November 1807–14 October 1874), was born in Hancock County, Georgia, but spent most of his life north of Villa Rica, Georgia. He married Mary Ann Stevens. He was a Methodist, a Master Mason, and a renowned singing teacher. He and his son W. S. Turner composed a great deal of unpublished music, but the manuscripts were lost after his death. He was a member of the revision committee for the 1850 *Sacred Harp*. He was vice president of the Southern Musical Convention during the period 1851–62, and was associated with the Chattahoochee Convention from its beginning in 1852 until his death, serving as chairman from 1865 to 1870 and in 1873. He was buried at Wesley Chapel near Villa Rica. His pupil J. S. James recalled:

> In leading music he never took his book or opened it. Every page and tune was perfectly familiar to him, and he rendered the music by notes as well as the words, called the pages, names of songs and sang them, keeping correct time without reference to the book.

270 CONFIDENCE

TURNER, M. H., lived in Coweta County, Georgia, and was a member of the Southern and Chattahoochee musical conventions during the 1850s. According to J. S. James, he taught music in Coweta County, and married and died there. He is listed in the 1850 census for Campbell County, which adjoined Coweta. A Mason, his name appears in an 1854 list of members of Haralson Lodge in Coweta County. WHEN I AM GONE was published in the 1850 appendix to *The Sacred Harp*. A possible identification is Memory Horatio Turner (1 December 1820–15 October 1860), son of Samuel Turner and Mahala Johnson Chapman, born in Roebuck, Spartanburg District, South Carolina, who "removed to Georgia," where he married Adaline Parsons. He moved to Rusk County, Texas, where he and Adaline appear on the 1860 census and where he died. He was buried in New Prospect Cemetery. A Martin H. Turner, born 7 December 1815, is another possible candidate.

339 WHEN I AM GONE [arranged]

TURNER, WILLIAM STEVENS (22 February 1835–12 March 1891), the son of J. R. Turner, was a farmer and Methodist minister. Born in Georgia, probably in Villa Rica, he married Martha Adelaide Harris and had several children; after 1877 he moved to Orange County, Florida, where he appears on the 1880 census, then moved to Fort Valley, Georgia, where he died and was buried in Oaklawn Cemetery. James reports that Turner wrote CONSECRATION in 1866 at Dark Corner Academy, in Douglas County, where it was sung the next day by his father's singing school.

370 MONROE

390 NEW PROSPECT

448 CONSECRATION

WADE, J. A. AND J. F., contributed, separately and together, a total of ten songs, most dated 1853 or 1854, to John G. McCurry's *Social Harp* (1855). J. S. James believed that they lived in South Carolina, although a James Adrian Clive Wade (17 October 1823–30 November 1886) was a resident of Hart County, Georgia, and a near contemporary of McCurry, as well as a direct ancestor of U.S. senator John Edwards of North Carolina (born 1953).

70 SAVE, MIGHTY LORD

WAKEFIELD, SAMUEL (6 March 1799–13 September 1895), was born in Path Valley, Cumberland County, Pennsylvania (now Perry County), the son of Irish-born Thomas Wakefield and Elizabeth Morton. At the age of fourteen he served as a drummer in the War of 1812. He showed musical talent at an early age, which he applied to playing the fiddle at local dances. He experienced religious conversion at a Methodist meeting in 1819; when he joined the church, an old lady cried out, "Thank God, the devil has lost his fiddler." He entered the ministry in 1820 and married Elizabeth Hough in 1821. During his many years in the ministry in western Pennsylvania, Wakefield was a tailor, singing teacher, state legislator, and a Mason. When he died in West Newton, Pennsylvania, at the age of ninety-six, he had 117 living descendants, including two great-great-grandchildren. His obituary states:

> He had a marked musical ability, and published nine books of music. He was also the author of "Wakefield's Theology," a recognized authority in the Methodist church. He built the first pipe organ west of the mountains, and it is now in Wakefield chapel at Uniontown. Until he was 80 years old he made all his own clothes, and even at the age of 75 he shod the horses on his place. When he was 90 years old he shingled the roof of his porch unaided. He was also an authority on horticulture, and introduced into this section of the State some of the choices[t] fruits that are seen in the farm and orchards.

He published several collections of sacred music in four shaped notes beginning in 1821, including *The Minstrel of Zion* (1845), containing settings of hymns by the

Reverend William Hunter of Pittsburgh. FATHERLAND was added to the 1870 appendix of *The Sacred Harp.* PRAY, BRETHREN, PRAY, which appears without attribution in the *Minstrel,* also appeared in the 1870 appendix, attributed to "Zion Minstrel," with a treble part credited to U. G. Wood.

    449 FATHERLAND

WALKER, WILLIAM (6 May 1809–24 September 1875), was born near the Tyger River in Union County, South Carolina, the son of Abraham Absalom Walker and Susannah Jackson. He grew up on Fairforest Creek and moved, with his parents, to Cedar Spring, near Spartanburg, about 1827. He began teaching singing schools around 1830. In 1832 he married Amy Shands Golightly (1811–98, sister of B. F. White's wife Thurza) and moved to Spartanburg, where he operated a bookstore. He taught singing schools and published four books, including the very successful *Southern Harmony and Musical Companion* (1835) and *Christian Harmony* (1867). He is buried in Magnolia Cemetery in Spartanburg. His tombstone reads:

> In Memory of Wm Walker A.S.H. [Author, Southern Harmony] Died Sept. 24, 1875 in the 67th year of his age. He was devoted Husband & kind Father. A consistent Baptist 47 years, Taught music 45 years. The Author of 4 books of sacred music. He rests from his labors. He died in the triumphs of faith.

Walker's compositions and arrangements are often melodic in every part and are models of dispersed composition; many are arrangements of songs in the oral tradition, as he acknowledged in the preface to *The Southern Harmony:*

> I have composed the parts to a great many good airs, (which I could not find in any publication, nor in manuscript,) and assigned my name as the author. I have also composed several tunes wholly, and inserted them in this work, which also bear my name. (iii)

    35 SAINTS BOUND FOR HEAVEN "by J. King
      and W. Walker"

    53 JERUSALEM [arranged]

    62 PARTING HAND [arranged]

    57 CHRISTIAN SOLDIER "Alto by William Walker"

    65 SWEET PROSPECT [arranged]

    129 HEAVENLY ARMOR

    130 MILLENNIUM

    134 THE CHRISTIAN'S HOPE

    141 COMPLAINER

145 WARRENTON "Alto by William Walker"

146 HALLELUJAH

149 THE TRUMPET "Treble and Alto
by William Walker"

161 SWEET HOME "Alto and Treble
by William Walker"

196 ALABAMA "Counter by William Walker"

207 LOUISIANA

213 THE GOOD OLD WAY

410 MUTUAL LOVE

WALLACE, CHARLENE (born 17 April 1929), was born in Mandeville, Georgia, the youngest of eleven children of Walter E. Wallace (1881–1969) and Maude Adeline Holcombe. Her sister Gladys Wallace was the wife of Buford McGraw. A textile worker at Arrow Shirt, and a lifelong singer, she was instructed in music by A. M. Cagle, E.I . McGuire, George D. Phillips, H. N. McGraw, Loyd Redding, and Hugh McGraw. For many years she has been caretaker of Holly Springs Church, an important location for Sacred Harp singing.

77 HOLCOMBE

WALLER, THOMAS, (ca. 1832-June 1862), son of Delaware native Joseph Waller and Mary Dent, was born in Upson County, Georgia. On 24 January 1856 he married Nancy Stephens. The couple had three children, two appearing in 1860 census records. On 11 May 1861 he enlisted in the Georgia Volunteer Infantry, Fifth Regiment, Company K, known as the "Upson Guards." He was promoted to sergeant in 1862, but took sick in the evacuation of Corinth, Mississippi, and died of dysentery at Okalona in June of that year. After his death his children attended the "poor school" in Upson County from 1866 to 1871. According to James he was "a good teacher, and about 30 years old when he died." In April 1854 he is mentioned along with H. S. Reese and E. T. Pound in the minutes of a "teachers' meeting" preceding the Southern Musical Convention in Marion County. He was a member of the 1859 revision committee and contributed one tune to that revision. LOVE DIVINE was first published in *The Organ* in the 1850s; it entered *The Sacred Harp* with the fourth edition of 1870.

30 LOVE DIVINE

WATSON, JOHN A., of Alabama, wrote PASSING AWAY in December 1872 for the 1873 edition of Walker's *Christian Harmony*. He may have been one of three John Watsons who lived in southeastern Alabama: John A. Watson (born 1808, of Henry County), John Watson (born 1826, of Henry or Barbour County), and John A. Watson (born 1851, of Barbour County).

445 PASSING AWAY

WEBSTER, JOSEPH PHILBRICK (22 March 1819–18 January 1875), was born in New Hampshire and settled in Elkhorn, Wisconsin; he was a pupil of Lowell Mason and George J. Webb. Joseph P. Webster was a music teacher, choir director, professional songwriter, and piano salesman. He composed some four hundred sacred and secular songs, but is best known for "In the Sweet By and By." With his wife Joanna he had four children, named Joseph Haydn Webster, Louis Beethoven Webster, Frederick Handel Webster, and Mary Webster. He was buried in Hazel Ridge Cemetery in Elkhorn. MARY'S GRIEF AND JOY (page 451) was arranged from his popular ballad "Zula Zong," published in 1860.

451 MARY'S GRIEF AND JOY
    "Arranged by B.F. White"

WELLS, LEE SCOTT (15 August 1887–February 1972), born in South Carolina, was a farmer, coal miner, and sawmill operator in Jasper, Alabama, and was instructed in music by T. J. Denson. He married Jeffie Burrow. In 1930 he traveled to New York as the leader of a group of seven singers who recorded Sacred Harp songs for the American Record Company; the other singers were Solon Hulsey, Grady Laramore, Mr. and Mrs. Dewey McCullar, Mrs. Sarah Wells Brom, and Miss Lois Wells. According to the *Jasper Daily Mountain Eagle*, "A representative of the recording company told Mr. Wells that he and his party sang better than any other party taken to New York to sing for the company. Every member of the party had a good time." His tune THE DYING FRIEND was published in the Denson revision of 1936.

399 THE DYING FRIEND

WEST, ELISHA (25 April 1756–after 1808), was born in North Yarmouth, Massachusetts (District of Maine). Around 1791 he settled in Woodstock, Vermont, where he was a farmer, carpenter, and singing teacher. He contributed tunes to the books of others and published his own *Musical Concert* in 1802. The year of his death is unknown. SHARON was printed in Nehemiah Shumway, *American Harmony* (1793), and EDOM was printed in Oliver Brownson, *A New Collection of Sacred Harmony* (1797).

200 EDOM

212 SHARON

WETMORE, TRUMAN SPENCER (12 August 1774–21 July 1861), the son of Abel Wetmore and Jerusha Hills, was born in Winchester, Litchfield County, Connecticut. As a young man he served as a chorister (song leader) in the local Congregational church. He married (1) Sylvia Spencer in October 1799; when she died a few months after their marriage, he took her surname as his own middle name. He then sought medical training in Torrington, Connecticut, and Albany, New York, where he also taught singing schools. After receiving his medical diploma, he set up his practice in Charlotte, Vermont, where he married (2) Elizabeth Jarvis in 1804. They returned to Winchester the following year, where their children were born, and where Wetmore continued his medical practice until 1850. He was buried in Winchester Cemetery. Local historian John Boyd recalled him as

> a well-read and successful physician of the old school, a poet of local celebrity, a musical composer (some of his tunes still being retained in the worship of the churches), a man of genial humor and tender feelings, and a chronicler of olden times.

Wetmore was a Mason, and he wrote a Masonic piece titled WESTERN STAR ANTHEM. He prepared a manuscript book called "Republican Harmony," containing his tunes and those of others, but only a few of his tunes were published, mostly by Stephen Jenks. According to his biographer,

> while sick with small pox, and pronounced by his physicians past recovery, his young friends, who were confined with him in what was termed the *pest house*, informed him he could not live, and desired him to compose a piece of music to be sung at his funeral. He consented, if they would furnish him with the *staves*, and turn him on his face. They did so, and the result was the piece called *Florida*, which is sung to this day, in all the places of Methodist worship, and also his entire recovery.

FLORIDA was published by Jenks in 1803.

36 AMERICA

203 FLORIDA

WHITE, BENJAMIN FRANKLIN (20 September 1800–5 December 1879), was the senior compiler of *The Sacred Harp*. The twelfth child of Robert and Mildred White, he was born near Cross Keys, Union County, South Carolina. After the death of his mother in 1807, he was raised by his older brother, Robert White Jr. According to family tradition, he attended only three brief summer terms of school and was self-taught in music. At the age of twelve, he volunteered as a fifer in the War of 1812; with his father's permission he served under Colonel Elijah Dawkins from April 1813 until December 1814. After the war he probably served in the South Carolina militia, as he was listed as "Captain." After his marriage in 1825 to Thurza Melvina Golightly, he moved to Spartanburg, where the couple were members of Cedar Springs Baptist Church. In 1833 Thurza's sister Amy Golightly married William Walker, who published his *Southern Harmony* in 1835. James claimed that White collaborated with William Walker on *The Southern Harmony* but was not given proper credit: only a single tune is attributed to him in that book. The consequent conflict is cited as a reason for White's move to Georgia. There is also evidence of a dispute involving Walker and White in 1839–41 over a commercial property near Spartanburg.

In 1842, B.F. White and his family moved to Harris County, Georgia, where he purchased a farm in Whitesburg. He was appointed a major in the Georgia militia in 1848. In the early 1850s he moved to Hamilton, where he became a prominent citizen, serving as clerk of the inferior court and as "superintendant" of a newspaper, *The Organ;* he was a member of the Masonic lodge in Hamilton. There is evidence that he may have boarded students in the Hamilton Female Seminary, including Sarah Lancaster. During the Civil War he helped train the local militia and was elected mayor of Hamilton. After the publication of *The Sacred Harp* in 1844, he helped organize the Southern Musical Convention (1845), which he served as president for twenty years, and the Chattahoochee Convention (1852). He supervised the revision of *The Sacred Harp* in 1850, 1959, and 1869. He retired to DeKalb County, Georgia, and was working on a fourth edition when he died in Atlanta following a fall on the street. On his deathbed, he sang, "plainly and distinctly," Justin Morgan's tune SOUNDING JOY (page 391). He is buried in Oakland Cemetery, Atlanta; his monument contains a sculpture of a Sacred Harp songbook. He was a lifelong Baptist. James wrote that Major White often taught music without charge to poor pupils. In a eulogy printed in the minutes of the Chattahoochee Convention, the author (probably J. P. Reese) wrote:

> Maj. White was never more at home than when surrounded with a band of sweet singers, especially when they seemed to have melody in their hearts as well as hosannas on their tongues. He was spirited and never failed to animate all whom he lead [*sic*], whether in church, social, school, or conventional gatherings. All were naturally drawn to him as he discoursed upon music and its charms.

68 ORTONVILLE "Arranged by B. F. White"

74 THE ENQUIRER

76 DESIRE FOR PIETY

80 SHOUTING SONG

81 BEACH SPRING

83 VALE OF SORROW

85 THE MORNING TRUMPET

88 DONE WITH THE WORLD

90 LOOK OUT

92 BURK

96 FEW HAPPY MATCHES [arranged]
    White and King

101 HOLY CITY

120 CHAMBERS [arranged from Holyoke]

133 HEBREW CHILDREN [arranged]

154 REST FOR THE WEARY
    "Original arrangement"

232 BAPTISMAL ANTHEM

323 SOFT MUSIC [arranged]

333 FAMILY CIRCLE "Rev. R. E. Brown &
    B. F. White"

341 THE LONE PILGRIM [arranged]

355 ANTHEM ON THE SAVIOR

361 LOVING JESUS [arranged] "White and Searcy"

369 SEND A BLESSING "B. F. White &
    L. L. Leadbeater"

376 HELP ME TO SING

388 THE HAPPY SAILOR [arranged]

451 MARY'S GRIEF AND JOY "Arranged by
    B. F. White"

496 THE ROCK THAT IS HIGHER THAN I
    "Arranged by B. F. W."

513 JOYFUL [arranged] "Treble by E. J. King"

565 THE HILL OF ZION "Original"

WHITE, BENJAMIN FRANKLIN, JR. "FRANK" (1 January 1845–8 January 1921),
son of B. F. White and Thurza Golightly, was born in Harris County, Georgia;
he lived in DeKalb County, Georgia, where he served as justice of the peace. He
also farmed in Gwinett County, where he appears in the 1880 census. A Methodist and a bass singer, he published *The New Sacred Harp* in 1884, along with his
brother, James Landrum White.

431 NEW BETHANY

WHITE, DAVID PATILLO (October 1828–23 October 1903), was born in Spartanburg, South Carolina, son of B. F. White and Thurza Golightly. At the age of twenty-one he is listed in the 1850 census as a music teacher, living with his parents; in that year he contributed five tunes to the 1850 appendix to *The Sacred Harp*. Soon after this time he visited southern Alabama with his father; he remained there and on 16 December 1852 married Celeste V. Brown, daughter of Reuben E. Brown, in Barbour County; they had ten children. The Whites settled in Henry County, where they are listed in the 1860 census. He later moved to Polk and then Cherokee County, Texas, where he was a farmer and justice of the peace. David and Celeste White were members of Mount Selman Baptist Church in Cherokee County. He served as secretary of the Central Texas Musical Convention in 1875. He died in Texas.

56 COLUMBIANA

271 RESTORATION

346 THE AMERICAN STAR [arranged]

362 NORWICH [arranged]

WHITE, JAMES LANDRUM (22 January 1847–8 March 1925), was the youngest son of B. F. White and Thurza Golightly. Born and raised in Harris County, Georgia, he spent most of his life in the Atlanta area as a farmer and singing teacher. He married Melinda Clark; they had four children. He died in Decatur and was buried in Ebenezer Cemetery. While he respected and took pride in his father's achievements, he repeatedly attempted, with mixed success, to modernize *The Sacred Harp* to make it more appealing to later generations of singers. According to J. S. James, White was active, though uncredited, in the 1870 revision of the *Sacred Harp*, the last produced during his father's lifetime, to which he contributed the tune EVENING. Next, J. L. White was co-compiler (with B. F. White Jr.) of *The New Sacred Harp* (1884), printed in seven shapes. He later published *The Sacred Harp*, fifth edition (two separate issues, 1909 and 1910); when these were not widely accepted by singers, he reissued in 1911 his father's *Sacred Harp*, fourth edition. This contained alterations and a supplement, drawn from his fifth edition, containing many modern gospel songs. This edition achieved some currency in parts of Georgia, Alabama, and Mississippi; it is still used in the Atlanta area and was reissued (2008) in a newly typeset edition. Professor White was a founder and the first president of the United Sacred Harp Musical Association in 1905, but he split with that group in 1911 when it adopted the *Original Sacred Harp* (the James edition).

WHITE, JESSE THOMAS (27 May 1821–28 July 1894), the son of Robert White Jr., was a nephew of B. F. White. Born in South Carolina, he may have moved to Georgia around 1840, when he requested a letter of dismission from Cedar Springs Baptist Church in Spartanburg County, South Carolina. Tom White married Caroline Penelope Ethridge and moved around 1850 to Mississippi, where he was clerk of Winston County. Around 1860 he moved to Smith County, Texas, where he farmed, ran a mill, and later operated a hotel in Tyler; he served as justice of the peace (1883) and was a member of the Masonic fraternity. He died at Mt. Pleasant, Titus County, at the home of his daughter; he and his wife were buried in the Masonic cemetery. While he lived in Georgia, he contributed ten songs to the first edition of *The Sacred Harp* (1844).

72 THE WEARY SOUL

82 EDGEFIELD [arranged]

89 THE CHURCH'S DESOLATION

122 ALL IS WELL [arranged]

WILLIAMS, AARON (1731–76) was probably born at Caldicot, Monmouthshire, Wales, the son of William Morgan. He was a London singing teacher, engraver, and music publisher who served as clerk of Scots Church, London Wall. He published several books of sacred music between 1763 and 1778. His *Universal Psalmodist* (1763) was reprinted in Newburyport, Massachusetts, before the American Revolution. The tune we know as ST. THOMAS was first published in *The Psalm-Singer's Help* (ca. 1769) by Thomas Knib.

34 ST. THOMAS

WILLIAMS, E. F., was a Georgia singer and a member of the Southern and Chattahoochee conventions. He contributed two tunes to the 1870 *Sacred Harp*.

458 FRIENDSHIP

WILLIAMS, J., has not been identified. He contributed THE TRUMPET to Josiah Leavitt's *Christian Lyre* (1831).

149 THE TRUMPET "Treble and Alto
    by William Walker"

WILLIAMS, WILLIAM LAFAYETTE (November 1833–21 September 1905), the eldest son of William Wesley Williams and Hester Minerva Fannin, was born in Georgia but raised in Chambers County, Alabama. On 21 July 1858 he married Henrietta Adeline Floyd in Tallapoosa County, where he is listed as a physician in the 1870 census. In 1880 Dr. Williams lived in Roanoke, Randolph County. Some time after this he retired to Texas, where several of his children had settled. He died at Gilmer, Upshur County. William L. Williams contributed several tunes to the 1850 and 1859 editions of the *Sacred Harp* and at least one tune to the Barnesville *Weekly Gazette* in 1869.

319 RELIGION IS A FORTUNE

335 RETURN AGAIN

429 CHRISTIAN'S DELIGHT [arranged]

WILSON, HUGH (1766–14 August 1824), shoemaker, schoolteacher, engineer, and sundial-maker, was a precentor (song leader) in the Scottish Seceder church. This melody of SACRED THRONE (page 569), credited to him in 1827, had been published earlier, and may be a traditional air. It was arranged by Hugh McGraw for the 1966 Denson revision.

569 SACRED THRONE

WILSON, JOHN (5 April 1595–22 February 1674), was an English singer, lutenist, and songwriter. Born at Faversham, Kent, he moved to London at an early age; he was active in the theatre and composed songs for the King's Men (William Shakespeare's theatrical company) during the years 1614–29. He was a member of the London waits (city musicians) and served Charles I as a court musician from 1635. On 10 March 1644 he took the doctorate in music at Oxford; he spent the years of the Commonwealth in Churchill, Oxfordshire. In 1656 he was named professor of music at Oxford, where he was known for his wit and musical skill. At the restoration of the monarchy Wilson resigned his professorship in 1661 to rejoin the court as a lutenist and gentleman of the Chapel Royal. He died at Westminster and was buried in the cloister of Westminster Abbey. He wrote more than two hundred songs, including sacred and dramatic songs and settings of Latin odes. Richard DeLong adapted the melody of CORLEY from the song "From the fair Lavinian shore," published in Wilson's *Cheerful Ayres or Ballads* (Oxford, 1660). In *The Seraph* (London, 1818) the melody appears as a hymn setting with the text "Hark, the herald angels sing."

510 CORLEY "Arr. Richard L. DeLong"

WOOD, ABRAHAM (30 July 1752–6 August 1804), the son of Samuel Wood and Kezia Moore, was born in Northborough, Massachusetts, where his father was a cloth merchant, and where he spent most of his life. A fuller by trade, he married Lydia Johnson in 1773; they had thirteen children. Wood was a drummer in the American Revolution, and in 1781 was appointed a captain in the militia. A Congregationalist, he was chorister (music director) for thirty-two years in his native town. He died at his home at the age of fifty-two. Along with William Billings, Captain Wood was one of the first American composers. His tunes were published by others as early as 1778, but his own publications were issued in the years 1789–1800; these include *The Columbian Harmony* (1793), with Joseph Stone. A manuscript of his tunes (twenty-six of them unpublished) is in the Northborough Historical Society. WORCESTER, in Andrew Law's *Select Harmony* (1778), was his first published tune.

195 WORCESTER

228 MARLBOROUGH

WOOD, FRANCIS C. (ca. 1824–after 1860), was born in Georgia. He moved to Chambers County, Alabama, where he married Evelina S. Webb in 1846 and appears in the 1850 and 1860 census. He was a blacksmith. According to J. S. James, he "was killed by a falling tree or limb," but it is not certain whether this anecdote refers to this Wood or to U. G. Wood, below.

277 ANTIOCH

WOOD, U. G., composed the treble part of PRAY, BRETHREN, PRAY in the 1870 appendix to *The Sacred Harp*.

167 PRAY, BRETHREN, PRAY
  "Treble by U. G. Wood"

WOODARD, THOMAS PICKENS (23 March 1888–23 December 1964), the son of Berry Newton Woodard and Jefferson Cutura Chappell, was born at Bowden, Georgia. A farmer, brickmason, and singing teacher, he moved with his family to Alabama at an early age. In 1910 he married Martha Elizabeth Dowda in Cullman County and settled at Helicon, Winston County, where he appears in the 1920 census. He was buried at Liberty Cemetery, Helicon. He wrote SOLDIER'S DELIGHT on 3 July 1918 to words by his brother, Clark Odis Woodard (1892–1965), but this fine minor tune was not published until it appeared in the 1960 appendix to the Denson revision.

487 SOLDIER'S DELIGHT

WOODBURY, ISAAC BAKER (23 October 1819–26 October 1858), was born in Beverly, Essex County, Massachusetts, the son of Isaac Woodbury and Nancy Baker. After studying music in London and Paris, he settled in Boston and New York as a church organist, teacher, editor, and writer; he founded the National Musical Convention as a training institute for music teachers. He published some fifteen sacred tunebooks and fourteen books of secular songs and school music. He suffered from tuberculosis and died in Charleston, South Carolina, on a trip to restore his health. His "Be kind to the loved ones at home," published around 1847, is the basis for E.T. Pound's arrangement, called THE LOVED ONES.

    413 THE LOVED ONES

WOOTTEN, TERRY (born 16 November 1954), the son of J. C. Wootten and Myrtle Kennamer, is a farmer, merchant, and singing teacher of Ider, Alabama. He married Sheila Rosser. A skilled singer and teacher, the tune attributed to him in *The Sacred Harp* was composed by Raymond Hamrick and credited to Terry Wootten in recognition of his dedicated service to Sacred Harp singing and his participation on the music committee for the 1991 revision.

    461 SHINING STAR

WRIGHT, GLEN (born 4 May 1962), is the son of David Wright and Rita McFarland. Born and raised in Natick, Massachusetts, he attended Colby College (B.A. 1984) and the University of Maine at Orono (M.M. in choral conducting, 1988). On 19 September 1992 he married Susan Mampre; they have one daughter. Introduced to the Sacred Harp by his mother, who heard it at a folk festival, he joined Norumbega Harmony. He currently lives in Rutland, Massachusetts, where he teaches music in an elementary school. Glen and Susan are avid gardeners, growing much of their family's food. Together they compiled and published *The Sacred Harper's Companion* in 1993.

    497 NATICK

WRIGHT, MARGARET JOHNSON (8 August 1918–19 March 1998), daughter of Dr. Ben Howard Johnson and Sarah Garner Beesley, was a music professor and organist. A graduate of Vanderbilt and the George Peabody College for Teachers, she taught from 1947 to 1977 at Middle Tennessee State University, Murfreesburo, where her husband, Neil H. Wright, was also a music professor and was chairman of the music department. She and her husband also raised and trained show horses. She founded the MTSU Sacred Harp Singers in 1947. JACOB'S VISION, printed in the 1960 appendix to the Denson revision, is based on a carol of the same name in an English collection, *Carols New and Old* (1871). The tune is a variant of MIDDLEBURY in the 1844 *Sacred Harp*.

    551 JACOB'S VISION

WYNN, MATTHEW MARK (15 June 1835–after 1897), the son of Sloman Wynn (sometimes spelled Wynne) and Mahala Camp, was born in Franklin County, Georgia, but grew up in Carroll County, where his parents are buried at Concord Methodist Church. He showed intellectual ability at an early age: at nineteen he was elected the first secretary of the Chattahoochee Convention in 1854. He also served in 1856 and 1865–66 and drafted that body's constitution following the 1866 session. He was a member of the Villa Rica Masonic Lodge. On 25 September 1859 he married Sarah Carolyn Garrison, daughter of Dr. Lovick Pierce Garrison of Carroll County.

About 1867 Mark Wynn moved to Texas, where he farmed and taught school, while remaining active and highly mobile as a singing teacher. He was secretary of the East Texas Singing Convention in 1869 and appears, with his growing family, in the 1870 census for Hunt County and the 1880 census for Hopkins County. From 1875 to 1877 he paid taxes on livestock in Camp County; in 1878 he was in Leesburg, Camp County, teaching in *The Temple Star* (1877), a seven-shape tunebook by Aldine S. Kieffer. In 1883 he was teaching school in Ladonia, Fannin County; from 1892 to 1897 he was living further west, in Brownville, Brown County, where he edited a newspaper, *Living Issues*. No trace of him has been found after this date. A photograph of him in middle age (plate 9) bears the imprint of a studio in Wolfe City, Hunt County, where his son S. L. Wynne was buried. The songs of Mark Wynn were first published in the 1870 edition of *The Sacred Harp* after his move to Texas. He also contributed a piece titled WHAT SHALL I DO in 1873 to *The Musical Million,* a Virginia periodical that promoted shape-notes.

    118 STOCKWOOD

    224 SAVE, LORD, OR WE PERISH

    263 DODDRIDGE

    450 ELDER

YATES, WILLIS ALVIN (1 December 1869–6 September 1950) was born in Villa Rica, Georgia, the son of Spartanburg, South Carolina, native Joel Pinkney Yates and Martha Jane Stewart. He married Octavia Moon in 1895 and settled some time after 1906 in Walker County, Alabama; he died at Jasper. He taught singing schools in Georgia as early as 1892 and remained active after his move to Alabama. He presided at the Walker County courthouse singing in 1928 and composed HEAVENLY HOME for the 1936 Denson revision.

    286 HEAVENLY HOME

SACRED HARP COMPOSERS, ARRANGED BY BIRTH DATE

The following table lists only those who contributed directly to *The Sacred Harp*, 1844–70 editions, to *Original Sacred Harp* (James edition, 1911, or Denson revisions, 1936–87), or to *The Sacred Harp*, 1991 edition.

· · ·

October 1776	John Mercer
about 1794	Reuben Ellis Brown
20 September 1800	Benjamin Franklin White
17 April 1803	Spencer Reed Penick
about 1803	Leonard P. Breedlove
8 November 1807	James R. Turner
15 February 1810	Edmund Dumas
1811	S. M. Brown
25 January 1812	Elphrey Heritage
about 1812	Israel Mayfield
7 July 1814	Zachariah Chambless
1816	James M.
26 October 1816	Richard F. M. Mann
12 September 1817	Lewis L. Ledbetter
25 October 1817	Absalom Ogletree
26 November 1817	William Thomas Power
8 March 1820	Oliver S. Bradfield
20 March 1820	John Smith Searcy
27 May 1821	Jesse Thomas White

1821	Elisha James King
22 December 1822	Thomas W. Carter
23 April 1823	William Williamson Parks
1824	Robert Henry Davis
1824	Richard Russell Osborne
about 1824	Francis C. Wood
2 February 1825	Matthew Sikes
11 January 1826	John Stringer Terry
13 April 1826	Shadrack P. Barnett
1826	James Lafayette Pickard
about 1827	Reuben Ellis Brown Jr.
about 1828	Jeremiah Troup Edmonds
11 March 1828	Elias Lafayette King
October 1828	David Patillo White
23 November 1828	Henry Smith Reese
23 November 1828	John Palmer Reese
16 January 1829	John Abner Zaccheus Shell
about 1830	W. F. Moore
about 1831	Cynthia Bass
about 1832	Thomas Waller
18 February 1832	Anna Lucinda Maria Atkinson Lancaster
18 January 1833	James Lloyd Meggs
2 February 1833	Edwin Theophilus Pound
15 April 1833	Calvin Ford Letson
about 1833	Frances Eva Parkerson
November 1833	William Lafayette Williams
28 April 1834	Sarah Lancaster
22 February 1835	William Stevens Turner
15 June 1835	Matthew Mark Wynn
23 December 1836	Melissa Ann Hendon
14 July 1838	Priscilla R. Lancaster
9 November 1838	James D. Arnold
21 August 1843	Henry Goodwin Mann
1 January 1845	Benjamin Franklin White Jr.
25 March 1845	Willis Dallas Jones
about 1847	Robert H. Reeves
March 1849	Jackson C. Brown
20 March 1849	Joseph Stephen James
30 May 1849	Burwell Stephen Aikin
25 March 1853	Augustus Jackson McLendon

11 October 1853	Sidney Seward Burdette Denson
9 April 1854	Seaborn McDaniel Denson
21 November 1858	Millard Fillmore McWhorter Sr.
21 February 1860	George Byron Daniell
7 January 1861	Amanda Symington Burdette Denson
20 January 1863	Thomas Jackson Denson
23 October 1863	Benjamin Edward Cunningham
14 June 1867	Hosea Anderson Parris
1 December 1869	Willis Alvin Yates
1 January 1875	John Marion Dye
5 March 1879	Otto Erastus Handley
4 February 1882	George Sebron Doss
4 March 1882	Lee Andrew McGraw
8 October 1882	Paine W. Denson
16 August 1883	Remus Adolphus Canant
18 November 1883	Henry Newton McGraw
5 October 1884	Alfred Marcus Cagle
17 March 1885	Anna Eugenia Denson Aaron
27 April 1885	Oscar Huston Frederick
9 January 1886	Abraham Allen Blocker
4 July 1887	Margaret Frances Denson Cagle
15 August 1887	Lee Scott Wells
23 March 1888	Thomas Pickens Woodard
23 December 1888	Henry Martin Blackmon
25 February 1890	Sidney Whitfield Denson
15 July 1890	Thomas Beatrice McGraw
12 August 1892	Robert E. Denson
12 April 1893	Floyd Monroe Frederick
3 July 1893	Jarusha Henrietta Denson Edwards
4 August 1897	Howard Burdette Denson
26 December 1897	Orin Adolphus Parris
11 September 1898	Palmer Godsey
17 November 1898	Cecil Houston Gilliland
25 December 1898	Jesse Monroe Denton
28 February 1905	James Adrian Ayers
5 September 1905	Priestley Miller
16 January 1906	Elbert Foy Frederick
1 February 1906	Doris Winn DeLong
14 February 1906	Harvey Roy Avery
21 September 1908	Susie Irene Kitchens Parker Denson

about 1910	Eula Denson Johnson
25 March 1911	Thomas Buford McGraw
16 June 1912	Elder James Elmer Kitchens
6 December 1912	Owel W. Denson
14 June 1915	Raymond Cooper Hamrick
13 October 1915	Loyd Richard Redding
28 February 1916	John Tilmon Hocutt
21 July 1917	Edgar Leon McGraw
8 August 1918	Margaret Johnson Wright
21 September 1927	Toney E. Smith
6 August 1928	Theodore Wallace Johnson
1 March 1929	Joyce Darlene Rape Harrison
17 April 1929	Charlene Wallace
11 September 1930	William J. Sheppard
20 February 1931	Hugh Winfred McGraw
1 April 1932	David Russell Grant
14 June 1932	Philip A. Taber
11 August 1943	Judy Hauff
21 January 1944	Frank Neely Bruce
16 April 1946	Philip Daniel Brittain
27 December 1946	Theodore Chelton Mercer Jr.
16 November 1954	Terry Wootten
3 August 1955	James P. Carnes
15 August 1955	David Ivey
2 November 1958	Bruce Randall
11 August 1959	Timothy Randall Gilmore
4 May 1962	Glen Wright
28 February 1963	Richard Lee DeLong

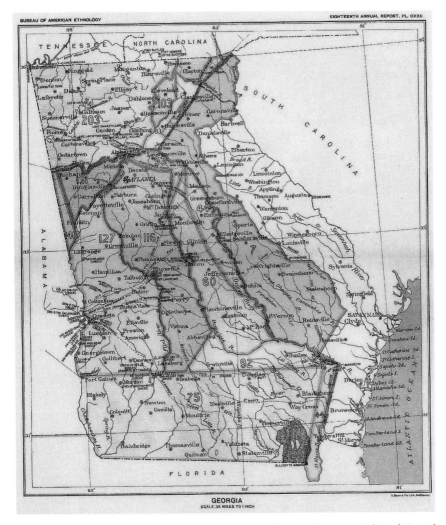

GEORGIA
SCALE, 35 MILES TO 1 INCH

1. "Georgia," in Charles C. Royce, *Indian Land Cessions in the United States*, in *Eighteenth Annual Report of the Bureau of American Ethnology to the Secretary of the Smithsonian Institution*, 1896–97, plate 122. The Creek cessions of 24 January 1826 are marked 127 and 131. Library of Congress, Geography and Map Division.

2. Detail from Samuel Augustus Mitchell, *A New Map of Georgia* (Philadelphia: Thomas, Cowperthwait, & Co., 1850). Courtesy of Birmingham, Alabama, Public Library Cartography Collection.

3. Thomas and Amanda Denson as newlyweds, with Amanda's parents, William H. and Julia Ann Burdette, 1878. Photograph courtesy of Michael Hinton.

4. Hugh McGraw. Photograph courtesy of Hugh McGraw.

5. "American Methodists proceeding to their camp meeting." One of fifty-four plates issued
to illustrate Jacques Gérard Milbert, *Itinéraire Pittoresque du Fleuve Hudson et des parties
latérales de l'Amérique du Nord, d'après les dessins originaux pris sur les lieux* (Paris, 1828–29),
"Pub. as the Act Directs March 1, 1829." Note that the participants are marching (in step) and
probably singing. Richard H. Hulan collection.

6. Elder John Leland.
Anonymous portrait, oil
on wood. Courtesy of
the Berkshire Museum,
Pittsfield, Massachusetts,
USA.

7. Elder Edmund Dumas.
Photograph courtesy of
Chloe Webb.

8. Reverend Henry Smith Reese.
Photograph courtesy of
Blake Adcock.

9. Matthew Mark Wynn.
Photograph courtesy of
Brad Preston.

10. Elder Joseph Thomas, the
"White Pilgrim." Portrait by
William Hillyer, 1835, donated by
Thomas's descendants to Elon
University. Photograph courtesy
of Belk Library Archives and
Special Collections, Elon
University, Elon, N.C.

PART FOUR

THE SONGS

THE SONGS OF THE
SACRED HARP

The following entries supply information about sources and attributions for words and music. Where the verses printed in *The Sacred Harp* are not at the beginning of the hymn, an effort has been made to specify the verse numbers in the original. The standard meter designations L.M., C.M., and S.M. indicate iambic meters. L.M. differs from 8888 (or 8s) in that the latter is anapestic, for example, "How tédious and tásteless the hóurs." H.M. represents the iambic meter 6666.4444 or occasionally 6666.88. X, Y, and Z indicate lines of 10, 11 and 12 syllables, respectively. Meter designations do not include recurrent refrains. Tunes first printed in *The Sacred Harp*, 1991 edition are marked with an asterisk. Attributions of alto parts dated 1902 are from *The Sacred Harp, Revised and Improved by W. M. Cooper* (1902).

· · ·

26　Samaria. L.M.D.
　　Words: Isaac Watts, 1719, Psalm 62.
　　Music: Maggie Denson Cagle, 1936; named for her mother-in-law,
　　Samaria Duke Cagle.

27　Bethel. C.M.
　　Words: William Cowper, 1772.
　　Music: Anonymous, in *The Sacred Harp*, 1844. Appears as Red Hill and
　　as Bethelsdorf in Hauser, *Hesperian Harp*, 1848; William Hauser, in *The
　　Olive Leaf*, 1878, dates his arrangement of Red Hill to 1841, implying that
　　the melody existed before that date.

28T AYLESBURY. S.M.
Words: Isaac Watts, 1719, Psalm 48, part 2.
Music: In John Chetham, *A Book of Psalmody*, [1717].

28B WELLS. L.M.
Words: Isaac Watts, 1709, Hymn 88, book 1.
Music: Israel Holdroyd, in *The Spiritual Man's Companion*, [1722].

29T FAIRFIELD. C.M.
Words: Edmund Jones, in Rippon, *Selection*, 1787.
Music: Hitchcock, in Law, *Rudiments of Music*, 1791.

29B TRIBULATION. C.M.
Words: Isaac Watts, 1707, Hymn 52, book 2.
Music: *Patterson's Church Music*, 1813. The tune is mentioned in a March 1812 letter of Lucius Chapin to Andrew Law as having been popular in Kentucky since about 1800; it may be by Amzi Chapin.

30T LOVE DIVINE. 8787.
Words: Charles Wesley, 1747.
Music: Thomas Waller, "Original. For the Organ," in *The Sacred Harp*, 1870 (p. 330); alto by S. M. Denson, 1911.

30B PROSPECT. L.M.
Words: Isaac Watts, 1707, Hymn 31, book 2.
Music: Graham, in Walker, *Southern Harmony*, 1835.

31T NINETY-THIRD PSALM. S.M.
Words: Philip Doddridge, 1755.
Music: Lucius Chapin, as BRENTFORD, in *A Collection of Tunes*, 1812; a variant of DELAY, in Ingalls, *Christian Harmony*, 1805.

31B WEBSTER. S.M.
Words: Isaac Watts, 1707, Hymn 30, book 2, altered.
Music: In Walker, *Southern Harmony*, 1835; a variant of NEW HOPE, in Davisson, *Supplement to the Kentucky Harmony*, 1820.

32T CORINTH. L.M.
Words: Joseph Grigg, 1765.
Music: John Massengale, in *The Sacred Harp*, 1844.

32B DISTRESS. L.M.
Words: Anne Steele, 1760.
Music: *Southern Harmony*, 1835.

33T WEEPING SAVIOR. S.M.
Words: Benjamin Beddome, in Rippon, *Selection*, 1787.
Music: E. J. King, in *The Sacred Harp*, 1844.

33B ABBEVILLE. S.M.
Words: Benjamin Beddome, in Rippon, *Selection*, 10th ed., 1800.
Music: E. J. King, 1844, a variant of THIRTIETH PSALM in *Patterson's
Church Music*, 1813, elsewhere attributed to Chapin, but itself a variant of
THE GENERAL DOOM in Ingalls, *Christian Harmony*, 1805. Alto after W. M.
Cooper, 1902.

34T THE GOSPEL POOL. S.M.
Words: John Newton, 1779.
Music: Edward Dumas, "Original," in *The Sacred Harp*, 1870 (p. 444).

34B ST. THOMAS. S.M.
Words: Isaac Watts, 1719, Psalm 95.
Music: Aaron Williams, in *The Psalm-Singer's Help*, [ca. 1769].

35 SAINTS BOUND FOR HEAVEN. P.M. [6663]
Words: "Original" in Elliott, *Sacred Lyre*, 1828.
Music: J. King and William Walker in *Southern Harmony*, 1840 appendix;
alto (i.e., second treble) by S. M. Denson, 1911.

36T AMERICA. S.M.
Words: Isaac Watts, 1719, Psalm 103, part 2.
Music: Truman S. Wetmore, in Benham, *Social Harmony*, 1798.

36B NINETY-FIFTH. C.M.
Words: Isaac Watts, 1707, Hymn 65, book 2.
Music: *Patterson's Church Music*, 1813; sometimes attributed to Colton or
Chapin. It is mentioned by Lucius Chapin as popular in Kentucky since
1800 in an 1812 letter to Andrew Law.

37T ESTER. L.M.
Words: *The Religious Telescope*, Feb. 2, 1842, "To the memory of Miss
Maria Roush, Bloom County, Kentucky."
Music: John S. Terry, 1869, in *The Sacred Harp*, 1870 (p. 437).

37B LIVERPOOL. C.M.
Words: In Hall, *A New collection of the most approved Hymns and Spiritual
Songs*, 1804.
Music: [Arranged by] M. C. H. Davis, in Walker, *Southern Harmony*, 1835; a
variant of BENEVOLENCE in Boyd, *Virginia Sacred Musical Repository*, 1818.

38T   WINTER. C.M.
Words: Isaac Watts, 1719, Psalm 147, verses 5 and 7.
Music: Daniel Read, in *The American Singing Book,* 1785.

38B   WINDHAM. L.M.
Words: Isaac Watts, 1709, Hymn 158, book 2.
Music: Daniel Read, in *The American Singing Book,* 1785; named for
Windham, Connecticut.

39T   DETROIT. C.M.
Words: Philip Doddridge, 1755.
Music: [Arranged by William] Bradshaw, in Davisson, *Supplement to the
Kentucky Harmony,* 1820. Previously printed without attribution in Lewis,
Beauties of Harmony, 1818.

39B   SHARPSBURG. C.M.
Words: Philip Doddridge, 1755.
Music: J. P. Reese and J. A. Z. Shell, 1869, in *The Sacred Harp,* 1870 (p.
440); alto by S. M. Denson, 1911; named for Sharpsburg, Coweta County,
Georgia.

40   LENOX. H.M.
Words: Charles Wesley, in *Hymns for New Year's Day,* 1750.
Music: Lewis Edson, in Jocelin, *Chorister's Companion,* 1782; named for
Lenox, Berkshire County, Massachusetts.

41   HOME IN HEAVEN. 9.X.9.X.
Words: William Hunter, in *Select Melodies,* 1843.
Music: As A HOME IN HEAVEN, W. W. Parks and M. H. Thomas, in
The Sacred Harp, 1870 (p. 411); arranged from A. Rich, in Hunter, *Select
Melodies,* 1843; alto by S. M. Denson, 1911.

42   CLAMANDA. L.M.
Words: In Mintz, *Collection of Hymns and Spiritual Songs,* 1806; attributed
to [John Poage] Campbell in Cleland, *Evangelical Hymns,* 2d ed., 1828.
Music: In Davisson, *Supplement to the Kentucky Harmony,* 1820; from an
eighteenth-century song tune; as "The Freemason's Farewell," in Bellamy
MS, Connecticut, ca. 1799, and elsewhere.

43   PRIMROSE HILL. C.M.
Words: Isaac Watts, 1707, Hymn 65, book 2.
Music: Anonymous, in *The Sacred Harp,* 1844; from a song tune, "On
Primrose Hill there dwelt a lass"; in Jenks, *Jovial Songster,* 1806, and

elsewhere. Another variant is Dudley, in Walker, *Southern Harmony*, 1840 appendix.

44   The Converted Thief. C.M.D.
      Words: Samuel Stennett, in Rippon, *Selection*, 1787.
      Music: William Moore, in *Columbian Harmony*, 1825. Alto in Walker, *Christian Harmony*, 1867.

45T   New Britain. C.M.
      Words: John Newton, 1779.
      Music: Anonymous, in Walker, *Southern Harmony*, 1835; a variant of Gallaher, in Shaw and Spilman, *Columbian Harmony*, 1829. Alto after Hauser, *Hesperian Harp*, 1848.

45B   Imandra New. YYYY.
      Words: In Mead, *General Selection*, 1807.
      Music: Anonymous in Walker, *Southern Harmony*, 1835. Alto after Walker, *Christian Harmony*, 1867.

46   Let Us Sing. P.M.
      Words: W. F. Moore, 1867.
      Music: "Words and Music arranged by W. F. Moore, March 3, 1867," in *The Sacred Harp*, 1870 (p. 461); arranged from Let Us Walk in the Light, in Waters, *Sabbath-School Bell*, [1859].

47T   Primrose. C.M.
      Words: Isaac Watts, 1707, Hymn 88, book 2.
      Music: Amzi Chapin. In its first publication, in *A Collection of Tunes*, 1812, under the name Twenty-Fourth, it is attributed to Lucius Chapin, but Lucius attributes it (under the name Orange) to Amzi in an 1812 letter to Andrew Law.

47B   Idumea. S.M.
      Words: Charles Wesley, 1763.
      Music: Ananias Davisson, in *Kentucky Harmony*, 1816. Alto in Walker, *Christian Harmony*, 1867.

48T   Devotion. L.M.
      Words: Isaac Watts, 1719, Psalm 92, part 1, verses 1, 5, and 7.
      Music: Alexander Johnson, in *Tennessee Harmony*, 1818. Alto in Walker, *Christian Harmony*, 1867.

48B   Kedron. L.M.
      Words: Charles Wesley, 1762.

Music: In Pilsbury, *United States' Sacred Harmony*, 1799. Alto in Walker, *Christian Harmony*, 1867.

49T OLD HUNDRED. L.M.
Words: Brady and Tate, *New Version of the Psalms of David*, 1696, Psalm 95.
Music: *Pseaumes octante trois de David*, 1551.

49B MEAR. C.M.
Words: Isaac Watts, 1719, Psalm 74.
Music: As MIDDLESEX, in Brown, *Sett of Tunes*, 1720.

50T MORTALITY. L.M.
Words: Isaac Watts, 1719, Psalm 90, verses 5, 6, and 8.
Music: Daniel Read, in *The American Singing Book*, 1785.

50B HUMILITY. 7777.
Words: William Hammond, 1745.
Music: *David Grant, 1988, in *The Sacred Harp*, 1991.

51 MY HOME. C.M.
Words: Verses by Samuel Stennett in Rippon, *Selection*, 1787.
Music: [Arranged by] C. F. Letson, in *The Sacred Harp*, 1870, from a revival tune; a variant is I WILL NOT TARRY HERE, by L. J. Jones in *The Southern Minstrel*, 1849.

52T ALBION. S.M.
Words: Isaac Watts, 1707, Hymn 30, book 2.
Music: Robert Boyd, in Davisson, *Kentucky Harmony*, 1816.

52B CHARLESTOWN. 8787.
Words: John Newton, 1779.
Music: As CHARLESTON, in Pilsbury, *United States' Sacred Harmony*, 1799.

53 JERUSALEM. L.M.
Words: Verses by John Cennick, 1743.
Music: William Walker, in *Southern Harmony*, 1835; arranged from WESLEY [C.M.] by Moore, in *Wyeth's Repository of Sacred Music*, 1810.

54 THE BLESSED LAMB. 8787.
Words: Verses 5 and 6 of "Brethren see my Jesus coming," in *Choice Selection of Hymns and Spiritual Songs*, 3d ed., 1827. Also as verses 5 and 6 of "Great Redeemer, friend of sinners," in Leavitt, *Christian Lyre*, 1830.
Music: Anonymous, in *The Sacred Harp*, 1870 (p. 454), probably from a song tune.

55 SISTER'S FAREWELL. C.M.D.
Words: A. J. McLendon, 1905.
Music: A. J. McLendon, 1905, in James, *Union Harp*, 1909. "In memory of
Bertha B. Brantly, daughter of Mr. and Mrs. J. D. Laminack."

56T COLUMBIANA. 8787.
Words: John Newton, 1779.
Music: D. P. White, in *The Sacred Harp*, 1850 (p. 331).

56B VILLULIA. C.M.
Words: John Newton, 1779.
Music: J. M. Day, in *The Sacred Harp*, 1850 (p. 331); a variant of VICKSBURG,
in Hauser, *Hesperian Harp*, 1848. The tune also appears as MANNON,
attributed to Nicholson, in a manuscript tunebook from Adams County,
Ohio, ca. 1820.

57 CHRISTIAN SOLDIER. C.M.
Words: Isaac Watts, *Sermons*, 1724; based on 1 Corinthians 16:13.
Music: [Arranged by] F. Price, in Walker, *Southern Harmony*, 1835. The
melody was published earlier, without attribution, in Clayton and Carrell,
Virginia Harmony (1831). Alto in Walker, *Christian Harmony*, 1867.

58 PISGAH. C.M.
Words: Richard Burnham, 1783.
Music: J. C. Lowry, in Davisson, *Kentucky Harmony*, 2d ed., 1817; the
second treble is from CHRISTIAN TRIUMPH, a variant setting of the same
melody in A. Johnson, *Tennessee Harmony*, 1818.

59 HOLY MANNA. C.M.
Words: George Askins, in Harrod, *Social and Camp-Meeting Songs, for the
Pious*, 1817.
Music: William Moore, in *Columbian Harmony*, 1825. Alto after W. M.
Cooper, 1902.

60 DAY OF WORSHIP. L.M.D.
Words: Anonymous, in Hauser, *Hesperian Harp*, 1848; perhaps by B. F.
Davis.
Music: B. F. and E. K. Davis, in Hauser, *Hesperian Harp*, 1848; alto by S. M.
Denson, 1911.

61 SWEET RIVERS. C.M.D.
Words: John Adam Granade, in *The Pilgrim's Songster*, 1804.
Music: William Moore, in *Columbian Harmony*, 1825. Alto by William
Hauser, 1848.

62   PARTING HAND. L.M.D.

Words: Credited variously to John Blain, 1818, and to Clement Nance. The earliest located occurrence, in Robert Foster's *Portsmouth Selection*, 1823 ed., may favor Nance, as a Christian Connexion minister and a contributor to the Portsmouth-based journal of that group.

Music: William Walker, in *Southern Harmony*, 1835, a variant of TRANQUILITY, in Ingalls, *Christian Harmony*, 1805. Alto by William Hauser, 1848.

63   CORONATION. C.M.

Words: Edward Perronet, 1779.

Music: Oliver Holden, in *The Union Harmony*, 1793.

64   NASHVILLE. P.M. [886.886]

Words: In *Hymns and Spiritual Songs for the Use of Christians* ("The Baltimore Collection," 1803 ed.); tentatively attributed to Rev. Mr. [John Poage] Campbell by Brown and Butterworth, *Story of the Hymns and Tunes*, 1907, p. 277n.

Music: Alexander Johnson, in *Tennessee Harmony*, 2d ed., 1821; alto after W. M. Cooper, 1902; a variant of KINGWOOD, page 266. Named for Nashville, Tennessee.

65   SWEET PROSPECT. C.M.

Words: Samuel Stennett, in Rippon, *Selection*, 1787.

Music: [Arranged by] William Walker, 1833, in *Southern Harmony*, 1835; a variant of NEW-MARKET by William Caldwell, in his *Union Harmony*, 1837. Alto in Walker, *Christian Harmony*, 1867.

66   JORDAN. C.M.

Words: Isaac Watts, 1707, Hymn 66, book 2.

Music: William Billings, in *Suffolk Harmony*, 1786.

67   COLUMBUS. C.M.D.

Words: In Mercer, *Cluster*, 1810.

Music: Anonymous in Walker, *Southern Harmony*, 1835; a variant of HOPEWELL, in Shaw and Spilman, *Columbian Harmony*, 1829. Alto by William Walker, 1866.

68T   SALEM. L.M.

Words: Isaac Watts, "Christ dying, rising and reigning," in *Horae Lyricae*, 2d ed., 1709, altered by Martin Madan, 1760.

Music: Stephen Bovell, in Davisson, *Kentucky Harmony*, 2d ed., 1817.

68B ORTONVILLE. C.M.
Words: John Newton, 1779.
Music: "Arranged by B. F. White," in *The Sacred Harp*, 1850 (p. 283), from
Thomas Hastings, in his *Manhattan Collection*, 1837. Alto by S. M. Denson,
1911.

69T MINISTER'S FAREWELL. C.M.D.
Words: "Brethren farewell," in Joshua Smith, *Divine Hymns*, 8th ed., 1797,
as modified in *Hymns and Spiritual Songs for the Use of Christians* ("The
Baltimore Collection"), 1803 ed.
Music: *Wyeth's Repository of Sacred Music, Part Second*, 1813.

69B FAREWELL TO ALL. L.M.D.
Words: John Blain or Clement Nance (as at page 62, above).
Music: J. P. Reese, "Original," in *The Sacred Harp*, 1870 (p. 398); alto by W.
M. Cooper, 1902.

70T GAINSVILLE. 7S.
Words: William Hammond, 1745.
Music: W. D. Jones, "Original," in *The Sacred Harp*, 1870, named after
Gainesville, Hall County, Georgia.

70B SAVE, MIGHTY LORD. L.M.
Words: Verses by John Cennick, 1743.
Music: J. A. and J. F. Wade, 1854, in McCurry, *Social Harp*, 1855; rearranged
by J. S. James in *Union Harp and History of Songs*, 1909.

71 LEANDER. C.M.D.
Words: Isaac Watts, 1707, Hymn 10, book 2, altered.
Music: Anonymous in A. Johnson, *Tennessee Harmony*, 1818; attributed to
Austin in *Tennessee Harmony*, 1821, and elsewhere; probably based on a
song tune. Alto in Walker, *Christian Harmony*, 1867.

72T THE WEARY SOUL. C.M.D.
Words: John Adam Granade, in *The Pilgrim's Songster*, 1804.
Music: [Arranged by] J. T. White, in *The Sacred Harp*, 1844, as THE WEARY
SOULS; a variant of FLORENCE on page 121. Alto after William Walker,
1866.

72B BELLEVUE. YYYY.
Words: "K___" in Rippon, *Selection*, 1787.
Music: [Arranged by] Z. Chambless, in *The Sacred Harp*, 1844; named for

Belleview, Talbot County, Georgia; a variant of Protection, in Funk, *Genuine Church Music*, 1832. Alto after B. P. Poyner, 1902.

73T CUSSETA. L.M.
Words: Isaac Watts, 1719, Psalm 51, part 1.
Music: John Massengale, in *The Sacred Harp*, 1844; named for Cusseta, Chattahoochee County, Georgia. Alto by W. M. Cooper, 1902.

73B ARLINGTON. C.M.
Words: Isaac Watts, 1707, Hymn 103, book 1.
Music: Ralph Harrison, in his *Sacred Harmony*, 1784; the melody is arranged from an air in *Artaxerxes* (1762) by Thomas A. Arne.

74T THE ENQUIRER. C.M.D.
Words: Isaac Watts, 1707, Hymn 103, book 1.
Music: B. F. White, in *The Sacred Harp*, 1844; alto by S. M. Denson, 1911.

74B KING OF PEACE. 7777.
Words: John Newton, 1779.
Music: [Arranged by] F. Price, in Walker, *Southern Harmony*, 1835; a variant of LOVEST THOU ME in Leavitt, *Christian Lyre*, 1831. Alto in Walker, *Christian Harmony*, 1867.

75 I WOULD SEE JESUS. C.M.D.
Words: Verse 1 anonymous; verses 2 and 3, Horatius Bonar, 1846.
Music: L. P. Breedlove, "Original," in *The Organ*, 1 March 1854; in *The Sacred Harp*, 1870; alto by S. M. Denson, 1911.

76T HOLINESS. 777777.
Words: John Cennick, before 1755.
Music: E. J. King, in *The Sacred Harp*, 1844; alto by S. M. Denson, 1911.

76B DESIRE FOR PIETY. L.M.
Words: In Dupuy, *Hymns and Spiritual Songs, Original and Selected*, 1811.
Music: B. F. White, in *The Sacred Harp*, 1844; alto by S. M. Denson, 1911.

77T THE CHILD OF GRACE. C.M.D.
Words: Charles Wesley, 1759.
Music: [Arranged by] E. J. King, in *The Sacred Harp*, 1844; a variant of DOVER, in Pilsbury, *United States' Sacred Harmony*, 1799. Alto after W. M. Cooper, 1902.

77B HOLCOMBE. C.M.
Words: Isaac Watts, 1719, Psalm 5.

Music: *Charlene Wallace, 1986, in *The Sacred Harp,* 1991. In honor of her mother, Maude Holcombe.

78   STAFFORD. S.M.
Words: Isaac Watts, 1719, Psalm 118, part 5.
Music: Daniel Read, in Jocelin, *The Chorister's Companion,* 1782; alto by Raymond Hamrick, 1971. Named for Stafford, Tolland County, Connecticut.

79   THE OLD SHIP OF ZION. P.M.
Words: In Bryan, *Songster's Companion,* 1837, altered.
Music: Thomas W. Carter, in *The Sacred Harp,* 1844.

80T   SHOUTING SONG. 8787.
Words: In Peak, *New Collection of Hymns and Spiritual Songs,* 3d ed., 1793.
Music: B. F. White, in *The Sacred Harp,* 1844; alto after W. M. Cooper, 1902.

80B   SERVICE OF THE LORD. L.M.
Words: Verse 5 of "O may I worthy prove to see," in *Hymns and Spiritual Songs for the Use of Christians* ("The Baltimore Collection," 1801).
Music: E. J. King, in *The Sacred Harp,* 1844; alto in *Original Sacred Harp,* 1911, probably by S. M. Denson.

81T   BEACH SPRING. 878747.
Words: Joseph Hart, 1759.
Music: B. F. White, in *The Sacred Harp,* 1844; named for Beech Springs, Harris County, Georgia. Alto after W. M. Cooper, 1902.

81B   COOKHAM. 7777.
Words: Charles Wesley, 1735.
Music: As CHRISTMAS, in *Harmonia Sacra,* 1754; alto in Walker, *Christian Harmony,* 1867. Named for Cookham, Berkshire, England.

82T   BOUND FOR CANAAN. 7676.
Words: Verses by John Leland, 1793.
Music: E. J. King, in *The Sacred Harp,* 1844; alto after W.M. Cooper, 1902.

82B   EDGEFIELD. 8888.
Words: John Newton, 1779.
Music: J. T. White, in *The Sacred Harp,* 1844; a variant of BETHANY, in [Howe], *The Psalm-Singer's Amusement,* [ca. 1804].

83T   VALE OF SORROW. P.M.
Words: In Battle, *Collection of Hymns & Spiritual Songs,* 1814.
Music: B. F. White, in *The Sacred Harp,* 1844; alto by W.M. Cooper, 1902.

83B   THE DYING MINISTER. C.M.
      Words: Berryman T. Hicks (1778–1839), in Walker, *Southern Harmony*,
      1835. "This song was composed by the Rev. B. Hicks (a Baptist minister of
      South Carolina,) and sent to his wife while he was confined in Tennessee
      by a fever of which he afterwards recovered" (p. 19).
      Music: Edmund Dumas, 1854, in *The Sacred Harp*, 1870 (p. 124); alto by
      S. M. Denson, 1911.

84   AMSTERDAM. 7676.7776.
      Words: Robert Seagrave, in *Hymns for Christian Worship*, 1742.
      Music: *A Collection of Tunes, . . . as they are commonly sung at the Foundery*
      ("The Foundery Collection," 1742). The melody is adapted from that
      of "Sei willkommen" by Johann Georg Hille (d. 1744) of Glaucha, near
      Halle, Germany. This version of the melody first appears in *The Divine
      Musical Miscellany*, 1754.

85   THE MORNING TRUMPET. 7676.
      Words: Verses by John Leland, 1793.
      Music: B. F. White, in *The Sacred Harp*, 1844.

86   POLAND. C.M.
      Words: Isaac Watts, 1719, Psalm 39, part 3.
      Music: Timothy Swan, in Brownson, *Select Harmony*, [1785].

87   SWEET CANAAN. L.M.
      Words: Verses in Mead, *General Selection*, 1807.
      Music: [Arranged by] E. J. King, in *The Sacred Harp*, 1844, from a revival
      tune, in *Revival Melodies*, 1842; Alto after W. M. Cooper, 1902.

88T   DONE WITH THE WORLD. L.M.
      Words: Verse by John Cennick, 1743.
      Music: B. F. White, in *The Sacred Harp*, 1844.

88B   MOUNT ZION. C.M.
      Words: Verse by Charles Wesley, 1739.
      Music: John Massengale, in *The Sacred Harp*, 1844.

89   THE CHURCH'S DESOLATION. 8787 D.
      Words: Anonymous in *The Sacred Harp*, 1844.
      Music: [Arranged by] J. T. White, in *The Sacred Harp*, 1844, from a song
      tune. A variant is MOURNING SOULS in Ingalls, *Christian Harmony*, 1805.

90   LOOK OUT. 8787 D.
      Words: In Courtney, *The Christian Pocket Companion* (1805) as "a new Song
      from Tennessee."

Music: B. F. White, in *The Sacred Harp,* 1844; alto after Anna L. Blackshear, 1902.

91 ASSURANCE. C.M.
Words: Isaac Watts, 1719, Psalm 27, part 1, verse 5.
Music: William Billings, in *The Psalm-Singer's Amusement,* 1781.

92 BURK. 7676.
Words: In Battle, *Collection of Hymns & Spiritual Songs,* 1814; considerably revised from the original; attributed to [John Poage] Campbell in Cleland, *Evangelical Hymns,* 2nd ed., 1826; also so attributed by Brown and Butterworth, *Story of the Hymns and Tunes,* 1906, p. 277n.
Music: B. F. White, in *The Sacred Harp,* 1844.

93 FROZEN HEART. L.M.
Words: Joseph Hart, 1762, "Oh! For a glance of heavenly day," greatly altered; verse 4 not by Hart.
Music: [Arranged by] E. J. King, in *The Sacred Harp,* 1844, from a song tune.

94 NEVER PART. C.M.
Words: Verse by Edmund Jones, 1787.
Music: [Arranged by] John Carwell, in *The Sacred Harp,* 1850 (p. 294); alto by S. M. Denson, 1911. From a revival chorus, in Himes, *Millennial Harp,* 1842.

95 VERNON. 8888.88.
Words: Charles Wesley, 1742.
Music: Amzi Chapin. Unattributed in *Patterson's Church Music,* 1813, it is mentioned in an 1812 letter of Lucius Chapin as the work of Amzi Chapin; a variant of FAREWELL HYMN, in Ingalls, *Christian Harmony,* 1805.

96 FEW HAPPY MATCHES. 886.886.
Words: Lady Huntingdon's *Collection of Hymns,* 1774, as altered in Rippon, *Selection,* 1787.
Music: [Arranged by] B. F. White and [E. J.] King, in *The Sacred Harp,* 1844, attributed to Crane in Jocelin, *Chorister's Companion,* 2d ed., 1788.

97 WE'LL SOON BE THERE. L.M.
Words: Verses in Mead, *General Selection,* 1807; altered, and with a different refrain.
Music: [Arranged by] Oliver Bradfield, in *The Sacred Harp,* 1859 (p. 397), from a song tune, "The Rose That All Are Praising," by Edward J. Loder. "Alto by J.P. Rees."

98   DULL CARE. C.M.

Words: Eighteenth-century English secular lyric; in Jenks, *Jovial Songster,* 1806, and elsewhere.

Music: [Arranged by] E. J. King, in *The Sacred Harp,* 1844, from a song tune, "The Friendly Society."

99   GOSPEL TRUMPET. L.M.

Words: In Broaddus and Broaddus, *Collection of Sacred Ballads,* 1790.

Music: [Arranged by] E. J. King, in *The Sacred Harp,* 1844, from VERMONT in Pilsbury, *United States' Sacred Harmony,* 1799.

100 THE BOWER OF PRAYER. YYYY.

Words: John Osborn of Lee, N.H., about 1815; perhaps based on "There's a bower of roses by Bendemeer's stream" by Thomas Moore.

Music: [Arranged by] E. J. King, in *The Sacred Harp,* 1844, from a song tune. Also in Hayden, *Introduction to Sacred Music,* 1835.

101T CANAAN'S LAND. C.M.D.

Words: In J. Lloyd, *Hymns on Select Passages of Scripture,* 1811.

Music: E. J. King, in *The Sacred Harp,* 1844; alto in Walker, *Christian Harmony,* 1873.

101B HOLY CITY. 7676 D.

Words: In Mead, *General Selection,* 1807.

Music: B. F. White, in *The Sacred Harp,* 1844; alto after W. M. Cooper, 1902.

102 FULFILLMENT. 9898 D.

Words: John Adam Granade, in *The Pilgrim's Songster,* 1804.

Music: E. J. King, in *The Sacred Harp,* 1844; alto by S. M. Denson, 1911.

Compare with variant at PARTING FRIENDS, page 267.

103 ANIMATION. C.M.

Words: Charles Wesley, 1759.

Music: Anonymous, in *The Sacred Harp,* 1844; alto by S. M. Denson, 1911.

104 THE LOVELY STORY. 8888 D.

Words: In Mercer, *Cluster,* 1810.

Music: [Arranged by] E. J. King, in *The Sacred Harp,* 1844; a variant of WELLINGTON, in Davisson, *Supplement to the Kentucky Harmony,* 3d ed., 1826.

105 JEWETT. C.M.

Words: Verses by John Newton, 1779.

Music: R. F. M. Mann, August 3, 1858, "Original," in *The Sacred Harp*, 1870 (p. 438); alto by S. M. Denson, 1911.

106   ECSTASY. 7676.
Words: Verses by John Leland, 1793.
Music: Thomas W. Carter, in *The Sacred Harp*, 1844.

107   RUSSIA. L.M.
Words: Isaac Watts, 1719, Psalm 62.
Music: Daniel Read, in *The American Musical Magazine*, no. 3, 1786–87.

108T   WEEPING SINNERS. 7777.
Words: Oliver Holden, in *The Young Convert's Companion*, 1806.
Music: J. P. Reese, "Original," in *The Sacred Harp*, 1870; alto in *Original Sacred Harp*, 1911, probably by S. M. Denson.

108B   THE TRAVELER. 7777.
Words: Verses by William B. Collyer, in Rippon, *Selection*, 29th ed. (1829), as "Haste, trav'ler, haste" (L.M.). Here altered (by dropping the first syllable in every line), but only slightly rewritten.
Music: "Arranged by A. Ogletree" in *The Sacred Harp*, 1870; a variant of MESSIAH by Samuel Wakefield in *The Ecclesiastic Harmony*, 1825; see also BOZRAH, in Walker, *Southern Harmony*, 1835.

109   CARNSVILLE. 7776 D.
Words: In Myers, *Zion Songster*, 3d ed., 1829.
Music: E. J. King, in *The Sacred Harp*, 1844; second treble by William Hauser, 1848; named for Carnesville, Franklin County, Georgia.

110   MOUNT VERNON. L.M.D.
Words: Broadside, "Hymn sung at Hartford, Conn., during religious services performed on the occasion of the death of George Washington, Dec. 27th, 1799."
Music: Stephen Jenks, in *The New-England Harmonist*, 1799; named for George Washington's home near Alexandria, Virginia.

111T   JOURNEY HOME. L.M.
Words: Verses in Mead, *General Selection*, 1807.
Music: R. F. M. Mann, November 15, 1868, "Original," in *The Sacred Harp*, 1870; alto in *Original Sacred Harp*, 1911, probably by S. M. Denson.

111B   TO DIE NO MORE. L.M.
Words: Verses by Isaac Watts, 1707, Hymn 31, book 2.

Music: "Set to music by Eld. E. Dumas, in 1856," in *The Sacred Harp*, 1870; arranged from a ballad tune, "The Three Ravens."

112   THE LAST WORDS OF COPERNICUS. C.M.D.
Words: Philip Doddridge, 1755.
Music: Sarah Lancaster, "Original; For the Organ," in *The Sacred Harp*, 1870; alto in *Original Sacred Harp*, 1911, probably by S. M. Denson.

113   THE PRODIGAL SON. C.M.
Words: Verses by John Newton, 1779.
Music: [Arranged by] E. J. King, in *The Sacred Harp*, 1844, from a revival tune.

114   SAINT'S DELIGHT. C.M.
Words: Verses by Isaac Watts, 1707, Hymn 65, book 2.
Music: F. Price, in Walker, *Southern Harmony*, 1835; alto by S. M. Denson, 1911.

115   EDMONDS. 7676 D.
Words: William H. Bozarth, Grayson County, Kentucky, 1818.
Music: Edmund Dumas. "Original," in *The Sacred Harp*, 1870, "In honor of Troup Edmonds"; alto by S. M. Denson, 1911.

116   UNION. Z8Z8 D.
Words: As "Dear sisters and brothers," in Cram, *Collection of Hymns and Poems*, 1815.
Music: E. J. King, in *The Sacred Harp*, 1844, from a song tune.

117   BABYLON IS FALLEN. 878787.
Words: First two verses by Richard McNemar in Wells, *Millennial Praises*, 1813; altered in Hauser, *Hesperian Harp*, 1848. The third verse, from neither source, may be the work of the arranger, W. E. Chute.
Music: Arranged by W. E. Chute in *The Musical Million 6* (December 1875); attributed to Chute in Hauser, *Olive Leaf*, 1878. Based on a Shaker melody for this text in an undated manuscript by Paulina Bryant in the Library of Congress.

118   STOCKWOOD. 8787 D.
Words: Samuel F. Smith, 1832.
Music: M. Mark Wynn, "Original," in *The Sacred Harp*, 1870.

119　Heaven's My Home. YYYY.
Words: Verse 1 anonymous; verses 2 and 3 by David Denham, in *The Saints' Melody*, 1837.
Music: R. H. Davis and J. S. Terry, in *The Sacred Harp*, 1870.

120　Chambers. 668.668.
Words: Isaac Watts, 1719, Psalm 93.
Music: "Arranged by B. F. White," in *The Sacred Harp*, 1870, from Savoy by Samuel Holyoke, in *The Columbian Repository of Sacred Harmony*, [1803]; alto by S. M. Denson, 1911.

121　Florence. C.M.D.
Words: Verse 1 by Philip Doddridge, 1755. Verse 2 begins a different hymn by John Adam Granade, from *The Pilgrim's Songster*, 1804.
Music: [Arranged by] T. W. Carter, in *The Sacred Harp*, 1844; alto by S. M. Denson, 1911; a variant of The Weary Soul on page 72, and of Redeeming Love by William Caldwell, in *Union Harmony*, 1837.

122　All Is Well. P.M. [8383.8883]
Words: Anonymous, in *Pious Songs: Social, Prayer, Closet, and Camp Meeting Hymns, and Choruses*, 3d ed., 1836. Inspired by the dying words of William McKendree (1757–1835).
Music: [Arranged by] J. T. White, *The Sacred Harp*, 1844; alto by W. M. Cooper, 1902; from a revival melody associated with this text, e.g., *Revival Melodies*, 1842.

123T　The Dying Christian. Y8Y8.
Words: Benjamin Francis, in *The Baptist Register*, 1795.
Music: [Arranged by] E. J. King, in *The Sacred Harp*, 1844; alto by S. M. Denson, 1911; a variant of Concord, in Caldwell, *Union Harmony*, 1837.

123B　Cross of Christ. C.M.D.
Words: Verse 1 in *Southern Harmony*, 1835; verse 2 from "The Son of God goes forth to war," by Reginald Heber, 1827.
Music: L. P. Breedlove, in *The Sacred Harp*, 1844; alto by William Walker, 1866.

124　Lover of the Lord. C.M.
Words: Verse by Charles Wesley, 1749.
Music: [Arranged by] R. H. Reeves, in *The Sacred Harp*, 1870 (p. 475), from a revival chorus.

125 EXPRESSION.
Words: Caleb Jarvis Taylor, in *Spiritual Songs,* 1804.
Music: *The Sacred Harp,* 1844, from a song tune; alto after W. R. McCoy,
1902. A variant is CHEERFUL, in Walker, *Southern Harmony,* 1835.

126 BABEL'S STREAMS. C.M.D.
Words: Verse 1, Scottish Psalter, Psalm 137; verse 2, perhaps by Stephen
Jenks.
Music: Stephen Jenks, in *The Royal Harmony of Zion,* 1810 (first half);
Stephen Jenks, *Christian Harmony,* 1811 (complete); alto after W. R. McCoy,
1902.

127 GREEN FIELDS. 8888.
Words: John Newton, in Cowper and Newton, *Olney Hymns,* 1779.
Music: Metcalf, *The Kentucky Harmonist,* 1818, from a song tune, "Farewell, ye green fields and sweet groves," in Thompson manuscript, ca.
1777, and elsewhere.

128 THE PROMISED LAND. C.M.
Words: Verses by Samuel Stennett, in Rippon, *Selection,* 1787.
Music: Matilda T. Durham, in Walker, *Southern Harmony,* 1835; alto after
Anna L. Blackshear, 1902.

129 HEAVENLY ARMOR. 7676.
Words: John Leland, 1793; "O when shall I see Jesus?"
Music: William Walker, 19 September 1828, in *Southern Harmony,* 1835; alto
by Anna L. Blackshear, 1902.

130 MILLENNIUM. P.M.
Words: In Foster, *Hymns, and Spiritual Songs* ("The Portsmouth Selec-
tion"), Second Part, 1818.
Music: William Walker, 1831, in *Southern Harmony,* 1835; alto after *Christian
Harmony,* 1867.

131T MESSIAH. C.M.D.
Words: Samuel Stennett, in Rippon, *Selection,* 1787.
Music: James P. Carrell, in Davisson, *Supplement to the Kentucky Harmony,*
2d ed., ca. 1823, perhaps in Carrell, *Songs of Zion,* 1821 (unlocated).

131B INVOCATION. 7676.7776
Words: Robert Seagrave, 1742.
Music: Walker, *Southern Harmony,* 1835; alto by Anna L. Blackshear, 1902.

132   SINNER'S FRIEND. LM.
Words: Verse from Isaac Watts, "Christ dying, rising and reigning," in
Horae Lyricae, 2d ed., 1709, altered by Martin Madan, 1760.
Music: "Arranged for the Organ" by J. P. Reese, in *The Sacred Harp,* 1870
(p. 472).

133   HEBREW CHILDREN. P.M.
Words: Anonymous in *The Sacred Harp,* 1844.
Music: [Arranged by] B. F. White, in *The Sacred Harp,* 1844, p. 78; from a
revival tune; alto by S. M. Denson, 1911.

134   THE CHRISTIAN'S HOPE. P.M. [8886D]
Words: In Harrod, *Social and Camp-Meeting Songs,* 7th ed., 1825.
Music: William Walker, in *Southern Harmony,* 1835; alto in Walker ,
Christian Harmony, 1867.

135   OLNEY. 8787 D.
Words: Robert Robinson, 1758.
Music: *Tennessee Harmony,* 1818, but apparently mentioned in a letter
by Lucius Chapin to Andrew Law in 1812 as a tune current since 1800 in
Kentucky; alto by S. M. Denson, 1911. Named for Olney, Buckingham-
shire, England, sometime home of the poets John Newton and William
Cowper.

136   MORALITY. YYYY.
Words: Hannah More, "Florella's Song," in *Search after Happiness* [written
in 1762], 1825 ed.
Music: *Wyeth's Repository of Sacred Music, Part Second,* 1813; alto in Walker,
Christian Harmony, 1867; from a song tune, "The Death Song of the
Cherokee Indian."

137   LIBERTY. C.M.
Words: Anonymous, perhaps by Stephen Jenks.
Music: Stephen Jenks, in *The Musical Harmonist,* 1800; alto by S. M.
Denson, 1911.

138T ADORATION. C.M.
Words: Anne Steele, 1760.
Music: W. W. Parks, "Original, for the Organ," in *The Sacred Harp,* 1870 (p.
439).

138B OGLETREE. C.M.
Words: Simeon Browne, 1720.

Music: S. M. Brown, "Original," in *The Sacred Harp*, 1870; alto by S. M. Denson, 1911; named for Absalom Ogletree.

139   ELYSIAN. P.M. [7676.7776]
Words: Richard Kempenfelt, 1777.
Music: *Southern Harmony*, 1835, a variant of HARRISONBURG, in Davisson, *Supplement to the Kentucky Harmony*, 2d ed., ca. 1822; alto in Walker, *Christian Harmony*, 1867; akin to "The Minstrel Boy."

140   SWEET SOLITUDE. L.M.
Words: Hannah More, "Sylvia's Song," in *Search after Happiness* [written in 1762], 1825 ed.
Music: *Southern Harmony*, 1835, arranged from a song tune; alto by S. M. Denson, 1911.

141   COMPLAINER. 7676 D.
Words: Anonymous in *Southern Harmony*, 1835.
Music: William Walker, in *Southern Harmony*, 1835; alto after *Christian Harmony*, 1867.

142   STRATFIELD. L.M.
Words: Isaac Watts, 1719, Psalm 90.
Music: Ezra Goff, in *The Worcester Collection*, 1786.

143   PLEYEL'S HYMN. C.M.D.
Words: Helen Maria Williams, 1790.
Music: Arranged from Ignaz Joseph Pleyel, *Symphonie concertante*, 1786, second movement, *Andante grazioso*, in Costellow, *Sunday's Amusement*, [ca.1801].

144   JUBILEE. 8787 D.
Words: In *Hymns and Spiritual Songs for the Use of Christians* ("The Baltimore Collection"), 1801.
Music: In Davisson, *Supplement to the Kentucky Harmony*, 1820.

145T   WARRENTON. 8787.
Words: Verses by Robert Robinson, 1758.
Music: *Young Convert's Pocket Companion*, 1822. Treble by William Walker, 1838; alto after William Walker, 1866.

145B   SWEET AFFLICTION. 8787.
Words: Samuel Pearce, in *Memoirs*, 1800.
Music: Arranged by Lowell Mason, in *The Boston Handel and Haydn Society Collection of Church Music*, 2d ed., 1823, from "Rousseau's Dream: An Air,

with Variations for the Piano-forte," by J. B. Cramer; arranged from an air in *Le Devin du Village,* by Jean-Jacques Rousseau, 1752. The Sacred Harp version is from *Southern Harmony,* 1840 appendix; alto by S. M. Denson, 1911.

146 HALLELUJAH. C.M.
Words: Verses by Charles Wesley, 1759.
Music: William Walker, in *Southern Harmony,* 1835; alto in *Christian Harmony,* 1867.

147T BOYLSTON. S.M.
Words: Isaac Watts, 1707, Hymn 93, book 2.
Music: Lowell Mason, in *The Choir,* 1832. Named for Boylston, Worcester County, Massachusetts.

147B LABAN. S.M.
Words: George Heath, 1781.
Music: Lowell Mason, in Mason and Hastings, *Spiritual Songs for Social Worship,* 1831.

148 JEFFERSON. 8787.
Words: John Newton, in Cowper and Newton, *Olney Hymns,* 1779.
Music: *Tennessee Harmony,* 1818; alto by Anna L. Blackshear, 1902.

149 THE TRUMPET. P.M. [YZZZ]
Words: Henry Hart Milman, 1827.
Music: J. Williams, in Leavitt, *Christian Lyre,* 1831; treble by William Walker, 1835; alto by William Walker, 1866.

150 AMITY. 668.668.
Words: Isaac Watts, 1719, Psalm 122.
Music: Daniel Read, in *The American Singing Book,* 1785.

151 SYMPHONY. P.M. [XXXXXX]
Words: Isaac Watts, 1719, Psalm 50, verse 2.
Music: Justin Morgan, in Benham, *Federal Harmony,* 1790.

152 SHEPHERDS REJOICE. C.M.D.
Words: Isaac Watts, "The Nativity of Christ," in *Horae Lyricae,* 1706.
Music: Leonard P. Breedlove, in *The Sacred Harp,* 1850 (p. 288); removed from the 1870 edition, it was "rearranged" and given an alto part by B. S. Aikin in 1908 and printed in James, *Union Harp,* 1909, and *Original Sacred Harp,* 1911.

153 RESURRECTED. P.M.
Words: In Hillman, *Revivalist*, 1869, as "My brother's going to wear that crown."
Music: Arranged by S. M. Denson, 1908, in James, *Union Harp*, 1909; treble by Sidney Denson; from a revival tune, "Away over Jordan," in *The Revivalist*, 1869.

154 REST FOR THE WEARY. 8787.
Words: Verses by Robert Robinson, 1758.
Music: "Original arrangement by B. F. W.[hite]" in *The Sacred Harp*, 1870 (p. 474); adapted from J. W. Dadmun, in *The Melodeon*, 1860.

155 NORTHFIELD. C.M.
Words: Isaac Watts, 1707, Hymn 21, book 1, verses 6 and 2.
Music: Jeremiah Ingalls, in *Village Harmony*, 5th ed., 1800. Named for Northfield, Franklin County, Massachusetts.

156 JESUS ROSE. P.M.
Words: Anonymous, in *The Sacred Harp*, 1870.
Music: H. S. Reese, in *The Sacred Harp*, 1870 (p. 473); alto by W. M. Cooper, 1902.

157 ESSAY. 7676 D.
Words: In Purify, *Selection of Hymns and Spiritual Songs*, 1823.
Music: Arranged by A. C. Clark, in Walker, *Southern Harmony*, 1840 appendix; alto by S. M. Denson, 1911; from a Scots song tune.

158 FUNERAL THOUGHT. P.M. [ZYZZ]
Words: Reginald Heber, 1818, in the periodical *Friendly Visitor*, edited by William Carus Wilson, 1824, "On the Death of an Infant."
Music: William Caldwell, in Caldwell, *Union Harmony*, 1837.

159 WONDROUS LOVE. P.M. [63.6663]
Words: In Dupuy, *Hymns and Spiritual Songs, Original and Selected*, 2d ed., 1812.
Music: James Christopher, in Walker, *Southern Harmony*, 1840 appendix; alto by S. M. Denson, 1911.

160T WAR DEPARTMENT. YYYY.
Words: Verse 10 of "From the realms where the day her first dawning extends," anonymous in the [Bennington] *Vermont Gazette*, 6 April 1803, as "The Triumph of Grace in the Wilderness."
Music: *Southern Harmony*, 1835.

160B TURN, SINNER, TURN. L.M.
       Words: In Kent, *Gospel Hymns*, 1811.
       Music: Arranged by E. J. King, in *The Sacred Harp*, 1844 (p. 105), from a
       revival song; alto by S. M. Denson, 1911.

161   SWEET HOME. YYYY.
       Words: David Denham, in *The Saints' Melody*, 1837.
       Music: Arranged, in *Southern Harmony*, 1840 appendix, from "Home,
       Sweet Home" by Henry Bishop, from the opera *Clari, or The Maid of
       Milan* (1823); also in W. R. Rhinehart, *American or Union Harmony*, 1831, H.
       Smith, *Church Harmony*, 1831, and Clayton and Carrell, *Virginia Harmony*,
       1831. Treble by William Walker, 1840; alto after William Walker, 1866.

162   PLENARY. C.M.
       Words: Isaac Watts, 1707, Hymn 63, book 2.
       Music: Arranged by A. C. Clark, in A. W. Johnson, *American Harmony*,
       1839, from a song tune, "Auld lang syne," in Thompson, *Select Collection of
       Original Scottish Airs*, 1802. Alto after Minnie Floyd, 1902.

163T MORNING. L.M.
       Words: Isaac Watts, "Christ dying, rising and reigning," in *Horae Lyricae*,
       2d ed., 1709, altered by Martin Madan, 1760.
       Music: Amos Pilsbury, in *United States' Sacred Harmony*, 1799; alto after
       Anna L. Blackshear, 1902.

163B CHINA. C.M.
       Words: Isaac Watts, 1707, Hymn 3, book 2.
       Music: Timothy Swan, in *New England Harmony*, 1801. James writes,
       "China is one of [Swan's] master-pieces, and illustrates his self-culture in
       the art of song."

164   DUANE STREET. L.M.D.
       Words: James Montgomery, "The Stranger," December 1826.
       Music: George Coles, 1835; treble by J. T. White; alto after Anna L.
       Blackshear, 1902.

165   FAMILY BIBLE. P.M.
       Words: In the *Charleston* [S.C.] *Courier*, 1818, a parody of "The Old Oaken
       Bucket" by Samuel Woodworth.
       Music: William Caldwell, in *Union Harmony*, 1837, a variant of a tune
       claimed by J. C. Lowry in Shaw and Spilman, *Columbian Harmony*, 1829;
       alto by B. P. Poyner, 1902.

166   STILL BETTER. 8787 D.

Words: Anonymous, in *The Sacred Harp,* 1870; perhaps by one of the cited composers.

Music: Israel Mayfield and J. L. Meggs, in *The Sacred Harp,* 1870 (p. 455); alto by Minnie Floyd, 1902.

167   PRAY, BRETHREN, PRAY. P.M.

Words: William Hunter, in Hunter and Wakefield, *The Minstrel of Zion,* 1845.

Music: Anonymous, in Hunter and Wakefield, *The Minstrel of Zion,* 1845; treble by U. G. Wood, in *The Sacred Harp,* 1870 (p. 467); alto by S. M. Denson, 1911.

168   COWPER. L.M.

Words: Verse 1, William Cowper in Cowper and Newton, *Olney Hymns,* 1779, verse 5 of "Almighty King! whose wondrous hand"; verse 2 by Ann Taylor in *Hymns for Infant Minds,* 1808.

Music: Oliver Holden, in *The Worcester Collection,* 8th ed., 1803; named for the poet William Cowper.

169   DARTMOUTH. S.M.D.

Words: Isaac Watts, 1719, Psalm 95.

Music: Stephen Jenks, in Jenks and Griswold, *The American Compiler,* 1803; alto by S. M. Denson, 1911.

170   EXHILARATION. L.M.

Words: *Hymns and Spiritual Songs for the Use of Christians* ("The Baltimore Collection"), 1801. The opening couplet is based on Brady and Tate, *New Version of the Psalms of David,* 1696, Psalm 106, verse 4.

Music: Thomas W. Carter, in *The Sacred Harp,* 1844; alto by S. M. Denson, 1911.

171   EXHORTATION. C.M.

Words: Isaac Watts, 1719, Psalm 5.

Music: Hibbard, in Griswold and Skinner, *Connecticut Harmony,* [1796].

172   HARMONY. 886.886.

Words: John Ogilvie, verse 10 of "Begin my soul th'exalted lay," Psalm 148, in Ogilvie, *Poems on Several Subjects,* 1762.

Music: Abner Ellis, in Jenks, *The Delights of Harmony; or, Norfolk Compiler,* 1805; alto after Anna L. Blackshear, 1902.

173 PHOEBUS. C.M.D.
Words: Isaac Watts, 1719, Psalm 5.
Music: William Billings, in *The New-England Psalm-Singer,* 1770.

174 PETERSBURG. L.M.D.
Words: John Logan, 1781.
Music: William Billings, in *Suffolk Harmony,* 1786.

175 HIGHLANDS OF HEAVEN. P.M. [6767 D]
Words: In *Hymn Book of the Methodist Protestant Church,* 1859.
Music: Arranged by J. D. Arnold, in *The Sacred Harp,* 1870 (p. 453); from
"The Braes o Balquhidder," by Robert Tannahill, in R. A. Smith, *Scottish
Minstrel,* 1821, set to a traditional Scots air; alto by S. M. Denson, 1911.

176T RAGAN. L.M.
Words: Verse 5 of "O may I worthy prove to see," in *Hymns and Spiritual
Songs for the Use of Christians* ("The Baltimore Collection"), 1801.
Music: Arranged by W. F. Moore, in *The Sacred Harp,* 1870; the melody
was learned from the Rev. Robert G. Ragan, Davisville, Alabama; alto by
S. M. Denson, 1911.

176B BLOOMING YOUTH. C.M.
Words: Thomas Gibbons, 1769.
Music: Henry G. Mann, "Original," in *The Sacred Harp,* 1870 (p. 442).

177 THE CHRISTIAN'S FLIGHT. P.M.
Words: Philip Doddridge, 1755.
Music: W. F. Moore, 1866, in *The Sacred Harp,* 1870 (p. 476).

178 AFRICA. C.M.
Words: Isaac Watts, 1707, Hymn 39, book 1.
Music: William Billings, in *The New-England Psalm-Singer,* 1770.

179 THE CHRISTIAN WARFARE. Y8Y8 D.
Words: Anonymous in *Southern Harmony,* 1835.
Music: *Southern Harmony,* 1835; alto by William Walker, 1866.

180 VERMONT. C.M.D.
Words: Isaac Watts, 1707, Hymn 9, book 1.
Music: William Billings, in *The Singing-Master's Assistant,* 1778.

181 EXIT. L.M.
Words: Isaac Watts, 1719, Psalm 90, verses 5–8.
Music: P. Sherman, in Peck, *Musical Medley,* 1808.

182   NEWBURGH. S.M.D.
       Words: Isaac Watts, 1719, Psalm 148.
       Music: Amos Munson, in Read, *The Columbian Harmonist, No. 2, with Additional Music,* [1798]; named for Newburgh, Orange County, New York.

183   GREENWICH. L.M.D.
       Words: Isaac Watts, 1719, Psalm 73.
       Music: Daniel Read, in Andrew Law, *Rudiments of Music,* 2d ed., 1785; named for Greenwich, Connecticut.

184   ENFIELD. C.M.D.
       Words: Elizabeth Rowe, *Miscellaneous Works,* 1739.
       Music: Solomon Chandler, in Oliver Brownson, *Select Harmony,* 1785; named for Enfield, Hartford County, Connecticut.

185   PILGRIM'S FAREWELL. L.M.
       Words: First verse in French, *Psalmodist's Companion,* 1793; complete (with refrain) in *The Western Missionary Magazine and Repository of Religious Intelligence* 1 (Washington, Pa., 1803).
       Music: In French, *Psalmodist's Companion,* 1793 (first part only); by Field, in French, *Harmony of Harmony,* 1802 (complete); alto after W. M. Cooper, 1902.

186   SHERBURNE. C.M.
       Words: Nahum Tate, 1702.
       Music: Daniel Read, in *The American Singing Book,* 1785.

187   PROTECTION. C.M.
       Words: Isaac Watts, 1719, Psalm 73, part 2.
       Music: P. Sherman, in Peck, *Musical Medley,* 1808.

188   SPRING. 8888.77.
       Words: Charles Wesley, verse 2 of "The voice of my beloved sounds."
       Music: In Boyd, *Virginia Sacred Musical Repository,* 1818; also in *David's Harp,* no date, perhaps 1818; possibly from a song tune; counter by [W. H.] Swan, 1848.

189   MONTGOMERY. C.M.D.
       Words: Isaac Watts, 1719, Psalm 63, "The Morning of a Lord's Day."
       Music: Justin Morgan, in Benham, *Federal Harmony,* 1790.

191   VIRGINIA. C.M.
       Words: Isaac Watts, 1719, Psalm 89, part 2, verse 4.
       Music: Oliver Brownson, in Jocelin, *Chorister's Companion,* 1782.

192   SCHENECTADY. L.M.D.
Words: Isaac Watts, 1719, Psalm 117.
Music: Nehemiah Shumway, in *The Easy Instructor*, 1805 ed.; named for
Schenectady, New York.

193   HUNTINGTON. L.M.D.
Words: Isaac Watts, 1719, Psalm 73.
Music: Justin Morgan, in Benham, *Federal Harmony*, 1790.

195   WORCESTER. S.M.D.
Words: Isaac Watts, 1707, Hymn 10, book 1.
Music: Abraham Wood, in Law, *Select Harmony*, 1778; named for Worcester, Massachusetts.

196   ALABAMA. C.M.D.
Words: Verse 8 (altered) of "The cross of Christ inspires my heart,"
anonymous in *Southern Harmony*, 1835.
Music: *Southern Harmony*, 1835; arranged from PRODIGAL, in A. Johnson,
Tennessee Harmony, 1818; counter (second treble) by William Walker, 1835.

197   GEORGIA. C.M.D.
Words: Anonymous in *Southern Harmony*, 1835.
Music: T. B. McGraw, 1935, in *Original Sacred Harp* (Denson revision), 1936.

198   GREEN STREET. C.M.
Words: Edward Perronet, 1779.
Music: In Collins, *Timbrel of Zion*, 1853; from an unknown British source.

200   EDOM. C.M.D.
Words: Isaac Watts, Psalm 147, "The Seasons of the Year."
Music: Elisha West, in Brownson, *New Collection of Sacred Harmony*, 1797.

201   PILGRIM. C.M.
Words: John Adam Granade, in *The Pilgrim's Songster*, 1804.
Music: Allen D. Carden, *Missouri Harmony*, 1820; alto after Anna L.
Blackshear, 1902. Based on a song tune; another variant is THE WEARY
TRAVELLER in Ingalls, *Christian Harmony*, 1805.

202   NEW LEBANON. L.P.M. [888.888]
Words: Isaac Watts, 1719, Psalm 19.
Music: P. Sherman, in Peck, *Musical Medley*, 1808.

203   FLORIDA. S.M.
Words: Isaac Watts, 1719, Psalm 55.

Music: Truman S. Wetmore, in Jenks and Griswold, *American Compiler*, 1803.

204 MISSION. L.M.D.
Words: In Wolcott, *Selection of Hymns and Spiritual Songs*, 1817.
Music: Arranged by Andrew Grambling, in Walker, *Southern Harmony*, 1835; a variant of ROAN in Davisson, *Supplement to the Kentucky Harmony*, 3d ed., 1826; alto after William Walker, 1866.

205 PLEASANT HILL. C.M.D.
Words: John Fawcett, 1782.
Music: William Nicholson, in Davisson, *Supplement to the Kentucky Harmony*, 1820.

206 CHRISTIAN'S HOPE. P.M. [8886]
Words: Arranged by H. A. Parris, 1907, in James, *Union Harp*, 1909; from a revival chorus in Walker, *Southern and Western Pocket Harmonist*, 1846.
Music: Arranged by H. A. Parris, 1907, in *Union Harmony*, 1909, from a revival tune.

207 LOUISIANA. 8787 D.
Words: Anonymous in *Southern Harmony*, 1835.
Music: William Walker, in *Southern Harmony*, 1835; alto in *Christian Harmony*, 1867; a variant is ZION'S CALL by William Caldwell, in *Union Harmony*, 1837.

208 TRAVELING ON. L.M.
Words: In French, *Psalmodist's Companion*, 1793.
Music: S. M. Denson and J. S. James, in *Original Sacred Harp*, 1911 (p. 508).

209 EVENING SHADE. S.M.
Words: John Leland, 1790.
Music: Stephen Jenks, in *The Delights of Harmony; or, Norfolk Compiler*, 1805; alto after Hauser, *Hesperian Harp*, 1848.

210 LENA. P.M. [887.887]
Words: Anonymous in *The Worcester Collection*, 5th ed., 1794; the complete hymn is in Smith and Jones, *Hymns, Original and Selected, for the Use of Christians*, 1804.
Music: Daniel Belknap, in *The Worcester Collection*, 5th ed., 1794.

211 WHITESTOWN. L.M.D.
Words: Isaac Watts, 1719, Psalm 107, last part, verses 3–4, "A Psalm for New-England."

Music: Howd, in Jenks, *Musical Harmonist,* 1800. Named for Whitestown, Oneida County, New York.

212　SHARON. P.M. [668.668]
Words: Isaac Watts, 1719, Psalm 133.
Music: Elisha West, in Shumway, *American Harmony,* 1793; alto by S. M. Denson, 1911.

213T　THE GOOD OLD WAY. L.M.
Words: In Mintz, *Spiritual Song Book,* 1805.
Music: William Walker, in *Southern Harmony,* 1835; alto in *Original Sacred Harp,* 1922, probably by S. M. Denson.

213B　WARNING. P.M. [6464]
Words: Credited to "Spiritual Songs" in Marks, *Hymns for Christian Melody,* 1832.
Music: Elphrey Heritage, in *The Sacred Harp,* 1870.

214　REPENTANCE. C.M.D.
Words: Isaac Watts, 1707, Hymn 106, book 2.
Music: [J. H.] Rollo, in Griswold and Skinner, *Connecticut Harmony,* 1796; alto by S. M. Denson, 1911.

215　NEW TOPIA. C.M.D.
Words: In Hall, *New collection of the most approved Hymns and Spiritual Songs,* 1804.
Music: Reubin Monday, in Davisson, *Kentucky Harmony,* 1816.

216　DELIGHT. H.M. [6666.4444]
Words: Isaac Watts, 1719, Psalm 121, verse 3.
Music: Simeon Coan, in Benham, *Social Harmony,* 1798.

217　BALLSTOWN. L.M.
Words: Isaac Watts, 1719, Psalm 84, part 2.
Music: Nehemiah Shumway, in *The Easy Instructor,* 1809 ed.; named for Ballstown, now Ballston, Saratoga County, New York.

218　MOUNT PLEASANT. C.M.
Words: Isaac Watts, 1709, Hymn 110, book 1.
Music: Deolph, in Shumway, *American Harmony,* 1793.

220　MOUNT ZION. S.M.D.
Words: Isaac Watts, 1707, Hymn 30, book 2, verses 9 and 10.
Music: Bartholomew Brown, in *The Worcester Collection,* 4th ed., 1792; alto by B. P. Poyner, 1902.

222 OCEAN. C.M.D.
Words: Isaac Watts, 1719, Psalm 107, part 5: "The Mariner's Psalm," altered by Joel Barlow, 1785.
Music: In Adgate, *Philadelphia Harmony*, 2d ed., 1789.

223 PORTUGUESE HYMN. P.M. [YYYX]
Words: Latin original by John F. Wade, 1743; English translation in B. Carr, *Musical Journal for the Piano Forte*, vol. 2, no. 29 (Philadelphia, 1800).
Music: Melody by John Wade in *An Essay on the Church Plain Chant*, 1782; also appears in manuscripts by Wade as early as 1750; alto after W. M. Cooper, 1902.

224 SAVE, LORD, OR WE PERISH. P.M. [ZZZZ]
Words: Reginald Heber, 1827.
Music: M. Mark Wynn, "Original," in *The Sacred Harp*, 1870.

225T REYNOLDS. C.M.
Words: Isaac Watts, 1719, Psalm 144, part 1.
Music: *Hugh McGraw, 1985, in *The Sacred Harp*, 1991; named for William J. Reynolds.

225B CHRISTMAS ANTHEM. [Ode.]
Words: In Totten, *Collection of the Most Admired Hymns and Spiritual Songs*, 3d ed., 1813.
Music: James M. Denson, in *The Sacred Harp*, 1844; alto after W. M. Cooper, 1902.

227 ODE ON LIFE'S JOURNEY. L.M.
Words: "Elegy" in Samuel Arnold, *Six Canzonets*, op. 13, 1778. The anonymous poem, consisting of 29 stanzas, beginning "When, young, life's journey I began," was used as a popular exercise for penmanship and grammatical parsing. Roswell C. Smith, *English Grammar on the Productive System* (1832), printed the poem with a transposed prose interpretation. E. J. King, who must have studied Smith's popular textbook, obscures the metrical scheme by setting the prose version of verse 1 followed by the poetic original of verse 4.
Music: E. J. King, in *The Sacred Harp*, 1844; alto by S. M. Denson, 1911.

228 MARLBOROUGH. C.M.
Words: Isaac Watts, 1719, Psalm 47.
Music: Abraham Wood, in Stone and Wood, *Columbian Harmony*, 1793; named for Marlborough, Middlesex County, Massachusetts.

229   IRWINTON C.M.D.
      Words: In Maxwell, *Hymns and Spiritual Songs*, London, 1759.
      Music: T. W. Carter, in *The Sacred Harp*, 1844 (p. 124); alto by S. M.
      Denson, 1911; a variant of HOPEWELL in Lewis, *Beauties of Harmony*, 5th
      ed., 1828; named for Irwinton, Wilkinson County, Georgia.

230   CONVERTING GRACE. C.M.
      Words: Brady and Tate, *New Version of the Psalms of David*, 1696, Psalm 42.
      Music: R. E. Brown Jr., in *The Sacred Harp*, 1859 (p. 392).

231   THOU ART PASSING AWAY. P.M. [ZZZZ]
      Words: In Pitts, *Zion's Harp*, stereotyped ed., 1852.
      Music: Arranged by George Coles from Henry Russell, "Wind of the
      Winter Night"; in Walker, *Southern Harmony*, 1854.

232   BAPTISMAL ANTHEM.
      Words: Matthew 3:1–4.
      Music: B. F. White, in *The Sacred Harp*, 1844; alto after Leila Underwood,
      1902.

234   REVERENTIAL ANTHEM.
      Words: Psalm 96:8–9, 11, 13.
      Music: E. J. King, in *The Sacred Harp*, 1844; alto by S. M. Denson, 1911.

235   LONG SOUGHT HOME. C.M.
      Words: Undated manuscript by "F. B. P.," ca. 1600, includes the first two
      verses; this text and chorus include verses 1, 2, and 7 (of 10) as found in
      Walker, *Southern Harmony*, 1847 ed.
      Music: William W. Bobo, in Walker, *Southern Harmony*, 1847 ed.; alto in
      Christian Harmony, 1867.

236   EASTER ANTHEM.
      Words: Luke 24:34; 1 Corinthians 15:20; Edward Young, *The Complaint, or
      Night Thoughts*, 1742–44, "Night the fourth: The Christian triumph."
      Music: William Billings, 1787.

240   CHRISTIAN SONG. [Ode. 8888.]
      Words: Anonymous in Ingalls, *Christian Harmony*, 1805.
      Music: Jeremiah Ingalls, in *Christian Harmony*, 1805; alto by William
      Walker, 1866.

242   ODE ON SCIENCE. L.M.
      Words: Jazaniah Sumner, 1798, for the semi-centennial of the Taunton
      Academy.

Music: Jazaniah Sumner, in Edson, *Social Harmonist*, 3d ed., 1803; alto by
Hugh McGraw, 1971.

245   CLAREMONT. [Ode.]
Words: Alexander Pope, "The Dying Christian, to His Soul," 1736, a
response to the Roman emperor Hadrian's "Animula vagula blandula"
(Little soul, wandering and pale).
Music: [Samuel] Temple and David Merrill, in Merrill, *Psalmodist's
Best Companion*, 1799. Named for Claremont, Sullivan County, New
Hampshire.

250   HEAVENLY VISION. [Anthem.]
Words: Revelation 7:9, 4:8b, 8:13, 11:15a, 6:15–17.
Music: Jacob French, in *The Worcester Collection*, 1786.

254   ROSE OF SHARON. [Anthem.]
Words: Song of Solomon 2:1–5, 7–8, 10–11.
Music: William Billings, in *The Singing-Master's Assistant*, 1778.

260   FAREWELL ANTHEM.
Words: Anonymous, in Jacob French, *The New American Melody*, 1789.
Music: Jacob French, in *The New American Melody*, 1789.

263   DODDRIDGE. [Ode. 878747.]
Words: In Goode, *Collection of Hymns for Public, Social, and Domestic
Worship*, 1847.
Music: M. Mark Wynn, "Original," in *The Sacred Harp*, 1870 (p. 463); alto
by Hugh McGraw, 1971.

266   KINGWOOD. 886.886.
Words: Thomas Greene, in *Poems on Various Subjects*, 1780.
Music: [Arranged by] R. D. Humphreys, in Davisson, *Supplement to the
Kentucky Harmony*, 1820; from a song or dance tune; a variant is NASH-
VILLE, page 64.

267   PARTING FRIENDS. P.M. [9898 D]
Words: Anonymous, in McCurry, *The Social Harp*, 1855.
Music: Arranged by John G. McCurry, 1846, in *The Social Harp*, 1855. "The
Author, when eight years old, learned the air of this tune from Mrs.
Catharine Penn." A variant of FULFILLMENT, page 102.

268   DAVID'S LAMENTATION. [Anthem.]
Words: 2 Samuel 18:33.

Music: William Billings, in *The Singing-Master's Assistant,* 1778; alto in *Kentucky Harmony,* 1816.

269 BEAR CREEK. L.M.
Words: Isaac Watts, 1719, Psalm 68, part 2.
Music: William Billings, as WASHINGTON, in *The Singing-Master's Assistant,* 1778; alto by G. B. Daniell, 1911.

270 CONFIDENCE. L.M.D.
Words: Charles Wesley, 1742.
Music: J. R. Turner, in *The Sacred Harp,* 1850.

271T ARKANSAS. L.M.
Words: In *Revival Melodies,* 1842.
Music: S. P. Barnett, "Original, for the Organ," in *The Sacred Harp,* 1870.

271B RESTORATION. L.M.
Words: Anonymous in Rippon, *Selection,* 1787.
Music: D. P. White, in *The Sacred Harp,* 1850 (p. 265); alto by S. M. Denson, 1911.

272 EXHORTATION. L.M.
Words: Isaac Watts, 1707, Hymn 91, book 1.
Music: Eliakim Doolittle, in Jenks, *Musical Harmonist,* 1800.

273 MILFORD. C.M.
Words: "An Hymn for Easter-Day," in Playford, *Divine Companion,* 2d ed., 1707.
Music: Joseph Stephenson, as EASTER DAY, in *Church Harmony,* 3d ed., [1760.] Named for Milford, New Haven County, Connecticut.

274T THE GOLDEN HARP. L.M.
Words: Verse 5 of "O may I worthy prove to see," in *Hymns and Spiritual Songs for the Use of Christians* ("The Baltimore Collection"), 1801.
Music: J. P. Reese, in *The Sacred Harp,* 1870.

274B ROLL JORDAN. L.M.
Words: Verses by Charles Wesley, 1758.
Music: A. W. and J. G. McCurry, 1853, in *The Social Harp,* 1855; alto by S. M. Denson, 1911.

275T LOVING-KINDNESS. L.M.
Words: Verses by Samuel Medley, 1782.
Music: J. P. [Reese] and S. R. Penick, in *The Sacred Harp,* 1850; alto by W. M. Cooper, 1902.

275B ROLL ON. L.M.
Words: Verse by Isaac Watts, 1707, Hymn 31, book 2.
Music: Cynthia Bass, in *The Sacred Harp*, 1850; alto by Anna L. Blackshear,
1902.

276 BRIDGEWATER. L.M.
Words: Isaac Watts, 1719, Psalm 117.
Music: Lewis Edson, in Jocelin, *Chorister's Companion*, 1782; named for
Bridgewater, Plymouth County, Massachusetts.

277 ANTIOCH. L.M.
Words: Verses by Samuel Medley, 1775.
Music: F. C. Wood, in *The Sacred Harp*, 1850; alto by J. W. and W. R.
McCoy, 1902.

278T LOVE SHALL NEVER DIE. C.M.
Words: Isaac Watts, 1709, Hymn 165, book 2.
Music: *Toney Smith, 1987, in *The Sacred Harp*, 1991.

278B TRAVELING PILGRIM. L.M.
Words: Verses from stanza 5 of "O may I worthy prove to see," in *Hymns
and Spiritual Songs for the Use of Christians* ("The Baltimore Collection"),
1801.
Music: H. S. Reese, in *The Sacred Harp*, 1850; alto by Anna L. Blackshear,
1902.

279 THE SHEPHERD'S FLOCK. L.M.
Words: Philip Doddridge, in Rippon, *Selection,* 1787.
Music: J. E. Kitchens, 1935, in *Original Sacred Harp* (Denson revision), 1936.

280 WESTFORD. L.M. [3 verses].
Words: Isaac Watts, 1707, Hymn 15, book 2.
Music: Daniel Read, in *The American Singing Book*, 1785; named for
Westford, Windham County, Connecticut.

282 I'M GOING HOME. L.M.
Words: Verses 5 and 3 of "O may I worthy prove to see," in *Hymns and
Spiritual Songs for the Use of Christians* ("The Baltimore Collection"), 1801.
Music: Leonard P. Breedlove, in *The Sacred Harp*, 1850; alto by S. M.
Denson, 1911.

283 SABBATH MORNING. C.M.
Words: Charles Wesley, 1763.

Music: H. N. McGraw, 1935, in *Original Sacred Harp* (Denson revision), 1936.

284 GARDEN HYMN. 886.886.
Words: In *Hymns and Spiritual Songs for the Use of Christians* ("The Baltimore Collection"), 1803 ed.; tentatively attributed to Rev. Mr. [John Poage] Campbell by Brown and Butterworth, *Story of the Hymns and Tunes*, 1906, p. 277n.
Music: As BALTIMORE, in Davisson, *Supplement to the Kentucky Harmony*, 3d ed., 1826; a variant is LOVE DIVINE in Ingalls, *Christian Harmony*, 1805.

285T ARNOLD. C.M.D.
Words: Charles Wesley, *Funeral Hymns*, 2d series, 1759.
Music: Leonard P. Breedlove, in *The Sacred Harp*, 1850; alto by S. M. Denson, 1911.

285B LAND OF REST. C.M.
Words: Anonymous in *The Religious Telescope*, 15 January 1837.
Music: H. S. Reese, in *The Sacred Harp*, 1850.

286 HEAVENLY HOME. C.M.
Words: Verse by Matthew Sikes, in *The Sacred Harp*, 1859.
Music: W. A. Yates, in *Original Sacred Harp* (Denson revision), 1936.

287 CAMBRIDGE. C.M.
Words: William Cowper, 1779.
Music: John Randall, in Addington, *Collection of Psalm Tunes*, 6th ed., 1786. Named for Cambridge, England.

288 WHITE. C.M.
Words: Attributed to "Farwell" in Dobell, *New Selection*, 1806.
Music: Edmund Dumas, 1856, in *The Sacred Harp*, 1870; "In honor of B. F. White."

289 GREENSBOROUGH. C.M.
Words: Isaac Watts, 1707, Hymn 66, book 2.
Music: John Mercer, in *The Sacred Harp*, 1850; named for Greensborough (now Greensboro), Greene County, Georgia.

290 VICTORIA. C.M.
Words: Verse by Isaac Watts, 1707, Hymn 9, book 2.
Music: Leonard P. Breedlove, in *The Sacred Harp*, 1850; alto by Lessie Green, 1902.

291   MAJESTY. C.M.D.
      Words: Attributed to Thomas Sternhold, in *The Whole Book of Psalms*
      ("The Old Version"), 1561 ed., Psalm 18, verses 9–10.
      Music: William Billings, in *The Singing-Master's Assistant,* 1778; alto by
      Hugh McGraw, 1971.

292   BEHOLD THE SAVIOR. C.M.D.
      Words: Samuel Wesley Sr., 1700.
      Music: Paine Denson, 1935, in *Original Sacred Harp* (Denson revision),
      1936.

293   AKERS. C.M.D.
      Words: Isaac Watts, 1707, Hymn 65, book 2; the final quatrain in Broaddus
      and Broaddus, *Collection of Sacred Ballads,* 1790.
      Music: T. J. Denson, 1935, in *Original Sacred Harp* (Denson revision), 1936;
      named for the composer's second wife, Lola Akers.

294   ROCKY ROAD. P.M.
      Words: In *The New Sacred Harp* (1884), verses from a revival song, "Oh
      my mudder's in de road," in "Fifty Cabin and Plantation Songs," in
      Armstrong, Ludlow, and Fenner, *Hampton and Its Students,* 1874.
      Music: J. C. Brown, arranged by Paine Denson, 1935, in *Original Sacred
      Harp* (Denson revision), 1936; a variant of a revival song arranged by
      Thomas P. Fenner in "Fifty Cabin and Plantation Songs," in Armstrong,
      Ludlow, and Fenner, *Hampton and Its Students,* 1874. The song also
      appeared as RUGGED ROAD in *The New Sacred Harp* (1884), and as ROCKY
      ROAD, arranged by J. C. Brown, in *Sacred Hymns and Tunes* (1913).

295   ODEM. C.M.
      Words: Isaac Watts, 1707, Hymn 7, book 1.
      Music: Leon McGraw, 1935, in *Original Sacred Harp* (Denson revision),
      1936; in honor of L. P. Odem of Loretto, Tennessee.

296   SARDINIA. C.M.D.
      Words: Isaac Watts, 1719, Psalm 35, part 2.
      Music: Castle, in Atwill, *New-York and Vermont Collection,* 2d ed., [1804].
      The town of Sardinia, Erie County, New York, was named for this tune in
      1821 by one of its early pioneers, Ezra Nott (1787–1864).

297   CONVERSION. C.M.
      Words: Isaac Watts, 1719, Psalm 126.
      Music: Supply Belcher, in *The Harmony of Maine,* 1794.

298 PROVIDENCE. C.M.
Words: Isaac Watts, 1719, Psalm 116, part 2.
Music: Curtis, in *Wyeth's Repository of Music, Part 2d*, 1820; alto after Anna
L. Blackshear, 1902; a variant is PATMOS, attributed to Carrell in Davisson,
Supplement to the Kentucky Harmony, 2d ed. [ca. 1823], and perhaps in
Carrell, *Songs of Zion*, 1821 (unlocated).

299 NEW JERUSALEM. C.M.
Words: Isaac Watts, 1707, Hymn 21, book 1.
Music: Jeremiah Ingalls, in *The Village Harmony*, 2d ed., 1796.

300 CALVARY. C.M.
Words: Isaac Watts, "Death and Eternity," in *Horae Lyricae*, 1706.
Music: Daniel Read, in *The American Singing Book*, 1785.

301 GREENLAND. C.M.D.
Words: Isaac Watts, Psalm 147, "The Seasons of the Year."
Music: W. F. Moore, 1867, "Original," in *The Sacred Harp*, 1870 (p. 302); alto
by S. M. Denson, 1911.

302 LOGAN. S.M.
Words: John Leland, 1790.
Music: T. J. Denson, 1908, in James, *Union Harp*, 1909.

303 HEAVENLY LAND. C.M.
Words: Isaac Watts, 1707, Hymn 66, book 2.
Music: *Jeff Sheppard, 1987, in *The Sacred Harp*, 1991.

304 MORGAN. C.M.D.
Words: Isaac Watts, Psalm 147, "The Seasons of the Year."
Music: *The Easy Instructor, Part II*, [1803].

306 OXFORD. C.M.D.
Words: Isaac Watts, "The Nativity of Christ," in *Horae Lyricae*, 1706.
Music: Arranged by John Massengale, in *The Sacred Harp*, 1850; a fuging
variant of HAMILTON, in Knight, *Juvenile Harmony*, 1825; alto by W. M.
Cooper, 1902.

308 PARTING FRIENDS. C.M.D.
Words: Charles Wesley, 1749.
Music: E. L. King, in *The Sacred Harp*, 1850; alto after J. M. C. Shaw, 1902.

309 LIVING LAMB. C.M.
Words: Verses from Isaac Watts, *Sermons*, 1724; based on 1 Corinthians
16:13.

Music: Arranged by C. A. Davis, in *The Sacred Harp*, 1850; from a revival song; alto after Lula Munny, 1902.

310   WEEPING SAVIOR. C.M.
Words: Verses by Isaac Watts, 1707, Hymn 9, book 2.
Music: Arranged by Edmund Dumas, in *The Sacred Harp*, 1870; from "Russian Air" in Moore, *Selection of Popular National Airs* [1818], where it is arranged by John Stevenson; alto by S. M. Denson, 1911.

311   SILVER STREET. S.M.
Words: Verses from Isaac Watts, 1719, Psalm 95.
Music: Isaac Smith, in Addington, *Collection of Psalm Tunes,* [1779]. Named for Silver Street Meeting House, London.

312T   SING TO ME OF HEAVEN. S.M.
Words: Mary Stanley Bunce Dana Shindler, in *The Religious Telescope*, 1840.
Music: John Massengale, in *The Sacred Harp*, 1850; probably based on a song tune; alto by Henrietta Spivey, 1902.

312B   RESTORATION. 8787.
Words: Verses by Robert Robinson, 1758.
Music: *The Southern Harmony*, 1835; alto in *The Hesperian Harp*, 1848.

313T   CONCORD. S.M.
Words: Isaac Watts, 1707, Hymn 30, book 2, verses 8, 9, and 10.
Music: Oliver Holden, in *The Union Harmony*, 1793.

313B   COBB. C.M.
Words: Verse 1 by Isaac Watts, 1707, Hymn 17, book 2; verse 2 by Isaac Watts, 1719, Psalm 145, part 2, verse 5.
Music: *P. Dan Brittain, 1971, in *The Sacred Harp*, 1991; in honor of Buell E. Cobb.

314   CLEBURNE. C.M.
Words: Edward Perronet, 1779.
Music: S. M. Denson, 1908, in James, *Union Harp*, 1909; named for Cleburne County, Alabama.

315   IMMENSITY. L.M.
Words: Isaac Watts, 1719, Psalm 139, part 1.
Music: Eliakim Doolittle, in *The Psalm Singer's Companion*, 1806.

316 NEW HOPE. L.M.D.
Words: Anne Steele, 1760.
Music: A. M. Cagle, 1908, in James, *Union Harp,* 1909.

317 JACKSON. L.M.
Words: In Clay, *Hymns and Spiritual Songs,* 1793.
Music: M. F. McWhorter, 1908, in James, *Union Harp,* 1909.

318 PRESENT JOYS. L.M.
Words: Joseph Cottle, *Hymns and Sacred Lyrics,* 1828, verses 1 and 6.
Music: A. M. Cagle, 1908, in James, *Union Harp,* 1909.

319 RELIGION IS A FORTUNE. 7676.
Words: Verses by John Leland, 1793.
Music: William L. Williams, in *The Sacred Harp,* 1850; alto by S. M.
Denson, 1911.

320 FUNERAL ANTHEM.
Words: Revelation 14:13.
Music: William Billings, in *The Singing-Master's Assistant,* 1778.

321 NEWNAN. C.M.D.
Words: Joseph Hart, *Hymns,* 1762, supplement.
Music: J. P. Reese, Original, in *The Sacred Harp,* 1859 (p. 368); alto by S.
M. Denson, 1911. Spelled NEWMAN in previous editions, it was correctly
spelled NEWNAN in the index of J. L. White's fourth edition with supple-
ment (1911); named for Newnan, Coweta County, Georgia.

322 MAN'S REDEMPTION. P.M. [9797]
Words: In Battle, *Collection of Hymns and Spiritual Songs,* 1814.
Music: S. M. Brown, "Original," in *The Sacred Harp,* 1870 (p. 321); alto by S.
M. Denson, 1911.

323T MULLINS. 8787.
Words: In Peak, *New collection of hymns and spiritual songs,* 3d ed., 1793.
Music: Edmund Dumas, in *The Sacred Harp,* 1870, "in honor of Eld. John
Mullins"; alto by S. M. Denson, 1911; a variant of HALLELUJAH, in *Wyeth's
Repository of Sacred Music, Part Second,* 1813.

323B SOFT MUSIC. P.M.
Words: Mary Stanley Bunce Dana Shindler, in *The Southern Harp,* 1841.
Music: Arranged by B. F. White, in *The Sacred Harp,* 1850; alto by S. M.
Denson, 1911; in *The Southern Harp,* 1841, from a German song tune, "Du,
du liegst mir im Herzen."

324 NORTH PORT. L.M.
     Words: Verses by John Cennick, 1743.
     Music: Dr. R. R. Osborne, in *The Sacred Harp*, 1850; bass by J. Smith;
     named for Northport, Tuscaloosa County, Alabama.

325 SOLDIER OF THE CROSS. C.M.
     Words: Isaac Watts, *Sermons*, 1724; based on 1 Corinthians 16:13.
     Music: George B. Daniell, in James, *Union Harp*, 1909.

326 WEARY PILGRIM. P.M. [7979.7888.88]
     Words: Caleb Jarvis Taylor, in *Spiritual Songs*, 1804.
     Music: Leonard P. Breedlove, in *The Sacred Harp*, 1850; alto after W. R.
     McCoy.

327 INVITATION. L.M.D.
     Words: Isaac Watts, 1707, Hymn 70, book 1; and Hymn 78, book 1, verse 7.
     Music: Jacob Kimball, in *Select Harmony*, [1784].

328 PRAISE GOD. C.M.D.
     Words: Charles Wesley, 1742.
     Music: S. M. Denson, in *Original Sacred Harp*, 1911 (p. 528).

329 VAIN WORLD ADIEU. P.M. [8888.883]
     Words: In Leavitt, *Seaman's Devotional Assistant*, 1830.
     Music: [Arranged by] Edmund Dumas, 1856, in *The Sacred Harp*, 1870;
     alto by S. M. Denson, 1911; a variant of a revival tune associated with this
     text, cf. SONNET in Mansfield, *American Vocalist*, 1848, and THE SAILOR'S
     HOME, claimed by W. M. Caudill and W. Walker, in *Southern Harmony*,
     1854.

330T HORTON. C.M.
     Words: Cento; verse 1, Frances Maria Cowper; verse 2, Amanda Burdette
     Denson; verse 3, unknown; verse 4, *Southern Harmony*, 1835; verse 5, Isaac
     Watts, 1707, Hymn 21, book 1, verse 6; Broaddus and Broaddus, *Collection
     of Sacred Ballads*, 1790. Named for the family of the composer's second
     wife.
     Music: Paine Denson, 1935, in *Original Sacred Harp* (Denson revision),
     1936.

330B FELLOWSHIP. S.M.
     Words: John Fawcett, in *Hymns adapted to the circumstances of Public
     Worship and Private Devotion*, 1782.
     Music: Paine Denson, 1935, in *Original Sacred Harp* (Denson revision),
     1936.

331   JESTER. P.M.
Words: S. M. Denson, 1908, in James, *Union Harp,* 1909.
Music: S. M. Denson, 1908, in James, *Union Harp,* 1909, "published in honor of Prof. N. D. Jester, of Franklin County, Ala."

332   SONS OF SORROW. 8s & 7s.
Words: In Harrod, *Social and Camp-Meeting Songs,* 7th ed., 1825; a fuller text, claimed by Selah Gridley, is in *Mill of the Muses,* 1828.
Music: In Hauser, *Hesperian Harp,* 1848; a variant of MOULDERING VINE by James P. Carrell, in Davisson, *Supplement to the Kentucky Harmony,* 2d ed., [ca. 1823]; "treble by Wm. Houser"; alto after Mrs. E. D. Martin, 1902.

333   FAMILY CIRCLE. 8787.
Words: Verses by Robert Robinson, 1758.
Music: R. E. Brown [Sr.] and B. F. White, in *The Sacred Harp,* 1850; alto after Anna L. Blackshear, 1902.

334   O COME AWAY. P.M.
Words: In Stowe, *Melodies for the Temperance Band,* 1856.
Music: *The Hesperian Harp,* 1848; from "Krambambuli," a German drinking song; "treble and alto by Wm. Houser."

335   RETURN AGAIN. 8787.
Words: Verses by John Newton, in Cowper and Newton, *Olney Hymns,* 1779.
Music: William L. Williams, in *The Sacred Harp,* 1850; alto by Anna L. Blackshear, 1902.

336   ETERNAL HOME. C.M.
Words: Isaac Watts, 1719, Psalm 90, part 1.
Music: S. M. Denson, in *Original Sacred Harp,* 1911 (p. 536).

337   MERCY'S FREE. P.M. [9393.8883]
Words: Two verses in *Pious Songs: Social, Prayer, Closet, and Camp Meeting Hymns, and Choruses,* 3d ed., 1836; the complete text (altered here) is in Brunson and Pitman, *Sweet Singer of Israel,* 1840.
Music: Leonard P. Breedlove, in *The Sacred Harp,* 1850; alto by William Walker, 1866.

338   SAWYER'S EXIT. P.M. [9898]
Words: Seymour Boughton Sawyer (1808–44), Methodist preacher of Montgomery, Alabama, in *The Sacred Harp,* 1850. "These words were

composed by Rev. S. B. Sawyer on the day of his death, with request that this tune should be set to them."
Music: Arranged by John Massengale, in *The Sacred Harp*, 1850; from a song tune, "Rosin the Beau."

339   WHEN I AM GONE. P.M. [X4X4.XXX4]
Words: Mary Stanley Bunce Dana Shindler, in *The Southern Harp*, 1841. Text altered, especially in verse 2.
Music: Arranged by M. H. Turner, in *The Sacred Harp*, 1850; alto by William Walker, 1866; from the song tune "Long, Long Ago" by Thomas Haynes Bayly.

340   ODEM. C.M.
Words: James Rowe (1865–1933), 1915.
Music: T. J. Denson, 1935, in *Original Sacred Harp* (Denson revision), 1936; in honor of Lonnie P. Odem of St. Joseph, Tennessee.

341   THE LONE PILGRIM. P.M. [Y8Y8]
Words: John Ellis, 1838, on visiting the grave of Joseph Thomas (1791–1835; see plate 10), an itinerant preacher known as the White Pilgrim; altered in *The Sacred Harp*, 1850. The popular text was published as a broadside.
Music: Arranged by B. F. White, in *The Sacred Harp*, 1850; alto after Minnie Floyd, 1902; a variant of MISSIONARY, OR WHITE PILGRIM, in Thomas Commuck, *Indian Melodies*, 1845, where the melody is called "a tradition of the New-York Indians."

342   THE OLD-FASHIONED BIBLE. P.M. [ZYZY D]
Words: In the *Charleston* [S.C.] *Courier*, 1818, a parody of "The Old Oaken Bucket" by Samuel Woodworth.
Music: Arranged by Leonard P. Breedlove, in *The Sacred Harp*, 1850, from "The Methodist and the Formalist," a revival tune.

343   HAPPY HOME. L.M.
Words: Anonymous in *The Sacred Harp*, 1859.
Music: J. P. Reese, in *The Sacred Harp*, 1859 (p. 377); alto by S. M. Denson, 1911.

344   RAINBOW. C.M.
Words: Isaac Watts, 1719, Psalm 65, part 2.
Music: Timothy Swan, in Brownson, *Select Harmony* [1785]; rearranged by Phil A. Taber, 1988, in *The Sacred Harp*, 1991.

345T JESUS IS MY FRIEND. L.M.

Words: Verse 6 of "There is a heaven above the skies," in *Hymns and Spiritual Songs for the Use of Christians* ("The Baltimore Collection"), 1803 ed.

Music: J. P. Reese, "Original," in *The Sacred Harp,* 1870.

345B I'M ON MY JOURNEY HOME. L.M.

Words: Verse in Mead, *General Selection,* 1807.

Music: Sarah Lancaster, "Original," in *The Sacred Harp,* 1859 (p. 393); alto by S. M. Denson, 1911.

346 THE AMERICAN STAR. P.M. [ZYZY D]

Words: John McCreery, verse 3 of "Come, strike the bold anthem, the war-dogs are howling," in *The Songster's Repository,* 1811.

Music: Arranged by D. P. White, in *The Sacred Harp,* 1850, from "The Humors of Glen," a song and dance tune in McLean, *A Collection of Favourite Scots Tunes* [ca. 1774].

347 CHRISTIAN'S FAREWELL. P.M. [44X.44X]

Words: Altered from "My brethren farewell" (meter 55Y.55Y) in B. Lloyd, *Primitive Hymns,* 1841, or 3d ed., 1845.

Music: *Raymond C. Hamrick, 1989, in *The Sacred Harp,* 1991.

348T AINSLIE. C.M.

Words: Berryman Hicks (1778–1839), in *Southern Harmony,* 1835. "This song was composed by the Rev. B. Hicks (a Baptist minister of South Carolina) and sent to his wife while he was confined in Tennessee by a fever of which he afterwards recovered" (p. 19).

Music: *Judy Hauff, 1988, in *The Sacred Harp,* 1991.

348B FLEETING DAYS. C.M.

Words: Isaac Watts, 1707, Hymn 58, book 2.

Music: Henry G. Mann, October 26, 1869, "Original," in *The Sacred Harp,* 1870 (p. 395).

349 A CROSS FOR ME. C.M.

Words: Thomas Shepherd, 1693.

Music: O. A. Parris, 1935, in *Original Sacred Harp* (Denson revision), 1936.

350 NATIVITY. C.M.

Words: Charles Wesley, 1739.

Music: Thomas Jarman, in *Sacred Harmony,* [ca. 1804]; rearranged, and the fuging section removed, by Phil A. Taber, 1988, in *The Sacred Harp,* 1991.

351 PITTSFORD. C.M.
Words: Isaac Watts, 1707, Hymn 87, book 2, verse 6.
Music: Hezekiah Moors, in *Province Harmony*, 1809; named for Pittsford, Rutland County, Vermont.

352 SWANTON. L.M.
Words: Isaac Watts, 1707, Hymn 69, book 1.
Music: Hezekiah Moors, in *Province Harmony*, 1809; named for Swanton, Franklin County, Vermont.

353 McGRAW. L.M.
Words: Isaac Watts, 1719, Psalm 145.
Music: *P. Dan Brittain, 1971, in *The Sacred Harp*, 1991; named for Hugh McGraw.

354T LEBANON. C.M.
Words: Anne Steele, 1756.
Music: *J. Monroe Denton, 1980, in *The Sacred Harp*, 1991.

354B HAPPY LAND. P.M. [6464.66664]
Words: Andrew Young, 1838.
Music: Arranged by L. P. Breedlove, in *The Sacred Harp*, 1850; alto by S. M. Denson, 1911; from Robert A. Smith's adaptation of a song tune, "I've come from a happy land."

355 ANTHEM ON THE SAVIOR.
Words: A prose homily, perhaps by B. F. White.
Music: B. F. White, in *The Sacred Harp*, 1850.

358 MURILLO'S LESSON. P.M. [YYYY D]
Words: Timothy Dwight, "Columbia," in *The American Musical Miscellany*, 1798; said to date from 1777 or 1778, when Dwight served as chaplain to the Continental forces. The first verse in the musical setting is the last verse of Dwight's poem. The second verse, originally the third, was underlaid in 1911, with the last couplet altered and Christianized.
Music: "Unknown" in *The Sacred Harp*, 1850; alto by S. M. Denson, 1911; from "Lesson by Morelli," a march tune, in *The Instrumental Assistant*, 1800, and elsewhere.

359 THE BRIDE'S FAREWELL. 8787.
Words: Miss M. L. Beevor, in *The Ladies' Pearl and Literary Gleaner*, August 1840.
Music: H. S. Reese, "Original," in *The Sacred Harp*, 1870 (p. 460).

360   THE ROYAL BAND. P.M. [ZYZY D]
      Words: In Mintz, *Spiritual Song Book*, 1805.
      Music: W. T. Power, in *The Sacred Harp*, 1850; alto by Anna L. Blackshear,
      1902.

361   LOVING JESUS. P.M. [887.X887]
      Words: Anonymous, in *The Sacred Harp*, 1850.
      Music: [B. F.] White and Searcy, in *The Sacred Harp*, 1850; alto by S. M.
      Denson, 1911; from the glee "Viva tutte le vezzose" by Felice Giardini;
      also popular as a fife tune.

362   NORWICH. C.M.D.
      Words: Isaac Watts, 1707, Hymn 91, book 2.
      Music: D. P. White, in *The Sacred Harp*, 1850; adapted from MALABAR by
      Samuel Holyoke, in *The Columbian Repository of Sacred Harmony*, 1803.

365   SOUTHWELL. 886.886.
      Words: Anonymous, in *The American Musical Magazine*, 1786–87; sug-
      gested by Samuel Stennett's "'Tis finished! so the Saviour cried."
      Music: Elihu Carpenter, in *The American Musical Magazine*, 1786–87.

367   CONSOLATION. C.M.D.
      Words: Annie Denson Aaron, in *Original Sacred Harp* (Denson revision),
      1936.
      Music: Annie Denson Aaron, in *Original Sacred Harp* (Denson revision),
      1936.

368   STONY POINT. 886.886.
      Words: *Social and Camp-Meeting Songs, for the Pious*, 7th ed., 1825.
      Music: *Judy Hauff, 1990, in *The Sacred Harp*, 1991.

369   SEND S BLESSING. P.M. [55X.55X]
      Words: John Gambold, 1748.
      Music: B. F. White and L. L. Ledbetter, in *The Sacred Harp*, 1859; alto after
      the Cooper revision, 1902.

370   MONROE. 8787 D.
      Words: Henry F. Lyte, 1824.
      Music: W. S. Turner, "Original," in *The Sacred Harp*, 1859; alto by W. R.
      McCoy, 1902.

371   HEAVENLY DOVE. C.M.
      Words: Isaac Watts, 1707.
      Music: Absalom Ogletree, in *The Sacred Harp*, 1859; adapted from TURNER
      by Abraham Maxim, in *The Oriental Harmony*, 1802.

372   ROCKPORT. S.M.D.
Words: George Heath, 1721.
Music: *James P. Carnes, 1989, in *The Sacred Harp,* 1991.

373   HOMEWARD BOUND. C.M.D.
Words: O. A. Parris, in *Original Sacred Harp* (Denson revision), 1936.
Music: Howard Denson, in *Original Sacred Harp* (Denson revision), 1936.

374   OH, SING WITH ME! L.M.D.
Words: Anonymous, in *The Sacred Harp,* 1859.
Music: Priscilla R. Lancaster, in *The Sacred Harp,* 1859; alto by Anna L. Blackshear, 1902.

375   LOVE THE LORD. C.M.
Words: Verse by Isaac Watts, 1707, Hymn 9, book 2.
Music: [Arranged by] J. P. Reese, in *The Sacred Harp,* 1859; alto after B. P. Poyner; a variant of HALLELUJAH by John Nash Bereman (1785–1853), in Shaw and Spilman, *Columbian Harmony,* 1829.

376   HELP ME TO SING. P.M. [9898D]
Words: In Mead, *General Selection,* 1807, altered.
Music: B. F. White, in *The Sacred Harp,* 1859; alto by Anna L. Blackshear, 1902.

377   ETERNAL PRAISE. L.M.
Words: Isaac Watts, 1719, Psalm 117.
Music: O. A. Parris, in *Original Sacred Harp* (Denson revision), 1936.

378T   HEAVENLY PORT. C.M.
Words: Verses from Samuel Stennett, in Rippon, *Selection,* 1787.
Music: Arranged by Edmund Dumas, August 8, 1859, in *The Sacred Harp,* 1859; alto by W. M. Cooper, 1902; from a revival song.

378B   NEVER TURN BACK. L.M.
Words: From verse 8 of "O may I worthy prove to see," in *Hymns and Spiritual Songs for the Use of Christians* ("The Baltimore Collection"), 1801; this couplet is based on verse 10 of Samuel Medley's "Now in a song of grateful praise," 1776.
Music: Arranged for *The Organ* by "J. P. Rees & Miss F. E. Parkerson"; in *The Sacred Harp,* 1870 (p. 381); alto by W. R. McCoy, 1902.

379   SPAN OF LIFE. C.M.D.
Words: Frances Maria Cowper, in *Original Poems on Various Occasions,* 1792.

Music: S. M. Brown, "Original," in *The Sacred Harp*, 1870; alto after J. W. McCoy, 1902.

380 LAWRENCEBURG. L.M.D.
Words: Isaac Watts, Hymn 31, book 2, 1707, verses 3 and 4.
Music: T. J. Denson, 1935, in *Original Sacred Harp* (Denson revision), 1936; named for Lawrenceburg, Tennessee.

381 SING ON. C.M.D.
Words: Anonymous, in *Original Sacred Harp* (Denson revision), 1936.
Music: T. B. McGraw, 1935, in *Original Sacred Harp* (Denson revision), 1936.

382 COSTON. C.M.D.
Words: As "Brethren farewell," in Joshua Smith, *Divine Hymns*, 8th ed., 1797.
Music: T. J. Denson, 1935, in *Original Sacred Harp* (Denson revision), 1936; named for W. T. Coston of Dallas, Texas.

383 ETERNAL DAY. C.M.D.
Words: Charles Wesley, 1759.
Music: J. P. Reese, "music original," in *The Sacred Harp*, 1859; alto after Anna L. Blackshear, 1902.

384 PANTING FOR HEAVEN. 8888 D.
Words: Verse 3 of "Ye angels who stand round the throne," by Maria de Fleury, in *Divine Poems, and Essays on Various Subjects*, 1791.
Music: S. M. Brown, "Original," in *The Sacred Harp*, 1870; alto altered from Minnie Floyd, 1902.

385T FIGHT ON. S.M.
Words: Verse 4 of "My soul be on thy guard" by George Heath, 1781.
Music: J. P. Reese, "Original," in *The Sacred Harp*, 1859; alto altered from W. L. McGee and W. R. McCoy, 1902.

385B CAN I LEAVE YOU? 8787.47.
Words: S. F. Smith, 1832; a parody of "Sweetest Love, I'll Not Forget Thee" by Thomas Moore.
Music: R. F. Ball, "Original," in *The Sacred Harp*, 1859 (p. 395); alto altered from J. W. Watson, 1902.

386 CHRIST OUR SONG. C.M.D.
Words: Isaac Watts, 1707, Hymn 20, book 1; and John Cennick, 1743, verse 4 of "Thou dear Redeemer, dying Lamb."
Music: T. B. McGraw, in *Original Sacred Harp* (Denson revision), 1936.

387 PENICK. C.M.
Words: Matthew Sikes, in *The Sacred Harp*, 1859.
Music: Matthew Sikes, in *The Sacred Harp*, 1859; alto by S. M. Denson, 1911; named in honor of Spencer Reed Penick.

388 THE HAPPY SAILOR. P.M.
Words: In Bryan, *Songster's Companion*, 1837; here altered, and with a new chorus. See page 79, above.
Music: Arranged by B. F. White, in *The Sacred Harp*, 1859; from a revival song; alto after Minnie Floyd, 1902.

389 FREDERICKSBURG. C.M.
Words: Anonymous, in *Original Sacred Harp* (Denson revision), 1936.
Music: O. H. Frederick, in *Original Sacred Harp* (Denson revision), 1936.

390 NEW PROSPECT. C.M.
Words: Anonymous, in *The Religious Telescope*, 15 January 1837.
Music: Arranged by W. S. Turner, in *The Sacred Harp*, 1859, from a revival song, in McLain, *Appendix to the Christian's Harp*, ca. 1835; alto after Anna L. Blackshear, 1902.

391 SOUNDING JOY. S.M.
Words: Isaac Watts, 1719, Psalm 19, part 2.
Music: Justin Morgan, in Benham, *Federal Harmony*, 1790; alto by S. M. Denson, 1911.

392 MANCHESTER. C.M.D.
Words: Isaac Watts, 1707; second half of verse 2 anonymous in Broaddus and Broaddus, *Collection of Sacred Ballads*, 1790.
Music: Paine Denson, in *Original Sacred Harp* (Denson revision), 1936.

393 ALEXANDER. C.M.
Words: Timothy R. Gilmore, 1986, in *The Sacred Harp*, 1991.
Music: *Timothy R. Gilmore, 1986, in *The Sacred Harp*, 1991; named for Mr. and Mrs. Roie Alexander of Oneonta, Alabama.

394 THE MESSIAH'S PRAISE. S.M.
Words: Benjamin Rhodes, 1787.
Music: R. F. M. Mann and James A. Spark, "Original," in *The Sacred Harp*, 1870; alto by S. M. Denson, 1911.

395 NEW BETHEL. C.M.D.
Words: Charles Wesley, 1739.
Music: L. A. McGraw, in *Original Sacred Harp* (Denson revision), 1936.

396 NOTES ALMOST DIVINE. 886.886.
Words: Samuel Medley, 1789.
Music: Paine Denson, in *Original Sacred Harp* (Denson revision), 1936.

397 THE FOUNTAIN. C.M.D.
Words: William Cowper, 1772.
Music: T. J. Denson, in *Original Sacred Harp* (Denson revision), 1936.

398 THE DYING BOY. C.M.D.
Words: Anonymous in *The Sacred Harp,* 1859.
Music: H. S. Reese, in *The Sacred Harp,* 1859.

399T THE DYING FRIEND. P.M. [8886]
Words: Lee S. Wells, in *Original Sacred Harp* (Denson revision), 1936.
Music: Lee S. Wells, in *Original Sacred Harp* (Denson revision), 1936.

399B HAPPY CHRISTIAN. 669.669.
Words: Charles Wesley, 1749.
Music: Arranged by B. E. Cunningham, in *Original Sacred Harp* (Denson
revision), 1936; a variant of SOLICITATION by P. Axton, in W. Moore,
Columbian Harmony, 1825.

400 STRUGGLE ON. L.M.
Words: Anonymous in *The Sacred Harp,* 1859.
Music: H. S. Reese, in *The Sacred Harp,* 1859; alto by S. M. Denson, 1911.

401 CUBA. P.M.
Words: Anonymous in *The Sacred Harp,* 1859.
Music: J. A. Bolen and H. S. Reese, in *The Sacred Harp,* 1859 [the first name
is printed as J. H. Bolen in 1870, presumably a correction]; alto by S. M.
Denson, 1911.

402 PROTECTION. 8888.88.
Words: Joseph Addison, 1712; paraphrase of Psalm 23.
Music: C. F. Letson, "Original," in *The Sacred Harp,* 1870.

403 HEAVENLY REST. C.M.
Words: August M. Toplady, 1759.
Music: John S. Terry, "Original," in *The Sacred Harp,* 1870; alto by S. M.
Denson, 1911.

404 YOUTH WILL SOON BE GONE. L.M.D.
Words: In Robinson, *New England Sunday School Hymn Book,* 1830.
Music: J. P. Reese, "Original," in *The Organ,* 6 June 1855; in *The Sacred
Harp,* 1870; alto by S. M. Denson, 1911.

405   THE MARCELLAS. 7777 D.
      Words: John Cennick, 1742.
      Music: Edmund Dumas, "Original," in *The Sacred Harp,* 1859; alto by S. M.
      Denson, 1911.

406   NEW HARMONY. 8787 D.
      Words: Verses 4, 2, and 3 of "O that I had some humble place," in P. D.
      Myers, *The Zion Songster,* 3d ed., 1829.
      Music: M. L. A. Lancaster, in *The Sacred Harp,* 1859.

407   CHARLTON. C.M.
      Words: Frances Maria Cowper, in *Original Poems on Various Occasions,*
      1792.
      Music: Leonard P. Breedlove, in *The Organ,* 3 May 1854; in *The Sacred Harp,*
      1859.

408   WEEPING MARY. P.M.
      Words: Anonymous in *The Sacred Harp,* 1859.
      Music: J. P. Reese, in *The Sacred Harp,* 1859; alto after W. M. Cooper, 1902.

409   PROMISED DAY. C.M.
      Words: Isaac Watts, 1707, Hymn 21, book 1, verses 6, 4, and 5.
      Music: L. M. Raiford, in *The Sacred Harp,* 1859; alto by S. M. Denson, 1911.

410T THE DYING CALIFORNIAN. 8787.
      Words: Kate Harris of Pascoag, Rhode Island, *The New England Diadem
      and Rhode Island Temperance Pledge,* 9 February 1850, "suggested on hear-
      ing read an extract of a letter from Captain Chase, containing the dying
      words of Brown Owen, who recently died on his passage to California."
      Music: R. F. Ball and Drinkard, in *The Sacred Harp,* 1859; rearranged, and
      alto added, by Howard Denson in *Original Sacred Harp* (Denson revision),
      1936.

410B MUTUAL LOVE. 7676 D.
      Words: John Leland, 1793.
      Music: William Walker, 1833, in *Southern Harmony,* 1835; alto in *Christian
      Harmony,* 1867; arranged by Howard Denson in *Original Sacred Harp*
      (Denson revision), 1936.

411   MORNING PRAYER. C.M.D.
      Words: In B. Lloyd, *Primitive Hymns,* 1841, or 3d ed., 1845.
      Music: T. J. Denson, in *Original Sacred Harp* (Denson revision), 1936.

412 NEW HOSANNA. L.M.
Words: Verses in John Dobell's *New Selection*, 1806, as "Awake, arise, and hail the morn."
Music: [Arranged by] H. S. Reese, in *The Sacred Harp*, 1859, from a revival song; see Collins, *Timbrel of Zion*, 1853, p. 319; alto by W. M. Cooper, 1902.

413 THE LOVED ONES. Y8Y8 D.
Words: Margaret Courtney (1822–62).
Music: [Arranged by] E. T. Pound, in *The Sacred Harp*, 1859; alto by S. M. Denson, 1911; from "Be Kind to the Loved Ones at Home," by Isaac B. Woodbury, 1847.

414 PARTING FRIENDS. C.M.D.
Words: Anonymous in *The Sacred Harp*, 1859.
Music: "Arranged by J. C. Graham," in *The Sacred Harp*, 1859 (p. 377, not in index); alto after Anna L. Blackshear, 1902.

415 EASTER MORN. 7777.
Words: Verse 1, *Lyra Davidica*, 1708, anonymous paraphrase of a Latin hymn, "Surrexit Christus hodie," altered in John Arnold, *Compleat Psalmodist*, 1749; verse 2, Thomas Scott, 1769, in *Gospel Magazine*, September 1775, as altered by Thomas Gibbons, in *Hymns Adapted to Divine Worship*, 1784.
Music: *David Ivey, 1988, in *The Sacred Harp*, 1991.

416 THE CHRISTIAN'S NIGHTLY SONG. P.M. [66X.66X]
Words: In Mead, *General Selection*, 1807; here verses 1 and 8 of 10.
Music: E. T. Pound, "Original," in *The Organ*, 17 May 1855; in *The Sacred Harp*, 1859; alto by Hugh McGraw, 1971.

417 WEEPING PILGRIM. P.M.
Words: Almost exclusively a chorus, in that only one word changes per verse; text is perhaps by the composer, J. P. Rees [*sic*].
Music: J. P. Rees [*sic*], in *The Sacred Harp*, 1859; alto by S. M. Denson, 1911.

418 REESE. C.M.
Words: Verses by Isaac Watts, 1709, Hymn 110, book 1.
Music: Edmund Dumas, "Original," in *The Sacred Harp*, 1859; alto by S. M. Denson, 1911; named in honor of John Palmer Reese.

419 MELANCHOLY DAY. C.M.D.
Words: Isaac Watts, 1707, Hymn 52, book 2.
Music: H. S. Reese, "Original," in *The Sacred Harp*, 1859; alto by S. M. Denson, 1911.

420 BISHOP. C.M.
Words: Octavia Bishop McGraw, 1935, in *Original Sacred Harp* (Denson revision), 1936.
Music: T. B. McGraw, 1935, in *Original Sacred Harp* (Denson revision), 1936; named for the composer's wife and her family.

421 SWEET MORNING. L.M.
Words: Verses from "Come ye that love the Lord, indeed," anonymous, in Broaddus and Broaddus, *Collection of Sacred Ballads*, 1790, altered.
Music: Arranged by H. S. Reese, in *The Sacred Harp*, 1859; alto by Anna L. Blackshear, 1902; from a revival song.

422 BURDETTE. C.M.
Words: Charles Wesley, 1742.
Music: Whitt Denson, in James, *Union Harp*, 1909; named for the composer's wife and her family.

423 GRANTVILLE. C.M.
Words: Isaac Watts, 1707. Hymn 65, book 2, verse 2.
Music: J. P. Reese, in *The Sacred Harp*, 1859; alto by S. M. Denson, 1911; named for Grantville, Coweta County, Georgia.

424 SWEET UNION. L.M.
Words: Samuel Medley, 1782.
Music: J. P. Reese, in *The Sacred Harp*, 1859; alto by S. M. Denson, 1911.

425 GOLDEN STREETS. P.M.
Words: This couplet is from the chorus of JERUSALEM, p. 53; its second line seems to have appeared first with that tune in *The Southern Harmony*, 1835.
Music: J. L. Pickard, in *The Sacred Harp*, 1859; alto after Anna L. Blackshear; a revival chorus.

426T KELLEY. C.M.D.
Words: Amanda Burdette Denson, 1908, in James, *Union Harp*, 1909.
Music: Amanda Burdette Denson, 1908, in James, *Union Harp*, 1909.

426B JASPER. C.M.
Words: Ottiwell Heginbotham, 1794.
Music: T. J. Denson, 1907, in James, *Union Harp*, 1909; named for Jasper, Walker County, Alabama.

428 WORLD UNKNOWN. S.M.
Words: Charles Wesley, 1763.

Music: H. S. Reese, "Original," in *The Sacred Harp*, 1859; alto by S. M. Denson, 1911.

429   CHRISTIAN'S DELIGHT. L.M.
Words: Verses by Samuel Ecking, 1778; detached chorus appears in *Pious Songs: Social, Prayer, Closet, and Camp Meeting Hymns, and Choruses*, 3d ed., 1836.
Music: William L. Williams, in *The Sacred Harp*, 1859; alto by S. M. Denson, 1911; from a revival tune.

430   ARBACOOCHEE. C.M.D.
Words: Isaac Watts, 1719, Psalm 35, part 2, as altered by Joel Barlow, 1785.
Music: S. M. Denson, 1908, in James, *Union Harp*, 1909; named for Arbacoochee, Cleburne County, Alabama. J. S. James adds by way of dedication that "the words are great favorites of Wyley J. James [Wiley Jones James, 1834–1924], who resides in Tallapoosa, Ga., and who is a great admirer of the old sacred songs."

431   NEW BETHANY. L.M.
Words: Harriet Auber, 1829.
Music: B. F. White Jr., "Original," in *The Sacred Harp*, 1870.

432   CHEVES. L.M.
Words: William P. Biddle and William J. Newborn, *The Baptist Hymn Book*, 1825.
Music: Oliver Bradfield, 1857, in *The Sacred Harp*, 1870; alto by S. M. Denson, 1911.

433   McKAY. C.M.D.
Words: Samuel Stennett, in Rippon, *Selection*, 1787; verses 2 and 3 of "On Jordan's stormy banks I stand."
Music: S. M. Denson, 1908, in James, *Union Harp*, 1909; in honor of Rev. S. M. McKay (Samuel Martin McKay, 1828–91) of Clay County, Alabama.

434   FILLMORE. L.M.
Words: Ottiwell Heginbotham, 1794.
Music: J. P. Reese, "for the Organ," in *The Sacred Harp*, 1870.

435   SACRED REST. L.M.
Words: Isaac Watts, 1719, Palm 92, part 1, verse 2.
Music: W. D. Jones, "Original," in *The Sacred Harp*, 1870.

436   MORNING SUN. L.M.D.
Words: In Wolcott, *Selection of Hymns and Spiritual Songs*, 1817.
Music: S. M. Denson, in *Original Sacred Harp*, 1911.

437   SIDNEY. C.M.D.
Words: Isaac Watts, Psalm 23, 1719; the second half of the text is
anonymous.
Music: Whitt Denson, 1908, in James, *Union Harp*, 1909; named for the
composer's mother, Sidney Burdette Denson.

438   THE MARRIAGE IN THE SKIES. C.M.D.
Words: Sidney Burdette Denson, in James, *Union Harp*, 1909.
Music: Sidney Burdette Denson, in James, *Union Harp*, 1909.

439   JORDAN. C.M.D.
Words: Samuel Stennett, in Rippon, *Selection*, 1787.
Music: A. M. Cagle, 1908, in James, *Union Harp*, 1909.

440   NORTH SALEM. C.M.
Words: Isaac Watts, 1707, Hymn 62, book 2.
Music: Stephen Jenks, in *The New-England Harmonist*, 1799; counter by
[W. H.] Swan, in *The Harp of Columbia*, 1848. Named for North Salem,
Westchester County, New York.

441   RAYMOND. C.M.
Words: Philip Doddridge, 1755.
Music: John G. McCurry, in *The Social Harp*, 1855; alto after *Christian
Harmony*, 1867; a major-mode adaptation of NORTH SALEM by Jenks, page
440.

442   NEW JORDAN. C.M.D.
Words: Samuel Stennett, in Rippon, *Selection*, 1787.
Music: *The Easy Instructor*, 10th ed., 1815; possibly by Nehemiah Shumway.

444   ALL SAINTS NEW. L.M.D.
Words: Isaac Watts, 1707, Hymn 31, book 2, verses 3 and 4.
Music: Amariah Hall, in *The Worcester Collection*, 3d ed., 1791; alto by S. M.
Denson, 1911.

445   PASSING AWAY. C.M.
Words: Verses from Charles Wesley, *Hymns for Children*, 1763.
Music: John A. Watson, December 1872, in Walker, *Christian Harmony*, 1873.

446   INFINITE DAY. L.M.D.
Words: Isaac Watts, 1707, Hymn 66, book 2.

Music: Ruth Denson Edwards, in *Original Sacred Harp* (Denson revision), 1936.

447 WONDROUS CROSS. L.M.D.
Words: Isaac Watts, 1707, Hymn 7, book 3.
Music: Paine Denson, July 4, 1932, in *Original Sacred Harp* (Denson revision), 1936.

448T CONSECRATION. 8888.88.
Words: Charles Wesley, verse 4 of "Behold the servant of the Lord," 1744.
Music: W. S. Turner, "Original," in *The Sacred Harp*, 1859 (p. 422).

448B THE GRIEVED SOUL. 7676 D.
Words: Joseph Hart, 1759.
Music: [Arranged by] Miss M. A. Hendon, in *The Sacred Harp*, 1859; alto by Julia Sellers, 1902; a variant of OHIO, in Knight, *Juvenile Harmony*, 1825.

449 FATHERLAND. P.M. [9878 D.]
Words: William Hunter, in *Select Melodies*, 1843.
Music: Samuel Wakefield, in Hunter, *Select Melodies*, 1843.

450 ELDER. 7777 D.
Words: In Ives, *Manual of Instruction in American Sunday-School Psalmody*, 1832.
Music: M. Mark Wynn, in *The Sacred Harp*, 1870.

451 MARY'S GRIEF AND JOY. 7777 D.
Words: John Newton, 1779.
Music: Arranged by B. F. White, in *The Sacred Harp*, 1870, from a song tune, "Zula Zong," by J. P. Webster, published 1860.

452 MARTIN. 7777 D.
Words: Charles Wesley, 1738.
Music: S. B. Marsh, in Hastings, *Musical Miscellany*, vol. 1 (1836); alto by S. M. Denson, 1911.

453 HOLLY SPRINGS. C.M.
Words: Verses by Isaac Watts, 1709, Hymn 110, book 1.
Music: H. N. McGraw, 1935, in *Original Sacred Harp* (Denson revision), 1936; named for Holly Springs Primitive Baptist Church, Bremen, Georgia.

454 THE BETTER LAND. L.M.
Words: O. A. Parris, 1935, in *Original Sacred Harp* (Denson revision), 1936.
Music: O. A. Parris, 1935, in *Original Sacred Harp* (Denson revision), 1936.

455   SOAR AWAY. H.M. [6666.88]
Words: Claimed by A. M. Cagle, in *Original Sacred Harp*, 1936. The
verses are from Charles Wesley, altered from verses 3 and 5 of "Jesus, my
strength, my hope" (S.M.), in *Hymns and Sacred Poems*, 1742.
Music: A. M. Cagle, 1935, in *Original Sacred Harp* (Denson revision), 1936.

456   SACRED MOUNT. C.M.D.
Words: Philip Doddridge, "Sing ye redeemed of the Lord," 1755, altered
to fit the structure of this chorus; the second opening couplet thus omits
his closing rhyme, "And let the prospect cheer your eye, / While laboring
up the hill."
Music: A. M. Cagle, 1935, in *Original Sacred Harp* (Denson revision), 1936.

457   WAYFARING STRANGER. 9898 D.
Words: As popularized, this was called "The Libby Prison Hymn,"
broadsides of which were sold for the relief of former Union soldiers
at the close of the Civil War. Its origin was among the United Brethren
in Christ, who had published its first English version in Bever's *Christian
Songster*, 1858; this was an adaptation of a German original, "Ein Pilgrim
bin auch ich auf Erden" (1816) by Isaac Niswander, a minister of the same
denomination in Rockingham County, Virginia.
Music: Arranged by John M. Dye, 1935, in *Original Sacred Harp* (Denson
revision), 1936, from a revival song.

458   FRIENDSHIP. 8787 D.
Words: John Newton, 1779.
Music: E. F. Williams, in *The Sacred Harp*, 1870; alto by Anna L.
Blackshear.

459   TOLLING BELL. P.M. [X4X4.XXX4]
Words: Mary Stanley Bunce Dana Shindler, in Dana, *Southern Harp*, 1841.
Music: Richard F. M. Mann, November 1, 1868, in *The Sacred Harp*, 1870; alto
after Anna L. Blackshear, 1902. "For Miss M. A. White and E. A. Mann."

460   SARDIS. P.M. [88.8884]
Words: In *Hymns and Spiritual Songs for the Use of Christians*, 2d ed., 1802.
Music: Sarah Lancaster, "Original," in *The Sacred Harp*, 1870 (p. 470).

461   SHINING STAR. C.M.D.
Words: A cento: the first four lines are by Nahum Tate, 1702; the next
four are anonymous. Verse 2 is from William Billings's SHILOH in *The
Suffolk Harmony*, 1786.
Music: *Terry Wootten, 1988, in *The Sacred Harp*, 1991.

462 FAITH AND HOPE. C.M.D.

Words: A cento: verse 1 is from "Oh once I had a glorious view," in Mercer, *The Cluster,* 3d ed., 1810; verse 2 is from Isaac Watts, 1707, Hymn 65, book 2, and from Broaddus and Broaddus, *Collection of Sacred Ballads,* 1790.

Music: A. M. Cagle, 1957, in *Original Sacred Harp* (Denson revision), 1960.

463 OUR HUMBLE FAITH. C.M.D.

Words: Verse 1, Isaac Watts, 1707, Hymn 11, book 3; verse 2 altered from verse 3 of "Now let our pains be all forgot," Isaac Watts, 1707, Hymn 16, book 3.

Music: G. S. Doss, 1959, in *Original Sacred Harp* (Denson revision), 1960.

464 SHEPPARD. S.M.

Words: Isaac Watts, 1707, Hymn 10, book 1.

Music: *Theodore Mercer, 1990, in *The Sacred Harp,* 1991; named in honor of Jeff and Shelbie Sheppard.

465 WHERE THERE'S NO TROUBLE AND SORROW. P.M.

Words: Claimed by Doris W. DeLong in *Original Sacred Harp* (Denson revision), 1960.

Music: Doris W. DeLong, in *Original Sacred Harp* (Denson revision), 1960.

466 HAYNES CREEK. C.M.

Words: Ingram Cobbin, 1843.

Music: *Joyce Harrison, 1988, in *The Sacred Harp,* 1991.

467 LISBON. S.M.

Words: Isaac Watts, 1707, Hymn 14, book 2.

Music: Daniel Read, in *The American Singing Book,* 1785; rearranged, with the fuging section removed, after Lowell Mason.

468 BRISTOL. L.M.D.

Words: Joseph Addison, 1712, a paraphrase of Psalm 19.

Music: Timothy Swan, in *Select Harmony,* [1785].

470 THE MERCY SEAT. L.M.

Words: Hugh Stowell, 1828.

Music: Loyd Redding, in *Original Sacred Harp* (Denson revision), 1960.

471 THE SAVIOR'S NAME. C.M.

Words: Frederick Whitfield, 1855.

Music: T. B. McGraw, in *Original Sacred Harp* (Denson revision), 1960.

472 AKIN. L.M.
Words: Isaac Watts, 1719, Psalm 139, part 1, verse 3.
Music: *P. Dan Brittain, 1971, in *The Sacred Harp*, 1991; named for E. G.
Akin of Carrollton, Georgia.

473 CARMARTHEN. H.M. [6666.88]
Words: Charles Wesley, 1741.
Music: *Musica Sacra, being a Choice Collection of Psalm and Hymn Tunes, and
Chants* [ca.1778].

474 MOUNT DESERT. C.M.
Words: Isaac Watts, 1719, Psalm 125.
Music: *Bruce Randall, 1985, in *The Sacred Harp*, 1991; named for Mount
Desert Island, Hancock County, Maine.

475 A THANKFUL HEART. C.M.
Words: Anne Steele, 1760.
Music: *John T. Hocutt, 1989, in *The Sacred Harp*, 1991.

476 THE THRONE OF GRACE. C.M.D.
Words: Isaac Watts, *Sermons,* 1721, verses 1 and 5.
Music: Buford McGraw, in *Original Sacred Harp* (Denson revision), 1960.

477 LORD, WE ADORE THEE. 7777.
Words: Owel W. Denson, in *Original Sacred Harp* (Denson revision), 1960.
Music: Owel W. Denson, in *Original Sacred Harp* (Denson revision), 1960.

478 MY RISING SUN. C.M.D.
Words: William Cowper, 1774.
Music: C. H. Gilliland, in *Original Sacred Harp* (Denson revision), 1960.

479 CHESTER. L.M.
Words: Verse 1 by Philip Doddridge, 1755; Verse 2, Isaac Watts, 1719, Psalm
19, verse 3.
Music: William Billings, in *The New-England Psalm-Singer,* 1770.

480 REDEMPTION. P.M. 9696.
Words: John T. Hocutt, 1959, in *Original Sacred Harp* (Denson revision),
1960.
Music: John T. Hocutt, 1959, in *Original Sacred Harp* (Denson revision),
1960.

481 NOVAKOSKI. S.M.
Words: Isaac Watts, 1707, Hymn 30, book 2.
Music: *P. Dan Brittain, 1989, in *The Sacred Harp*, 1991.

482 MULBERRY GROVE. P.M. [88888]
Words: Verse 1 by H. Wood, in *The Sacred Harp,* 1870; verse 2 by A. M.
Cagle, in *Original Sacred Harp* (Denson revision), 1966.
Music: J. P. Reese, in *The Sacred Harp,* 1870 (p. 94).

483 ETERNAL LIGHT. C.M.
Words: Isaac Watts, 1709, Hymn 103, book 1.
Music: H. N. McGraw, in *Original Sacred Harp* (Denson revision), 1960.

484 HEAVENLY UNION. P.M. [88887]
Words: In Mintz, *Spiritual Song Book,* 1805.
Music: *Neely Bruce, 1989, in *The Sacred Harp,* 1991.

485 NEW AGATITE. C.M.
Words: Edward Perronet, 1779.
Music: *Theodore W. Johnson, 1990, in *The Sacred Harp,* 1991. Named for
Agatite Street, Chicago.

486 BENEFICENCE. L.M.D.
Words: Brady and Tate, *New Version of the Psalms of David,* 1696, Psalm
112.
Music: William Billings, in *The Suffolk Harmony,* 1786. "Selected by
Raymond Hamrick" in *Original Sacred Harp* (Denson revision), 1960.

487 SOLDIER'S DELIGHT. L.M.
Words: C. O. Woodard, 1918.
Music: T. P. Woodard, 1918, in *Original Sacred Harp* (Denson revision),
1960.

488 AS WE GO ON. L.M.
Words: O. H. Handley, in *Original Sacred Harp* (Denson revision), 1960.
Music: O. H. Handley, 1959, in *Original Sacred Harp* (Denson revision),
1960.

489 THE SAVIOR'S CALL. 6666.
Words: Edward Caswall, *Lyra Catholica,* 1849; "from the Spanish."
Music: Elphrey Heritage, in *The Sacred Harp,* 1870 (p. 433).

490 MY SHEPHERD GUIDES. C.M.D.
Words: Era Tidwell Godsey, 1959.
Music: Palmer Godsey, 1959, in *Original Sacred Harp* (Denson revision),
1960.

491   OH, WHAT LOVE. P.M. [779.778]
Words: Eula Denson Johnson, in *Original Sacred Harp* (Denson revision), 1960.
Music: Eula Denson Johnson, January 20, 1960, in *Original Sacred Harp* (Denson revision), 1960.

492   INVOCATION. P.M.
Words: Isaac Watts, 1707, Hymn 82, book 2, verses 1 and 6, altered.
Music: *Raymond C. Hamrick, 1982, in *The Sacred Harp*, 1991.

493   AMANDA RAY. C.M.
Words: Verses 6 and 10 of "I am alone, dear Master," by Frances R. Havergal, in *Under the Surface*, 1874.
Music: Whitt Denson, January 15, 1960, in *Original Sacred Harp* (Denson revision), 1960.

494   BIG CREEK. P.M. [9797]
Words: Anonymous in *The Sacred Harp*, 1991.
Music: *Richard L. DeLong, 1986, in *The Sacred Harp*, 1991; named for Big Creek Primitive Baptist Church, Alpharetta, Georgia.

495   THE MIDNIGHT CRY. P.M. [7676.7777]
Words: In Burdett, *Baptist Harmony*, 1834.
Music: *Southern Harmony*, 1835; alto by S. M. Denson, 1911.

496   THE ROCK THAT IS HIGHER THAN I. YYYY.
Words: Attributed to "Bennet" in Dobell, *New Selection*, 1806.
Music: Arranged by B. F. White, in *The Sacred Harp*, 1870 (p. 340); alto by Minnie Floyd, 1902; from a revival tune in *The Minstrel of Zion*, 1845.

497   NATICK. 7777.
Words: Thomas Hastings, in Mason and Hastings, *Spiritual Songs for Social Worship* (1831).
Music: *Glen Wright, 1989, in *The Sacred Harp*, 1991; named for Natick, Middlesex County, Massachusetts.

498   THE RESURRECTION DAY. P.M. [6X6X.6X86]
Words: John T. Hocutt, in *Original Sacred Harp* (Denson revision), 1960.
Music: John T. Hocutt, 1959, in *Original Sacred Harp* (Denson revision), 1960.

499 AT REST. S.M.
Words: Verses 1–2 from "O where shall rest be found" by James Montgomery, 1825; verse 3 by Floyd M. Frederick, added to *The Sacred Harp* in 1991.
Music: Floyd M. Frederick, 1959, in *Original Sacred Harp* (Denson revision), 1960.

500 LIVING HOPE. C.M.D.
Words: Verses by Isaac Watts, 1707, Hymn 26, book 1.
Music: Hugh W. McGraw, 1959, in *Original Sacred Harp* (Denson revision), 1960.

501 O'LEARY. S.M.
Words: Philip Doddridge, 1755.
Music: *Theodore Mercer, 1990, in *The Sacred Harp,* 1991; named for Stephen D. and Mary Rose O'Leary.

502 A CHARGE TO KEEP. S.M.D.
Words: Charles Wesley, 1762.
Music: Paine Denson, 1959, in *Original Sacred Harp* (Denson revision), 1960.

503 LLOYD. S.M.
Words: Verse 1 from Isaac Watts, 1719, Psalm 45; the remainder from Isaac Watts, 1707, Hymn 93, book 2, "My God, my life, my love," verses 3 and 6.
Music: *Raymond C. Hamrick, 1980, in *The Sacred Harp,* 1991; named for Loyd Redding.

504 WOOD STREET. L.M.
Words: Brady and Tate, *New Version of the Psalms of David,* 1696, Psalm 137.
Music: *Judy Hauff, 1986, in *The Sacred Harp,* 1991; named for Wood Street, Chicago, Illinois.

505 WHERE CEASELESS AGES ROLL. L.M.
Words: Owel W. Denson, in *Original Sacred Harp* (Denson revision), 1960.
Music: Robert E. Denson, 1959, in *Original Sacred Harp* (Denson revision), 1960.

506 THE ARK. C.M.
Words: Verse in Mercer, *The Cluster,* 3d ed., 1823; chorus based on phrases in later verses.
Music: J. A. Ayers, in *Original Sacred Harp* (Denson revision), 1966.

507 SERMON ON THE MOUNT. [Anthem.]
     Words: Matthew 5:1–3, 5.
     Music: A. M. Cagle, 1959, in *Original Sacred Harp* (Denson revision), 1960.

510 CORLEY. 7777.
     Words: Marcus M. Wells, in *The New York Musical Pioneer,* November 1858.
     Music: Arranged by Richard L. DeLong, 1988, in *The Sacred Harp,* 1991,
     from a song tune, "From the fair Lavinian shore," by John Wilson, in
     Cheerful Ayres or Ballads, 1660; adapted as a hymn tune in Whitaker, *The
     Seraph,* 1818; named for the composer's grandmother, Dollie Corley.

511 THE GREAT REDEEMER. L.M.
     Words: Anne Steele, 1760.
     Music: E. Foy Frederick, 1959, in *Original Sacred Harp* (Denson revision),
     1960.

512 THE SPIRIT SHALL RETURN. [Anthem.]
     Words: Ecclesiastes 12:2, 6, 7.
     Music: J. E. Kitchens, 1959, in *Original Sacred Harp* (Denson revision), 1960.

513 JOYFUL. C.M.
     Words: Verses in Isaac Watts, *Sermons,* on "Holy Fortitude," 1724.
     Music: [Arranged by] B. F. White, in *The Sacred Harp,* 1844 (p. 166); treble
     by E. J. King; alto after B. P. Poyner, 1902. A variant of a revival tune in
     Himes, *Millennial Harp,* 1842, based on a song tune "The seven joys of
     Mary."

515 FEDERAL STREET. L.M.
     Words: Isaac Watts, 1709. Hymn 139, book 2.
     Music: H. K. Oliver, 1832, in Mason, *Boston Academy Collection of Church
     Music,* 1835; named after Federal Street, Boston, Massachusetts.

516 DELONG. L.M.D.
     Words: Clement Nance or John Blain; from the same text as at page 62
     above.
     Music: *Hugh W. McGraw, 1985, in *The Sacred Harp,* 1991; named after the
     DeLong family.

517 MARS HILL. C.M.
     Words: Isaac Watts, 1719, Psalm 119, part 4.
     Music: Hugh W. McGraw, 1959, in *Original Sacred Harp* (Denson revision),
     1960.

518 HEAVENLY ANTHEM
Words: Psalm 19:1–4, 7–8, 11, 14.
Music: Paine Denson, 1950, in *Original Sacred Harp* (Denson revision),
1960.

521 PARTING FRIENDS. C.M.D.
Words: Anonymous in Walker, *Southern Harmony,* 1835.
Music: R. A. Canant, 1959, in *Original Sacred Harp* (Denson revision), 1960.

522 YE HEEDLESS ONES. L.M.D.
Words: In Wolcott, *Selection of Hymns and Spiritual Songs,* 1817.
Music: A. M. Cagle, 1959, in *Original Sacred Harp* (Denson revision), 1960.

523 PLEYEL'S HYMN. 7777.
Words: John Newton, 1779.
Music: Arranged from Ignaz Joseph Pleyel, String Quartet in G major,
1788, *Andante,* in *Select Hymns for Voice and Harpsichord,* [ca. 1790].

524 THE TWENTY-THIRD PSALM. [Anthem.]
Words: Psalm 23.
Music: Paine Denson, 1950, in *Original Sacred Harp* (Denson revision),
1960.

527 MY LIFE AND BREATH. C.M.
Words: Samuel Stennett, in Rippon, *Selection,* 1787, verses 3, 4, and 5 of
"Majestic sweetness sits enthroned."
Music: Hugh W. McGraw, 1959, in *Original Sacred Harp* (Denson revision),
1960.

528 SHOWERS OF BLESSINGS. C.M.D.
Words: Isaac Watts, 1719, Psalm 147.
Music: [Arranged by] A. A. Blocker, 1959, in *Original Sacred Harp* (Denson
revision), 1960; the melody is from GRAFTON, by Joseph Stone, in *The
Columbian Harmony,* 1793.

530 A GLAD NEW SONG. C.M.D.
Words: Jonathan B. Atchinson, in *Gospel Hymns,* no. 6, 1891.
Music: T. B. McGraw, 1959, in *Original Sacred Harp* (Denson revision),
1960.

531 DURA. L.M.
Words: H. M. Blackmon, in *Original Sacred Harp* (Denson revision), 1960.
Music: H. M. Blackmon, 1959, in *Original Sacred Harp* (Denson revision),
1960; named for Blackmon's wife Dura Ann Campbell.

532 PEACE AND JOY. 8787 D.
Words: John Bowring, 1825.
Music: Paine Denson, 1959, in *Original Sacred Harp* (Denson revision),
1960.

534 NEW GEORGIA. C.M.D.
Words: Paine Denson, in *Original Sacred Harp* (Denson revision), 1960;
an assemblage of phrases from several hymns of the eighteenth and
nineteenth centuries.
Music: Ruth Denson Edwards, 1959, in *Original Sacred Harp* (Denson
revision), 1960.

535 SHAWMUT. S.M.
Words: Charles Wesley, 1759.
Music: Lowell Mason, in *The Boston Academy Collection of Church Music*,
1835. Shawmut is a transcription of the native Massachuset name for the
site of Boston, Massachusetts.

536 SWEET MAJESTY. C.M.D.
Words: Isaac Watts, 1707, Hymn 91, book 2.
Music: A. M. Cagle, 1959, in *Original Sacred Harp* (Denson revision), 1960.

538 HAMPTON. L.M.
Words: Isaac Watts, 1719, Psalm 148, verses 6 and 12 of "Loud hallelujahs
to the Lord."
Music: Eliakim Doolittle, in *The Psalm Singer's Companion*, 1806.

539 SUPPLICATION. L.M.
Words: Floyd M. Frederick, 1959, in *Original Sacred Harp* (Denson revision), 1960.
Music: Floyd M. Frederick, 1959, in *Original Sacred Harp* (Denson revision), 1960; mistakenly attributed to E. Foy Frederick.

540 NIDRAH. S.M.
Words: Samuel Stennet, in Rippon, *Selection*, 1787, verses 1 and 6.
Music: *Raymond C. Hamrick, 1982, in *The Sacred Harp*, 1991. Named for
Nidrah Plantation near Leslie, Georgia.

541 HOME OF THE BLEST. C.M.D.
Words: "O. P." in *The Missionary Minstrel*, 1826.
Music: Doris W. DeLong, 1959, in *Original Sacred Harp* (Denson revision),
1960.

542 I'LL SEEK HIS BLESSINGS. S.M.
Words: Adapted by A. M. Cagle, 1959, from Isaac Watts, 1719, Psalm 55,
"Let sinners choose their course."
Music: A. M. Cagle, 1959, in *Original Sacred Harp* (Denson revision), 1960.

543 THOU ART GOD. C.M.
Words: Isaac Watts, 1719, Psalm 90, verses 3 and 2.
Music: Ruth Denson Edwards, 1959, in *Original Sacred Harp* (Denson revision), 1960.

544 PRAISE HIM. L.M.
Words: Verses 4, 6, and 9 of "O may I worthy prove to see," in *Hymns and Spiritual Songs for the Use of Christians* ("The Baltimore Collection"), 1801.
Music: H. N. McGraw, in *Original Sacred Harp* (Denson revision), 1960.

545 THE PILGRIM'S WAY. 8787 D.
Words: In *Lexington Collection,* 2d ed., 1805, in twelve verses, condensed to six by John Totten and other early Methodist compilers. The second half of the single verse here is a sort of synopsis of the original text, which graphically describes both heaven and hell.
Music: Irene Parker Denson, 1959, in *Original Sacred Harp* (Denson revision), 1960.

546 MY BRIGHTEST DAYS. C.M.
Words: Isaac Watts, 1707, Hymn 54, book 2.
Music: O. A. Parris, 1959, in *Original Sacred Harp* (Denson revision), 1960.

547 GRANVILLE. L.M.
Words: Isaac Watts, 1719, Psalm 89, part 6.
Music: *Judy Hauff, 1986, in *The Sacred Harp,* 1991.

548 WOOTTEN. P.M.
Words: Hugh W. McGraw, 1976, in *The Sacred Harp,* 1991.
Music: *Hugh W. McGraw, 1976, in *The Sacred Harp,* 1991; named for the Wootten family.

549 PHILLIPS FAREWELL. L.M.
Words: George Donahoo Phillips, 1962.
Music: *Hugh W. McGraw, 1962, in *The Sacred Harp,* 1991.

550 BLISSFUL DAWNING. C.M.
Words: Isaac Watts, 1707, Hymn 54, book 2.
Music: A. M. Cagle, 1959, in *Original Sacred Harp* (Denson revision), 1960.

551 JACOB'S VISION. P.M. [YZZZ]
Words: In Bramley and Stainer, *Christmas Carols New and Old*, [1871].
Music: Arranged by Margaret Wright, 1959, in *Original Sacred Harp*
(Denson revision), 1960, from Bramley and Stainer, *Christmas Carols New
and Old*, [1871]; a variant of MIDDLEBURY, by Humphreys, in Davisson,
Supplement to the Kentucky Harmony, 1820, and in *The Sacred Harp*, 1844.

553 ANTHEM ON THE BEGINNING.
Words: John 1:1–10.
Music: Paine Denson, 1959, in *Original Sacred Harp* (Denson revision), 1960.

556 PORTLAND L.M.
Words: Isaac Watts, 1719, Psalm 92, part 1.
Music: Abraham Maxim, in *The Oriental Harmony*, 1802; named for
Portland, Maine.

558 LIVING STREAMS. L.M. [4 stanzas]
Words: R. B. Robertson, Psalm 23, in *The Psalter: The Scottish Version of the
Psalms Revised*, 1872.
Music: T. B. McGraw, in *Original Sacred Harp* (Denson revision), 1960.

560 MY HOME. P.M.
Words: H. Roy Avery, 1959, in *Original Sacred Harp* (Denson revision),
1960.
Music: H. Roy Avery, 1959, in *Original Sacred Harp* (Denson revision), 1960.

562 INFINITE DELIGHT. C.M.D.
Words: Verse 1, from verses 8 and 9 of "How long shall death, the tyrant,
reign?" in Isaac Watts, *Horae Lyricae*, 1706; verse 2 from verses 3 and 4 of
"When the last trumpet's awful voice," in *Translations and Paraphrases in
Verse*, 1781, based on 1 Corinthians 15:52–58.
Music: T. B. McGraw, 1959, in *Original Sacred Harp* (Denson revision), 1960.

564 ZION. C.M.D.
Words: John T. Hocutt, 1959, in *Original Sacred Harp* (Denson revision),
1960.
Music: John T. Hocutt, 1959, in *Original Sacred Harp* (Denson revision),
1960.

565 THE HILL OF ZION. S.M.
Words: Isaac Watts, 1707, Hymn 30, book 2, verses 9–10.
Music: B. F. White, "Original," in *The Sacred Harp*, 1859 (p. 380); alto by S.
M. Denson, 1911.

566 HEBRON. L.M.
Words: Isaac Watts, 1707, Hymn 80, book 1.
Music: Lowell Mason, in *Boston Handel and Haydn Society Collection of Church Music,* 9th ed., 1830; in *The Sacred Harp,* 1850, (p. 264).

567 THE GREAT DAY. P.M.
Words: Anonymous, in *The Sacred Harp,* 1859.
Music: J. P. Reese, in *The Sacred Harp,* 1859 (p. 386); "as sung by Judge Falkerner of Al'a."

568 I WANT TO GO TO HEAVEN. C.M.
Words: J. E. Kitchens, in *Original Sacred Harp* (Denson revision), 1960.
Music: J. E. Kitchens, 1959, in *Original Sacred Harp* (Denson revision), 1960 (p. 574).

569T EMMAUS. C.M.
Words: Anne Steele, 1760.
Music: *Raymond C. Hamrick, 1975, in *The Sacred Harp,* 1991.

569B SACRED THRONE. C.M.
Words: John Kent, 1835.
Music: Hugh Wilson, in R. A. Smith, *Sacred Music . . . Sung at St. George's,* 1825; treble and alto by Hugh McGraw, 1966.

570 FAREWELL TO ALL. C.M.D.
Words: Berryman Hicks (1778–1839), in *Southern Harmony,* 1835. See the note to the song on page 83B.
Music: *Hugh W. McGraw, 1985, in *The Sacred Harp,* 1991.

571 PENITENCE. Y8Y8D.
Words: Joseph Swain, 1791; verses 3 and 4 combined, then 1 and 2 (of 10), of "O thou in whose presence my soul takes delight."
Music: Raymond C. Hamrick, in *Original Sacred Harp* (Denson revision), 1966.

572 THE LAMB OF GOD. [Anthem.]
Words: Matthew 3:1; John 1:29.
Music: Priestley Miller, in *Original Sacred Harp* (Denson revision), 1966.

573 HARPETH VALLEY. C.M.
Words: Samuel Longfellow, verses 3 and 4 of "O still in accents sweet and strong," in *Hymns of the Spirit,* 1864.
Music: A. M. Cagle, in *Original Sacred Harp* (Denson revision), 1966.

7

SOURCES
FOR THE SONGS

Psalm and Hymn Books

Allen, Richard. *A Collection of Spiritual Songs and Hymns Selected from Various Authors.* Philadelphia: John Ormrod, 1801. Reprint ed. with introduction by J. Roland Braithwaite, Philadelphia: Mother Bethel African Methodist Episcopal Church, 1987.

The American Musical Miscellany: A collection of the newest and most approved songs set to music. Northampton, Mass.: Andrew Wright, 1798.

Barlow, Joel. *Dr. Watts's imitation of the Psalms of David / corrected and enlarged by Joel Barlow; to which is added a collection of hymns; the whole adapted to the state of the Christian Church in general.* [Hartford: Barlow & Babcock, 1785.] 4th ed. Hartford: Hudson & Goodwin, n.d. [1791].

Battle, Elisha. *A Collection of Hymns & Spiritual Songs, for Public and Family Worship.* Raleigh, N.C.: Minerva Press by A. Lucas, 1814.

Bever, Joseph. *The Christian Songster.* Dayton, Ohio: Printing establishment of the United Brethren in Christ, 1858.

Biddle, William P., and William J. Newborn. *The Baptist Hymn Book, in Two Parts.* Washington City [D.C.]: Columbian Office, by John S. Meehan, 1825.

Brady, Nicholas, and Nahum Tate. *A New Version of the Psalms of David, Fitted to the Tunes Used in Churches.* London: M. Clark, 1696.

———. *A Supplement to the New Version of Psalms, by Dr. Brady and Mr. Tate.* London: J. Heptinstall, 1700.

Broaddus, Andrew. *The Dover Selection of Spiritual Songs.* Richmond: Drinker & Morris, 1828.

———. *The Virginia Selection of Psalms, Hymns, and Spiritual Songs.* Richmond: R. I. Smith, 1836.

Broaddus, Richard, and Andrew Broaddus. *Collection of Sacred Ballads.* n.p.: 1790.

Brunson, Albert, and Charles Pitman. *The Sweet Singer of Israel: A Collection of Hymns and Spiritual Songs.* Pittsburgh: C. H. Kay & Co., 1840.

Bryan, David. *The Songster's Companion: A Selection of Hymns and Spiritual Songs*. Jacksonville, Ala.: J. F. Grant, 1837.

Burdett, Staunton S. *The Baptist Harmony*. Philadelphia: T. W. Ustick, 1834.

Caswall, Edward. *Lyra Catholica*. London: James Burns, 1849.

A Choice Collection of Hymns and Spiritual Songs. Designed for the Use of the Pious of All Denominations. Newbern [N.C.]: Watson & Hall, 1807.

A Choice Selection of Hymns and Spiritual Songs. 3d ed. Montpelier, Vt.: G. W. Hill, 1827.

A Choice Selection of Hymns and Spiritual Songs, Designed for the Use of the Pious. Philadelphia: Dickinson & Heartt, 1805.

Clay, Eleazar. *Hymns and Spiritual Songs*. Richmond [Va.]: John Dixon, 1793.

Cleavland, Benjamin. *Hymns on different spiritual subjects*. Norwich, Conn.: John Trumbell, 1792.

Cleland, Thomas. *Evangelical Hymns*. 2d ed. Lexington, Ky.: T. T. Skillman, 1828.

Cottle, Joseph. *Hymns and Sacred Lyrics*. London: T. Cadell, 1828.

Courtney, John, Sr. *The Christian's Pocket Companion; Being a Collection of Hymns and Spiritual Songs; for the Use of Christians: A Number Never Before Published*. Richmond: John Courtney, Sr., 1805.

Cowper, Frances Maria, and William Cowper. *Original Poems on Various Occasions*. London: J. Deighton, J. Mathews, & R. Faulder, 1792.

Cowper, William, and John Newton. *Olney Hymns*. London: W. Oliver, 1779.

Cram, Nancy Gove. *A Collection of Hymns and Poems*. Schenectady, N.Y.: For the Compiler, 1815.

de Fleury, Maria. *Divine Poems and Essays on Various Subjects*. London: M. de Fleury, 1791.

Denham, David. *The Saints' Melody. A new selection of upwards of one thousand hymns . . . Designed as a companion to Dr. Watts's Psalms & Hymns, with some originals, etc.* London: R. Banks, 1837.

Dobell, John. *A New Selection of Seven Hundred Evangelical Hymns*. London: Williams & Smith, 1806.

Doddridge, Philip. *Hymns founded on Various Texts in the Holy Scriptures*. Salop [England]: J. Eddowes & J. Cotton, 1755.

Dupuy, Starke. *Hymns and Spiritual Songs, Original and Selected*. Frankfort, Ky.: William Gerard, 1811.

Elliott, John. *The Sacred Lyre, comprising Psalms, Hymns and Spiritual Songs*. Lancaster [Pa.]: Mary Dickson, 1828.

An Essay on the Church Plain Chant. London: J. P. Coghlan, 1782.

Fawcett, John. *Hymns Adapted to the Circumstances of Public Worship, and Private Devotion*. Leeds: G. Wright & Son, 1782.

Foster, Robert. *Hymns, and Spiritual Songs, Original and Selected* ("Portsmouth Selection"), Second Part. Portsmouth, N.H.: R. Foster, 1818.

Gibbons, Thomas. *Hymns Adapted to Divine Worship*. J. Buckland & C. Dilly, 1784.

Goddard, Josiah. *A new and beautiful collection of select hymns and spiritual songs*. Conway, Mass.: Theodore Leonard, 1798.

Goode, William. *A Collection of Hymns for Public, Social, and Domestic Worship*. Richmond: M. E. Church, South, 1847.

Granade, John Adam. *The Pilgrim's Songster*. Lexington, Ky.: Daniel Bradford, 1804.

Graves, Absalom. *Hymns, Psalms, and Spiritual Songs.* [Louisville, 1825.] 2d ed., Cincinnati: Dodge, L. Hommedieu, & Hammond, 1829.

Greene, Thomas. *Poems on Various Subjects.* London: H. Goldney, 1780.

Gridley, Selah. *The Mill of the Muses.* Exeter, N.H.: T. Gridley, 1828.

Hall, Salmon. *A New collection of the most approved Hymns and Spiritual Songs.* Newbern, N.C.: for S. Hall, 1804.

Harrod, John J. *Social and Camp-Meeting Songs, for the Pious.* Baltimore: J. J. Harrod, 1817.

Hart, Joseph. *Hymns, &c. Composed on Various Subjects.* London: J. Hart, 1762.

Havergal, Frances Ridley. *Under the Surface.* London: James Nisbet & Co., 1874.

Hinde, Thomas S. *The Pilgrim's Songster.* Chillicothe, Ohio: Fredonian Press, 1815.

Hunter, William. *Select Melodies.* Cincinnati: Methodist Book Concern, 1843.

Hymn Book of the Methodist Protestant Church. Baltimore: Book Concern of the Methodist Protestant Church, 1859.

Hymns and Spiritual Songs for the Use of Christians, Including a Number Never Before Published (by 1806, known as "The Baltimore Collection"). Baltimore: M'Crea & Barnhill, 1801.

Kent, John. *Gospel Hymns. An Original Collection. To Which Is Added, an Appendix, Containing a Number of Select Hymns.* London: 1803, reprint: Boston, 1811.

Kolb, George. *The Spiritual Songster: Containing a Variety of Camp-meeting, and other hymns.* Frederick-Town, Md.: George Kolb, 1819.

Leavitt, Joshua. *The Seaman's Devotional Assistant, and Mariners' Hymns.* New York: Sleight & Robinson, 1830.

The Lexington Collection, being a Selection of Hymns and Spiritual Songs, from the Best Authors. Together, with a Number Never Before Published, 2d ed. Lexington, Ky.: Joseph Charless, 1805.

Lloyd, Benjamin. *The Primitive Hymns.* Wetumpka, Ala.: 1841.

Lloyd, John. *Hymns on Select Passages of Scripture: With others usually sung at Camp-Meetings, &c.* Chambersburg, Pa. [J. Lloyd] and Poughkeepsie, N.Y. [Paraclete Potter], 1811.

Longfellow, Samuel, and Samuel Johnson. *Hymns of the Spirit.* Boston: Ticknor & Fields, 1864.

Lyra Davidica: Or, A Collection of Divine Songs and Hymns. London: J. Walsh, 1708.

Marks, David. *Hymns for Christian Melody.* Dover, N.H.: Free-Will Baptist Connection, 1832.

Maxwell, James. *Hymns and Spiritual Songs, in three books.* London: J. Fuller, 1759.

Mead, Stith. *A General Selection of the Newest and Most Admired Hymns, and Spiritual Songs.* Richmond: Seaton Grantland, 1807.

Mercer, Jesse. *The Cluster.* 3d ed. Augusta, Ga.: Hobby & Bunce, 1810.

Mintz, David B. *Collection of Hymns and Spiritual Songs, Mostly New.* Newbern, N.C.: John M'Williams & Christopher D. Neale, 1806.

———. *The Spiritual Song Book, Designed as an Assistant for the Pious of all Denominations.* Halifax, N.C.: Abraham Hodge, 1805.

The Missionary Minstrel. Comp. by O. P. London: James Nisbet, 1826.

More, Hannah. *Search after Happiness; and Other Poems; Sacred Dramas; and Essays on Various Subjects.* London, T. & J. Allman, 1825 [written in 1762].

Myers, Peter D. *The Zion Songster: A collection of Hymns and Spiritual Songs, generally sung at Camp and Prayer Meetings, and in Revivals of Religion.* 3d ed. New York: M'Elrath & Bangs, 1829.

Noel, Silas M. *A Hymn Book Containing a Copious Selection of Hymns and Songs, from the Best Authors.* Frankfort, Ky.: Gerard & Berry, 1814.

Occum, Samson. *A Choice Collection of Hymns and Spiritual Songs.* New London, Conn., 1774.

Ogilvie, John. *Poems on Several Subjects.* London: G. Keith, 1762.

Parkinson, William. *A Selection of Hymns and Spiritual Songs, in Two Parts.* New York: John Tiebout, 1809.

Peak, John. *A New Collection of Hymns and Spiritual Songs.* Windsor, Vt.: Alden Spooner, 1793.

Pearce, Samuel. *Memoirs of the Late Rev. Samuel Pearce, A.M., Minister of the Gospel in Birmingham.* 2d ed. Clipstone [England]: J. W. Morris, 1800.

Pious Songs: Social, Prayer, Closet, and Camp Meeting Hymns, and Choruses. 3d ed. Baltimore: Armstrong & Berry, 1836.

Pitts, Fountain E. *Zion's Harp.* [Nashville, 1846.] Stereotype edition, much enlarged. Louisville: John P. Morton & Co., 1852.

The Psalms Hymns, and Spiritual Songs, of the Old & New Testament: Faithfully Translated into English Meetre (the "Bay Psalm Book"), 9th ed. Boston: Printed by B. Green and J. Allen for Michael Perry, 1698.

The Psalms of David, According to the Version Approved by The Church of Scotland ("The Scottish Psalter"). Edinburgh: J. Dickson & P. Hill, 1792.

The Psalter: The Scottish Version of the Psalms Revised, and the New Versions Adopted by the United Presbyterian Church of North America. Pittsburgh: United Presbyterian Board of Publication, 1872.

Pseaumes octante trois de David. Geneva: Jean Crespin, 1551.

Purify, John. *A Selection of Hymns and Spiritual Songs, in Two Parts.* Raleigh, N.C.: Bell & Lawrence, 1823.

Rippon, John. *A Selection of Hymns from the Best Authors, Intended to Be an Appendix to Dr. Watts's Psalms and Hymns.* New York: William Durrell, 1792.

Robinson, David F. *The New England Sunday School Hymn Book.* Hartford, Conn.: D. F. Robinson & Co., 1830.

Rowe, Elizabeth. *Miscellaneous Works in Prose and Verse.* London: R. Hett & R. Dodsley, 1739.

Seagrave, Robert. *Hymns for Christian Worship, Partly Composed and Partly Collected from Various Authors.* London: n.p., 1742.

Smith, Elias, and Abner Jones. *Hymns, Original and Selected, for the Use of Christians.* Boston: Manning & Loring, 1804.

Smith, Joshua. *Divine Hymns or Spiritual Songs, for the Use of Religious Assemblies, and Private Christians.* Portsmouth, N.H.: John Melcher, [1791].

Smith, Robert Archibald. *Sacred Music . . . Sung at St. George's Church, Edinburgh.* Edinburgh: Alexander Robertson, 1825.

———. *The Scottish Minstrel: A Selection from the Vocal Melodies of Scotland, Ancient and Modern.* Edinburgh: Purdie, [1821–24].

The Songster's Repository. New York: Nash & Dearborn, 1811.

Spalding, Joshua. *The Lord's Songs: A Collection of Composures in Metre, Such as Have Been*

Most Used in the Late Glorious Revivals; Dr. Watts's Psalms and Hymns Excepted. Salem, Mass.: Joshua Cushing, 1805.

Stowe, Phineas. *Melodies for the Temperance Ship.* Boston: Phineas Stowe, 1856.

Taylor, Ann. *Hymns for Infant Minds.* London: T. Conder, 1808.

Taylor, Caleb Jarvis. *Spiritual Songs.* Lexington, Ky.: Joseph Charless, 1804.

Totten, John. *A Collection of the most admired hymns and spiritual songs, with the choruses affixed as usually sung at camp-meeting, &c., with others suited to various occasions.* New York: John C. Totten, 1809.

Translations and Paraphrases in Verse of Several Passages of Sacred Scripture. Edinburgh: J. Dickson, 1781.

Watts, Isaac. *Horae Lyricae. Poems, chiefly of the lyric kind.* London: S. & D. Bridge, 1706.

————. *Hymns and Spiritual Songs, in three books.* London: J. Humfreys, 1707.

————. *Hymns and Spiritual Songs, in three books.* Corrected and much enlarged. London: John Humphries, 1709.

————. *The Psalms of David Imitated in the Language of the New Testament, and apply'd to the Christian State and Worship.* London: J. Clark, 1719.

Wells, Seth W. *Millennial Praises.* Hancock, [Mass.]: Josiah Tallcott Jr., 1813.

[Wesley, Charles]. *A Collection of Hymns for the use of the People called Methodists.* London: J. Paramore, 1780. [Compiler John Wesley's preface states, "The majority are by Charles Wesley."]

[————]. *Funeral Hymns* [2d series]. London: n.p., 1759.

————. *Hymns for Children.* Bristol: E. Farley, 1763.

Wesley, John, and Charles Wesley. *Hymns and Sacred Poems.* [3d ed.] Bristol: F. Farley, 1742.

[————.] *Hymns for New Year's Day.* London: R. Hawes, [1750].

Whitaker, John. *The Seraph.* London: Button, Whitaker & Co., 1818.

The Whole Book of Psalms, Collected into English Metre, by Thomas Sternhold, John Hopkins, and others ("The Old Version"). [London: John Day, 1562.] Cambridge: John Hayes, 1676.

Wolcott, T. *A Selection of Hymns and Spiritual Songs, for those who wish to Praise God.* Portland, Me.: A. & J. Shirley, 1817.

The Young Convert's Companion: Being a Collection of Hymns for the Use of Conference Meetings, Original and Selected. Boston: E. Lincoln, 1806. (The compiler was Oliver Holden; it has a number of his tunes in the back, and he claims them with the initial H. in the index.)

Young, Edward. *The Complaint, or Night Thoughts on Life, Death, and Immortality.* London: R. Dodsley, 1742–44.

Tunebooks

Addington, Stephen. *A Collection of Psalm Tunes.* 6th ed. London: S. Addington, 1786.

Adgate, Andrew. *The Philadelphia Harmony.* 2d ed. Philadelphia: John McCulloch, 1789.

Arnold, John. *The Compleat Psalmodist.* London: Robert Brown, 1749.

Atwill, Thomas. *The New-York and Vermont Collection.* 2d ed. Albany: B. Buckley, [1804].

Belcher, Supply. *The Harmony of Maine.* Boston: Thomas & Andrews, 1794.

Benham, Asahel. *Federal Harmony*. New Haven: A. Morse, 1790.

———. *Social Harmony*. [Wallingford, Conn.,] 1798.

Billings, William. *The Continental Harmony*. Boston: Thomas & Andrews, 1794.

———. *The New-England Psalm-Singer*. Boston: Edes & Gill, 1770.

———. *The Psalm-Singer's Amusement*. Boston: W. Billings, 1778.

———. *The Singing-Master's Assistant*. Boston: Draper & Folsom, 1778.

———. *The Suffolk Harmony*. Boston: J. Norman, 1786.

Boyd, James M. *The Virginia Sacred Musical Repository*. Winchester, Va.: J. Foster, 1818.

Bramley, H. R., and John Stainer. *Christmas Carols New and Old*. London, [1871].

Brown, Simeon. *A Sett of Tunes in Three Parts*. London: Matthews, [1720].

Brownson, Oliver. *A New Collection of Sacred Harmony*. Simsbury, Conn.: O. Brownson, 1797.

———. *Select Harmony*. [Connecticut: n.p., 1785].

Butts, Thomas. *Harmonia Sacra*. London: Thomas Butts, [1754].

Caldwell, William. *Union Harmony, or Family Musician*. Maryville, Tenn.: F. A. Parham, 1837.

Carden, Allen D. *The Missouri Harmony*. Cincinnati: Morgan, Lodge & Co., 1820.

Chetham, John. *A Book of Psalmody*. London: William Pearson, [1717].

Clayton, David L., and James P. Carrell. *Virginia Harmony*. Winchester, Va.: Samuel H. Davis, 1831.

A Collection of Tunes . . . As They Are Commonly Sung at the Foundery ("The Foundery Collection"). London: A. Pearson, 1742.

[*A Collection of Tunes printed for John Logan*]. 1812.

Collins, T. K., Jr. *The Timbrel of Zion*. Philadelphia: T. K. Collins Jr., 1853.

Commuck, Thomas. *Indian Melodies*. New York: G. Lane and C. B. Tippett, 1845.

Costellow, Thomas, *Sunday's Amusement: A Selection of Sacred Music, as Sung at Bedford Chapel*. London: E. Riley, [ca. 1801].

Dadmun, J. W. *Army Melodies*. Boston: Benjamin B. Russell, 1861.

———. *The Melodeon*. Boston: J. P. McGee, 1860.

Dana, Mary. *The Southern Harp*. Boston: Parker & Ditson, 1841.

Davisson, Ananias. *The Kentucky Harmony*. Harrisonburg, Va.: A. Davisson, 1816.

———. *Supplement to The Kentucky Harmony*. Harrisonburg, Va.: A. Davisson, 1820.

The Divine Musical Miscellany. London: William Smith, 1754.

Doolittle, Eliakim. *The Psalm Singer's Companion*. New Haven: E. Doolittle, 1806.

Edson, Lewis, Jr. *The Social Harmonist*, 3d ed. New York: Sage & Clough, 1803.

French, Jacob. *Harmony of Harmony*. Northampton, Mass.: Andrew Wright, 1802.

———. *The New American Melody*. Boston: John Norman, 1789.

———. *The Psalmodist's Companion*. Worcester: I. Thomas, 1793.

Funk, Joseph. *Genuine Church Music*. Winchester, Va.: J. W. Hollis, 1832.

Griswold, Elijah, and Thomas Skinner. *Connecticut Harmony*. [Simsbury, Conn., 1796].

Harrison, Ralph. *Sacred Harmony*. London: T. Williams, [1784].

Hastings, Thomas. *The Manhattan Collection*. New York: Ezra Collier and Gould & Newman, 1837.

———. *Musical Miscellany*. Vol. 1. New York, 1836.

Hauser, William. *The Hesperian Harp*. Philadelphia: T. K. & P. G. Collins, 1848.

————. *The Olive Leaf.* Wadley, Ga.: Hauser & Turner, 1878.

Hayden, A. S. *Introduction to Sacred Music.* Pittsburgh: Johnson and Stockton, 1835.

Hillman, Joseph. *The Revivalist.* Troy, N.Y.: J. Hillman, 1869.

Himes, Joshua V. *The Millennial Harp.* Boston: Joshua V. Himes, 1843.

Holden, Oliver. *The Union Harmony.* Boston: Thomas & Andrews, 1793.

Holdroyd, Israel. *The Spiritual Man's Companion.* London: William Pearson, [1722].

Holyoke, Samuel. *The Columbian Repository of Sacred Harmony.* Exeter, N.H.: Henry Ranlet, [1803].

————. *Harmonia Americana.* Boston: Thomas & Andrews, 1791.

[Howe, Solomon.] *The Psalm-Singer's Amusement.* [Greenwich, Mass., ca. 1804.]

Hunter, William, and Samuel Wakefield. *The Minstrel of Zion.* Philadelphia: Sorin & Ball, 1845.

Ingalls, Jeremiah. *The Christian Harmony, or Songster's Companion.* Exeter, N.H.: Henry Ranlet, 1805.

Ives, Elam. *Manual of Instruction in American Sunday-School Psalmody.* Philadelphia: American Sunday School Union, 1832.

James, J. S. *Union Harp and History of Songs.* Atlanta: J. S. James, 1909.

Jarman, Thomas. *Sacred Harmony.* London: Henry Thompson, [ca. 1804].

Jenks, Stephen. *The Christian Harmony.* Dedham, Mass.: H. Mann, 1811.

————. *The Delights of Harmony; or, Norfolk Compiler.* Dedham, Mass.: H. Mann, 1805.

————. *The Jovial Songster.* Dedham, Mass.: H. Mann, 1806.

————. *The Musical Harmonist.* New Haven: Amos Doolittle, 1800.

————. *The New-England Harmonist.* Danbury, Conn.: Douglas & Nichols, 1799.

————. *The Royal Harmony of Zion.* Dedham, Mass.: H. Mann, 1810.

Jenks, Stephen, and Elijah Griswold. *The American Compiler of Sacred Harmony.* Northampton, Mass.: [Andrew Wright], 1803.

Jocelin, Simeon. *The Chorister's Companion.* New Haven: Amos Doolittle, 1782.

Johnson, Alexander. *Tennessee Harmony.* Cincinnati: Morgan, Lodge, & Co., 1818.

Johnson, Andrew W. *The American Harmony,* 2d ed. Nashville: W. H. Dunn, 1839.

Jones, L. J. *The Southern Minstrel.* Philadelphia: Grigg, Elliott, & Co., 1849.

Kieffer, A. S. *The Temple Star.* Singer's Glen, Va.: Ruebush, Kieffer, & Co., 1877.

Knight, William C. *The Juvenile Harmony.* Cincinnati: Morgan, Lodge, & Fisher, 1825.

Law, Andrew. *The Musical Primer.* Cheshire, Conn.: William Law, 1793.

————. *Rudiments of Music,* 3d ed. [Cheshire, Conn.: William Law], 1791.

————. *Select Harmony.* Cheshire, Conn.: [William Law], 1778.

Leavitt, Joshua. *The Christian Lyre.* New York: Jonathan Leavitt, 1830–31.

Lewis, Freeman. *The Beauties of Harmony.* 3d ed. Pittsburgh: Cramer & Spear, 1818.

Little, William, and William Smith. *The Easy Instructor.* [Philadelphia, 1801.]

Mansfield, D. H. *The American Vocalist.* Boston: Charles H. Pierce, 1848.

Mason, Lowell. *The Boston Academy Collection of Church Music.* Boston: Carter, Hendee & Co., 1835.

————. *The Boston Handel and Haydn Society Collection of Church Music.* 2d ed. Boston: Richardson & Lord, 1823.

————. *The Choir.* Boston: Carter, Hendee, & Co., 1832.

————. *The New Carmina Sacra.* Boston, 1856.

Mason, Lowell, and Thomas Hastings. *Spiritual Songs for Social Worship.* 1831.

Mason, Lowell, and Timothy Mason. *The Sacred Harp or Eclectic Harmony.* Boston: Shepley & Wright, 1838.

Maxim, Abraham. *The Oriental Harmony.* Exeter, N.H.: Henry Ranlet, 1802.

Maynard, Ezekiel. *A New Selection of Sacred Music.* Baltimore: Ezekiel Maynard, 1822.

McCurry, J. G. *The Social Harp.* Philadelphia: T. K. Collins Jr., 1855.

McLain, Lazarus B. *Appendix to the Christian's Harp* [n.p.: ca. 1835], bound with Samuel Wakefield, *The Christian's Harp,* 1832.

McLean, Charles. *A Collection of Favourite Scots Tunes.* Edinburgh: N. Stewart, [ca. 1774].

Merrill, David. *The Psalmodist's Best Companion.* Exeter, N.H.: Henry Ranlet, 1799.

Metcalf, Samuel L. *The Kentucky Harmonist.* Cincinnati: Morgan, Lodge, & Co., 1818.

Moore, Thomas. *A Selection of Popular National Airs, with Symphonies and Accompaniments by Sir John Stevenson.* London: J. Power, 1818.

Moore, William. *The Columbian Harmony.* Cincinnati: Morgan, Lodge, & Fisher, 1825.

Moors, Hezekiah. *The Province Harmony.* Boston: J. T. Buckingham, 1809.

Musica Sacra, Being a Choice Collection of Psalm and Hymn Tunes, and Chants . . . As They Are Used in . . . the Countess of Huntingdon's Chapels, in Bath, Bristol, &c. Bath: W. Gye, [ca.1778].

Parris, O. A. *Christian Harmony. Book 1.* Birmingham: Christian Harmony Publishing Co., 1954.

Patterson, Robert. *Patterson's Church Music.* Pittsburgh: R. & J. Patterson, 1813.

Peck, Daniel. *The Musical Medley.* Dedham, Mass.: H. Mann, 1808.

Pilsbury, Amos. *The United States' Sacred Harmony.* Boston: Thomas & Andrews, 1799.

Playford, Henry. *The Divine Companion.* London: William Pearson, 1701.

Playford, John. *A Brief Introduction to the Skill of Musick.* London: J. Playford, 1654.

———. *Psalms & Hymns in Solemn Musick.* London: W. Godbid, 1671.

———. *The Whole Book of Psalms.* London: W. Godbid, 1677.

The Psalms Hymns, and Spiritual Songs, of the Old & New-Testament ("The Bay Psalm Book"), 9th ed. Boston: Michael Perry, 1698.

The Psalm-Singer's Help. London: Thomas Knibb, [ca. 1769].

Read, Daniel. *The American Singing Book.* New Haven: [D. Read], 1785.

———. *The Columbian Harmonist, No. 2, with Additional Music.* New Haven: D. Read, [1798].

Reed, Ephraim. *The Musical Monitor, or New-York Collection of Devotional Church Music.* Ithaca: Mack & Searing, 1820.

Revival Melodies, or Songs of Zion, Dedicated to Elder Jacob Knapp. Boston: John Putnam, 1842.

Rhinehart, W. R. *American or Union Harmony.* Chambersburg, Pa.: Henry Ruby, 1831.

Sankey, Ira D., James McGranahan, and George C. Stebbins. *Gospel Hymns, No. 6.* New York: Biglow & Main, 1891.

Select Harmony. Newburyport: Daniel Bayley, [1784].

Select Hymns for Voice and Harpsichord. London: J. Carr, [ca. 1790].

Shaw, Benjamin, and Charles H. Spilman. *The Columbian Harmony.* Cincinnati: Lodge, L'Hommedieu & Hammond, 1829.

Shaw, Oliver, Amos Albee, and H. Mann. *The Columbian Sacred Harmonist*. Dedham, Mass.: H. Mann, 1808.

Shumway, Nehemiah. *The American Harmony*. Philadelphia: John McCulloch, 1793.

Smith, Henry. *Church Harmony*. Chambersburg, Pa.: Henry Ruby, 1831.

[Smith, Isaac?] *A Collection of Psalm Tunes*. London: Mrs. Davenhill & Mr. Buckland, [1779].

Smith, William. *The Easy Instructor, Part II*. [Hopewell, N.J.:] William Smith & Co., [1803].

Stephenson, Joseph. *Church Harmony*. 3d ed. London: J. Rivington & J. Fletcher, [1760].

Stone, Joseph, and Abraham Wood. *The Columbian Harmony*. [Worcester, Mass.: n.p., 1793].

Swan, Timothy. *The New England Harmony*. Northampton, Mass.: Andrew Wright, 1801.

Swan, W. H., and M. L. Swan. *The Harp of Columbia*. Knoxville: The Authors, 1848.

Thompson, George. *A Select Collection of Original Scottish Airs*. London, 1802.

Tufts, John. *Introduction to the Art of Singing Psalm-Tunes*. Boston: Samuel Gerrish, 1721.

Village Harmony. 5th ed. Exeter, N.H.: Henry Ranlet, 1800.

Wakefield, Samuel. *The Christian's Harp*. Pittsburgh: Johnston & Stockton, 1832.

———. *The Ecclesiastic Harmony*. Pittsburgh: Eichbaum & Johnston, 1825.

Walker, William. *The Christian Harmony*. Philadelphia: E. W. Miller and William Walker, 1867.

———. *The Southern and Western Pocket Harmonist*. Philadelphia: Thomas, Cowperthwait, & Co., 1846.

———. *The Southern Harmony and Musical Companion*. New Haven: Nathan Whiting, 1835.

Walter, Thomas. *The Grounds and Rules of Musick*. Boston: Samuel Gerrish, 1721.

Waters, Horace. *The Sabbath-School Bell*. New York: Horace Waters, [1859].

White, J. L., and B. F. White, Jr. *The New Sacred Harp*. Atlanta: S. P. Richard & Son, 1884.

Wilson, John. *Cheerful Ayres or Ballads*. Oxford: W. Hall, 1660.

The Worcester Collection of Sacred Harmony. Worcester: Isaiah Thomas, 1786.

Wyeth, John. *Wyeth's Repository of Sacred Music*. Harrisburgh, Pa.: John Wyeth, 1810.

———. *Wyeth's Repository of Sacred Music, Part Second*. Harrisburgh, Pa.: John Wyeth, 1813.

The Young Convert's Pocket Companion. Boston: J. Loring, 1822.

NOTES

Introduction

1. Steel, "Lazarus J. Jones," 123–24.
2. *Original Sacred Harp* [James edition], 29.
3. Ibid., 49.
4. Ibid., 82.
5. Ibid., 277.

Chapter 1: The Origins of the Sacred Harp

1. Cobb, *Sacred Harp*, 131.
2. This notation was invented by the Philadelphia merchant John Connelly, who on 10 March 1798 signed over his rights to the system to Little and Smith. See Smith, *Easy Instructor*, Part II, p. [2]; Crawford, *Andrew Law*, 175.
3. James, *Brief History*, 29–30.
4. Eskew, "Georgia Origins," 25–35.
5. Personal communication from Mike White.
6. They are M. C. H. Davis, Matilda Durham, Andrew Grambling, F. F. Price, Isaac Neighbours, A. C. Clark, and one "Graham"; White did not reprint his own tune JERUSALEM from the 1835 *Southern Harmony*.
7. WONDROUS LOVE was likewise reprinted in *The Sacred Harp* without its attribution to James Christopher.
8. James, *Brief History*, 31–32.
9. Steel, *Stephen Jenks*, lxxi.
10. Ringwalt, *American Encyclopaedia of Printing*, 107–8.
11. Cobb, *Sacred Harp*, 69.
12. Adams, *Typographia*, 34, 351–52.
13. Bishop, *History of American Manufactures*, 643–46.

14. [David Warren Steel and others.] "Sacred Harp Singing FAQ" http://www.mcsr .olemiss.edu/~mudws/faq/.

15. Hauser, *Hesperian Harp*, iii.

16. Cobb, *Sacred Harp*, 85–87.

17. UCLA Law and Columbia Law School, *Copyright Infringement Project*. http://cip .law.ucla.edu/ s.v. Cooper v. James, 213 F. 871 (D.C. N.D. Ga., 1914), http://cip.law.ucla .edu/cases/case_cooperjames.html.

18. Jackson, "Fa-Sol-La Folk," 6–10.

19. Turner, *Frontier in American History*, 38.

Chapter 2: The Chattahoochee Valley

1. "American Indian Land Cessions in Georgia," in *About North Georgia*, http:// ngeorgia.com/history/indianla.html.

2. "Georgia's Land Lottery," in *About North Georgia*, http://ngeorgia.com/history/ lotteries.html.

3. University of Virginia, *Historical Census Browser*. Retrieved from the University of Virginia, Geospatial and Statistical Data Center: http://fisher.lib.virginia.edu/ collections/stats/histcensus/index.html.

4. Fussell, *Chattahoochee Album*.

Chapter 3: The Westward Migration

1. *Barnesville Gazette*, undated clipping, ca. 1869.

Chapter 4: The Sacred Harp and the Civil War

1. U.S. Census figures for 1860 show 397,967 slaveowners among 8,289,782 free citizens in the states that allowed slavery, or 4.8 percent; figures for Georgia are somewhat higher: 41,084 slaveowners of 595,088 free citizens, or 6.9 percent. Data from the University of Virginia, *Historical Census Browser*. Retrieved from the University of Virginia, Geospatial and Statistical Data Center: http://fisher.lib.virginia.edu/collections/ stats/histcensus/ index.html.

2. James Madison, *Letters and Other Writings* (1865), 3:516, quoted in Meacham, *American Lion*, 93.

3. *The Organ*, 31 October 1855.

4. *The Organ*, 6 June 1855. Other area newspapers were more blatant in favoring secession, for example, the [Columbus] *Corner Stone*, published by attorney James N. Bethune, also known as the owner of the slave pianist Blind Tom. See Phillips, *Georgia and State Rights*, 193.

5. Wetherington, *Plain Folks' Fight*, 126–29.

6. Cobb, *Sacred Harp*, 76–77.

7. Ann Lancaster papers, Georgia State Library.

8. Hauser, *Olive Leaf*, [4].

9. Calhoun *Monitor-Herald*, 7 May 1903.

Chapter 5: Musical Families

1. Cooke, "American Psalmodists," 7–25.
2. Scholten, "The Chapins."
3. Shull, "John Logan," 22–49.
4. *New Grove Dictionary of Music*, s.v. Lupo.
5. Ann Lancaster papers, Georgia State Library.
6. Ibid.

Chapter 6: Professions and Occupations

1. Crawford, *America's Musical Life*, 127–30.
2. Cooke, "Itinerant Yankee Singing Masters," 17–19.

Chapter 7: Teachers and Tradition

1. *Whole Book of Psalms* [Bay Psalm Book], 9th ed., 419.
2. Chute, *Chute Family*, 58.
3. J. M. Hamrick, *Life of James Martin Hamrick*. http://www.ronsattic.com/jmhamric .htm.

Chapter 8. The Styles of Sacred Harp Music

1. Seeger, "Contrapuntal Style," 490.
2. Abbott Ferris, "Sacred Harp Singing," in Library of Congress, Archive of Folk Culture, notes to AFS 2735–3153: 419 discs made by Herbert Halpert in the South between March 15 and June 15, 1939, under the joint sponsorship of the Library of Congress and the Folk Arts Committee of the WPA. http://www.mcsr.olemiss.edu/~mudws/articles/ meridian.html.
3. Saal, "Sacred Singout," 108–9.
4. Jackson, *White Spirituals*, 16–19.
5. Temperley, "John Playford and the Metrical Psalms," 338–40.
6. Ibid., 340.
7. Ibid., 357.
8. Crawford, *America's Musical Life*, 25.
9. Sedley, "Playford's *Dancing Master*," www.innertemplelibrary.org.uk/newsletter/ Archive/newsletter14.doc.
10. Temperley, "John Playford and the Metrical Psalms," 357.
11. Halsey, *Diary of Samuel Sewall*, 538.
12. Quoted in Appel, *The Music of the Bay Psalm Book*, 10–11.
13. Lowens, *Music and Musicians*, 33–45.
14. Quoted in Kroeger, *Complete Works of William Billings*, 4:32–33.
15. Samuel Griswold Goodrich, quoted in Steel, *Stephen Jenks: Collected Works*, xiii.
16. Holyoke, *Harmonia Americana*, 4, quoted in Crawford, *American Studies and American Musicology*, 23.

17. Law, *Musical Primer*, 2d ed., 8, quoted in Crawford, *Andrew Law*, 105–6.

18. Crawford, *American Studies and American Musicology*, 27–28.

19. Crawford, *Andrew Law*, 175.

20. Maynard, *New Selection*, [3].

21. Davisson, *Kentucky Harmony*, 2d ed. Other signs omitted by Davisson include the hold (fermata), emphasis (staccato), direct (custos), and the C clef.

22. *The Organ*, 2 February 1856, quoted in Bealle, *Public Worship, Private Faith*, 134–36.

23. Seeger, "Contrapuntal Style," 484–86.

24. Ibid., 488.

25. Horn, "Quartal Harmony," 564–81; Horn, *Sing to Me of Heaven*, chap. 8; Tallmadge, "Folk Organum," 47–65.

26. McCurry, *Social Harp*, 14.

27. Ibid.

28. The piece is subtitled "Chant" in the round-note *Sacred Harp or Eclectic Harmony* (1838) by Lowell and Timothy Mason; in Lowell Mason's *New Carmina Sacra* (1856), the first and third phrases are for solo voice accompanied by instruments, and the second and fourth are sung by the choir.

29. Cobb, *Sacred Harp*, 85–87.

30. Vaughn, *Approaching 150*, 16–17.

Chapter 9: Frontiers of the American Hymn

1. Dow's first-person experience song, "O that poor sinners did but know, / What I for them do undergo!" was widely published (by himself, his wife Peggy, and many others), though not in the *Sacred Harp*. Hinde did not publish his own poetry, but a number of samples of it survive with his personal papers, preserved among the Lyman Draper manuscripts at the Wisconsin Historical Society.

2. Conclusions in this and the following paragraph are based in part on unpublished research notes on Broaddus shared with me by Paul A. Richardson (Stamford University) and long-standing exchanges about Joshua Smith with David W. Music (Baylor University). Their most recent study is Music and Richardson, *"I Will Sing the Wondrous Story."*

3. Ibid., especially chap. 3 and its references.

4. *Celebration of the Hundredth Anniversary*, 39.

5. There is no better discussion of this than that found in Irving Lowens's introduction to the reprinted 1820 edition of John Wyeth's *Repository of Sacred Music, Part Second*, also printed in Lowens, *Music and Musicians*.

6. See Hulan, "Camp-Meeting Spiritual Folksongs," chap. 2.

7. A good bit is known about Sarah Jones, apart from her somewhat veiled career as a hymn writer. See Lyerly, "Tale of Two Patriarchs," 490–508.

8. For a broader treatment of the black presence in the American folk hymn tradition, see Hulan, "Camp-Meeting Spiritual Folksongs," chap. 7.

9. The first two editions of Allen's compilation and their relation to the "Baltimore

Collection" have been examined in detail in J. Roland Braithwaite's introduction to the 1987 reprint of Allen, *Collection of Hymns and Spiritual Songs*.

10. A comprehensive Web resource on the Stone-Campbell "Restoration Movement" is maintained by Hans Rollmann of the Memorial University of Newfoundland. Some of the referenced Charless and Bradford imprints are available on Stone's page there: www.mun.ca/rels/restmov/people/bstone.html.

11. McNemar wrote many hymns that were popular among the Shakers but only two that had any circulation in the broader religious community, outside the cultural islands that were their colonies. One is found at p. 117 in *The Sacred Harp*. For the other, see Patterson, *Shaker Spiritual*, 157.

Chapter 10. Sketches of Selected Poets and Hymn Writers

1. For Leland's religious biography and baptism story see Moore, "Writers of Early Virginia Baptist History (3): John Leland," 579–93.

2. Music and Richardson, *"I Will Sing the Wondrous Story,"* 147–50 et passim. His relationship with Madison and political influences are explored in Emerson Proctor, "John Leland," at www.chuckbaldwinlive.com/read_johnleland.html. A fine account of the Mammoth Cheese is in Harriman, "Most Excellent"; the quotation is from Benedict, *General History* 1:440–41.

3. Price, *Holston Methodism*, 3:130–31.

4. The effort to obtain Granade's journal is described in Dow, *History of Cosmopolite*, 318. See generally Hulan, "John Adam Granade," 77–87. Additional hymns are credited to Granade in Hauser, *Olive Leaf*. These attributions do not appear to be reliable, but it is possible that either Hauser or his correspondent William Chute had a copy of Granade's original *Pilgrim's Songster*, and if so, that some of them are based on it.

5. Fry, "Early Camp-Meeting Song Writers," 214–15. For Taylor's hymn about Cane Ridge see Hulan, "American Revolution in Hymnody," 201.

6. For Askins's ministerial career see *Minutes Taken at the Several Annual Conferences of the Methodist Episcopal Church*, vol. 1, especially his obituary on 277–78. Jonathan Stamper is quoted (from a poorly cited periodical called *Home Circle*) in Redford, *History of Methodism in Kentucky*, 451.

7. Collins, *Historical Sketches of Kentucky*, 1:462; Green, *Historic Families of Kentucky*, 50–60 et passim. A modern study of the camp-meeting movement that gives the appropriate weight to its roots in Scotch-Irish summer sacramental meetings is Conkin, *Cane Ridge: America's Pentecost*.

BIBLIOGRAPHY

1. Sources for Chapter 11: Biographical Sketches of the Composers

Many of the URLs (Internet addresses) may be obsolete, but some may be retrieved from the Way Back Machine at www.archive.org/.

Aaron, Anna Eugenia "Annie" Denson
    Composer information from Hugh McGraw.

Aikin, Burwell Stephen
    Original Sacred Harp, 479.
    RootsWeb, wc.rootsweb.ancestry.com/cgi-bin/igm.cgi?op=GET&db=hfamilytree
        &id=I4034
    USGenWeb Archives. files.usgwarchives.net/ga/pike/obits/a/aikin91940b.txt

Arne, Thomas Augustine
    New Grove Dictionary of Music and Musicians.

Arnold, James D.
    RootsWeb, archiver.rootsweb.ancestry.com/th/read/GAMONROE/2006–09/
        1157832020
    USGenWeb Archives, files.usgwarchives.net/special/afas/volume2/vol2no3.txt

Avery, Harvey Roy
    Composer information from Hugh McGraw.

Ayers, James Adrian
    Composer information from Hugh McGraw.
    Newspaper obituary from Hugh McGraw, source unknown.

Ball, R. F.
    James, *Brief History,* 121.

Barnett, Shadrack P. "Shade"

RootsWeb, archiver.rootsweb.com/th/read/FIELDER/2001–08/0998925429

RootsWeb, archiver.rootsweb.com/th/read/BARNETT/2002–06/1024578430

Bass, Cynthia

Original Sacred Harp, 275.

RootsWeb, wc.rootsweb.com/cgi-bin/igm.cgi?op=GET&db=:1897412&id=I1355

Bayly, Thomas Haynes

New Grove Dictionary of Music and Musicians.

Belcher, Supply

New Grove Dictionary of Music and Musicians.

Metcalf, *Writers and Compilers*, 83–84.

Owen, "Supply Belcher."

Davenport, "Maine's Sacred Tunebooks."

Belknap, Daniel

Metcalf, *Writers and Compilers*, 146–48.

New Grove Dictionary of Music and Musicians.

Steel, *Daniel Belknap.*

Billings, William

Metcalf, *Writers and Compilers*, 51–64.

McKay and Crawford, *William Billings of Boston.*

New Grove Dictionary of Music and Musicians.

Blackmon, Henry Martin

Composer information from Hugh McGraw.

Blocker, Abraham A.

Church of Jesus Christ of Latter-Day Saints, FamilySearch Internet Genealogy
Service.

Descendants of Joseph Blocker, www.geocities.com/heartland/ranch/1805/
blocker.htm

Bobo, William W.

Sparks, *History of Padgett's Creek*, 79–80.

RootsWeb, wc.rootsweb.ancestry.com/cgi-bin/igm.cgi?op=GET&db=wilson
-templeton&id=I6943

RootsWeb, wc.rootsweb.ancestry.com/cgi-bin/igm.cgi?op=GET&db
=kgt2&id=I3805

Bolen, J. H.

Original Sacred Harp, 401.

Bovell, Stephen

    Sanders, *Presbyterianism in Paris and Bourbon County*, 7, 12, 205, 221.

    RootsWeb, wc.rootsweb.ancestry.com/cgi-bin/igm.cgi?op=GET&db=susan
      _wood&id=I10906

    www.genealogy.com/users/r/i/c/RandalRichardson/FILE/0003page.html

Boyd, Robert

    Music, "Ananias Davisson, Robert Boyd, Reubin Monday, John Martin, and Archi-
    bald Rhea in East Tennessee," 72–84.

    RootsWeb, wc.rootsweb.com/cgi-bin/igm.cgi?op=GET&db=stwatkins&id=I775

Bradfield, Oliver S.

    RootsWeb, wc.rootsweb.ancestry.com/cgi-bin/igm.cgi?op=GET&db
    =kpw&id=I125

    RootsWeb, wc.rootsweb.ancestry.com/cgi-bin/igm.cgi?op=GET&db
    =joan&id=I0174

Bradshaw, William

    www.tngenweb.org/sevier/webbbs/queries/index.cgi?read=2811

Breedlove, Leonard P.

    James, *Brief History*, 113.

    Original Sacred Harp, 282.

    Childs, *They Tarried in Taylor*, 7, 20–21, 97, 101.

    Davidson, *Rockaway in Talbot*, 2:27, 29, 105, 265–66, 278, 301, 359–63; 3:88–89.

    "Incorporation of Various Academies," USGenWeb Archives, files.usgwarchives
    .org/ga/talbot/history/academy.txt

Brittain, Philip Daniel

    Composer information from Hugh McGraw.

Brown, Bartholomew

    Metcalf, *Writers and Compilers*, 150–52.

Brown, Jackson C.

    Carroll County Times, 13 May 1881.

    Original Sacred Harp, 521.

Brown, Reuben E.

    Morrell, *Flowers and Fruits*, 322–23.

    Ozark (Ala.) *Tribune*, Sept. 13, 1904.

    Watson, *Forgotten Trails*, 170.

    Original Sacred Harp, 333.

    RootsWeb, archiver.rootsweb.ancestry.com/th/read/ALDALE/2001–02/
    0983325640

Brown, Reuben E., Jr.
RootsWeb, archiver.rootsweb.ancestry.com/th/read/ALDALE/2001–02/
0983325640

Brown, S. M.
Carroll County Times, 15 April 1881.
Original Sacred Harp, 321.

Brownson, Oliver
Metcalf, *Writers and Compilers,* 65.
Crawford, "Massachusetts Musicians," 613–14.
New Grove Dictionary of Music and Musicians.

Bruce, Frank Neely
New Grove Dictionary of Music and Musicians.

Cagle, Alfred Marcus
Composer information from Hugh McGraw and Mike Hinton.
Biographical notes, typescript by Linda Traywick.

Cagle, Margaret Frances "Maggie" Denson
Composer information from Hugh McGraw and Amanda Brady.

Caldwell, William
Wood, *Drifting Down Holston River Way,* 21–24.
Music, "William Caldwell's *Union Harmony.*"
RootsWeb, wc.rootsweb.ancestry.com/cgi-bin/igm.cgi?op=GET&db
=:2412974&id=I516524333

Canant, Remus Adolphus
Composer information from Hugh McGraw.

Carnes, James P.
Composer information from Hugh McGraw.

Carpenter, Elihu
Crawford, "Massachusetts Musicians," 615.
RootsWeb, wc.rootsweb.com/cgi-bin/igm.cgi?op=GET&db=:1565855&id=I14044

Carrell, James P.
RootsWeb, rootsweb.ancestry.com/~varussel/probate/jamespcarrell.html

Carter, Thomas W.
Original Sacred Harp, 106.
RootsWeb, homepages.rootsweb.com/~jeanette/ezekiel.htm
personal.lig.bellsouth.net/m/s/msaffold/dekcen50.htm

Carwell, John

    www.accessgenealogy.com/scripts/data/database.cgi?file=Data&report
=SingleArticle&ArticleID=0023557

Castle

    No biographical sources located.

Chambless, Zachariah

    RootsWeb, wc.rootsweb.ancestry.com/cgi-bin/igm.cgi?op=GET&db
=karenchambliss&id=I4654

    USGenWeb Archives, files.usgwarchives.org/ga/monroe/wills/chamb.txt

    USGenWeb Archives, files.usgwarchives.org/ga/talbot/cemeteries/chamb.txt

Chandler, Solomon

    Crawford, "Massachusetts Musicians," 616.

    Kroeger and Callahan, "The 'Other' Billings."

    RootsWeb, www.rootsweb.ancestry.com/~nygreen2/cemetery_papers_9.htm

Chapin, Amzi

    Scholten, "The Chapins."

Chapin, Lucius

    Scholten, "The Chapins."

Christopher, James

    http://www.halosites.com/upload/pictures/4292005112632/documents/
Cemetery/Cemetary%20Records%20for%20Sharon.pdf

    http://boards.ancestry.com/surnames.leatherwood/236.1.2.1.1.1.1.1.1/mb.ashx

Chute, William Edward

    Chute, *Chute Family.*

    RootsWeb, freepages.genealogy.rootsweb.ancestry.com/~chute/np40
.htm#rnn656

    RootsWeb, wc.rootsweb.ancestry.com/cgi-bin/igm.cgi?op=GET&db
=craigsharrow&id=I451205

Clark, Alexander C.

    Original Sacred Harp, 157.

Coan, Simeon

    Fulton, *Coan Genealogy,* 187–88.

    RootsWeb, wc.rootsweb.ancestry.com/cgi-bin/igm.cgi?op=GET&db
=jchoo&id=I22562

Coles, George

    RootsWeb, freepages.genealogy.rootsweb.ancestry.com/~woolsey/books/
elijah1771/colesgeorge1792_1858.html

Commuck, Thomas

Commuck, "Sketch of the Brothertown Indians."

Page, *Thomas Commuck and His Indian Melodies.*

www.library.wisc.edu/etext/WIReader/WER0439.html

Crane

No biographical sources located.

Cunningham, Benjamin Edward

Composer information from Hugh McGraw.

Curtis

No biographical sources located.

Dadmun, John William

Metcalf, *Writers and Compilers,* 315–16.

Official Minutes of the Ninetieth Session, 95–96.

Daniell, George B.

Original Sacred Harp, 534.

Church of Jesus Christ of Latter-Day Saints, *FamilySearch Internet Genealogy Service.* Ancestral File: AF97-105199

www.findagrave.com/cgi-bin/fg.cgi?page=gr&GRid=14816247

hammondsfamily.com/genealogy/indilist.php?view=preview&surname =DANIELL&falpha=G

Davis, B. F.

Hauser, *Hesperian Harp,* 258.

Davis, C. A.

No biographical sources located.

Davis, E. K.

Hauser, *Hesperian Harp,* 258.

Davis, Martin C. H.

RootsWeb, wc.rootsweb.com/cgi-bin/igm.cgi?op=GET&db=roots-by -jen&id=I2776

Davis, Robert Henry

The Heritage of Pike County, 27, 54.

RootsWeb, wc.rootsweb.com/cgi-bin/igm.cgi?op=GET&db=cmacchia&id=I1696

RootsWeb, wc.rootsweb.com/cgi-bin/igm.cgi?op=GET&db=winnwinn&id=I15

RootsWeb, ftp.rootsweb.com/pub/usrgenweb/al/military/11ala.txt

Davisson, Ananias

    Music, "Ananias Davisson, Robert Boyd, Reubin Monday, John Martin, and Archibald Rhea in East Tennessee."

    Harley, "Ananias Davisson."

Day, J. M.

    No biographical sources located.

DeLong, Doris Winn

    Composer information from Hugh McGraw and Kenneth DeLong.

DeLong, Richard Lee

    Composer information from Hugh McGraw and Richard DeLong.

Denson, Amanda Symington Burdette

    Composer information from Hugh McGraw, Mike Hinton, and Amanda Brady.
    Denson, *Denson Families in America*.

Denson, Howard Burdette

    Composer information from Hugh McGraw, Mike Hinton, and Amanda Brady.

Denson, James M.

    Composer information from Hugh McGraw.

    USGenWeb Archives, files.usgwarchives.net/la/bienville/history/hist2.txt

    RootsWeb, wc.rootsweb.ancestry.com/cgi-bin/igm.cgi?op=GET&db
    =corkys&id=I33594

Denson, Owel W.

    Composer information from Hugh McGraw and R. E. Denson.

Denson, Paine W.

    Composer information from Hugh McGraw and Mike Hinton.
    Denson, *Denson Families in America*.

Denson, Robert E.

    Composer information from Hugh McGraw and Amanda Brady.

Denson, Seaborn McDaniel

    Composer information from Hugh McGraw.

    Denson, *Denson Families in America*.

Denson, Sidney Seward Burdette

    Denson, *Denson Families in America*.

    USGenWeb Archives, files.usgwarchives.org/al/lowndes/military/civilwar/
    whburdette.txt

Denson, Sidney Whitfield "Whitt"

    Composer information from Hugh McGraw, R. E. Denson, and Julietta Haynes.

Denson, Susie Irene Kitchens Parker
Composer information from Hugh McGraw.

Denson, Thomas Jackson
Composer information from Hugh McGraw, Mike Hinton, and Amanda Brady.
Denson, *Denson Families in America.*

Denton, J. Monroe
Information from Hugh McGraw and Dollie Miller.
Montgomery and Green, *Biographical Sketches.*

Deolph or DeWolf.
Perry, *Charles D'Wolf of Guadaloupe,* 68–69.
Crawford, "Massachusetts Musicians," 616–17.
RootsWeb, wc.rootsweb.ancestry.com/cgi-bin/igm.cgi?op=GET&db
=stone1343&id=I9640

Doolittle, Eliakim
Metcalf, *Writers and Compilers,* 152–53.
Cooke, "American Psalmodists," 7–11.
RootsWeb, wc.rootsweb.com/cgi-bin/igm.cgi?op=GET&db=83152&id=I02639.

Doss, George Sebron
Clipping from unidentified newspaper, 1963.
Composer information from Hugh McGraw.

Drinkard
RootsWeb, wc.rootsweb.ancestry.com/cgi-bin/igm.cgi?op=GET&db=:3250321&id
=I634220313 09 01 20

Dumas, Edmund
James, *Brief History,* 107.
History of the Baptist Denomination, 198–99.
The Organ, 14 February 1855.
GenForum, genforum.genealogy.com/cgi-bin/pageload.cgi?edmund::dumas::693
.html
RootsWeb, wc.rootsweb.ancestry.com/cgi-bin/igm.cgi?op=GET&db
=rldumas&id=I23715

Durham, Matilda T.
RootsWeb, wc.rootsweb.ancestry.com/cgi-bin/igm.cgi?op=GET&db
=:3232287&id=I2411

Dye, John Marion
Knippers, *Who's Who Among Southern Singers and Composers,* 46–47.
Information from Donald Howard, Alabaster, Ala.

RootsWeb, wc.rootsweb.com/cgi-bin/igm.cgi?op=GET&db=rawboots2&id
=I41467

RootsWeb, www.rootsweb.ancestry.com/~alshelby/cemMtEra.html

Edmonds, Jeremiah Troup

James, *Brief History,* 121.

RootsWeb, wc.rootsweb.ancestry.com/cgi-bin/igm.cgi?op=GET&db
=mcclendon1&id=I261

Edson, Lewis

Lowens, *Music and Musicians,* 178–93.

Crawford, "Massachusetts Musicians," 617–18.

Edwards, Jarusha Henrietta "Ruth" Denson

Composer information from Hugh McGraw.

Information from Hugh McGraw, Mike Hinton, and Amanda Brady.

Ellis, Abner

Lamson, *History,* 63.

Slafter, "Schools and Teachers," 99.

RootsWeb, wc.rootsweb.ancestry.com/cgi-bin/igm.cgi?op=GET&db
=rtate&id=I14890

Frederick, Elbert Foy

Composer information from Hugh McGraw.

Frederick, Floyd Monroe

Composer information from Hugh McGraw.

Frederick, Oscar Huston

Composer information from Hugh McGraw.

French, Jacob

Metcalf, *Writers and Compilers,* 88–89.

Genuchi, "Life and Music of Jacob French."

Giardini, Felice

New Grove Dictionary of Music and Musicians.

Gilliland, Cecil Houston

Composer information from Hugh McGraw.

Gilmore, Timothy R.

Composer information from Hugh McGraw.

Godsey, Palmer

Composer information from Hugh McGraw.

RootsWeb, wc.rootsweb.com/cgi-bin/igm.cgi?op=GET&db=graywolf1980&id
=I0988

Goff, Ezra Whiting

Crawford, "Massachusetts Musicians," 618.

RootsWeb, wc.rootsweb.ancestry.com/cgi-bin/igm.cgi?op=GET&db
=geolarson2&id=I137060

missar.org/search.htm

Graham

No biographical sources located.

Graham, J. C.

Original Sacred Harp, 377.

Grambling, Andrew

www.bobmerritt.com/family/matthewmerritt/aqwno8.htm

RootsWeb, wc.rootsweb.ancestry.com/cgi-bin/igm.cgi?op=GET&db
=claydeeweaver&id=I09018

Grant, David Russell

Composer information from Hugh McGraw.

Hall, Amariah

RootsWeb, wc.rootsweb.ancestry.com/cgi-bin/igm.cgi?op=GET&db
=halldb&id=I2425

Hamrick, Raymond Cooper

Composer information from Hugh McGraw.

www.usgennet.org/usa/ga/county/baldwin/berry.html

Handley, Otto Erastus "O. H."

Composer information from Hugh McGraw.

RootsWeb, wc.rootsweb.com/cgi-bin/igm.cgi?op=GET&db=mawj1&id=I021

Harrison, Joyce Darlene Rape

Composer information from Hugh McGraw.

hatcherfamilyassn.com/getperson.php?personID=I41211&tree=WmtheIm

Harrison, Ralph

Lightwood, *Hymn Tunes and Their Story*, 162–63.

Thornber, *Social History of Cheshire*, www.thornber.net/cheshire/ideasmen/
crossst.html

Hastings, Thomas

Metcalf, *Writers and Compilers*, 194–99.

New Grove Dictionary of Music and Musicians.

Reynolds, *Companion to the Baptist Hymnal*, 390–30.

Hauff, Judy

Composer information from Hugh McGraw and Judy Hauff.

Hauser, William
    Jackson, *White Spirituals*, 70–74.
    Patterson, "William Hauser's *Hesperian Harp* and *Olive Leaf*."
    Scott, "Tunebooks of William Hauser."

Hendon, M. A.
    RootsWeb, wc.rootsweb.com/cgi-bin/igm.cgi?op=GET&db=:694650&id
        =I32826601
    RootsWeb, wc.rootsweb.com/cgi-bin/igm.cgi?op=GET&db=:1188773&id=I04498

Heritage, Elphrey
    James, *Brief History*, 112.
    RootsWeb,wc.rootsweb.ancestry.com/cgi-bin/igm.cgi?op=GET&db
        =micjosaur&id=I0187

Hibbard
    Crawford, *Core Repertory*, xlvii.

Hitchcock
    No biographical sources located.

Hocutt, John Tilmon
    Composer information from Hugh McGraw.

Holden, Oliver
    Metcalf, *Writers and Compilers*, 124–34.
    Music, *Oliver Holden*.
    New Grove Dictionary of Music and Musicians.
    Reynolds, *Companion to the Baptist Hymnal*, 338–39.

Holdroyd, Israel
    Temperley, *Music of the English Parish Church*, 428.

Holyoke, Samuel
    Metcalf, *Writers and Compilers*, 114–20.
    Eskew and Kroeger, *Selected Works of Samuel Holyoke and Jacob Kimball*.
    New Grove Dictionary of Music and Musicians.

Howd
    genonthehoof.familytreeguide.com/getperson.php?personID=I6332&tree
        =T1&PHPSESSID=246968fb30a74364190b51812a00ebf5

Humphreys, R. D.
    No biographical sources located.

Ingalls, Jeremiah
    Crawford, "Massachusetts Musicians," 619–21.
    Metcalf, *Writers and Compilers*, 121–24.

New Grove Dictionary of Music and Musicians.

Klocko, "Jeremiah Ingalls's *The Christian Harmony.*"

Ivey, David

Composer information from Hugh McGraw.

James, Joseph Stephen

Campbell, "Old Can Be Used Instead of New."

Vinson, "As Far From Secular, Operatic, Rag-time, and Jig Melodies as Is Possible."

RootsWeb, wc.rootsweb.ancestry.com/cgi-bin/igm.cgi?op=GET&db=spirit&id =I00311

Jarman, Thomas

New Grove Dictionary of Music and Musicians.

Weston, "A Northamptonshire Composer: Thomas Jarman of Clipston."

Immanuel's Ground: Warwick's West Gallery Quire, www.immanuelsground.com/ composers/Thomas_Jarman.htm

Jenks, Stephen

Metcalf, *Writers and Compilers,* 154–57.

Steel, *Stephen Jenks.*

Original Sacred Harp, 540.

Johnson, Alexander

Music, "Alexander Johnson and the *Tennessee Harmony.*"

Johnson, Eula Denson

Composer information from Hugh McGraw.

Johnson, Theodore Wallace

Composer information from Hugh McGraw and Theodore Wallace Johnson.

Jones, Willis Dallas

James, *Brief History,* 116.

Original Sacred Harp, 70.

RootsWeb, wc.rootsweb.ancestry.com/cgi-bin/igm.cgi?op=GET&db=:3086304 &id=I167

Kimball, Jacob

Metcalf, *Writers and Compilers,* 111–14.

Eskew and Kroeger, *Selected Works of Samuel Holyoke and Jacob Kimball.*

King, Elias Lafayette

James, *Brief History,* 121.

Davidson, *Rockaway in Talbot,* 3:116–17.

King, Elisha James

    Cobb, *Sacred Harp*, 68–70.

    James, *Brief History*, 105–6.

    Original Sacred Harp, 308.

    Davidson, *Rockaway in Talbot*, 3:111–16.

    RootsWeb, wc.rootsweb.ancestry.com/cgi-bin/igm.cgi?op=GET&db
      =mccook&id=I12

King, J.

    No biographical sources located.

Kitchens, James Elmer

    Composer information from Hugh McGraw.

    Montgomery and Green, *Biographical Sketches*.

Lancaster, M. L. A., P. R., and Sarah

    James, *Brief History*, 115–16.

    RootsWeb, wc.rootsweb.com/cgi-bin/igm.cgi?op=GET&db=bertiesong&id
      =I4432.

    www.webcom.com/hamlet/genealogy/

        Lancaster, Anna Lucinda Maria Atkinson "Ann"

        James, *Brief History*, 115–16.

        Ann Lancaster diaries and letters, Georgia State Library.

        RootsWeb, wc.rootsweb.ancestry.com/cgi-bin/igm.cgi?op=GET&db
          =:1915952&id=I603021453

        Lancaster, Priscilla R. "Sid"

        RootsWeb, wc.rootsweb.ancestry.com/cgi-bin/igm.cgi?op=GET&db
          =:1915952&id=I603021458

        Lancaster, Sarah "Sally"

        James, *Brief History*, 111–12.

        RootsWeb, wc.rootsweb.ancestry.com/cgi-bin/igm.cgi?op=GET&db
          =:1915952&id=I579561577

        RootsWeb, worldconnect.rootsweb.com/cgi-bin/igm.cgi?op=GET&db
          =:1915952&id=I579561546

        GenForum, genforum.genealogy.com/cgi-bin/pageload.cgi?washington
          ::hagler::193.html

        RootsWeb, wc.rootsweb.com/cgi-bin/igm.cgi?op=GET&db=:1915952&id
          =I579561530

Ledbetter, Lewis L.

    RootsWeb, wc.rootsweb.com/cgi-bin/igm.cgi?op=GET&db=laura47&id=I48493

    USGenWeb Archives, files.usgwarchives.org/ga/jenkins/cemeteries/habersha.txt

Letson, Calvin Ford

 RootsWeb, wc.rootsweb.com/cgi-bin/igm.cgi?op=GET&db=:2409836&id
 =I515033211

Lowry, James C.

 No biographical sources located.

Mann, Henry Goodwin

 RootsWeb, wc.rootsweb.com/cgi-bin/igm.cgi?op=GET&db=georand&id=I7356

Mann, Richard. F. M.

 Original Sacred Harp, 95.

 Milledgeville Asylum records, Georgia State Library.

 RootsWeb, wc.rootsweb.ancestry.com/cgi-bin/igm.cgi?op=GET&db
 =bigmann&id=I1631

Marsh, Simeon Butler

 Metcalf, *Writers and Compilers*, 225–27.

 Reynolds, *Companion to the Baptist Hymnal*, 368–69.

Mason, Lowell

 Metcalf, *Writers and Compilers*, 211–18.

 New Grove Dictionary of Music and Musicians.

 Bealle, *Public Worship, Private Faith*, chap. 1.

 Pemberton, *Lowell Mason*.

 Mason, *Hymn-Tunes of Lowell Mason*.

 Reynolds, *Companion to the Baptist Hymnal*, 370–71.

Massengale, John

 www.usgennet.org/usa/ga/county/macon/newspapers/columbus_enq_pg_2
 .htm

Maxim, Abraham

 Metcalf, *Writers and Compilers*, 161–63.

 Davenport, "Maine's Sacred Tunebooks."

Mayfield, Israel

 Hueytown Historical Society, Family Histories, *Genealogies, Stories and Links for
 Families of Southwest Jefferson County*, s.v. "Descendants of Isaac Israel Mayfield."
 www.hueytown.org/historical/Families/Isaac_Israel_Mayfield_Descendants
 .pdf

McCurry, Alexander W.

 Patterson, introduction to McCurry, *Social Harp*.

 RootsWeb, wc.rootsweb.ancestry.com/cgi-bin/igm.cgi?op=GET&db
 =:992767&id=I426

McCurry, John Gordon

    Jackson, *White Spirituals* 74–80.

    Patterson, introduction to McCurry, *Social Harp.*

    The Organ, articles by B. F. White and Edmund Dumas, noted by Robert L.
        Vaughn.

    RootsWeb, wc.rootsweb.ancestry.com/cgi-bin/igm.cgi?op=GET&db
        =davidhbrown&id=I427

    RootsWeb, wc.rootsweb.com/cgi-bin/igm.cgi?op=GET&db=:992767&id=I427

McGraw, Edgar Leon

    Composer information from Hugh McGraw.

McGraw, Henry Newton "Bud"

    Composer information from Hugh McGraw.

McGraw, Hugh Winfred

    Composer information from Hugh McGraw.

    GenForum, genforum.genealogy.com/mcgraw/messages/796.html

McGraw, Lee Andrew

    Composer information from Hugh McGraw.

    www.mcgrawonline.us/FamHistDarrellI.html

McGraw, Thomas Beatrice

    Composer information from Hugh McGraw.

McGraw, Thomas Buford

    Composer information from Hugh McGraw.

McLendon, Augustus Jackson

    RootsWeb, wc.rootsweb.com/cgi-bin/igm.cgi?op=GET&db=blackman
        -farmer&id=I177524

McWhorter, Millard Fillmore

    Composer information from Hugh McGraw.

Meggs, James Lloyd

    Hueytown Historical Society, Family Histories, *Genealogies, Stories and Links for*
        families of southwest Jefferson County. s.v. "Isaac Meigs' Descendants."
        www.hueytown.org/historical/Families/Isaac_Meigs_Descendants.pdf

    RootsWeb, wc.rootsweb.ancestry.com/cgi-bin/igm.cgi?op=REG&db
        =:3323147&id=I19639

Mercer, John

    Original Sacred Harp, 289.

    RootsWeb, wc.rootsweb.ancestry.com/cgi-bin/igm.cgi?op=GET&db
        =memmathis&id=I12623

RootsWeb, wc.rootsweb.ancestry.com/cgi-bin/igm.cgi?op=GET&db
     =jmljr&id=I99116

Mercer, Theodore Chelton, Jr.

Composer information from Hugh McGraw and Ted Mercer.

Merrill, David

RootsWeb, wc.rootsweb.ancestry.com/cgi-bin/igm.cgi?op=GET&db
     =:2927056&id=I1115

Miller, Priestley

Composer information from Hugh McGraw.

Monday, Reubin

Music, "Ananias Davisson, Robert Boyd, Reubin Monday, John Martin, and Archi-
     bald Rhea in East Tennessee."

Moore, W. F.

James, *Brief History*, 118.

RootsWeb, ftp.rootsweb.com/pub/usgenweb/al/cleburne/newspapers/
     gnw132newspape.txt

users.htcomp.net/JCGS/1892History/Johnson/Alvarado.htm

Moore, William

Music, "William Moore's Columbian Harmony."

Moors, Hezekiah

RootsWeb, wc.rootsweb.ancestry.com/cgi-bin/igm.cgi?op=GET&db
     =ragtimer&id=I4183

Morelli

No biographical sources located.

Morgan, Justin

Metcalf, *Writers and Compilers*, 66–68.

Bandel, *Sing the Lord's Song in a Strange Land*.

Crawford, "Massachusetts Musicians," 622.

Munson, Amos

Cooke, "American Psalmodists," 7–11.

RootsWeb, wc.rootsweb.com/cgi-bin/igm.cgi?op=GET&db=:2910310&id=I184971

RootsWeb, wc.rootsweb.ancestry.com/cgi-bin/igm.cgi?op=GET&db
     =:3117953&id=I98805

Nicholson, William

Hauser, *Olive Leaf,* 75.

Ogletree, Absalom
  J. S. James, *Brief History,* 103–5.
  RootsWeb, wc.rootsweb.com/cgi-bin/igm.cgi?op=GET&db=dkcoleman&id
    =I0891

Oliver, Henry Kemble
  Metcalf, *Writers and Compilers,* 230–33.

Osborne, Richard R.
  RootsWeb, wc.rootsweb.ancestry.com/cgi-bin/igm.cgi?op=GET&db
    =:1854812&id=I10513
  boards.ancestry.com/thread.aspx?mv=flat&m=192&p=localities.northam.usa
    .states.alabama.counties.pickens
  RootsWeb, wc.rootsweb.ancestry.com/cgi-bin/igm.
    cgi?op=GET&db=poole&id=I1107
  RootsWeb, wc.rootsweb.ancestry.com/cgi-bin/igm.cgi?op=GET&db
    =gwmayfield&id=I49276

Parkerson, Frances Eva
  Original Sacred Harp, 381.
  RootsWeb, homepages.rootsweb.ancestry.com/~palmrtre/gentr.htm

Parks, William Williamson
  Original Sacred Harp, 439.
  RootsWeb, wc.rootsweb.ancestry.com/cgi-bin/igm.cgi?op=GET&db=
    mrwm326&id=I3795

Parris, Hosea Anderson
  Original Sacred Harp, 506.
  RootsWeb, wc.rootsweb.ancestry.com/cgi-bin/igm.cgi?op=GET&db
    =lorenejones&id=I05901

Parris, Orin Adolphus
  Composer information from Hugh McGraw.

Penick, Spencer Reed
  James, *Brief History,* 118.
  Original Sacred Harp, 387.
  The Organ, 14 February 1855.
  RootsWeb, wc.rootsweb.ancestry.com/cgi-bin/igm.cgi?op=GET&db=wadleyv
    &id=I12295
  USGenWeb Archives, files.usgwarchives.org/ga/houston/cemeteries/evergr2.txt

Pickard, James Lafayette
  Graham, *Baptist Biography,* 2:258–61.
  RootsWeb, wc.rootsweb.com/cgi-bin/igm.cgi?op=GET&db=:2759277&id=I501

RootsWeb, wc.rootsweb.com/cgi-bin/igm.cgi?op=GET&db=randyj2222&id=I48705

GenForum, genforum.genealogy.com/pickard/messages/375.html

Pilsbury, Amos

Kroeger, "Yankee Tunebook from the Old South," 154–62.

Music, "Seven 'New' Tunes," 403–47.

Pleyel, Ignaz Joseph

New Grove Dictionary of Music and Musicians.

Pound, Edwin Theophilus

James, *Brief History,* 59–62, 114

History of Lamar County, 392–93.

(Barnesville, Georgia) *News-Gazette,* 26 June, 1919, obituary.

RootsWeb, wc.rootsweb.com/cgi-bin/igm.cgi?op=GET&db=surface&id=I4399

Power, William Thomas

Original Sacred Harp, 360.

RootsWeb, wc.rootsweb.ancestry.com/cgi-bin/igm.cgi?op=GET&db=lfot-1&id=I4213

RootsWeb, wc.rootsweb.ancestry.com/cgi-bin/igm.cgi?op=GET&db=sideboard&id=I00815

Price, F.

RootsWeb, wc.rootsweb.com/cgi-bin/igm.cgi?op=GET&db=tamara&id=I3989

Raiford, L. M.

Original Sacred Harp, 409.

RootsWeb, wc.rootsweb.ancestry.com/cgi-bin/igm.cgi?op=GET&db=lrossg&id=I0778

Randall, Bruce

Composer information from Hugh McGraw and Bruce Randall.

Randall, John

New Grove Dictionary of Music and Musicians.

Read, Daniel

Crawford, "Massachusetts Musicians," 622–23.

Metcalf, *Writers and Compilers,* 94–99.

New Grove Dictionary .

Kroeger, *Daniel Read.*

Redding, Loyd Richard

Composer information from Hugh McGraw.

Reese, Henry Smith
  James, *Brief History*, 108.
  Graham, *Baptist Biography*, 2:293–95.

Reese, John Palmer
  James, *Brief History*, 94–99.

Reeves, R. H.
  Original Sacred Harp, 475.
  "Muster Roll," www.angelfire.com/tx/RandysTexas/csareserve1/page12.html
  USGenWeb Archives, files.usgwarchives.net/ga/carroll/military/civilwar/
    rosters/fani.txt

Rich, A.
  No biographical sources located.

Rollo, John Hall
  RootsWeb, wc.rootsweb.ancestry.com/cgi-bin/igm.cgi?op=GET&
    db=norfield&id=I0552

  Rousseau, Jean-Jacques
  New Grove Dictionary of Music and Musicians.

Russell, Henry
  New Grove Dictionary of Music and Musicians.

Searcy, John Smith
  RootsWeb, wc.rootsweb.ancestry.com/cgi-bin/igm.cgi?op=GET&db
    =thweatt2222&id=I403

Shell, John Abner Zaccheus
  Original Sacred Harp, 293.
  web.infoave.net/~danshell/fam00487.htm
  RootsWeb, *Newnan Herald*, mhrising.com/newspapers/Georgia/newnan
    _herald%201865.htm
  searches.rootsweb.ancestry.com/usgenweb/archives/ga/coweta/newspapers/
    homenews155nnw.txt

Sheppard, William Jefferson
  Composer information from Hugh McGraw and Jeff Sheppard.

Sherman, P.
  RootsWeb, wc.rootsweb.ancestry.com/cgi-bin/igm.cgi?op=GET&db
    =wilson2000&id=I1631

Shumway, Nehemiah
  RootsWeb, wc.rootsweb.ancestry.com/cgi-bin/igm.cgi?op=GET&db
    =tsmith&id=I118428

Sikes, Matthew

    Original Sacred Harp, 387.

    RootsWeb, wc.rootsweb.ancestry.com/cgi-bin/igm.cgi?op=GET&db
      =town_mar&id=I17963

    GenForum, genforum.genealogy.com/cgi-bin/print.cgi?sikes::905.html

Smith, Isaac

    Temperley, *Music of the English Parish Church.*

    Lightwood, *Hymn Tunes and Their Story,* 161–62.

Smith, Toney E.

    Composer information from Hugh McGraw.

Spark, James A.

    No biographical sources located.

Stephenson, Joseph

    Sydenham, *History of the Town and County of Poole,* 341.

Stone, Joseph

    Metcalf, *Writers and Compilers,* 85–86.

    Kroeger, *Joseph Stone.*

Sumner, Jazaniah

    Nason, *Monogram,* 37–39.

    RootsWeb, wc.rootsweb.ancestry.com/cgi-bin/igm.cgi?op=GET&db=julian
      _sloan2&id=I0125

Swan, Timothy

    Crawford, "Massachusetts Musicians," 623–25.

    Metcalf, *Writers and Compilers,* 103–7.

    New Grove Dictionary of Music and Musicians.

    Cooke, *Timothy Swan.*

Taber, Philip A.

    Composer information from Hugh McGraw.

    Tennessee death certificate, cited by *FamilySearch Internet Genealogy Service.*

Temple, Samuel

    RootsWeb, wc.rootsweb.ancestry.com/cgi-bin/igm.cgi?op=GET&db
      =abrahamtemple&id=P3209184725

Terry, John Stringer

    James, *Brief History,* 112.

    RootsWeb, wc.rootsweb.ancestry.com/cgi-bin/igm.cgi?op=GET&db
      =4roses&id=I189

Thomas, M. H.

  www.usgennet.org/usa/ga/county/fulton/walton/waltonmarriages.pdf

Turner, James R.

  James, *Brief History*, 91–94.

  Original Sacred Harp, 270.

Turner, M. H.

  Original Sacred Harp, 339.

  RootsWeb, wc.rootsweb.ancestry.com/cgi-bin/igm.cgi?op=GET&db
    =shelb68&id=I955

  RootsWeb, wc.rootsweb.ancestry.com/cgi-bin/igm.cgi?op=GET&db
    =:2349697&id=I510408495

  USGenWeb Archives, files.usgwarchives.org/ga/coweta/deeds/grantort.txt

Turner, William Stevens

  James, *Brief History*, 137.

  Original Sacred Harp, 370.

  RootsWeb,wc.rootsweb.com/cgi-bin/igm.cgi?op=GET&db=mceachin&id
    =I09344

Wade, J. A. and J. F

  Patterson, introduction to McCurry, *Social Harp*.

  Original Sacred Harp, 70.

  www.wargs.com/political/edwards.html

  RootsWeb, wc.rootsweb.ancestry.com/cgi-bin/igm.cgi?op=GET&db=pkd&id
    =I6823Ja86a

Wakefield, Samuel

  Albert, *History of the County of Westmoreland*, 257.

  Storey, *History of Cambria County*, 3:53–56.

  Wiley, *Biographical and Portrait Cyclopedia of Cambria County*, 420–22.

Walker, William

  Landrum, *History of Spartanburg County*, 491–95.

  Eskew, "William Walker's *Southern Harmony*," 137–48.

  Jackson, *White Spirituals*, 55–69.

Wallace, Charlene

  Composer information from Hugh McGraw and Charlene Wallace.

Waller, Thomas

  Original Sacred Harp, 330, 426.

  The Organ, 17 May 1854.

  www.geocities.com/Heartland/Meadows/4386/waller.htm

RootsWeb, wc.rootsweb.ancestry.com/cgi-bin/igm.cgi?op=GET&db
=:2878842&id=I560763672

RootsWeb, www.rootsweb.com/~gaupson/1866page.htm

USGenWeb Archives, files.usgwarchives.net/ga/upson/history/1869.txt

USGenWeb Archives, files.usgwarchives.net/ga/upson/military/civilwar/k-5.txt

Watson, John A.

No biographical sources located.

Webster, Joseph Philbrick

Reynolds, *Companion to the Baptist Hymnal,* 456.

www.pdmusic.org/webster.html

Wells, Lee Scott

Composer information from Hugh McGraw.

West, Elisha

Kroeger, *Two Vermont Composers.*

Wetmore, Truman Spencer

Steel, "Truman S. Wetmore and His 'Republican Harmony,'" 75–89.

White, Benjamin Franklin

James, *Brief History,* 11–20, 27–37.

Jackson, *White Spirituals,* 81–93.

Clarke, *Chronology,* www.abstractmath.org/fasola/whitebio.htm

White, Benjamin Franklin, Jr. "Frank"

James, *Brief History,* 46–47.

White, David Patillo

James, *Brief History,* 45.

White, James Landrum

James, *Brief History,* 41–44.

White, Jesse Thomas

James, *Brief History,* 51.

Williams, Aaron

Reynolds, *Companion to the Baptist Hymnal,* 462.

Williams, E. F.

Original Sacred Harp, 458.

Williams, J.

No biographical sources located.

Williams, William Lafayette
James, *Brief History*, 121.
www.flemingmultimedia.com/Genealogy/williamsdesc.html

Wilson, Hugh
Reynolds, *Companion to the Baptist Hymnal*, 465.

Wilson, John
New Grove Dictionary of Music and Musicians.

Wood, Abraham
Metcalf, *Writers and Compilers*, 85–87.
Kroeger, *Abraham Wood.*
New Grove Dictionary of Music and Musicians.

Wood, F. C.
Original Sacred Harp, 277.
RootsWeb, wc.rootsweb.ancestry.com/cgi-bin/igm.cgi?op=GET&db
=gilead07&id=I059312
RootsWeb, wc.rootsweb.com/cgi-bin/igm.cgi?op=GET&db=thorntonr&id
=I08059

Wood, U. G.
No biographical sources located.

Woodard, Thomas Pickens
Composer information from Hugh McGraw.

Woodbury, Isaac Baker
Metcalf, *Writers and Compilers*, 281–85.
New Grove Dictionary of Music and Musicians.

Wootten, Terry
Information from Hugh McGraw and David Ivey.

Wright, Glen
Composer information from Hugh McGraw and Glen Wright.

Wright, Margaret Johnson
Composer information from Hugh McGraw.

Wynn, Matthew Mark
Original Sacred Harp, 118, 463.
James, *Brief History*, 109.
Boozer, *Long, Long Ago*, 107.
RootsWeb, wc.rootsweb.ancestry.com/cgi-bin/igm.cgi?op=GET&db
=:3000146&id=I586914125

Yates, Willis Alvin

> RootsWeb, wc.rootsweb.ancestry.com/cgi-bin/igm.cgi?op=GET&db=bubba4444
> &id=I00493

2. *The Sacred Harp:* Editions and Revisions in Chronological Order

White, B. F., and E. J. King. *The Sacred Harp.* Philadelphia: T. K. and P. G. Collins, 1844.

White, B. F., and E. J. King. *The Sacred Harp.* [2d ed.] Philadelphia: T. K. and P. G. Collins, 1850.

White, B. F., and E. J. King. *The Sacred Harp.* [3d ed.] New and much improved and enlarged edition. Philadelphia: S. C. Collins, 1859.

White, B. F., and E. J. King. *The Sacred Harp.* 4th edition, entirely remodeled. Philadelphia, S. C. Collins, [1870].

White, B. F. *The Sacred Harp.* Revised and improved by W. M. Cooper. [Cooper revision.] Dothan, Ala.: W. M. Cooper & Co., 1902. Successive editions appeared in 1909, 1927, 1949, 1960, 1992, 2000, and 2006.

White, B. F. *The Sacred Harp,* 5th edition, entirely remodeled and improved . . . by J. L. White and others. Atlanta: J. L. White, 1909. A variant issue was published in 1910.

White, B. F. *The Sacred Harp,* 4th edition, with supplement, by J. L. White and others. Atlanta: J. L. White, 1911. Reprinted in 1958 and 2008.

Original Sacred Harp. Revised, corrected and enlarged. [James edition.] Atlanta, 1911. Reprinted in 1927 and 1964.

Original Sacred Harp (Denson Revision). Cullman, Ala.: Sacred Harp Publishing Company, 1936. New material was added in 1960 and 1966; minor revisions were made in 1971, 1977, and 1987.

The Sacred Harp, 1991 Revision. Bremen, Ga.: Sacred Harp Publishing Co., 1991.

3. General Bibliography

Adams, Thomas F. *Typographia: A Brief Sketch of the Origin, Rise, and Progress of the Typographic Art, with Practical Directions for Conducting Every Department in an Office.* 4th ed. Philadelphia: L. Johnson and Co., 1854.

Albert, George Dallas. *History of the County of Westmoreland, Pennsylvania.* Philadelphia: L. H. Everts & Co., 1882.

The American Catalog, 1905–1907: Containing a record, under title, author, subject and series of the books published in the United States, recorded from January 1, 1905 to December, 1907, together with a directory of publishers. New York: Office of The Publishers Weekly, 1908.

Appel, Richard G. *The Music of the Bay Psalm Book, 9th Edition (1698).* I.S.A.M. Monographs, no. 9. Brooklyn: Institute for Studies in American Music, 1975.

Armstrong, Mary F., Helen W. Ludlow, and Thomas P. Fenner. *Hampton and Its Students, . . . With Fifty Cabin and Plantation Songs.* Boston: G. F. Putnam, 1874.

Bandel, Betty. *Sing the Lord's Song in a Strange Land: The Life of Justin Morgan.* Rutherford, N.J.: Fairleigh Dickinson University Press, 1981.

Bastin, Bruce. *Red River Blues: The Blues Tradition in the Southeast.* Urbana: University of Illinois Press, 1986.

Bealle, John. "New Strings on the Old Harp: The 1991 Revision of the Sacred Harp." *Tributaries* 1 (1994): 5–23.

———. *Public Worship, Private Faith: Sacred Harp and American Folksong.* Athens: University of Georgia Press, 1997.

Belcher, Joseph. *Historical Sketches of Hymns, Their Writers, and Their Influence.* Philadelphia: Lindsay & Blakiston, 1859.

Benedict, David. *A General History of the Baptist Denomination in America and Other Parts of the World.* Two volumes. Boston: Lincoln and Edmands, 1813.

Bishop, J. Leander. *A History of American Manufactures, 1608–1860.* 3d ed. Philadelphia: Edward Young & Co., 1868.

Bohlman, Philip, ed. *Music in American Religious Experience.* Oxford: Oxford University Press, 2006.

Boozer, Harriett Farris. *Long, Long Ago, 1776–1976: A Genealogical Record of the Farris, Wells, Keltner, Wynne, Russell and Roberts Families in America.* Sandy Springs, Ga.: The Author, 1976.

Boswell, George W. "Verse and Music in the Sacred Harp." *Southern Folklore Quarterly* 34 (1970): 53–61.

Bransford, Steve. "Blues in the Lower Chattahoochee Valley." *Southern Spaces,* 16 March 2004, www.southernspaces.org/2004/blues-lower-chattahoochee-valley.

Britton, Allen P. "The Singing School Movement in the United States." *International Musicological Society Congress Report* 8 (1961): 89–99.

Britton, Allen P., Irving Lowens, and Richard Crawford. *American Sacred Music Imprints, 1698–1810: A Bibliography.* Worcester: American Antiquarian Society, 1990.

Brown, A. Peter. "Musical Settings of Anne Hunter's Poetry: From National Song to Canzonetta." *Journal of the American Musicological Society* 47 (Spring 1994): 39–89.

Brown, Theron, and Hezekiah Butterworth. *The Story of the Hymns and Tunes.* New York: American Tract Society, 1907.

Bruce, Dickson D., Jr. *And They All Sang Hallelujah: Plain-Folk Camp-Meeting Religion, 1800–1845.* Knoxville: University of Tennessee Press, 1974.

Buechner, Alan Clark. "Thomas Walter and the Society for Promoting Regular Singing in the Worship of God: Boston, 1720–1723." In *New England Music: The Public Sphere, 1600–1900.* Boston: Boston University, for the Dublin Seminar for New England Folklife, 1998, pp. 48–60.

———. *Yankee Singing Schools and the Golden Age of Choral Music in New England, 1760–1800.* Boston: Boston University, for the Dublin Seminar for New England Folklife, 2003.

Campbell, Gavin James. "'Old Can Be Used Instead of New': Shape-Note Singing and the Crisis of Modernity in the New South, 1880–1920." *Journal of American Folklore* 110 (Spring 1997): 169–88.

Celebration of the Hundredth Anniversary of the Incorporation of Conway, Massachusetts. Northampton: Bridgman & Childs, 1867.

Cheek, Curtis Leo. "The Singing School and Shape-Note Tradition: Residuals in Twentieth-Century American Hymnody." Ph.D. diss., University of Southern California, 1968.

Childs, Essie. *They Tarried in Taylor.* Warner Robbins, Ga.: Central Georgia Genealogical Society, 1992.

Church of Jesus Christ of Latter-Day Saints. FamilySearch Internet Genealogy Service. www.familysearch.org.

Chute, William Edward. *A Genealogy and History of the Chute Family in America.* Salem, Mass.: [The Author], 1894.

Clarke, Donald Stephen. "A Chronology of the Life of Benjamin Franklin White." www.abstractmath.org/fasola/whitebio.htm.

Cobb, Buell E. "The Sacred Harp: Rhythm and Ritual in the Southland." *Virginia Quarterly Review* (Autumn 1974): 187–97.

———. *The Sacred Harp: A Tradition and Its Music.* Athens: University of Georgia Press, 1978.

Collins, Lewis. *Historical Sketches of Kentucky.* Maysville, Ky. and Cincinnati: J. A. and U. P. James, 1847.

Commuck, Thomas. "Sketch of the Brothertown Indians." *Wisconsin Historical Collections* 4 (1859): 291–98. www.library.wisc.edu/etext/WIReader/WER0439.html.

Conkin, Paul. *Cane Ridge: America's Pentecost.* Madison: University of Wisconsin Press, 1990.

Cooke, Nym. "American Psalmodists in Contact and Collaboration, 1770–1820." Ph.D. diss., University of Michigan, 1990.

———. "Itinerant Yankee Singing Masters in the Eighteenth Century." In *Itinerancy in New England and New York.* The Dublin Seminar for New England Folklife: Annual Proceedings 1984. Boston: Boston University, 1986.

———, ed. *Timothy Swan: Psalmody and Secular Songs.* Madison, Wis.: A-R Editions, 1997.

———. "William Billings: Representative American Psalmodist?" *Quarterly Journal of Music Teaching and Learning* 7 (Spring 1996): 57–60.

Crawford, Richard. *The American Musical Landscape.* Berkeley: University of California Press, 1993.

———. *American Studies and American Musicology: A Point of View and a Case in Point.* I.S.A.M Monographs, no. 4. Brooklyn: Institute for Studies in American Music, 1975.

———. *America's Musical Life: A History.* New York: Norton, 2001.

———. *Andrew Law, American Psalmodist.* Evanston: Northwestern University Press, 1968. Reprint, New York: Da Capo, 1981.

———, ed. *The Core Repertory of American Psalmody.* Madison, Wis.: A-R Editions, 1984.

———. "Massachusetts Musicians and the Core Repertory of Early American Psalmody." In *Music in Colonial Massachusetts, 1830–1820.* Boston: Colonial Society of Massachusetts, 1985, pp. 583–629.

———. "'Much Still Remains to Be Undone': Reformers of Early American Hymnody." *The Hymn* 35 (October 1984): 204–8.

———. "Musical Learning in Nineteenth-Century America." *American Music* 1 (Spring 1983): 1–11.

———. "Watts for Singing: Metrical Poetry in American Sacred Tunebooks, 1761–1785." *Early American Literature* 11 (1976): 139–46.

Davenport, Linda G. "Maine's Sacred Tunebooks, 1800–1830: Divine Song on the Northeast Frontier." Ph.D. diss., University of Colorado, 1991.

Davidson, William H. *A Rockaway in Talbot.* West Point, Ga.: The Author, 1983.

Denson, M. E. *Reverend Levi Phillips Denson (1819–1889): Denson Families in America.* Paducah, Ky.: Turner, 1997.

Dow, Lorenzo. *History of Cosmopolite.* 5th ed. Wheeling, Va.: Joshua Martin, 1848.

Downey, James C. "Joshua Leavitt's 'The Christian Lyre' and the Beginning of the Popular Tradition in American Religious Song." *Latin American Music Review* 7 (Autumn–Winter, 1986): 149–61.

———. "The Music of American Revivalism." Ph.D. diss., Tulane University, 1968.

Ellington, Charles Linwood. "The Sacred Harp Tradition of the South: Its Origin and Evolution." Ph.D. diss., Florida State University, 1969.

Ellis, Joseph. *American Creation.* New York: Knopf, 2007.

Eskew, Harry. "Andrew W. Johnson's *The Eclectic Harmony:* A Middle Tunebook in Middle Tennessee." *Notes* 58 (December 2001): 291–301.

———. "Georgia Origins of *The Sacred Harp.*" *Viewpoints: Georgia Baptist History* 20 (2006): 25–35.

———. "William Walker's *Southern Harmony:* Its Basic Editions." *Latin American Music Review* 7 (1986): 137–48.

Eskew, Harry, and Karl Kroeger. *Selected Works of Samuel Holyoke (1762–1820) and Jacob Kimball (1761–1826).* Music of the New American Nation 12. New York: Garland, 1998.

Fatout, Paul. "Threnodies of the Ladies' Books." *Musical Quarterly* 31 (October 1945): 464–78.

Fawcett-Yeske, Maxine, ed. *Two Connecticut Composers: The Collected Works of Eliakim Doolittle (1772–1850) and Timothy Olmstead (1759–1848).* New York: Garland, 1999.

Finney, Theodore M. "The Third Edition of Tufts' *Introduction to the Art of Singing Psalm-Tunes.*" *Journal of Research in Music Education* 14 (1963): 163–70.

Fry, Benjamin St. James. "The Early Camp-Meeting Song Writers." *Methodist Review,* series 4, 11 (1859): 214–15.

Fuld, James J., and Mary Wallace Davidson. *18th-Century American Secular Music Manuscripts: An Inventory.* MLA Index & Bibliography Series 20. Philadelphia: Music Library Association, 1980.

Fulton, Ruth Coan. *Coan Genealogy, 1697–1982.* Poutsmouth, N.H.: Peter E. Randall, 1983.

Furnas, J. C. *The Americans: A Social History of the United States, 1587–1914.* New York: Putnam, 1969.

Fussell, Fred C. *A Chattahoochee Album: Images of Traditional People and Folksy Places Around the Lower Chattahoochee Valley.* Eufala, Ala.: Historic Chattahoochee Commission, 2000.

Genuchi, Martin C. "The Life and Music of Jacob French (1754—1817), Colonial American Composer." Ph.D. diss., University of Iowa, 1964.

[Gilson, Franklin Howard.] *Music-Book Printing. With Specimens.* Boston: F. H. Gilson Co., 1897.

Goff, James R. *Close Harmony: A History of Southern Gospel*. Chapel Hill: University of North Carolina Press, 2002.

Graham, Balus Joseph Winzer, ed. *Baptist Biography*. Atlanta: Index Printing Company, 1920.

Green, Thomas Marshall. *Historic Families of Kentucky*. Cincinnati: Robert Charles & Co., 1889.

Hadamer, Armin. "O Come, Come Away: Temperance, Shape Notes, and Patriotism." *Song and Popular Culture* 45 (2000):109–20.

Hamrick, James Martin. *A Sketch of the Life of James Martin Hamrick*. Carrollton, Ga.: Times Job Department, 1902. www.ronsattic.com/jmhamric.htm.

Harley, Rachel Augusta Brett. "Ananias Davisson: Southern Tune-Book Compiler." Ph.D. diss., University of Michigan, 1972.

Harriman, John C. "'Most Excellent—far farm'd and far fetch'd Cheese': An Anthology of Jeffersonian-Era Poetry," *American Magazine and Historical Chronicle* 2 (Autumn–Winter 1986–97: 1–26.

Hatchett, Marion J. *A Companion to the New Harp of Columbia*. Knoxville. University of Tennessee Press, 2003.

———. "Early East Tennessee Shape-Note Tunebooks." *The Hymn* 46 (1995): 28–46.

———. "Three Little-Known West Tennessee Four-Shape Shape-Note Tunebooks." *The Hymn* 42 (1991): 10–16.

Hauser, William. *The Hesperian Harp*. Philadelphia: T. K. & P. G. Collins, 1848.

———. *The Olive Leaf*. Wadley, Ga.: Hauser & Turner, 1878.

The Heritage of Pike County, Alabama. Clanton, Ala.: Heritage Publishing Consultants, 2001.

Herman, Janet. "Sacred Harp Singing in California: Genre, Performance, Feeling." Ph.D. diss., University of California at Los Angeles, 1997.

History of Lamar County. Barnesville, Ga.: Barnesville News-Gazette, 1932.

History of the Baptist Denomination in Georgia, together with Biographical Sketches of Prominent Baptists. Atlanta: James P. Harrison, 1881.

Horn, Dorothy D. "English Sources of American Folk Hymns: Additions to the Jackson Lists." *Southern Folklore Quarterly* 28 (1964): 222–27.

———. "Quartal Harmony in the Pentatonic Folk Hymns of the Sacred Harp." *Journal of American Folklore* 71 (October–December 1958): 564–81.

———. *Sing to Me of Heaven: A Study of Folk and Early American Materials in Three Old Harp Books*. Gainesville: University of Florida Press, 1970.

House, Myron. "The Use of *The Sacred Harp* at Bethesda Church, Carroll, County, Georgia, at the Time of the Civil War." *National Sacred Harp Newsletter* 3 (April 1988).

Hueytown Historical Society. *Family Histories, Genealogies, Stories and Links for Families of Southwest Jefferson County*. www.hueytown.org/historical/Families/Family%20Histories.htm.

Hulan, Richard H. "The American Revolution in Hymnody." *The Hymn* 35 (October 1984): 199–203.

———. "Camp-Meeting Spiritual Folksongs: Legacy of the 'Great Revival in the West.'" Ph.D. diss., University of Texas, 1978.

———. "John Adam Granade: Wild Man of Goose Creek." *Western Folklore* 33 (1974): 77–87.

Immanuel's Ground: Warwick's West Gallery Quire. www.immanuelsground.com/.

Jackson, George Pullen. *Another Sheaf of White Spirituals.* Gainesville: University of Florida Press, 1952.

———. "Buckwheat Notes." *Musical Quarterly* 19 (October 1933): 393–400.

———. *Down East Spirituals and Others: Three Hundred Songs Supplemental to the Author's Spiritual Folk-Songs of Early America.* New York: Augustin, 1939.

———. "The Fa-Sol-La Folk." *Musical Courier* 93, no. 11 (1926): 6–7, 10.

———. "Some Factors in the Diffusion of American Religious Folksongs." *Journal of American Folklore* 65 (October–December 1952): 365–69.

———. *Spiritual Folk-Songs of Early America: Two Hundred and Fifty Tunes and Texts with an Introduction and Notes.* New York: Augustin, 1937.

———. *The Story of the Sacred Harp, 1844–1944: A Book of Religious Folk Song as an American Institution.* Nashville: Vanderbilt University Press, 1944.

———. *White and Negro Spirituals: Their Life Span and Kinship.* New York: Augustin, 1943.

———. *White Spirituals in the Southern Uplands: The Story of the Fasola Folk, Their Songs, Singings, and "Buckwheat Notes."* Chapel Hill: University of North Carolina Press, 1933.

James, Joseph Stephen. *A Brief History of the Sacred Harp and Its Author, B.F. White, Sr., and Contributors.* Douglasville, Ga.: New South Book and Job Print, 1904.

Johnson, Charles A. "Camp Meeting Hymnody." *American Quarterly* 4 (Summer 1952): 110–26.

Jones, Thomas G. *Reports of Cases Argued and Determined in the Supreme Court of Alabama, During December Term, 1876.* Montgomery, Ala.: Joel White, 1879.

Julian, John. *A Dictionary of Hymnology Setting Forth the Origin and History of Christian Hymns of All Ages and Nations.* London: John Murray, 1892. Reprint, New York: Dover, 1957.

Kelton, Mai Hogan. "Living Teacher-Composers of the Sacred Harp." *Tennessee Folklore Society Bulletin* 51 (Winter 1985): 137–43.

Klocko, David G. "Jeremiah Ingalls's *The Christian Harmony: Or, Songster's Companion* (1805)." Ph.D. diss., University of Michigan, 1978.

Knippers, Ottis J. *Who's Who among Southern Singers and Composers.* Hot Springs National Park, Ark.: Knippers Brothers [1937].

Koegel, John. "'The Indian Chief' and 'Morality': An Eighteenth-Century British Popular Song Transformed into a Nineteenth-Century American Shape-note Hymn." In *Music in Performance and Society: Essays in Honor of Roland Jackson,* ed. Malcolm Cole and John Koegel. Warren, Mich.: Harmonie Park, 1997, pp. 437–508.

Kroeger Karl, ed. *Abraham Wood: The Collected Works.* Music of the New American Nation 6. New York: Garland, 1996.

———. *The Complete Works of William Billings.* 4 vols. Boston: The American Musicological Society & The Colonial Society of Massachusetts, 1990.

———. *Daniel Read: Collected Works.* Madison, Wis.: A-R Editions, 1995.

———. *Joseph Stone: The Collected Works.* Music of the New American Nation 10. New York: Garland, 1996.

———. *Two Vermont Composers: The Collected Works of Elisha West (1752–ca.1808) and Justin Morgan (1747–1798).* Music of the New American Nation 7. New York: Garland, 1997.

———. "A Yankee Tunebook from the Old South: Amos Pilsbury's *The United States Sacred Harmony.*" *The Hymn* 32 (1981): 154–62.

Kroeger, Karl, and Joan R. Callahan. "The 'Other' Billings: The Life and Music of Nathaniel Billings (1768–1853), an Early American Composer." *Notes* 60 (December 2003): 377–92.

Lamson, Alvan. *A History of the First Church and Parish in Dedham.* Dedham, Mass.: Merman Mann, 1839.

Landrum, John Belton O'Neall. *History of Spartanburg County.* Atlanta: Franklin Printing and Publishing Co., 1900.

Larkin, Jack. *The Reshaping of Everyday Life, 1790–1840.* New York: Harper & Row, 1988.

Lightwood, James T. *Hymn Tunes and Their Story.* London: C. H. Kelly, 1906. Reprint, Whitefish, Mont.: Kessinger, 2007.

Lorenz, Ellen Jane. *Glory, Hallelujah! The Story of the Campmeeting Spiritual.* Nashville: Abingdon, 1978.

Lowens, Irving. *Music and Musicians in Early America.* New York: Norton, 1964.

Lyerly, Cynthia Lynn. "A Tale of Two Patriarchs; or, How a Eunuch and a Wife Created a Family in the Church." *Journal of Family History* 28 (October 2003): 490–508.

Marini, Stephen A. *Sacred Song in America: Religion, Music, and Public Culture.* Urbana: University of Illinois Press, 2003.

Mason, Henry Lowell. *Hymn-Tunes of Lowell Mason: A Bibliography.* Cambridge, Mass.: [Harvard] University Press, 1944.

———. *The New Carmina Sacra.* Boston, 1856.

Mason, Lowell, and Timothy Mason. *The Sacred Harp or Eclectic Harmony.* Boston: Shepley & Wright, 1838.

Maynard, Ezekiel. *A New Selection of Sacred Music.* Baltimore: Ezekiel Maynard, 1822.

McCormick, Davd W. "Oliver Holden, Composer and Anthologist." D.S.M. diss., Union Theological Seminary, 1963.

McCurry, John G. *The Social Harp,* ed. Daniel W. Patterson and John F. Garst. Facsimile ed. Athens: University of Georgia Press, 1973.

McKay, David P., and Richard Crawford. *William Billings of Boston: Eighteenth-Century Composer.* Princeton, New Jersey: Princeton University Press, 1975.

McKenzie, Wallace. "The Alto Parts in the 'True Dispersed Harmony' of *The Sacred Harp* Revisions." *Musical Quarterly* 73 (1989): 153–71.

———. "Anthems of the Sacred Harp Tunesmiths." *American Music* 6 (Autumn 1988): 247–63.

Meacham, Jon. *American Lion: Andrew Jackson in the White House.* New York: Random House, 2008.

A Memorial and Biographical History of Johnson and Hill Counties, Texas. Chicago: Lewis Publishing Co., 1892.

Metcalf, Frank J. *American Writers and Compilers of Sacred Music.* New York: Abingdon, 1925.

Miller, Kiri, ed. *The Chattahoochee Musical Convention, 1852–2002: A Sacred Harp Historical Sourcebook.* Carrollton, Ga.: Sacred Harp Museum, 2002.

———. "'First Sing the Notes': Oral and Written Traditions in Sacred Harp Transmission." *American Music* 22 (Winter 2004): 475–501.

———. *Traveling Home: Sacred Harp Singing and American Pluralism.* Urbana: University of Illinois Press, 2008.

Miller, Perry. *The Life of the Mind in America: From the Revolution to the Civil War.* New York: Harcourt, 1965.

Minutes Taken at the Several Annual Conferences of the Methodist Episcopal Church for the Years 1773–1828. New York: T. Mason and G. Lane, 1840.

Mitchell, George. *In Celebration of a Legacy: The Traditional Arts of the Lower Chattahoochee Valley.* Rev. ed. Columbus, Ga.: Columbus Museum of Arts and Sciences, 1998.

Mitchell, Henry C. "The Sacred Harp Singing Group as an Instance of Non-Formal Education." Ph.D. diss., Florida State University, 1976.

Montgomery, David, and Mark Green. *Biographical Sketches of Primitive or Old School Baptist Ministers.* Lampasas, Tex.: Primitive Baptist Heritage Corp., 2001. primitivebaptist .info/mambo//content/view/832/36/.

Moore, John S. "Writers of Early Virginia Baptist History (3): John Leland." *Virginia Baptist Historical Register* 13 (1974): 579–93.

Morley, Thomas. *A Plain and Easy Introduction to Practical Music.* 2d ed. Edited by R. Alec Harman. New York: Norton, 1963.

Morrell, Z. N. *Flowers and Fruits from the Wilderness; or, Thirty-Six Years in Texas and Two Winters in Honduras.* Boston: Gould & Lincoln, 1872.

Music, David W. "Alexander Johnson and the *Tennessee Harmony*." *Current Musicology* 37–38 (1984): 59–73.

———. "Ananias Davisson, Robert Boyd, Reubin Monday, John Martin, and Archibald Rhea in East Tennessee, 1816–26." *American Music* 1 (1983): 72–84.

———. "Early Hymnists of Tennessee." *The Hymn* 31 (1980): 246–51.

———. "A New Source for the Tune 'All Is Well.'" *The Hymn* 29 (April 1978): 76–82.

——— ed. *Oliver Holden (1765–1844): Selected Works.* Music of the New American Nation 13. New York: Garland, 1998.

———. *A Selection of Shape-Note Folk Hymns from Southern United States Tune Books, 1816–1861.* Madison, Wis.: A-R Editions, 2005.

———. "Seven 'New' Tunes in Amos Pilsbury's *United States' Sacred Harmony* (1799) and Their Use in Four-Shape Shape-Note Tunebooks of the Southern United States before 1860." *American Music* 13 (Winter 1995): 403–47.

———. "Tunes by Lowell Mason and Thomas Hastings in Southern Shape-Note Tune Books of the Early Nineteenth Century." *Journal of Musicological Research* 26 (October 2007): 325–52.

———. *We'll Shout and Sing Hosanna: Essays on Church Music in Honor of William J. Reynolds.* Fort Worth: School of Church Music, Southwestern Baptist Theological Seminary, 1998.

———. "William Caldwell's *Union Harmony* (1837): The First East Tennessee Tunebook." *The Hymn* 38 (July 1987): 16–22.

———. "William Moore's *Columbian Harmony* (1825)." *The Hymn* 36 (1985): 16–19.

Music, David W., and Paul A. Richardson. *"I Will Sing the Wondrous Story": A History of Baptist Hymnody in North America.* Macon: Mercer University Press, 2008.

Nason, Elias. *A Monogram on Our National Song.* Albany: Joel Munsell, 1869.

The New Grove Dictionary of American Music. Ed. H. Wiley Hitchcock and Stanley Sadie. 4 vols. London: Macmillan, 1986.

The New Grove Dictionary of Music and Musicians. 2d ed. Ed. Stanley Sadie. 29 vols. London: Macmillan, 2001. www.grovemusic.com.

Norton, Kay. "Who Lost the South?" *American Music* 21 (Winter 2003): 391–411.

Official Minutes of the Ninetieth Session of the New England Conference of the Methodist Episcopal Church. Boston: A. Mudge & Son, 1889.

Owens, Jessie Ann. *Composers at Work: The Craft of Musical Composition, 1450–1600.* New York: Oxford University Press, 1997.

Page, James P. *Thomas Commuck and His Indian Melodies: Wisconsin's Shape-Note Tunebook.* Madison, Wis.: The Author, 1989.

Patterson, Daniel W. *The Shaker Spiritual.* Princeton: Princeton University Press, 1979.

———. "William Hauser's *Hesperian Harp* and *Olive Leaf*: Shape-Note Tunebooks as Emblems of Change and Progress." *Journal of American Folklore* 101 (January–March 1988): 23–36.

Pemberton, Carol Ann. *Lowell Mason: His Life and Work.* Ann Arbor: UMI Research Press, 1985.

Perry, Calbraith B. *Charles D'Wolf of Guadaloupe, His Ancestors and Descendants.* New York: T. A. Wright, 1902.

Phillips, Ulrich Bonnell. *Georgia and State Rights: A Study of the Political History of Georgia from the Revolution to the Civil War, with Particular Regard to Federal Relations.* [American Historical Association monograph.] Washington, D.C.: Government Printing Office, 1902.

Playford, John. *An Introduction to the Skill of Music.* 12th ed. Intro. by Franklin B. Zimmerman. New York: Da Capo, 1972.

Plunkett, John, ed. *Newspaper Accounts from the* Atlanta Constitution *and* Atlanta Journal *of the United Sacred Harp Musical Association, 1904–1956.* Atlanta: Privately collected and printed, 2004.

Porter, Ellen Jane. "The 'Her' in the Hymn, or Who Was the Mysterious 'Pilgrim Stranger'?" *The Hymn* 35 (July 1984): 143–46.

———. "A Treasure of Campmeeting Spirituals." Ph.D. diss., Union Graduate School, 1978.

Porter, Ellen Jane, and John F. Garst. "More Tunes in Captain Kidd Meter." *The Hymn* 30 (1979): 252–62.

Price, Milburn. "Miss Elizabeth Adams' Music Book: A Manuscript Predecessor of William Walker's *Southern Harmony.*" *The Hymn* 29 (1978): 70–75.

Price, Richard N. *Holston Methodism: From Its Origin to the Present Time.* Five vols. Nashville: Publishing House of the Methodist Episcopal Church, South, 1906.

Prucha, Francis Paul. *American Indian Treaties: The History of a Political Anomaly.* Berkeley: University of California Press, 1997.

Redford, Albert H. *The History of Methodism in Kentucky.* 2 vols. Nashville: Southern Methodist Publishing House, 1870.

Reynolds, William J. "Benjamin Franklin White: The Sacred Harp Man." Dedicatory speech, Hamilton, Georgia, 27 October 1984. biographies.texasfasola.org/bfwhite .html.

———. *Companion to the Baptist Hymnal*. Nashville: Broadman, 1976.

Rhoads, Mark D. "Reformers and Resisters: Changing Tastes in American Protestant Church Music, 1800–1860." Plenary address presented at the Hymn Society conference, DePauw University, Indiana, July, 2006.

Ringwalt, John Luther. *American Encyclopaedia of Printing*. Philadelphia: Menamin & Ringwalt, 1871.

Rollman, Hans. *The Restoration Movement Pages*. 1995–2006. www.mun.ca/rels/ restmov/.

Rose, Richard Wayne. "The Psalmist: A Significant Hymnal for Baptists in America During the Nineteenth Century." D.M.A. diss., Southwestern Baptist Theological Seminary, 1991.

Saal, Hubert, with Joseph B. Cumming Jr. "Sacred Singout," http://www.mcsr.olemiss .edu/~mudws/articles/singout.html.

Sanders, Robert Stuart. *Presbyterianism in Paris and Bourbon County, Kentucky, 1786–1961*. Louisville, Ky.: Dunne, 1961.

Scholten, James W. "The Chapins: A Study of Men and Sacred Music West of the Alleghenies, 1795–1842." Ed.D. diss., University of Michigan, 1972.

Scott, Joseph Dennie. "The Tunebooks of William Hauser (*The Hesperian Harp, The Olive Leaf*)." D.M.A. thesis, New Orleans Baptist Theological Seminary, 1987.

Sedley [Sir Stephen]. "Playford's *Dancing Master*." *Inner Temple Newsletter* 14 (October 2008) www.innertemplelibrary.org.uk/newsletter/Archive/newsletter14.doc.

Seeger, Charles. "Contrapuntal Style in the Three-Voice Shape-Note Hymns." *Musical Quarterly* 26 (October 1940): 483–93.

Shull, Carl N. "John Logan: His Life and Work as a Singing Teacher on the Virginia and North Carolina Frontiers, 1792–1813." *Augusta Historical Bulletin* 16 (Spring 1980): 22–49.

Silverman, Kenneth. *A Cultural History of the American Revolution*. New York: Crowell, 1976.

Slafter, Carlos. "The Schools and Teachers of Dedham." *Dedham Historical Register* 4 (1893): 15–17, 55–60, 95–100, 153–56.

Sluder, Claude K. "The Ketcham Tune-book: Examples of 18th-Century Hymnody in Indiana." *Current Musicology* 23 (1977): 79–89.

Smith, Roswell Chamberlain. *English Grammar on the Productive System: A Method of Instruction Recently Adopted in Germany and Switzerland, in the Place of the Inductive System. Designed for Schools and Academies*. Boston: Richardson, Lord, & Holbrook, 1831.

Smith, William. *The Easy Instructor, Part II*. [Hopewell, N.J.:] William Smith & Co., [1803].

Southall, Geneva Handy. *Blind Tom, the Black Pianist-Composer (1849–1908): Continually Enslaved*. Lanham, Md.: Scarecrow, 1999.

Sparks, Claude Ezell. *A History of Padgett's Creek Baptist Church*. Union, S.C.: Counts, 1967.

Steel, David Warren, ed. *Daniel Belknap (1771–1815): The Collected Works*. Music of the New American Nation 14. New York: Garland, 1998.

————. "Early Shape-Note Singing in the Shenandoah Valley." Lecture presented to the Singers Glen Music and Heritage Festival, Singers Glen, Virginia, 1997.

————. "John Wyeth and the Development of Southern Hymnody." In *Music from the Middle Ages through the Twentieth Century: Essays in Honor of Gwynn McPeek*. ed. Carmelo P. Comberiati and Matthew C. Steel. New York: Gordon & Breach, 1988, pp. 357–74. www.mcsr.olemiss.edu/~mudws/wyeth.html.

————. "Lazarus J. Jones and *The Southern Minstrel* (1849)." *American Music* 6 (Summer 1988): 123–57.

————. "Men of Rough Exteriors: The Biographies of Southern Tunebook Compilers." Paper presented to the Sonneck Society, Pittsburgh, 1987.

————. "Sacred Harp Singing Today: A Cultural Geography." Lecture presented to the Church Music Symposium, Mercer University, Atlanta, 1988.

————. "Sacred Music in Early Winchester." *Connecticut Historical Society Bulletin* 45 (April 1980): 33–44.

————, ed. *Stephen Jenks: Collected Works*. Madison, Wis.: A-R Editions, 1995.

————. "Truman S. Wetmore and His 'Republican Harmony,'" *Connecticut Historical Society Bulletin* 45 (July 1980): 75–89.

Storey, Henry Wilson. *History of Cambria County, Pennsylvania*. New York: Lewis, 1907.

Stribling, Cynthia. "Joshua Leavitt's *The Christian Lyre*: An Historical Evaluation." M.M. thesis, William Carey College, 1976.

Sydenham, John. *The History of the Town and County of Poole*. Poole, England: Sydenham, 1839.

Taddie, Daniel. "Solmization, Scale, and Key in Nineteenth-Century Four-Shape Tunebooks: Theory and Practice." *American Music* 14 (Spring 1996): 42–64.

Tallmadge, William H. "Folk Organum: A Study of Origins." *American Music* 2 (Autumn 1984): 47–65.

————. "The Nomenclature of Folk Hymnody." *The Hymn* 30 (October 1979): 240–42.

Temperley, Nicholas. *The Hymn Tune Index: A Census of English-Language Hymn Tunes in Printed Sources from 1535 to 1820*. New York: Oxford University Press, 1998. Online search: hymntune.library.uiuc.edu .

————. "John Playford and the Metrical Psalms." *Journal of the American Musicological Society* 25 (1972): 331–78.

————. "John Playford and the Stationers' Company." *Music and Letters* 54 (1973): 203–12.

————. *The Music of the English Parish Church*. Cambridge: Cambridge University Press, 1979.

————. "The Origin of the Fuging Tune." *RMA Research Chronicle* 17 (1981): 1–32.

Temperley, Nicholas, and Charles G. Manns and Joseph Herl. *Fuging Tunes in the Eighteenth Century*. Detroit Studies in Music Bibliography no. 49. Detroit: Information Coordinators, 1983.

Thomas, M. Halsey, ed. *The Diary of Samuel Sewall, 1674–1729*. New York: Farrar, Straus and Giroux, 1973.

Thornber, Craig. *Social History of Cheshire in the Late 18th and Early 19th Centuries: Industrial and Intellectual Revolution in the North West: Men of Ideas and Action*. www.thornber.net/cheshire/htmlfiles/socialhist.html.

Tilley, Jessica. "Death in Sacred Harp." M.A. thesis, Georgia State University, 2007.

Turner, Frederick Jackson. *The Frontier in American History*. New York: Henry Holt & Company, 1920.

Turner, Steve. *Amazing Grace: The Story of America's Most Beloved Song*. New York: Harper-Collins, 2002.

UCLA Law and Columbia Law School. *Copyright Infringement Project*. 2002–2007. cip.law.ucla.edu.

University of Georgia Libraries. *Digital Library of Georgia*. 1996–2009. dlg.galileo.usg.edu.

University of Virginia Library. *Historical Census Browser*. fisher.lib.virginia.edu/collections/stats/histcensus/index.html.

Vaughn, R. L. *Approaching 150: A Brief History of the East Texas Musical Convention and Sacred Harp in East Texas*. Mount Enterprise, Texas: Waymark, 2005.

Vinson, Duncan. "'As Far From Secular, Operatic, Rag-Time, and Jig Melodies As Is Possible': Religion and the Resurgence of Interest in *The Sacred Harp*, 1895–1911." *Journal of American Folklore* 119 (Fall 2006): 413–43.

Wallace, James B. "Stormy Banks and Sweet Rivers: A Sacred Harp Geography." *Southern Spaces* 4 (June 2004). www.southernspaces.org/2007/stormy-banks-and-sweet-rivers-sacred-harp-geography.

Watson, Fred S. *Forgotten Trails: A History of Dale County, Alabama, 1824–1966*. Birmingham: Banner Press, 1968.

Webb, George E., Jr. *Tennessee Hymnals and Tune Books, 1813–1865: A Bibliographical Checklist*. Paris, Tenn.: George E. Webb Jr., 1994.

Weston, Stephen J. "A Northamptonshire Composer: Thomas Jarman of Clipston." *Northamptonshire Past and Present* 8 (1993–94): 385–91.

Wetherington, Mark V. *Plain Folks' Fight: The Civil War and Reconstruction in Piney Woods Georgia*. Chapel Hill: University of North Carolina Press, 2005.

The Whole Book of Psalms, Collected into English Metre, by Thomas Sternhold, John Hopkins, and others ("The Old Version"). [London: John Day, 1562.] Cambridge: John Hayes, 1676.

Wilcox, Glenn C. "E.T. Pound and Unorthodox Musical Notation." In *Festival Essays for Pauline Alderman: A Musicological Tribute*, ed, Burton L. Karson. Provo, Utah: Brigham Young University Press, 1976, pp. 195–208.

Wiley, Samuel T., ed. *Biographical and Portrait Cyclopedia of Cambria County, Pennsylvania*. Philadelphia: Union Publishing Co., 1896.

Willhide, J. Lawrence. "Samuel Holyoke: American Music Educator." Ph.D. diss., University of Southern California, 1954.

Williams, Hermine Weigel. *Thomas Hastings: An Introduction to His Life and Music*. Bloomington, Ind.: iUniverse, 2005.

Wilson, Ruth Mack. *Connecticut's Music in the Revolutionary Era*. Hartford: American Revolution Bicentennial Commission, 1980.

Wood, Mayme Parrott. *Drifting Down Holston River Way*. Maryville, Tenn.: Marion R. Mangrum, 1966.

Woods, William F. "The Evolution of Nineteenth-Century Grammar Teaching." *Rhetoric Review* 5 (Autumn 1986): 4–20.

WorldConnect Project. wc.rootsweb.ancestry.com/.

Worst, John. "New England Psalmody, 1760–1810: Analysis of an American Idiom." Ph.D. diss., University of Michigan, 1974.

Yeary, Mark Jerome. "Back and Fourth: Tracing the Theoretical Categorization of the Perfect Fourth in Medieval and Renaissance Treatises." Student paper, University of Chicago, 2004.

Zon, Bennett. "The Origin of 'Adeste fideles.'" *Early Music* 24 (May 1996): 279–88.

INDEX

Page numbers in bold refer to principal author and song references. Titles of songs that appear in the 1991 revision of *The Sacred Harp* are followed by the page number in parentheses, with "t" and "b" designating the top or bottom song as is the custom.

Aaron, Annie Denson, 27, 28, **82–83**, 110
Aaron, Newton Byrd, 82
ABBEVILLE (33b), 129–30, **181**
Abel, Frederick L., 134
accidentals, 47
Adams, Thomas F., 6–7
ADORATION (138t), 145, **197**
AFRICA (178), 86–87, **203**
African Americans: camp meeting participa-
   tion, 59, 64; H. S. Reese and, 150; lining out
   traditions of, 40; musical influence of, 13;
   religious opposition to slavery, 73; revival
   choruses and, 64; Richard Allen as hymn
   compiler, 63–64, 73; slavery in singing areas,
   13, 16, 258n1, 258n4
African Methodist Episcopal Church, 63
Aikin, Burwell Stephen, **83**, 199
AINSLIE (348t), 121–22, **221**
AKERS (293), 110–11, **214**
Akers, Lola, 214
AKIN (472), 91, **236**
Akin, E. G., 236
ALABAMA (196), 5, **205**
Alabama Music Hall of Fame, 115
Alabama State Sacred Harp Musical Associa-
   tion, 114, 120

ALBION (52t), 88, **184**
Aldridge, Robert, 118
ALEXANDER (393), 118, **226**
Allen, Richard, 63–64, 73
ALL IS WELL (122), 168, **195**
ALL SAINTS NEW (444), 51, 119, **232**
Almaliach, Ambrose de ("Lupo"), 24–25
"Almighty King! whose wondrous hand," 202
alto (counter): in the 1859 revision, 51; altered
   alto parts, 52; Amanda Burdette Denson
   role in composing, 105–6, 109; Cooper-James
   lawsuit, 10; historical styles and, 46–47; in
   James revision, 26, 28, 103; Seaborn Denson
   role in composing, 28, 105–6, 108, 109; Sidney
   Denson role in composing, 109
AMANDA RAY (493), 109–10, **238**
AMERICA (36t), 164, **181**
American Harmony, The (1793), 112, 155, 163
American Music Group, 94
American or Union Harmony (1831), 47
American Singing-Book, The (1785), 149–50
AMERICAN STAR, THE (346), 11, 167, **221**
American Vocalist, The (1848), 100
AMITY (150), 149–50, **199**
AMSTERDAM (84), **190**
ANIMATION (103), **192**
ANTHEM ON THE BEGINNING (553), 107, **244**
ANTHEM ON THE SAVIOR (355), 116, 165–66, **222**
anthems, 8, 43, 117
ANTIOCH (277), xiii, 50–51, 170, **212**
Arab Courthouse Singing, 120
ARBACOOCHEE (430), 108, **231**
Arbacoochee (Alabama), 26, 108

DAVID WARREN STEEL is an associate professor of music and southern culture at the University of Mississippi.

RICHARD H. HULAN is an independent scholar of American folk hymnody.

Traveling the High Way Home: Ralph Stanley and the World of Traditional
Bluegrass Music   *John Wright*

Carl Ruggles: Composer, Painter, and Storyteller   *Marilyn Ziffrin*

Never without a Song: The Years and Songs of Jennie Devlin, 1865–1952
Katharine D. Newman

The Hank Snow Story   *Hank Snow, with Jack Ownbey and Bob Burris*

Milton Brown and the Founding of Western Swing   *Cary Ginell, with special assistance
from Roy Lee Brown*

Santiago de Murcia's "Códice Saldívar No. 4": A Treasury of Secular Guitar Music
from Baroque Mexico   *Craig H. Russell*

The Sound of the Dove: Singing in Appalachian Primitive Baptist Churches
Beverly Bush Patterson

Heartland Excursions: Ethnomusicological Reflections on Schools of Music
Bruno Nettl

Doowop: The Chicago Scene   *Robert Pruter*

Blue Rhythms: Six Lives in Rhythm and Blues   *Chip Deffaa*

Shoshone Ghost Dance Religion: Poetry Songs and Great Basin Context   *Judith Vander*

Go Cat Go! Rockabilly Music and Its Makers   *Craig Morrison*

'Twas Only an Irishman's Dream: The Image of Ireland and the Irish in American
Popular Song Lyrics, 1800–1920   *William H. A. Williams*

Democracy at the Opera: Music, Theater, and Culture in New York City, 1815–60
Karen Ahlquist

Fred Waring and the Pennsylvanians   *Virginia Waring*

Woody, Cisco, and Me: Seamen Three in the Merchant Marine   *Jim Longhi*

Behind the Burnt Cork Mask: Early Blackface Minstrelsy and Antebellum American
Popular Culture   *William J. Mahar*

Going to Cincinnati: A History of the Blues in the Queen City   *Steven C. Tracy*

Pistol Packin' Mama: Aunt Molly Jackson and the Politics of Folksong   *Shelly Romalis*

Sixties Rock: Garage, Psychedelic, and Other Satisfactions   *Michael Hicks*

The Late Great Johnny Ace and the Transition from R&B to Rock 'n' Roll
James M. Salem

Tito Puente and the Making of Latin Music   *Steven Loza*

Juilliard: A History   *Andrea Olmstead*

Understanding Charles Seeger, Pioneer in American Musicology   *Edited by
Bell Yung and Helen Rees*

Mountains of Music: West Virginia Traditional Music from *Goldenseal*   *Edited by
John Lilly*

Alice Tully: An Intimate Portrait   *Albert Fuller*

A Blues Life   *Henry Townsend, as told to Bill Greensmith*

Long Steel Rail: The Railroad in American Folksong (2d ed.)   *Norm Cohen*

The Golden Age of Gospel   *Text by Horace Clarence Boyer; photography by Lloyd Yearwood*

Aaron Copland: The Life and Work of an Uncommon Man   *Howard Pollack*

Louis Moreau Gottschalk   *S. Frederick Starr*

The University of Illinois Press
is a founding member of the
Association of American University Presses.

———————————————————————

Designed by Kelly Gray
Composed in 10.5/13.5 Dante
with Shadowed Serif display
by Jim Proefrock
at the University of Illinois Press
Manufactured by Sheridan Books, Inc.

University of Illinois Press
1325 South Oak Street
Champaign, IL 61820-6903
www.press.uillinois.edu